**Robo Sacer**

# CRITICAL MEXICAN STUDIES

CRITICAL MEXICAN STUDIES
*Series editor: Ignacio M. Sánchez Prado*

Critical Mexican Studies is the first English-language, humanities-based, theoretically focused academic series devoted to the study of Mexico. The series is a space for innovative works in the humanities that focus on theoretical analysis, transdisciplinary interventions, and original conceptual framing.

Other titles in the series:

*The Restless Dead: Necrowriting and Disappropriation*, by Cristina Rivera Garza

*History and Modern Media: A Personal Journey*, by John Mraz

*Toxic Loves, Impossible Futures: Feminist Living as Resistance*, by Irmgard Emmelhainz

*Drug Cartels Do Not Exist: Narcotrafficking in US and Mexican Culture*, by Oswaldo Zavala

*Unlawful Violence: Mexican Law and Cultural Production*, by Rebecca Janzen

*The Mexican Transpacific: Nikkei Writing, Visual Arts, and Performance*, by Ignacio López-Calvo

*Monstrous Politics: Geography, Rights, and the Urban Revolution in Mexico City*, by Ben Gerlofs

# Robo Sacer

Necroliberalism and Cyborg Resistance in Mexican and Chicanx Dystopias

David S. Dalton

Vanderbilt University Press
*Nashville, Tennessee*

Copyright 2023 Vanderbilt University Press
All rights reserved
First printing 2023

Cover image by Mario A. Chacon, from *Lunar Braceros*.

Library of Congress Cataloging-in-Publication Data
on file LCCN 2022034903

ISBN 978-0-8265-0537-8 (Paperback)
ISBN 978-0-8265-0538-5 (Hardcover)
ISBN 978-0-8265-0539-2 (EPUB)
ISBN 978-0-8265-0540-8 (Web PDF)

For Ariadna, Davidcito, Dan Armando, and Isadora

# Contents

Acknowledgments  ix

INTRODUCTION: Defining the Robo Sacer in a Necroliberal World  1

PART I. DENATURALIZING GREATER-MEXICAN *ZOĒ*: THE EARLY STAGES OF NAFTA (1992–2001)

1  Reimagining the Sanctity of Expendable Life: Necroliberal Markets and Secularly Holy Cyborgs in Cherríe Moraga's *Heroes and Saints* and Guillermo del Toro's *Cronos*  33

2  Existing in the Necroliberal Order Online: Robo-Sacer Subjectivity in Pepe Rojo's "Ruido gris" and Ernest Hogan's *Smoking Mirror Blues*  65

PART II. NAFTA AFTER THE TRANSITION: WORKER EXPENDABILITY IN A NECROLIBERAL AGE (2006–2018)

3  Hacking the *Bios*: Disposable Braceros and Bare Life in Alex Rivera's *Sleep Dealer* and Rosaura Sánchez and Beatrice Pita's *Lunar Braceros 2125-2148*  93

4  Robo-Sacer Resistance and Feminicide: Gabriela Damián Miravete's "Soñarán en el jardín" and Carlos Carrera and Sabina Berman's *Backyard/El traspatio*  125

5  Guns, Narcos, and Low-Tech Cyborgs: Magical Realism, SF, and the Posthuman in Julio Hernández Cordón's *Cómprame un revólver* and Rudolfo Anaya's ChupaCabra Trilogy  159

| | |
|---|---|
| CONCLUSION. The Limits of Robo-Sacer Resistance | 191 |
| Notes | 203 |
| References | 269 |
| Index | 313 |

# Acknowledgments

From its inception, *Robo Sacer* was always going to be an ambitious project. The idea of an Agambian cyborg in Mexican and Chicanx dystopian fictions certainly interested me, but the project entailed numerous hurdles. I wish to extend my gratitude to the people who have been there to lend an ear as I have embarked on this study. I originally began thinking about the notion of robo sacer as a PhD student at the University of Kansas while taking a course on transnational race and performance with Nichole Hodges Persley. She was instrumental to helping me to think through and theorize how cyborg theory interfaced not only with gender and sexuality, but with race as well. Indeed, both of my books were born in classes that I took with her. Stuart Day was also a valuable resource as I first began developing this idea. I eventually decided to leave *Robo Sacer* to the side as I worked on my first book, *Mestizo Modernity*. Nevertheless, I'm very grateful to the mentors at KU who helped me to articulate my notion of robo sacer. I'm also grateful to colleagues like Jacob Rapp and Ezekiel Stear, both of whom read (very) early drafts of what would eventually become this manuscript. Their encouragement helped me to take confidence in my ideas and to develop them to their full potential.

This book has placed me in contact with an array of academic fields. I am especially grateful to my wonderful colleagues in (Greater-)Mexican studies and in Latin American science fiction studies for their support. In alphabetical order, I would like to voice my gratitude to the people who have read over drafts, attended different conference presentations, or simply talked with me about my ideas through chat or in person: Enrique Ajuria Ibarra, Susan Antebi, Pablo Brescia, J. Andrew Brown, Olivia Cosentino, Ángel

Díaz, Rodrigo Figueroa Obregón, Carolyn Fornoff, Miguel García, Mónica García Blizzard, M. Elizabeth Ginway, Rachel Haywood Ferreira, Emily Hind, Rebecca Janzen, Yunuen Ylce Mandujano-Salazar, Emily Maguire, Diana Montaño, Samanta Ordóñez Robles, Edmundo Paz Soldán, Amanda Petersen, Sara Potter, Brian Price, David Ramírez Plascencia, Elissa Rashkin, and Stephen Tobin. Their comments have challenged and invigorated me as they have helped me to make the strongest arguments possible. Sara Potter and Stephen Tobin have both humored me on multiple occasions with long conversations—through the Messenger app, no less—about the intersections of posthuman and transhuman discourses on gendered and racialized bodies. Many of these conversations lasted hours at a time. Truly, this project would not have come into fruition without the support and comments of all of these excellent colleagues. Their deep knowledge of Mexican studies and/or Latin American science fiction studies was a powerful resource. I'm so fortunate to belong to a community of scholars who so freely gives of their time to help one another to succeed professionally. This book would not be the same without them. I hope I can pay it forward and help others with their projects in the future as well.

I'm also grateful to the entire team at Vanderbilt University Press. They have ensured a smooth process at every juncture along the way. Ignacio M. Sánchez Prado expressed confidence in the text when he encouraged me to send this manuscript to his series, *Critical Mexican Studies*. Zack Gresham has been a pleasure to work with; a professional to the core. He has made the submission process easy, painless, and pressure free while at the same time ensuring things happen in an expeditious manner. He has also been a strong advocate for this project both with the press and beyond. Mexicanist colleagues: if you are wondering where to publish your monograph, you should consider Vanderbilt. Joell Simth-Borne did a fantastic job copyediting this manuscript, and Andrew Ascherl created the book's wonderful index.

I would be amiss if I were to ignore the excellent support I have received from the University of North Carolina, Charlotte. I am especially grateful to my colleagues in the Department of Languages and Culture Studies and to my colleagues in the Latin American Studies Program. My chair, Michele Bissiere, and associate chair, Anabel Aliaga-Buchenau, have been incredibly supportive by validating my research and ensuring I have the resources necessary to complete the project. The former directors of the Latin America Studies program, Carlos Coria and Jürgen Buchenau, have also been an absolute pleasure to work with over the last several years. In alphabetical order, I would like to express my gratitude to the following faculty members I have worked with in the Department of Languages and

Culture Studies and/or Latin American studies at Charlotte: Benny Andrés, José Manuel Batista, Oscar de la Torre, Michael Doyle, Erika Edwards, Javier García León, Maryrica Lottman, Concepción Godev, Eric Hoenes, Jeffrey Killman, Chris Mellinger, Andrea Pitts, Anton Pujol, Mónica Rodríguez, Carmen Soliz, and Allison Stedman. Many of these colleagues have gone to different presentations on campus that I have done in conjunction with this project; all of them have helped to build our strong programs in Spanish and/or Latin American studies that make UNC, Charlotte such a special place to work. I look forward to Charlotte's continued growth in Latin American, US-Latinx, and Hispanic studies.

Last but certainly not least, I'm grateful for the support of my family. My parents instilled in me the importance of reading, writing, and education from a young age. When I was a child, they would take me to Kinko's to bind the novellas and stories that I wrote in a way that looked professional. Their support made me want to be an author. And now I am! I'm also grateful to my children, all of whom are still quite young. They have watched me sift through an array of books and then return to write on the computer. My oldest jokes that my books are my prized possession, and he knows he's more than a little correct. In all seriousness, they are my great inspiration in my research and writing. I'm so grateful for the support they have given me as I have worked on this and other major projects. My successes belong just as much to them as they do to me. They have made it possible for me to do this. I hope my children find it inspiring to see their dad writing and publishing books, and I want them to know that they can and should aspire to do whatever they want. I'm especially grateful to Ariadna, who is always so supportive of me, especially when I have to go into writer mode for long periods of time. She is my partner in crime, and I can't imagine being on this crazy ride that we call life without her. I love her very much; I'm so fortunate to have her in my life.

A fragment of Chapter 2 was published in Spanish as "El consumo de la muerte en las televisiones nacionales: El necroliberalismo y la nación cyborg en 'Ruido gris' de Pepe Rojo," *Balajú: Revista de cultura y comunicación* 11 (2019): 3–26. It has been reprinted here with the permission of the editor, Elissa Rashkin. Another fragment of Chapter 2 was published in Spanish as "Reclamando el ciberespacio para los subalternos: Resistencia robo sacer en *Smoking Mirror Blues* de Ernest Hogan," in *Recalibrando los circuitos de la máquina: Imaginarios tecnológicos y ciencia ficción en la narrativa hispánica del siglo XXI*, edited by Jonatán Martín and Patricio Sullivan, 219–34 (Valencia: Albatros, 2022). This has also been reprinted with permission from the editor, Vicente Soler. Finally, a fragment of Chapter 3 was published as "*Robo Sacer*: 'Bare Life' and Cyborg Labor beyond the Border in Alex Rivera's *Sleep Dealer*," *Hispanic Studies Review* 1 (2016): 15–29. Once again, this segment has been reprinted with the permission of the editor, Carl Wise. I am also grateful to Mario A. Chacón who granted me the rights to include two of his illustrations in this book.

INTRODUCTION
# Defining the Robo Sacer in a Necroliberal World

On March 23, 2020, Texas lieutenant governor Dan Patrick appeared on the Fox News program *Tucker Carlson Tonight* to argue that the United States should abandon its COVID-related shutdowns and reopen. He went on to say, "no one reached out to me and said: 'as a senior citizen, are you willing to take a chance on your survival in exchange for keeping the America that all America loves for your children and grandchildren?' And if that's the exchange, I'm all in."[1] In making this statement, the lieutenant governor effectively called for as many as 2 percent of (mostly elderly) Texans and Americans to be ready to sacrifice their lives in order to promote the so-called American Dream, which he equated with unabated commerce. As he invoked the potential of death as prerequisite to a healthy economy, the lieutenant governor promulgated what I term necroliberal discourse: he signaled the market-based, ne(cr)oliberal economy as a Benjaminian state of emergency, or an Agambian state of exception, that must be protected at all costs.[2] Not surprisingly, Patrick received harsh criticism from progressive media and social media users for his comments. That said, upon closer inspection, it would appear that, far from disagreeing with the lieutenant governor about the fact that some lives must be risked to move the economy forward, these critics tended to center their attention, perhaps unconsciously, on the *types* of lives that Patrick had cast as expendable: elderly, upper-middle class, and white.

This fact rings clear when we note that the media remained relatively silent as agricultural corporations like Tyson continued to require their majority-Latinx meatpackers to work in close quarters without adequate personal protective equipment (PPE).[3] Meatpacking plants soon became hot spots for infection and transmission, but the political and economic pressure to keep them open remained enormous.[4] On April 28, 2020, then president

Donald Trump signed Executive Order 13917, which required meatpacking factories to remain open "to ensure a continued supply of protein for Americans."[5] Tellingly, the order remained silent on how meatpacking plants should ensure the safety of their workers. The executive order thus codified the devaluation of meatpackers' health and lives, marking them as expendable cyborgs whose value extended no further than their function in operating industrial machinery to produce food for consumers.[6] The extent of the dehumanization of immigrant meatpackers became especially clear in an egregious case in Iowa, where, in an attempt to create a "morale booster," managers at a Tyson Foods pork plant started a betting pool where they guessed which employees would take ill with COVID-19 next.[7] The dehumanization of meatpackers throughout the country reflected, in large part, their legal status: most were undocumented workers from countries like Mexico.[8] As such, they lacked citizenship claims that would have allowed them to more effectively contest the dangerous working conditions that corporate and government policies had imposed upon them.[9]

Viewed together, Patrick's words and the handling of meatpacking plants provide important insights into the biopolitical logic that undergirded US policy during the pandemic. In a Foucauldian sense, the state viewed its commitment to public health as key to its claims to legitimacy.[10] At the same time, however, Michel Foucault argues that biopower requires "the controlled insertion of bodies into the machinery of production."[11] In the case of a pandemic-ridden society, any attempt to assert biopower necessarily required the state to call on certain segments of the population—the elderly in Patrick's case; mostly undocumented, mostly Mexican and Latinx immigrants in the case of meatpacking plants—to bear a disproportionate amount of risk so that others could consume without interruption. Not surprisingly, the state played a proactive role in determining which lives and bodies deserved greater or lesser protection as it sought to maintain the exceptional state of market-based capitalism intact.[12]

The Italian theorist Giorgio Agamben proves particularly useful in examining the US response to COVID-19. Centering his analysis on the fact that biopolitical states base their legitimacy on their ability to preserve life even as they constantly kill, he postulates the theory of *homo sacer*. Reaching back to ancient Greece, he identifies two terms: *bios* and *zoē*, both of which translate as life in Italian and English. These words denote very different types of existence: *bios* refers to the fully human, Aristotelean good life that entails political autonomy. *Zoē*, a term that forms the root of zoology, refers to those whose lives exist outside the political sphere.[13] Under normal circumstances, the *zoē* can live decent lives, though their lack of access to citizenship precludes them from advocating for their own interests. Nevertheless, during states of exception—a "no-man's land between public law and political fact, and between the juridical order and life"—the state (or another "sovereign" actor) interpellates the *zoē* into *homo sacer* status.[14] For Agamben, *homines sacri* (the plural of *homo sacer*) are subjects who live beyond the protection of the law. As such, they "may be killed and yet not sacrificed," or even murdered, because society extends no value to their "bare lives" or even to their deaths.[15] In its most extreme articulations, like the Holocaust, the designation of *homo sacer* allows for the systematic extermination of entire communities. The COVID-19 crisis shows how states of exception can become so normalized that people may not even realize they exist. For example, most onlookers would probably have correctly identified public health as an important state of exception that world leaders sought to protect as they confronted the virus. Nevertheless, as the actions and statements of government leaders in the United States made clear, the drive to maintain commerce represented an even deeper institutionalized state of exception. This drive to consume led elected officials to call on both the elderly and migrants to potentially sacrifice their lives for the (supposedly) greater economic good.

The tensions between COVID-19 and the ne(cr)oliberal economy played out in more places than just the United States. Leaders throughout Latin America grappled with how best to handle the crisis as well.[16] This held especially true in Mexico, where the supposedly left-wing populist Andrés Manuel López Obrador resisted calls for economic shutdowns. In the early days of the pandemic, his ally, Puebla governor Luis Miguel Barbos Huerta, infamously proclaimed, "if you are rich you are in danger; if you are poor, no. We, the poor, are ... immune" (si son ricos tienen el riesgo; si son pobres no, los pobres estamos ... inmunes).[17] This statement made no sense at a scientific level, and the governor's claims of being poor were, of course, laughable. That said, his words reflected the fact that, in the earliest days of the pandemic, rich Mexicans had taken ill at higher rates because they could more easily cross international borders and enter countries where the virus had already taken hold.[18] Nevertheless, Barbos Huerta's statement underscored López Obrador's left-wing austerity that aimed to flatter working-class Mexicans while at the same time calling on them to contribute to the economy and ensure the continued flow of goods and services, even if this would expose them to physical harm.[19] As the pandemic progressed, Mexico became one of the hardest-hit countries in the Western Hemisphere.[20] Nevertheless, López Obrador continued to resist calls for shutdowns. Similar to his US counterparts, the Mexican president ultimately viewed the continued functioning of the market as an objective that was worth risking the lives of his own citizens, the majority of whom, as of this writing, belonged to the poor and working-class communities that had fueled his election in 2018.[21]

Capitalist expansion clearly represented a state of exception that political authorities in both the United States and Mexico strove to protect despite the presence of a lethal virus that made physical interactions dangerous. In many cases, both countries' national policies brought into the open biopolitical divisions that Mexican and Chicanx literary and cultural producers had identified through dystopian fictions since the earliest moments of the neoliberal period, and probably earlier.[22] At a personal level, one of the things that most drew my attention during the early stages of the pandemic was the extent to which government policies resembled those of the works I had studied for this project. The balance of this book discusses how dystopian fictions from Greater Mexico—a term that includes both Mexico and its diasporas, particularly those in the United States—aid us in theorizing contemporary (bio)politics on both sides of the US-Mexico border during the neoliberal period.[23] It is perhaps telling that Chicanx and Mexican literary and cultural producers imagine an array of forms of resistance predicated on rethinking humanity's (and the body's) relationship with technology. On the one hand, *Robo Sacer: Necroliberalism and Cyborg Resistance in Mexican and Chicanx Dystopias* highlights how technologies of production play a key role in casting Mexican and Chicanx workers as mere extensions of a dehumanizing, capitalist machine. On the other hand, however, the book also shows how technology provides an avenue of resistance by allowing marginalized individuals (and communities) to seize a political voice and advocate for themselves.

Some readers may find the juxtaposition of Mexican and Chicanx dystopian fictions problematic given the tensions that have existed between these communities since at least the early part of the twentieth century.[24] Nevertheless, a shared solidarity has also developed in recent years as increased migration under the North America Free Trade Agreement (NAFTA) has put Mexican and Chicanx communities into greater contact one with another. The Mexican government has, for example, undertaken steps to strengthen its ties with its diaspora.[25] As it compares these two Greater-Mexican nations, *Robo Sacer* builds on previous scholarship from critics like Marissa K. López and Lysa Rivera. In addressing the cultural ties between Chicanx populations and other US-Latinx populations more generally, for example, M. López has argued that a "politics of form" creates a shared set of identities that "can be culturally leveraged" in ways that suggest a shared racial, or ethnoracial, condition.[26] Looking southward, *Robo Sacer* asserts a similar set of circumstances as they relate to Chicanx and Mexican communities, particularly regarding their literary and cultural production. Certainly, we should recognize the distinctive social and political contexts on both sides of the US-Mexico border, but we should also note the shared struggles that these Greater-Mexican communities face as they navigate a world dominated by US-sponsored neoliberalism. Perhaps one of the most enduring similarities between Mexican and Chicanx populations is a perpetual construct of foreignness from the imperial center that justifies the continued economic exploitation of both.[27]

A few definitions are in order, particularly as they relate to Mexican diasporic communities in the United States, which have used an array of terms to refer to themselves over the years: Mexican, Mexican American, Chicano, Chicana, Chicanx, etc.[28] Throughout this book, I use the identitary terms that individual thinkers, cultural producers, and critics embrace for themselves in their given historical moment.[29] For example, I use the term Chicano when discussing the 1960s Chicano Movement and the term Chicana when referring to Chicana feminism. I also employ the term Chicanx—which has developed cultural currency within activist and academic circles in recent years due to its ability to include nonbinary, female, and male subjectivities—when engaging recent literary, scholarly, and cultural production.[30] Terms like Latinx and Chicanx certainly have their detractors, particularly among thinkers like Nicole Trujillo-Pagán, who views the terms Latinx and Chicanx as examples of linguistic imperialism that impose Anglocentric norms on the Spanish language.[31] In an attempt to reconcile the drive to move past the gender binary with that of keeping the term pronounceable in Spanish, Trujillo-Pagán proposes the term Latino/a/x, itself a difficult term to read, write, or even pronounce. Clearly, there is no perfect way to refer to Mexican and Latin American diasporic communities in the United States. While I am sympathetic to Trujillo-Pagán's position, I view Chicanx (and Latinx) as the most practical and inclusive terms currently available in English for referring to these communities.[32] As such, I use Chicanx and Latinx as umbrella terms that cover Chicana, Chicano, and Chicanx or Latina, Latino, and Latinx subjectivities respectively.

This language facilitates the interrogation of contemporary constructs of race, gender, sexuality, and identity that sits at the heart of *Robo Sacer*. That said, the book seeks to avoid the pitfalls of essentialist readings that view multiculturalism through a "neoliberal aesthetics" that would depoliticize racial difference by ignoring its socioeconomic implications.[33] Rather, my analysis reverberates with M. López's call for critical discussions of race to focus on "material inequalities" rather than simply "representational otherness."[34] Given that racial formation has always been a biopolitical project that uses phenotype and other interpellations of the body to assign people their roles in the economy, a materialist focus proves essential to my analysis.[35] Mexican and Chicanx dystopian fiction provides valuable tools for interrogating the commodification of Mexican and Chicanx bodies that has hastened since the rise of neoliberalism.[36] Lysa Rivera alludes to this fact when she asserts that Chicanx (and, one could add, Mexican) writers have used "the critical dystopian gaze of cyberpunk to probe how technological innovation and global capitalism have created a vast North American underclass—Chicana/os in the United States and mestiza/os in Mexico—whose labor feeds the consumer class and whose land serves as its dumping ground."[37] Given this backdrop, it should come as no surprise that Mexican and Chicanx dystopian fictions would speak to one another in valuable ways. The works discussed in *Robo Sacer* foreground how global capital interfaces with people's biopolitical status on both sides of the border. The following section theorizes robo-sacer being and resistance. Afterward, I discuss my decision to focus on dystopian literary and cultural production from Greater Mexico.

## ROBO-SACER RESISTANCE: POLYSPATIALITY, CYBORG IDENTITY, AND THE POLITIZATION OF THE *ZOĒ*

Throughout this book, I define robo sacer as a cyborg articulation of Giorgio Agamben's *homo sacer*. The works that I analyze suggest that unbalanced access to technology relegates Mexican and Chicanx individuals to a technologically bare existence. As such, the role of technology in perpetuating an oppressive social order proves key. The book's most important intervention centers around the potential for robo-sacer resistance, which occurs when oppressed individuals and communities employ technologies of domination in subversive ways that reject the reigning biopolitics. In this way, robo-sacer resistance parallels Gloria Anzaldúa's "Coatlicue State," where people become both subjects and objects.[38] Robo-sacer identity alludes to the deep, symbolic relationship between the body and society that is so common in Latin American literary and cultural production.[39] Indeed, the figure underscores José Manuel Valenzuela Arce's observation that "power is inscribed in the body, it is introjected, introduced in it, and it becomes the central site for diverse battles for control and resistance" (el poder se inscribe en el cuerpo, se introyecta, introduce en él y deviene ámbito central de diversas luchas de control y resistencia).[40] In each of the fictions analyzed in this book, the authors imagine ways that a character's corporeal, robo-sacer resistance allegorically represents a communitarian struggle against dehumanizing ideologies that normalize the deadly expansion of capital.

The notion of robo sacer further engages Ignacio M. Sánchez Prado's theorization of "'markets of precaritization,' which undermine the possible subjective territorializations of the Mexican population and pose complex vectors of affectivity and brutality that profoundly transform both the processes of individual and collective subjectivation into the social body and the articulation of bodies to the logic of capital" ("mercados de precarización" que socavan las posibles territorializaciones subjetivas de la población mexicana y plantean complejos vectores de afectividad y brutalidad que transforman de manera profunda tanto los procesos de subjetivación individual y colectiva hacia adentro del cuerpo social como la articulación de los cuerpos a la lógica del capital).[41] Certainly, Sánchez Prado does not explicitly theorize the technologized body here. Rather, he follows an array of scholars of neoliberalism like Wendy Brown, who charges neoliberal policies with viewing people solely in terms of their "human capital," a term that she defines as a person's integration into the capitalist machine.[42] As the previously mentioned case of migrant meatpackers in towns throughout the United States poignantly demonstrates, people who carry out necessary labor in the market economy frequently find themselves dehumanized precisely due to their role in the market(s) of production. Such workers come to embody what Judith Butler calls "precarious life," or those discursively unnamed, generally "foreign," people whom the market casts as killable.[43] Robo-sacer resistance centers its social critiques on precisely these constructs of precarity and expendability. In tying people's lives and deaths to the maintenance of a market economy, the dystopian works discussed in this book strive to expose the ideological beliefs that continue to cast Greater-Mexican lives as expendable.

My focus on Mexican and Chicanx literary and cultural production leads me to foreground the interrelationship between cyborg condition and constructs of race and ethnicity. In this way, *Robo Sacer* diverges from M. López's assertion that contemporary posthumanism has come to concern itself with "philosophical domains where race, ethnicity and inequality appear to have little purchase."[44] Indeed, Mexican and Chicanx dystopian fictions constantly juxtapose cyborg identity and technoculture with race, ethnicity, and subaltern studies. Cyborg condition frequently serves to mark Greater-Mexican lives as bare and expendable, a fact that Sergio González Rodríguez has explored in great depth.[45] Building on that argument, *Robo Sacer* explores how the so-called digital divide has played an outsized role in identifying who belongs to the so-called *bios* and who belongs to the supposed *zoē* by producing inequitable access to technology. On the one hand, this book follows the lead of thinkers like Manuel Castells, who theorizes the ramifications of a network society whose principal hubs exist in the Global North and, as a result, necessarily exacerbate the social and economic marginalization of the developing world.[46] On the other hand, this book challenges the assertion of Joseba Gabilondo, who in 1995 argued that "there is no such thing/subject as a 'postcolonial cyborg,' because postcolonial subject positions are always left outside cyberspace."[47] Gabilondo's assertion may have rung true in the mid-1990s, but by the third decade of the twenty-first century, marginalized and postcolonial subjects access and use digital technologies with frequency.[48] Indeed, Mexican and Chicanx actors have come to use technology in post- and decolonial ways that allow them to stand against a global order that would prefer to ignore and exploit them. As such, they leverage an ambiguous, cyborg subjectivity to advocate for a more inclusive world.

Given the nature of this study, I necessarily apply a broad definition that postulates a cyborg as any body—human or not—that forms a symbiotic relationship with any sort of technology.[49] Cyborgs could be people who use smartphones and internet, people with prosthetic extensions inserted into their bodies, people who have been vaccinated, or people who use low-tech tools like firearms as metaphorical extensions of themselves. This broad definition opens itself to understandable criticisms: if all people are cyborgs, then the term could lose much of its discursive potential. That said, I have previously argued that "this more inclusive definition of cyborg identity proves useful in untangling the intimate relationships between race, gender, technology, and the body."[50] My assertion reverberates with the thought of Donna Haraway, who characterizes the cyborg as a "floating signifier" whose discursive meaning necessarily shifts depending on the given sociopolitical context.[51] At its core, cyborg identity proves useful to interrogating different interpellations of the body, particularly those based on gender, sexuality, race, class, and a host of other demarcations tied to embodiment. Technologized bodies often force reconceptualizations of the body that call into question previous understandings of the overriding body politics and biopolitics.[52] Cyborg feminists have taken advantage of the ways these hybrid identities trouble gender-based constructs of performativity.[53] This does not mean that cyborg identity necessarily brings about a utopian refashioning of the reigning biopolitics, however. As Haraway notes, the cyborg is itself the product of a "hostile science" that has long excluded women and, one could add, people of color, from its ranks.[54]

Clearly, liberation does not automatically result from challenging current constructs of the body. Rather, emancipation must stem from a critical methodology to replace current modes of oppression with a more inclusive order.

In the end, any successful methodology of robo-sacer resistance must engage the unequal ties to citizenship that Mexican and Chicanx people face when compared to their more privileged (mostly white North American and European) counterparts. Once again, Agamben provides valuable insight: if *bios* refers to those who live an Aristotelean good life imbued with a political voice, then *zoē* refers to the subaltern whose weak ties to citizenship strip them of any political voice.[55] We see this clearly among Chicanx communities that exist in a state of perpetual precarity within the United States. In a world that views economics as a zero-sum endeavor, many US actors view any Chicanx success in the social sphere as a threat to continued Anglo-Saxon cultural dominance. Many scholars and activists have asserted ties to cultural citizenship and "liminal legality" as a means through which people from marginalized communities—particularly immigrants in the United States—can assert their right to wield a political voice.[56] That said, R. Andrés Guzmán asserts that "cultural citizenship is grounded on an identitarian logic [. . .] that undermines its political objectives and compels it to reproduce some of the very exclusions against which it agitates."[57] Even when individuals can claim a degree of cultural citizenship, their very act of doing so validates the relegation of others to the periphery. Viewed in this light, Héctor Amaya's assertion of citizenship as a "technology of power" takes on a deeper meaning.[58] In his estimation, it would seem that simply demanding citizenship rights may not be enough. Robo-sacer resistance may thus be at its most effective when it deconstructs the very notion of exclusive forms of citizenship, thus allowing marginal actors to seize a political voice without buoying a system that will keep others down.

Several Chicana theorists, particularly Chela Sandoval and Catherine S. Ramírez, speak precisely to this idea through their discussions of cyborg identity as a means to deconstruct both the patriarchy and racial oppression. As Sandoval argues, all women, particularly women of color, must negotiate a symbolic cyborg subjectivity in their daily lives due to the hybrid nature inherent to their embodied experience.[59] For her part, C. Ramírez explicitly argues that cyborg identity sits at the heart of Gloria Anzaldúa's mestiza consciousness.[60] Both theorists ultimately concur that cyborg identity sparks a type of "radical mestizaje"—or an overtly political articulation of Anzaldúa's mestiza consciousness—in which oppressed individuals recognize their shared marginalization and work together to challenge the status quo.[61] Sandoval's view of cyborg politics as intrinsically oppositional sits at the heart of my own theorization of robo sacer. When robo-sacer actors take advantage of their ties to technology to speak against oppression, they denaturalize the necroliberal state of exception and coerce repressive forces into acknowledging both their humanity and, crucially, their political voice. If Spivak is correct that the subaltern loses their subalternity when they engage in political discourse, then we should read robo-sacer resistance as nothing less than a politicization of the *zoē* catalyzed through a cybernetic communion that facilitates radical mestizaje.[62] In demanding their place within the political sphere, robo-sacer actors build a more accepting political order that expresses skepticism of divisions of *bios* and *zoē*.

*Robo Sacer* thus adds to previous scholarship by interrogating how cyborg subjectivity interfaces with the biopolitical context on both sides of the US-Mexico border. As such, it engages Haraway's assertion that "the cyborg is not subject to Foucault's biopolitics; the cyborg simulates politics, a much more potent field of operations."[63] The book largely disagrees with the first half of Haraway's argument. Indeed, the cyborg's resistant potential necessarily reflects its ability to contest the reigning biopolitics. Rosi Braidotti gets at this point when she asserts that "a focus on the vital and self-organizing powers of Life/*zoe* undoes any clear-cut distinctions between living and dying. It composes the notion of *zoe* as a posthuman yet affirmative life force."[64] Similar to the cyborg, she views *zoē* as a liminal construct that troubles the reigning hierarchies of life. Certainly, she follows this line of argumentation to advocate against anthropocentric paradigms, but she also highlights the fact that, when viewed critically, constructs of *zoē*—especially when juxtaposed with cyborg imageries—denaturalize the bio- and necropolitical context at large.[65] Viewed in this light, cyborgs *simulate* politics by providing a means through which the *zoē* can demand their dignity and assert their place in the *bios*. Throughout the neoliberal period, cyborg characters from Mexican and Chicanx dystopian fiction tend to employ their hybrid subjectivities to interface with the biopolitical order in ways that denaturalize the necroliberal state of exception. In so doing, they challenge their own relegation to robo- and *homo sacer* status.

That said, *Robo Sacer* strives to avoid a naïve optimism about technology's potential to usher in a new, liberated order.[66] Rather, it attempts to theorize the role of technology in creating both modes of oppression and means of resistance in contemporary society. In so doing, it grapples with the question of whether or not the resistant potential of cyborg politics exists beyond the discursive realm, and it suggests that robo-sacer resistance provides a powerful means to challenge a dehumanizing status quo.[67]

As it discusses subversive uses of technology among Mexican and Chicanx actors, the book challenges notions of "imported magic," or the belief that technology always exists as a foreign transplant when used in Latin America.[68] While technologies of domination generally enter the South from the North, Mexican and Chicanx actors can make these foreign technologies their own by using them in innovative ways.[69] This, in turn, opens spaces for liberation, particularly when marginalized actors proactively proclaim their rights to *bios* and seize a political voice for themselves.[70] The potential for robo-sacer resistance allows us to move beyond the critique of certain strains of Agambian thought, particularly those that nullify the potential for resistance and liberation.[71] That said, representations of technology remain "magical" in other respects. For example, cyborg subjectivities often take on a quasi-religious semblance that, similar to saints and talismans, "inscribe themselves into a cultural history conformed by a magical condition" (se inscriben en una historia cultural conformada por una condición mágica).[72] In other cases, foreign technologies take on an ambiguous aura as different characters use them in subversive ways to denaturalize interpellations of the body that mark them as expendable.

Ultimately, Greater-Mexican dystopian fiction tends to view technology, and particularly the internet, as a tool for facilitating resistance due to its penchant for fomenting polyspatial solidarity. Originally coined by the Chicano activist Ricardo Domínguez, the term *polyspatial* refers to a communion of people across space who converge at a single digital site.[73] Domínguez imagined polyspatiality as a means through which Chicanx activists like himself could support faraway actors like the Ejército Zapatista de Liberación Nacional. He founded the online hacktivist group Electronic Disturbance Theater (EDT), which organized numerous virtual sit-ins against symbolic targets: the Frankfurt Stock Exchange, the US Department of Defense, the website of then Mexican president Ernesto Zedillo, and many others.[74] The activists employed FloodNet—a simple java applet that would reload every three seconds—in order to amplify their presence and (hopefully) crash targeted servers.[75] The activists never illegally breached anyone's machine; rather, EDT framed its actions as civil disobedience.[76] EDT has not been without its critics; Chris Hables Gray, for example, argues that electronic disobedience "is not good politics so much as it is mischief, low-grade sabotage, and an effective generator of publicity."[77] The fictions discussed in this book largely disagree with Gray's analysis; while the thinker voices legitimate concerns about free speech, he remains silent on the potential of polyspatial resistance to bring about social change.[78] Many of the fictions discussed in this book imagine how cyborg actors can find supporters from all over the world by using internet technologies to bring like-minded actors together. In this way, they imagine polyspatial solidarity as the most important fruit of robo-sacer resistance: it is through this means that activist movements achieve critical mass and imbue the marginalized classes with a political voice. Viewed in this light, resistance takes on a posthuman flavor as actors from throughout the world come together to decry necroliberal systems of domination throughout the world.

If the resistant, often polyspatial, cyborg functions as the protagonist of this book, then the necroliberal market of death serves as its principal antagonist. *Robo Sacer* follows the lead of Pierre Bourdieu, who views the neoliberal shift of the 1980s and 1990s as one in which "casualization of employment is part of a *mode of domination* of a new kind, based on the creation of a generalized and permanent state of insecurity."[79] Indeed, the book views the necroliberal order as an institutionalized state of exception that necessarily codes Mexican and Chicanx lives as expendable in a quest to accrue ever more capital.[80] Similar to terms like "gore capitalism," "necropolitics," "necropolitical capitalism," "necrocapitalism," and "necropolitical neoliberal projects" (necropolítica de los proyectos neoliberals), the term *necroliberalism* highlights how economic imperatives for ever-increasing production and consumption tend to produce heavy costs in human lives.[81] Furthermore, in focusing on an international economic imperative, the term allows us to look beyond the state in our understanding of how people are coded as *bios* or *zoē*.[82] Certainly, the state, both Mexican and US, remains a central unit of analysis throughout this book. As Irmgard Emmelhainz notes, the contemporary Mexican (and, one could add, US) state occupies itself with guaranteeing commerce regardless of the politics of any particular government that may hold power.[83] That said, rather than viewing it as a largely autonomous entity, my focus on necroliberalism as a transnational state of exception highlights the fact that nation-states frequently negotiate drives and interests that exist beyond their borders as they carry out biopolitical projects. *Robo Sacer* allows us to question the extent to which structures outside the state—particularly those associated with transnational financial interests—lead to dehumanizing discourses in different countries' domestic and international politics. Certainly, the transnational nature of the necroliberal order plays out in different ways among people of Mexican descent on both sides of the US-Mexico border.

The term *necroliberalism* also draws explicitly on Achille Mbembe's groundbreaking theorization of necropolitics as "the trajectories by which the state of exception and the relation of enmity have become the normative basis of the right to kill. In such instances, power (which is not necessarily state power) continuously refers and appeals to the exception, emergency, and fictionalized enemies."[84] Numerous scholars have noted that Mbembe, as a scholar from the African nation of Cameroon, develops a theory of power that applies especially well to the so-called Third World given his direct engagement of coloniality.[85] Ariadna Estévez, for example, asserts that "in the Third World, instead of biopolitics there is necropolitics" (en el tercer mundo, en vez de biopolítica hay una necropolitica).[86] Perhaps for this very reason, Mbembe's notion of necropolitics reverberates particularly well with my theorization of robo sacer and the necroliberal state of exception. Indeed, Mbembe asserts that technology—or the robotically adjusted life—plays an integral role in meting out death upon the killable.[87] The Cameroonian theorist signals two key breaks with Agamben: first, the "right to kill," far from a byproduct of the desire to uphold the *bios* at the expense of the *zoē*, becomes the central tenet of political power; second, his understanding of necropolitics causes him to identify institutions beyond the state, such as the market, that can exert power over life and death. My own term of *necroliberalism* dovetails nicely with Mbembe's thought insofar as we both view a political economy of death to exist in a way that transcends both sovereignty and the state.

Agamben and Mbembe share a great deal of common ground, and many of the foremost critics of neoliberalism within the Mexican academy have worked to reconcile these two particular thinkers.[88] Estévez, for example, notes that Mbembe's necropolitics refers to a context where the Agambian state of exception is especially permanent.[89] Indeed, Mbembe's work frames the act of killing not as the protection of the so-called good life but as the central question of governance. Sayak Valencia argues that "necropolitics is a reinterpretation and stark iteration of biopower and the capacity for upending it. [...] Necropolitics is important because it re-situates the body at the center of the action without any interference. The bodies of *dystopian* dissidents and ungovernables are now those which hold power over the individual body of the population in general."[90] Both Mbembe's necropolitics and Agamben's *homo sacer* biopolitics prove valuable in teasing out my own theorization of the necroliberal state of exception. Together, they provide tools to theorize the competing drives of biopower—which, according to Foucault, refers to the "diverse techniques for achieving the subjugation of bodies and the control of populations"—and "necropower," or the state's imperative to mete out death upon the killable, often in a way that completely erases the stories of individuals and entire communities.[91] Agamben and Mbembe converge most explicitly with their discussions of the politics surrounding borders, which become exceptional sites that sovereign states invoke to dehumanize foreigners and separate *bios* from *zoē*.⁹² *Robo Sacer* intervenes at precisely this juncture by showing cyborg discourses that call into question the relegation of racial others, particularly those of Greater Mexico, to *zoē* and *homo sacer* status. This is not the first book to explore the role of race and ethnicity in constructing full and bare life.⁹³ Indeed, Mbembe theorizes race and racism as central components of the necropolitical order.⁹⁴ Nevertheless, the focus on the Greater-Mexican context provides a new angle from which to explore these relationships.

The degree to which cyborg subjectivity interfaces with the biopolitical and necropolitical context becomes clear in light of Mbembe's assertion that, during the age of neoliberalism, "it is no longer certain that the human person is very distinct from the object, the animal, or the machine."⁹⁵ On its surface, this reverberates with Haraway's famous deconstruction of the human/animal/machine ontologies of ages past.⁹⁶ That said, the thinkers frame these deconstructions in antithetical ways. For Haraway, this juxtaposition has decentered the primacy of the human and allowed us to foreground the experiences of both the nonhuman and the dehumanized.⁹⁷ Mbembe, however, views this deconstruction as the result of a neoliberal ideology that commodifies bodies, viewing them only in terms of consumption. The robo-sacer lens allows us to reconcile both Mbembe's and Haraway's ideas about the deconstruction of the human. On the one hand, robo-sacer bodies validate Mbembe's misgivings by showing how different people can find themselves interpellated into *zoē* as society at large conflates their bodies with machines for production. Valencia makes this point especially clear when she states that, in neoliberal society, "we [Mexican workers] lose our *property rights to our own bodies*."⁹⁸ In this case, the deconstruction of human, animal, and machine strips people of their rights by casting workers as replaceable cogs in the machine of global commerce. On the other hand, however, the theoretical lens of robo sacer permits a radical deconstruction not only of race and gender, but of biopolitics itself. As such, the possibility of robo-sacer resistance reflects a degree of optimism by imagining how members of the purported *zoē* can deconstruct restrictive power differentials—and challenge "radical disenchantment"—through cyborg actions that denaturalize their dehumanized state.⁹⁹

Beyond its clear invocation of necropolitics, the term *necroliberalism* is also a useful play on words that looks and reads almost exactly like the term *neoliberalism*: the economic order that has overseen the expansion of these markets of death since the Washington Consensus and, especially, the passage of NAFTA. If Ángel Rama identifies the Mexican Revolution as the moment that heralded Mexico's—and even Latin America's—decade-late entrance into the twentieth century, then one could argue that Mexico entered the twenty-first century in 1994 with the implementation of its free trade agreement with the United States and Canada.[100] Indeed, most scholars attribute other key moments that occurred at the turn of the century, particularly Vicente Fox's presidential victory that ended seventy-one consecutive years of governance by the Partido Revolucionario Institucional (PRI) and the decision by Felipe Calderón to use the military to combat expanding drug trafficking, as direct results of the neoliberal transition, which resulted in greater electoral democracy on the one hand and greater human rights violations on the other.[101] That NAFTA could have such apparently contradictory effects throughout the country should come as no surprise to those familiar with the discussions that surrounded its creation.

NAFTA ultimately reconfigured the biopolitical landscape in Mexico itself by shifting priorities toward greater integration with the international economy. As Gareth Williams argues, during most of the twentieth century, Mexican modernity was "predicated on the permanent application of state power in the construction of social order, rather than on the self-limitation of state power via a legal system guaranteeing individual rights and limiting public power."[102] He thus characterizes the Mexican exception as one that dealt less explicitly with commerce and more with the establishment of a strong state that could ensure economic and political stability. Certainly, we should note that Williams argues against using Agamben to theorize Mexican biopolitics.[103] That said, his argument reflects his focus on the pre-neoliberal context, where the notion of a killable *homo sacer* made less sense. By the end of the twentieth century, however, the state had clearly identified the accruement of capital as an institutionalized state of exception that continuously justified the loss of life within the country in the service of the market. A central tenet of post-NAFTA biopolitics was the drive to attract foreign investment to Mexico through a robust state apparatus committed to defending property rights and other conditions necessary for commerce.[104] Throughout the twentieth century, and, one could argue, into the twenty-first, Mexican biopolitics has not centered on any commitment to individual rights. Rather, in the tradition of Roberto Esposito, the state has aimed to inoculate its population against the social threats that it apparently has posed to itself.[105] That said, the distinctions between the Mexican exception and the US exception—and the biopolitical practices that emerge as a result—have become less distinct as neoliberalism has taken hold.

The NAFTA negotiations provide one of the clearest windows into the thinking that characterized the expendability of the entire Greater-Mexican population. The negotiators spent significant time discussing the rights of corporations and the movement of goods—Mexican, US, and Canadian—across borders, but the final agreement remained silent on the free transit of labor.[106] Kevin R. Johnson goes as far as asserting that US officials failed to see the connection between free trade and migration.[107] NAFTA thus normalized the free flow of goods across borders even as it refused to codify a means through which people could legally move between countries as free trade invariably disrupted their economies. Far from creating programs to help Mexican peasants who lost their jobs as a result of NAFTA, US policymakers instead chose to militarize the border with a focus on blocking major immigration hubs in big cities.[108] These policies resulted in potential migrants choosing more dangerous routes that led many to die in the desert. Abraham Acosta has argued convincingly that these actions along the border reflected the fact that US policymakers viewed potential migrants as *homo sacer* subjects whose lives did not deserve the protection of the state.[109] US policy held that Mexicans could exist as consumers of US products or as producers of relatively inexpensive raw materials, but they could not be allowed to labor legally in the country.

Nevertheless, NAFTA itself created the conditions that forced millions of Mexicans to migrate either to the United States or to urban centers within Mexico. In no sector was this more pronounced than among Indigenous farmers who lost their competitive edge almost overnight to subsidized products, principally corn, from the United States. As a result, rural Mexicans abandoned their *milpas* (traditional fields dedicated to subsistence agriculture) and incorporated themselves into the global economy.[110] Viewed against this backdrop, NAFTA codified distinctions between *bios* and *zoë* by marking Mexican bodies as expendable vessels meant to produce and consume in the global economy. Displaced Indigenous migrants played an especially important role in this process; they migrated to places like Ciudad Juárez, where they would provide maquiladora labor that elites hoped to spread across the Mexican side of the border region. These same workers would further fuel Mexican modernity by spending their wages in national and global markets.[111] Of course, maquiladora work has long been associated with violence and death, a fact that I explore in depth in Chapter 3 and, especially, in Chapter 4. As marginalized individuals took on work in these sweatshops, they became literal cyborgs. Global capitalists ceased to view them as human in a legal and economic sense, instead viewing them as cogs in the machine of the global economy. If they died while producing inexpensive trinkets for international consumers, then another person would quickly take their place. Despite promises of a utopian entrance into modernity, the implementation of NAFTA had produced a dehumanizing dystopia.¹¹² Mexican and Chicanx literary and cultural producers thus began to question different tenets of the new economic order through an array of creative expressions.

## UTOPIA, DYSTOPIA, AND NAFTA IN MEXICAN AND CHICANX THOUGHT

Utopian and dystopian discourses have abounded in Latin America since the earliest days of the contact period. Miguel López-Lozano has written extensively on the utopian underpinnings of the writings of Columbus, who referred to the islands that he visited in Edenic terms.¹¹³ Interestingly, the study of utopianism began when the English thinker Sir Thomas More published his classic *Utopia* in Latin in 1516, precisely when European colonizers began to explore the new world.¹¹⁴ More built on the Greek term *ou-topos*, which means "no place," but he also created a pun: *ou-topos* sounds similar to *eu-topos*, which means "a good place."¹¹⁵ The term *dystopia* dialogues more directly with the meaning of eu-topos, as it denotes a "bad place." Certainly, the divisions between utopia and dystopia are difficult—if not impossible—to identify. Vivien Greene notes, "more often than not, [...] utopian fiction shows its underside, for the idea of utopia is frequently intertwined with notions of dystopia, an experiment that takes a tragic turn."¹¹⁶ The dystopian fictions that I discuss throughout this book challenge different utopian narratives whose pernicious underbellies have proven disastrous in Mexican and Chicanx circles. The main utopia that these dystopian fictions deconstruct is that of NAFTA and the neoliberal order. That said, they also critique exclusionary articulations of mestizaje and the patriarchal hegemony that permeated much of postrevolutionary Mexican thought and the Chicano Movement. The dystopian fictions discussed in this book prove especially valuable as they denaturalize—regardless of the source—a critical, utopian narratives of progress.

Perhaps the single most prevalent utopian discourse that these texts confront is that of NAFTA as a utopian institution that embodies the triumphalist advances of a post–Cold War neoliberal order. Indeed, the dystopian fictions discussed in *Robo Sacer* dovetail almost perfectly with the lifespan of that agreement. The United States, Canada, and Mexico started negotiating NAFTA in 1992, and the administrations of Donald Trump, Justin Trudeau, and Andrés Manuel López Obrador agreed to phase it out—albeit with a new free trade agreement called the United States-Mexico-Canada Agreement (USMCA)—in 2018. As such, this selection of works provides valuable insights into how strategies for resisting the necroliberal onslaught of US and global capital evolved as NAFTA's effects became more apparent. On its face, NAFTA embodied many ideals of left-leaning governments throughout the Americas as it heralded a hitherto unprecedented level of regional integration.[117] It is for this reason that an array of business leaders and academics welcomed the agreement with the hope that it would lead to Mexican and Latin American modernity.[118] Of course, many of the intellectuals of the time period—including those who embraced NAFTA with open arms—recognized that an acritical celebration of the supposed NAFTA utopia would make it much harder to confront any problems that would invariably arise as a result of trade liberalization. Carlos Monsiváis emphasized this when he wrote:

> The formulation of a utopian dream is, in fact, the renunciation of any problematization; it is to believe that the simple act of signing the agreement ends centuries of backwardness and scarcity. Long before we know what NAFTA will look like, the cultural dream hails it as the end of the country's marginalization (read: that of the governing class) in the world as it enters globalization, prosperity, and the First World by means of the North American Free Trade Agreement.
>
> *La formulación ensoñadora o utópica es, de hecho, la renuncia a cualquier problematización, es dar por sentado que el solo acto de la firma liquida los siglos de atraso y escasez. Mucho antes de que sepamos en qué consistirá el TLC, el sueño cultural le declara el fin de sitio arrinconado de la nación (léase su clase dirigente) en el mundo, a la globalización, a la prosperidad, al Primer Mundo por vía del Tratado de Libre Comercio.*[119]

As Monsiváis so powerfully asserts, the administrations of Carlos Salinas de Gortari and his successors celebrated NAFTA as a means through which Mexico could enter modernity. Their utopian language downplayed legitimate concerns that different stakeholders expressed both during and after the negotiations.

One particularly pointed critique came from Jorge G. Castañeda, who argued that NAFTA represented a particularly brutal integration under the auspices of "radical" US capitalism.[120] NAFTA had certainly integrated the countries of North America, but it had done so on terms that increased inequality and cast Mexican and Chicanx lives as inferior to those of white Anglo-Saxons in the United States and Canada. The Mexican government continued to support the deal even as it became apparent that its citizens, particularly those in rural areas, had suffered severe displacement and marginalization as a result of neoliberal policies.[121] The Mexican state's puzzling behavior makes sense when we consider Emmelhainz's assertion that NAFTA and neoliberalism are two interrelated manifestations of an Althusserian "common sense," or an ideology that, in the words of Stuart Hall, encompasses "the regime of the 'taken for granted.'"[122] For Althusser, ideology exists beyond materiality and history as a construct that creates an imaginary relationship between individuals and their surroundings.[123] In the case of NAFTA, neoliberalism functioned as a common sense that resisted criticism precisely because the populations of Mexico, the United States, and Canada generally agreed with the capitalist logics of supply and demand that undergirded the agreement.[124] Given this fact, most government officials—and perhaps the population at large—accepted the utopian premise even as the agreement demanded concessions in the short term. Official discourses held that NAFTA would benefit the country in the long run. That said, thinkers like Armando Bartra have called for a new utopian vision to arise in opposition to that of NAFTA and neoliberalism. As he argues, such an ideal would create a world where Mexican (and Chicanx) politics can move beyond "exhaust[ing] itself in parties that alternate in power" while generally maintaining the status quo.[125]

The dystopian fictions of Greater Mexico prove especially useful at this juncture. Rather than simply reify electoral democracy—which often does little more than change the face of oppression while maintaining the status quo for the most marginalized sectors of society—they call for new ways to imagine the social order.[126] Most, though certainly not all, of the dystopian fictions discussed in this book come in the form of science fiction (SF) or other fantastic genres or modes.[127] The focus on SF specifically takes on renewed significance when we consider John Rieder's observation that Western (particularly US and British) SF—both dystopian and not—generally "transposes the positions of colonizer and colonized."[128] Indeed, SF authors from the colonial center frequently recast Western European and US society as the Indigenous inhabitants of a world overrun by aliens, robots, zombies, or a host of other external enemies.[129] Rieder's excellent study foregrounds the socially committed nature of much SF, but his emphasis on literary and cultural production from the colonial center makes it difficult to consider how the political projects of SF shift when articulated from a postcolonial subject position. Other scholars, however, have written about SF from postcolonial contexts, and they have shown that the specter of colonialism is, if anything, even more overt in these fictions than in those of the colonial center. Where Rieder analyzes SF's ability to estrange the colonial center from its privileged position, these scholars show how writers from marginalized communities use SF, speculative fiction, and the fantastic to denaturalize the biopolitical conditions that continue to relegate them to the periphery.

Clearly, Latin American and US-Latinx SF operate in a plain distinct from that which Rieder theorizes. Beyond simply noting that inequality exists, these traditions of SF also identify strategies of resistance. In many ways, then, these SF traditions reverberate with Achille Mbembe's characterization of Afrofuturism, which he defines as:

> a literary, aesthetic, and cultural movement that emerged [. . .] during the second half of the twentieth century. It combines science fiction, reflections on technology in its relations with black cultures, magic realism, and non-European cosmologies, with the aim of interrogating the past of the so-called colored peoples and their condition in the present. Afrofuturism rejects outright the humanist postulate, insofar as humanism can constitute itself only by relegating some other subject or entity (living or inert) to the mechanical status of an object or an accident.[130]

Central to Mbembe's observation is the fact that Afrofuturism (and other related traditions) does not conform to the generic demands of so-called Western literature and cultural studies. Indeed, one could argue that the aesthetic rupture among SF, magical realism, horror, and other related genres is a necessary component of the movement's overall rejection of Western humanism as an ideology. As Afrofuturism—and, one could add, US-Latinx and Latin American dystopian fictions—break with generic divisions imposed by the colonial center, they create new methodologies for imagining alliances capable of challenging imperial mindsets and structures of power.

While borrowing heavily from their Afrofuturist comrades, Chicanafuturist writers and cultural producers have developed a thriving tradition of their own that exists independently of other literary and cultural modes. Catherine Ramírez coined the term *Chicanafuturism* in an article about the art of Marion C. Ramírez.[131] As she explains, "Chicanafuturism explores the ways that new and everyday technologies, including their detritus, transform Mexican American life and culture. It questions the promises of science, technology, and humanism for Chicanas, Chicanos, and other people of color."[132] Chicanafuturist—and variations like Chicanxfuturist—literary and cultural production ultimately questions how discourses of modernity have interfaced with the lived experience of communities of color. Not surprisingly, these fictions tend to engage questions of oppression while at the same time imagining means of resistance. Similar to the Afrofuturist traditions that Mbembe highlights, Lysa Rivera argues that Chicanafuturist literary and cultural production "repurposes the 'familiar memes of science fiction' to imagine, interrogate, and invent not only new political realities but also new cultural identities."[133] As I have shown previously, in many cases, Chicanafuturist cultural producers achieve this by placing SF in dialogue with magical realism, fantasy, the Gothic, and other adjacent genres and modes.[134] Building on Mbembe, it would seem that Chicanx authors do not merely produce innovative storytelling strategies when they combine different fantastic genres and modes. Rather, they undertake subversive strategies for criticizing the status quo.

Mbembe's discussion of Afrofuturism provides valuable tools for approaching SF from Latin America south of the Río Grande as well. Certainly, no one has coined a term like *Latin-Americanfuturism*, but critics like M. Elizabeth Ginway have argued that it is often more fruitful to use the term speculative fiction rather than SF when discussing texts from this region.[135] Indeed, the umbrella term of *speculative fiction* allows for the interchange of genres and modes—SF, fantasy, magical realism, etc.—without maintaining divisions that English-language literary and cultural producers have insisted on for decades.[136] In so doing, this terminology de-emphasizes many of the rigid divisions that critics from the outside have attempted to impose on the region's literary and cultural production.[137] Speculative fiction has grown in prominence in Mexico in recent years. As Carlos Gerardo Zermeño Vargas argues, "it is important to note that the study of these fictional forms is very timely, and that the classical semantics of the marvelous, horror, and science fiction fit easily in contemporary mass culture" (es preciso reconocer que el estudio de estas formas ficcionales tiene ahora plena vigencia, y es que las semánticas clásicas de lo maravilloso, el terror y la ciencia ficción tienen cabida fácil en la cultura de masas contemporánea).[138] Viewed in this light, despite historical marginalization, an array of fantastic genres and modes are taking on greater visibility and prestige in the study of (Greater-) Mexican letters.

Speaking broadly on the Latin American context, Silvia Kurlat Ares asserts that SF functions as a means through which cultures "read processes of social and cultural transformation, especially since the advent of modernity" (lee[n] procesos de transformación social y cultural, especialmente a partir del advenimiento de la modernidad).[139] This argument takes on especial currency in the Greater-Mexican ne(cr)oliberal period as literary and cultural producers have come to use dystopian fictions to decry the dehumanizing effects of transnational capital(ism) in their communities.[140] Clearly, SF provides a valuable tool for approaching dystopian (and utopian) themes given its penchant for imagining future technologies.[141] That said, dystopian (and utopian) literature comes in myriad forms. Often rooted in SF or the fantastic, it can also reflect a real-world aesthetic taking place in the present day or even the past. As López-Lozano asserts, dystopian fiction provides "the means for Mexican and Chicano authors to question fundamental tenets of Latin American culture such as the Western model of industrialized capitalism as the only possible pattern for the economic development of the hemisphere."[142] Mexican and Chicanx dystopian literary and cultural production thus provides a powerful tool for denaturalizing the necroliberal order by taking the insatiable desire for capitalist expansion to its logical, dehumanizing conclusion.

At the same time, utopian texts have proven attractive for imagining enticing futures that combat the discriminatory realities of the present. Nevertheless, these utopias have, themselves, often projected heavy-handed attitudes about the proper articulations of community identities. This perhaps holds most true with regard to the utopian ideal of mestizaje that re-emerged in Mexico with a vengeance following the Revolution before spreading across the border to Chicanx communities by the mid-twentieth century. Proponents throughout Greater Mexico envisioned racial hybridity as a means to promote an interracial and interethnic communion throughout Mexico and its diasporas. José Vasconcelos's *La raza cósmica* became the principal text on the ideal when it inscribed mestizaje in a triumphal narrative that placed Mexico and Latin America at the center of a racialized, utopian world history. This text—and an earlier one called *Prometeo vencedor*—dabbled with what we would now refer to as SF.[143] Viewed in this light, SF and utopia became key genres to the production of lettered documents that influenced policymaking throughout Mexico.[144] The fetishization of mestizaje and mexicanidad would abate by the 1960s and 1970s in Mexico, but a modified Vasconcelianism took root in the Mexican diaspora in the United States during precisely those decades.[145] Once more, a combination of utopian ideals and SF aesthetics came together to produce politically motivated, ethnoracial projects of emancipation.

One especially important utopian narrative entered the official Chicano imaginary in 1969, when a group of activists met in Denver, Colorado, to pen "El Plan Espiritual de Aztlán." The manifesto identified the US Southwest—broadly, and perhaps conveniently, defined to include all of the territories claimed by the United States following the Mexican-American War and the Texas Revolution—as the mythic land of Aztlán, the ancient homeland of the Mexica, the nation that eventually gave rise to the Aztecs.[146] The term *Chicano*, which derives from Mexica, thus referred specifically to a supposed ancestral inheritance that imbued contemporary Chicanos with a powerful claim to the land. Throughout the late 1960s and into the 1970s, Chicano activists, both men and women, deliberately tied their presence in the US Southwest to a mythic past by asserting themselves as the ancestral heirs to those lands.[147] Viewed in this light, terms like *Chicano* and its derivatives (particularly *Chicana* and *Chicanx*) have always functioned as overtly political labels that are "consciously and critically assumed" by the most militant members of the community.[148] Rafael Pérez-Torres argues that, "as a symbol of unity, Aztlán indicates a type of cultural nationalism that is distinct from—though meant to work hand-in-hand with—social activism."[149] Indeed, the imaginary of Aztlán created shared feelings of community that permitted Chicano activists to speak out against oppressive forces that relegated them to the periphery by forging an imagined nation that could articulate its own interests and goals.

Aztlán as conceived during the 1960s and 1970s called attention to the racialized and ethnic oppression that people of Mexican descent faced in the United States. Nevertheless, Chicano activists used the ideal to foreground the experience of men to the point of erasing, minimizing, and ignoring the contributions and demands of female Chicanas.[150] The scholar/playwright Cherríe Moraga famously stated that "what was right about Chicano nationalism was its commitment to preserving the integrity of the Chicano people. [...] What was wrong about Chicano nationalism was its institutionalized heterosexism, its inbred machismo, and its lack of cohesive national political strategy."[151] Indeed, the utopian drive of Aztlán remains a powerful imaginary among Chicanx communities into the present despite the problems that accompanied its earliest imaginings. Dylan A. T. Miner, for example, argues that the discursive value of the Aztlán utopia comes precisely from its ability to "enable critical inquiry and dialogue among competing positions."[152] The myth of Aztlán thus held (and holds) great potential precisely because it provided a site from which marginalized Chicano (and later Chicana and Chicanx) voices could speak. As these different members of Chicanx society coalesced around a shared ideal, they forged a dialogue not only between Chicanos and their oppressors, but among different segments of the Chicanx population itself.

During the 1980s, an array of queer and female Chicana activists began to question the ideological underpinnings that withheld Chicanas from Chicano discourse. At the same time, these Chicana feminists also pushed back against white feminism, which frequently ignored, and at times even opposed, Chicana political interests.[153] Chicana feminism thus emerged as Chicanas interrogated the intersections of race and gender within their communities. It was from this backdrop that Gloria Anzaldúa posited a (particularly queer) "mestiza consciousness" as the means through which Chicanas and Chicanos could reconcile their presence in the United States with their Mexican (Spanish and mestiza/x) and Indigenous ancestries.[154] Her goal, of course, was to "[undo] the legacies of patriarchy, homophobia, and European imperialism in the New World."[155] Viewed in this light, Anzaldúa's mestiza consciousness became explicitly utopian as it dared to call out a dystopian present within contemporary Chicano thought and white feminist thought and thus imagine a future free from racism, sexism, and homophobia.[156] Her writings stood at the fore of the Chicana-feminist movement that left a deep mark on her community by using the notion of utopia to inspire Chicanos, Chicanas, and their allies to aspire toward a more just order.

In many ways, Anzaldúa's theorizations of mestizaje set the stage for Haraway's cyborg manifesto. Nevertheless, Claire Taylor and Thea Pitman bemoan the overall silence from the academic community about the interface of mestizaje—particularly a racialized mestizaje—with cyborg theory.[157] Indeed, they highlight the fact that much Latin American and US-Latinx cultural production emphasizes the enthnoracial repercussions of technological hybridity by juxtaposing it with racial hybridity.[158] That said, the similarities between Haraway and Anzaldúa extend beyond a shared fetishization of hybridity. Both thinkers also situate their work within the reigning paradigms of science and technology.[159] This is not to say that cyborg and mestiza/x identities should be viewed as wholly interchangeable; rather, each represents different strategies for hybridity. The two ideals generally work toward similar inclusive ends, but technological and racial/ethnic hybridity can, at times, produce very different methodologies of disruption. Perhaps one of the most interesting shared characteristics of Anzaldúa's (and even Vasconcelos's) mestizaje and Haraway's cyborg is that each of these ideals builds on utopian articulations of SF to imagine their resistant potential. Chela Sandoval, for example, notes that Anzaldúa viewed her mestiza utopia as a "science fiction world-of-possibility born of privilege, oppression, hope, and horror."[160] For her part, C. Ramírez asserts deep ties between Anzaldúa and the literary production of the Afrofuturist author Octavia E. Butler.[161] More recently, Susana Ramírez has emphasized "how we can view [Anzaldúa] more directly as a sci-fi writer" by identifying the many SF stories (published and not) that she wrote throughout her life.[162] In highlighting not only Anzaldúa's affinity for SF but her own production of the genre, S. Ramírez provides a framework that allows us to approach the utopian discourse of *Borderlands/La frontera* at a deeper level. Beyond theorizing a hybridized subjectivity that resists the oppressive tendencies of US (Anglo) culture, Anzaldúa explicitly engages tropes of utopia, futurity, and even SF to communicate her ideal.

That Anzaldúa would express her mestiza consciousness through a utopian, SF-inspired essay fits current trends in critical theory. For example, Michael Hardt and Antonio Negri argue that dystopian fictions like cyberpunk provide a powerful discursive blueprint for a necessary refashioning of the body prerequisite to a radical reconceptualization of (neoliberal) society.[163] *Robo Sacer* builds on their assertion to show that dystopian literature provides an especially poignant vantagepoint from which to view the excesses of late capitalism. As they show the oppressive underbelly of their own fictional societies—which invariably bear the vice of runaway consumerism—these dystopian fictions denaturalize the utopian discourses that continue to abound in contemporary society. In highlighting how oppressive forces use technology as a tool for domination, these fictions reverberate with the words of Emmelhainz, who asserts that, in the neoliberal era, "control of the psyche is based on the biogenetic wiring that creates a subjectivity from which emerge techno-biological and techno-cognitive automatisms" (se basa en el control de la psique social a través del cableado biogenético que crea subjetividades y que emergen de automatismos tecno-biológicos y tecno-cognitivos).[164] That said, these fictions refuse to give in to total pessimism; rather, they imagine a resistant potential that continues to exist even in the most dystopian of contexts. As these fictions identify the techno-biological processes that continue to marginalize people of Mexican descent on both sides of the border, they also lay the groundwork for a subversive robo-sacer subject. These actors acknowledge the technological infrastructure that relegates them to the periphery. Rather than simply give up, however, they choose to lean into the technologies that surround them, donning them in a subversive light that delegitimizes the continued marginalization of Mexican and Chicanx subjects on both sides of the border.

## ORGANIZATION OF THE BOOK

I have organized the book in a way that allows us to consider different challenges that the necroliberal order has imposed on Greater Mexico. I have divided it into two sections and five chapters. Part 1, "Denaturalizing Greater-Mexican *Zoē*: The Early Stages of NAFTA (1992–2001)" consists of two chapters that engage texts written during the earliest years of NAFTA. The fictions that I engage here interrogate constructs of Mexican and Chicanx killability and *zoē*. They do not engage the specifics of NAFTA because the agreement had not been in place long enough for people to understand its precise ramifications. Rather, these fictions employ a speculative mode to imagine strategies through which Mexican and Chicanx individuals can contest their relegation to *zoē* through transgressive uses of technology. Part 2, "NAFTA after the Transition: Expendable Life in a Necroliberal Age (2006–2018)," looks at dystopias that came out after the ramifications of NAFTA had become more visible. Unlike the works discussed in the earlier section, these engage specific labor conditions that have emerged in NAFTA's wake, particularly the expansion of the maquiladora industry, the consolidation of transnational capital, and the explosion of the drug trade. The chapters imagine different types of robo-sacer activism through which oppressed classes can resist racism, feminicide, and drug violence.

Each section considers dystopias from both Mexican and Chicanx cultural producers, a fact that allows us to view the resistant potential of robo-sacer subjectivity from multiple vantagepoints. In this way, the book promotes a cross-cultural dialogue between Mexican and Chicanx narrative and cultural production. Most of the chapters juxtapose a work of Mexican fiction with a Chicanx one. That said, Chapter 3 deals with the dehumanization of cheap immigrant and Chicanx labor—subjects that are primarily Chicanx and US Latinx in nature. At the same time, Chapter 4 deals with the subject of feminicide, which has traditionally received greater attention within Mexican studies. Viewed together, Chapter 3 and Chapter 4 provide valuable insights into the different dimensions of the necroliberal dehumanization of racial and gender Others as they are incorporated into a life/*zoē*-consuming economy. In both cases, literary and cultural producers view technology as a means of both perpetuating and resisting the necroliberal order. Without further ado, let us turn to the chapters themselves.

Chapter 1, "Reimagining the Sanctity of Expendable Life: Necroliberal Markets and Secularly Holy Cyborgs in Cherríe Moraga's *Heroes and Saints* and Guillermo del Toro's *Cronos*," discusses how the neoliberal shift posed threats to Mexican and Chicanx lives even prior to the implementation of NAFTA. If the sacral nature of Agamben's *homo sacer* results from its killability, which becomes the means through which the state builds its own sovereignty, then the robo-sacer subjects of these fictions draw their sanctity from their ties to folk Catholicism and their ability to foment rebellion.[165] Produced during the early stages of the NAFTA negotiations in 1992, both works show the misgivings that Mexican and Chicanx thinkers felt about the expansion of free trade. Moraga and del Toro enunciate their critiques of the necroliberal order through secularly holy cyborg protagonists: Jesús Gris in *Cronos* (1993), Cerezita in *Heroes and Saints* (1992). Each character's ties to the cybernetically sacred denaturalizes societal constructs that relegate them to killable, bare life. The murder of these secularly holy cyborgs in both works serves not only to call into question the dehumanization of the protagonists but to chip away at the biopolitical underpinnings that would code others as expendable as well. These robo-sacer protagonists differ qualitatively from Agamben's *homo sacer* in that their deaths take on a sacrificial dynamic that ultimately catalyzes revolution—either metaphorical as in *Cronos* or real as in *Heroes and Saints*—against necroliberal interests.

Chapter 2, "Existing in the Necroliberal Order Online: Robo-Sacer Subjectivity in Pepe Rojo's 'Ruido gris' and Ernest Hogan's *Smoking Mirror Blues*," discusses two narratives that emerged a few years after the passage of NAFTA. Both speculative texts imagine a near future where capitalism has gone from simply tolerating the deaths of the *zoē* in its pursuit of profits to a place where death becomes a marketable end in and of itself. In both narratives, greedy television companies broadcast the deaths of *homo sacer* subjects on live television in order to increase ratings. The narratives thus imagine a further specialization of necroliberal markets where death itself becomes a lucrative commodity. All people can find themselves interpellated into bare life if a camera captures them in the moments prior to their deaths. Technology, particularly television broadcasts, plays an integral role in casting the characters of both narratives as killable. Furthermore, the protagonists of these narratives—a young, unnamed protagonist in "Ruido gris" ("Gray Noise" 1996) and an artificial intelligence (AI) rendering of the Aztec god of mischief Tezcatlipoca in *Smoking Mirror Blues* (2001)—can only conceive of effective resistance through the integrated circuit. Ultimately, Rojo and Hogan provide a split verdict about the efficacy of online resistance: both works suggest that technologies like television and internet provide a powerful space from which to undermine the status quo. Nevertheless, they prove less optimistic about the possibility of establishing a more democratic order. While members of the so-called *zoē* can scramble the political conditions in their respective contexts, neither one can instill a more democratic order in its place.

Chapter 3, "Hacking the *Bios*: Disposable Braceros and Bare Life in Alex Rivera's *Sleep Dealer* and Rosaura Sánchez and Beatrice Pita's *Lunar Braceros 2125–2148*," engages two speculative fictions that assert that the neoliberal order dehumanizes Chicanx, Mexican, US-Latinx, and Latin American workers throughout the hemisphere. In both *Sleep Dealer* (2008) and *Lunar Braceros* (2009), corporate interests align themselves with a necroliberal state that sucks labor and money from migrant workers. Both fictions imagine a necroliberal North American state that uses its technological superiority to police and perpetuate its hegemony. Rivera imagines a US-Mexico border region marked by a massive wall and drone surveillance. Sánchez and Pita tell of a future nation-state called Cali-Texas that sends the poor to reservations on earth and to labor camps on the moon. Even so, these works are among the most optimistic—even if only tentatively so—discussed throughout *Robo Sacer*. In each case, the necroliberal state's overdependence on technological superiority opens a space through which dedicated hackers can infiltrate the system and assert their political voice. Both works end before the main characters have completed a successful revolution, but they also conclude with the optimistic belief that oppressed people will continue to find ways to resist and reshape politics well into the future. In both works, robo-sacer activism proves especially valuable when hackers infiltrate the integrated circuit and undermine necroliberal interests from within cyberspace.

Chapter 4, "Robo-Sacer Resistance and Feminicide: Gabriela Damián Miravete's 'Soñarán en el jardín' and Carlos Carrera and Sabina Berman's *Backyard/El traspatio*," discusses the ethics of representation as it pertains to victims of feminicide in Mexico. The chapter begins with a discussion of *Backyard/El traspatio* (2009), a feature film that recreates many of the theories and narratives surrounding the mid-1990s feminicides in Ciudad Juárez. The producers framed the movie as resistant because it drew attention to the serial murder of women. Nevertheless, the film's use of a slasher aesthetic evinces its focus on profit over ethics. Beyond problematic shots that seem to fetishize murdered women's bodies, the film also adopts a slasher morality that blames sexually active women for getting themselves killed. The result is a film of questionable ethics whose ruminations on robo-sacer resistance feel like an afterthought. The primary prerogative is to exploit the stories of the desparecidas for profit. My reading of this story informs my discussion of "Soñarán en el jardín," ("They Will Dream in the Garden," 2018) which narrates the life of Marisela, a feminist activist who attempts to resurrect victims of feminicide through holograms of the dead that she infuses with public records, family photographs, and social media. The story optimistically alludes to the potential of using avatars and online mobilization as a "methodology of the oppressed" through which Mexican women can assert "joint kinship" against a murderous patriarchy.[166] At the same time, it also highlights an oppositional ethics and biopolitics between Marisela and the state. Because those in power exploit the spectral nature of the holograms to self-congratulatorily proclaim that they have ended the scourge of feminicide, they undermine attempts to resurrect the desparecidas.

Chapter 5, "Guns, Narcos, and Low-Tech Cyborgs: Magical Realism, SF, and the Posthuman in Julio Hernández Cordón's *Cómprame un revólver* and Rudolfo Anaya's ChupaCabra Trilogy," builds on Sophie Esch's characterization of firearms as "prosthes[es] for citizenship."[167] Produced in the wake of the devastating drug war that has intensified significantly since 2006, both Anaya's trilogy (2006–2018) and Hernández Cordón's film (2018) view drug trafficking as a quintessentially necroliberal enterprise that feeds on the lifeforce of Mexican and Chicanx bodies in a quest for ever-increasing profits. Both cultural producers situate their fictions at the threshold between traditional SF and magical realism, a fact that becomes especially important as they narrate their fictions from the point of view of female narrators who experience different degrees of marginalization. The fictions articulate violence and weapons in a way that builds on both SF and magical realism. On the one hand, armed resistance embodies the resistant potential of Haraway's cyborg as the oppressed use tools meant for their domination to assert their political voice. On the other hand, the use of weapons in both texts plays a central role in enunciating a magical-real mode: in *Cómprame un revólver* (*Buy Me a Gun*), the director juxtaposes acts of violence with magical-real imageries. For his part, Anaya imagines weapons as talismans that produce a mystical cyborg subjectivity that foments a mestiza/x communion with the past. In the end, both works provide a critical commentary about the prevalence of weapons in society. When the only means of resistance is to recreate the very structures of power that have marginalized so many, structural reform proves all but impossible.

Through these chapters, I show how an array of Mexican and Chicanx dystopian fictions have envisioned technology as both an agent of oppression and a means of resistance. Of course, beyond simply shedding light on the individual fictions studied, the case studies found herein also shed greater light on the biopolitical and necropolitical context that has emerged in NAFTA's wake. An array of thinkers has theorized the cyborg body from throughout the so-called Third World.[168] *Robo Sacer* contributes to those studies through its in-depth discussion of the nature of the robo-sacer body and resistance in dystopian literary and cultural production from Greater Mexico. Beyond its clear resonance with the dystopian traditions that it engages directly, this book also sheds light on the role of technology—and particularly that of the digital divide—in creating biopolitical conditions throughout Latin America and the developing world more generally. Ultimately, *Robo Sacer* invites its readers to imagine the potential for robo-sacer resistance in a necroliberal world that constantly interpellates people from marginal communities into bare life, *zoē*, and even *homo sacer* status.

# Part I. Denaturalizing Greater-Mexican *Zoē*

The Early Stages of NAFTA (1992–2001)

CHAPTER 1
# Reimagining the Sanctity of Expendable Life

Necroliberal Markets and Secularly Holy Cyborgs in Cherríe Moraga's *Heroes and Saints* and Guillermo del Toro's *Cronos*

The early 1990s posed significant challenges for Greater-Mexican cultural producers who attempted to navigate a society where a combination of electoral democracy and deregulated capitalism had emerged as the predominant blueprint for a modern nation-state. During these years, Mexican and Chicanx authors and cultural producers decried the further radicalization of neoliberalism in their work. One common theme that appeared across much cultural production was the question of how the continued advancement of unfettered capitalism would exacerbate the markets of death that had plagued the most vulnerable members of these societies for decades. It was against this backdrop that the Chicana intellectual and playwright Cherríe Moraga wrote and staged the play *Heroes and Saints* (1992) and Guillermo del Toro wrote and directed the film *Cronos* (1993).[1] These works differ significantly one from another, but they converge in their criticism of a necroliberal order that funds itself by draining Mexican, Mexican American, and Chicanx bodies and lives. Furthermore, both works present robo-sacer heroes whose cyborg articulations of secular sanctity encourage a reevaluation of what it means for killable life to be holy. The protagonists of *Heroes and Saints* and *Cronos* become secular saints who sacrifice themselves in a messianic way that sanctifies their resistance against necroliberal capitalism by challenging the validity of constructs of Mexican (and third-world) bare life and *zoē*.

The secularly sacred cyborg protagonists of these works challenge Giorgio Agamben's understanding of the sacrosanct nature of the *homo sacer* (a term that literally means sacred man). Regarding the sanctity of killable life, Agamben asserts that "the form of its exclusion (that is, of its capacity to be killed), has thus offered the key by which not only the sacred tests of sovereignty but also the very codes of political power will unveil their mysteries."[2] *Homines sacri*, then, are "sacred men" precisely because their liminal bodies straddle the division between *bios* and *zoē*, and the regulation of their existence becomes the very site of sovereignty. When hegemonic actors extralegally kill them with impunity, they validate the status quo and legitimize their claims to power. The protagonists of both the play and the film belong to a class of *zoē* whose right to life goes only as far as their ability to participate in the economy. Nevertheless, these characters' willingness to die for their communities sets them apart from traditional *homines sacri*. As they give their lives, these characters highlight how hegemonic society codes them as expendable on the one hand, even as they prove their undeniable humanity—and even holiness—on the other. The characters' will to action imbues them with a degree of agency that Agamben ignores in his own theorization of bare life, which implicitly rejects *homo sacer* autonomy. Instead, the protagonists of *Cronos* and *Heroes and Saints* sacrifice themselves and cement their roles as secular saints.[3] The act of sealing their resistance with their blood catalyzes a broader resistance against the necroliberal order.

A brief discussion of both works will facilitate our discussion.

*Heroes and Saints* takes place in the agricultural community of McGlaughlin, California, a fictional town whose federally funded, inexpensive housing has been constructed on top of land previously used for disposing of pesticides and other harmful chemicals. This results in an unusually high number of cancer cases and birth defects afflicting the town. No case of disease or birth defects takes on greater prominence than that of Cerezita Valle, a teenage girl who was born as a head with no body.[4] She achieves a degree of mobility through her *raite* (ride), a platform that she sits upon and can move with the help of a remote control that she keeps under her chin. An activist to the core, Cerezita instructs the town's children to hang the dead bodies of the deceased victims of childhood cancer on crosses. These actions capture the attention of the press. Cerezita meets a leftist priest named Juan who encourages her to go out in public so that she can inspire a movement against an agricultural industry that knowingly poisons the drinking water. For her part, Cerezita helps Juan to eschew the more conservative aspects of his faith so that he can better advocate for the interests of his flock. The climax occurs when the two characters enter a cornfield to crucify a recently deceased child. A team of sharpshooters fires on them from a helicopter, and Cerezita dies. The people of McGlaughlin respond by destroying the fields. Cerezita's sacrificial death thus spurs the people of McGlaughlin to political consciousness and action. Her unique articulation of cyborg identity and the sacred thus positions her as the ideal critic of those necroliberal policies that willingly contaminate and destroy Mexican and Chicanx bodies in the name of profit maximization.

*Cronos* tells the story of Jesús Gris, an Argentine expat who operates a modest antique shop in Mexico City, where he raises his granddaughter, Aurora, who has not spoken since the death of her parents.[5] His life undergoes drastic change when he acquires a baroque angel. Hidden within, he finds the Cronos Device, an insect-like gadget that can grant eternal life to its wearer. This immortality comes with a catch: the person who uses it becomes a vampire-like being who must drink human blood. Unbeknownst to Jesús, two wealthy foreign businessmen, the elderly Dieter de la Guardia and his nephew, Ángel de la Guardia, also seek the device. Ángel does not know of the device's power, but he runs errands for Dieter in hopes that he can inherit his uncle's factory and pay for a nose job. When the duo of robber barons realize that Jesús has the device in his possession, they attempt to extract it from him through increasingly violent means. At one point, Ángel beats Jesús, locks him in his car, and pushes it off of a cliff. Jesús is resurrected, but his new undead condition perturbs him. He visits Dieter in his factory to ask what has happened to him. The businessman informs him that he is now a bloodsucking creature of the night. When Jesús asks for a way out, Dieter attempts to stab him through the heart, but Aurora hits the man on the head and knocks him out. Ángel then arrives and a battle ensues between Jesús and Ángel. Jesús finally grabs his antagonist and hurtles them both to the ground several stories below. Ángel dies, but Aurora revives her grandfather with the Cronos Device. A desire to feed on Aurora's blood overcomes Jesús. He manages to resist the urge to kill her and instead destroys the device to avoid future temptation. He dies shortly thereafter, but Aurora is now safe.

As these summaries show, *Cronos* and *Heroes and Saints* center on secularly holy characters who invoke Christ and the Virgin of Guadalupe, the two holiest figures in Greater-Mexican Catholicism. In so doing, these protagonists emphasize their own *bios* as well as that of their communities at large. The secular sanctity of Cerezita and Jesús operates within a religious and spiritual framework of sacredness that reverberates with a significant body of scholarship on secular sainthood in the region. Within Latin America, major political figures often attain a type of secular canonization by carrying out revolutionary behavior on behalf of the people. Phyllis Passariello has written extensively on Che Guevara's secular sanctity, while Desirée A. Martin has discussed a similar condition among such figures as César Chávez, Pancho Villa, and Subcomandante Marcos.[6] Indeed, Martin provides valuable insights about secular sainthood in the borderlands that we can extrapolate for our own discussion of the secularly holy cyborgs of *Heroes and Saints* and *Cronos*:

> As figures that assume a sacred aura, in part because of their secular roles as political, revolutionary, or cultural icons, these saints perform and embody the contradiction of human and divine reflected in secular sanctity. Some of these secular saints remain on the margins, others insert themselves into or are appropriated by the center, and some shift back and forth between center and periphery. All of them bring the margins to the forefront, particularly during historical and political moments of crisis that shape and challenge state formation and national identity.[7]

This quote emphasizes the fact that secular sanctity tends to reflect not a person's miraculous actions in the spiritual realm—though these may exist—but the way that a person changes the sociopolitical context in which they live. Viewed through this lens, the fictional protagonists of *Heroes and Saints* and *Cronos* clearly qualify as secular saints: their actions continue to loom large in the economic and political order even after their deaths. Those characters who kill Cerezita and Gris lump them with a faceless *zoē* whom they can kill with impunity, but other marginalized people see these same characters as fully human victims of the excesses of a necroliberal order. Far from validating the status quo, the deaths of Jesús and Cerezita denaturalize economic systems that would code any human(s) as expendable.

In sacrificing their lives for a secular cause, these cybernetic, secular saints come to embody Christological sacrifice and thus implicitly reject Agamben's assertion that *homo sacer* lives cannot be sacrificed.[8] That said, at least at first, this sacrifice is only legible to members of the oppressed class who already recognize their shared humanity. In both works, the protagonists willingly give their lives for the liberation of other marginalized people. Their secular appropriation of saintly figures—particularly Christ and the Virgin—suggests a type of "spiritual mestizaje," a term that refers to the popular fusion of traditional Catholicism with marginalized forms of spirituality and even politics.[9] When Gloria Anzaldúa coined this term, she stated, "in our very flesh, (r)evolution works out the clash of cultures. It makes us crazy constantly, but if the center holds, we've made some kind of evolutionary step forward. *Nuestra alma el trabajo*, the opus, the great alchemical work; spiritual *mestizaje*, a 'morphogenesis,' an inevitable unfolding. We have become the quickening serpent movement."[10] Here Anzaldúa speaks of a mestiza cosmology that allows subaltern and marginalized peoples to live authentic lives free from the dogmas of the hegemony. Beyond living authentically, both Cerezita and Jesús also refashion the religious traditions of the hegemony and articulate a resistant and subversive popular spirituality in its stead. Secular sanctity thus creates a resistant potential that parallels that of Haraway's cyborg. Just as the technologically hybrid body's ambiguous nature can make it illegible to society at large, these secular saints' ambivalent articulations of secular and sacred subjectivity produce a type of spiritual mestizaje that imbues them with resistant potential.[11]

The cyborgian and secularly holy discourses of each of the aforementioned fictions buoy a shared political project, but they also reverberate with very different generic traditions. Both works fit within a dystopian framework: *Cronos* takes place in 1997, four years after the film's release and after the implementation of NAFTA, which would occur in 1994; *Heroes and Saints* speaks to the dystopian realities Mexican migrant workers had been facing for decades, and which continue in different forms into the present.[12] The dystopian elements of these works open certain dialogues with SF, particularly the focus on technology's role in oppressing marginalized bodies. At the same time, the works view cyborg identity as a means to achieve secular sainthood and spiritual mestizaje through the modes of Gothic horror (*Cronos*) and magical realism (*Heroes and Saints*). We can thus learn a great deal from both of these dystopias as we interrogate the dialogue between SF and other related modes and genres. Critics often demand clear-cut divisions between genres like SF, horror, fantasy, and magical realism; nevertheless, such scholarly approaches often fail to explain literary conditions as they exist on the ground. Indeed, despite an almost total critical silence surrounding the intersection of SF and magical realism in Latin American literature, both modes engage similar subject matters like (post)colonialism and the onset of modernity.[13] Scholars have dedicated more time to parsing out the relationship between Gothic horror and science fiction.[14] Some have asserted that the genres engage technological advancement in very different ways: Gothic horror warns of the dangers of mad science, while SF frames technological advancement as an indicator of "progress and intelligence."[15] These generalizations may capture the particularities of each of the aforementioned genres in broad strokes—particularly in the US context—but they still leave a degree of ambiguity that makes it difficult to adequately classify certain works as one or the other.

This holds especially true with the cinema of del Toro (and especially *Cronos*), which, according to Gabriel Eljaiek-Rodríguez, "moves constantly between horror cinema and fantastic cinema" (se mueve constantemente entre el cine horror y el cine fantástico).[16] The difficulty in classifying *Cronos* becomes all the more apparent when we consider the words of Vivian Carol Sobchack, who asserts that "the horror film is primarily concerned with the individual in conflict with society or with some extension of himself, the SF film with society and its institutions in conflict with each other or with some alien other."[17] Both facets of this attempted differentiation between the genres adequately describes different components of *Cronos*. Jesús's internal battles with the Cronos Device and his bloodlust jibe with Sobchack's definition of horror, which plays up the individual's internal conflict. Nevertheless, given that the film emphasizes Jesús's antagonistic relationship with Dieter and Ángel de la Guardia, the director also pushes a societal critique that corresponds more clearly to SF. Sobchack's definition thus suggests that, while *Cronos* looks like a horror film on the surface, its politics align more precisely with SF. This is not to downplay the significance of Gothic horror in the film. Indeed, much of *Cronos*'s allegorical weight emerges through the generic tension between SF and horror that emerges as it balances individual- and societal-level conflicts. For example, Jesus's ability to overcome the temptation to consume human blood occurs at the individual level and reverberates with horror themes and aesthetics. Yet this personal domination marks him as a secularly sacred Christological cyborg who can worthily resist unfettered international capitalism.[18] We cannot satisfactorily classify *Cronos* as only Gothic, horror, or SF because the production intertwines elements from all of these traditions through its narratological and political discourse.

In a similar way, Moraga uses the intersection of SF and magical realism to imbue her main protagonist with a redemptive glow. The play thus shows the value of placing SF and magical realism in conversation one with another, despite the fact that almost no scholarship has interrogated the slippage between these literary genres. The competition between SF and magical realism in Latin America continues to play out in the criticism and in popular thought. Nevertheless, as *Heroes and Saints* shows, cultural producers have often toyed with both genres in ways that challenge clear divisions between them. Unlike horror, which is a genre in and of itself, magical realism is a literary mode that can appear in many genres. That said, the most prominent magical-real literature tends to take place in a real-world setting where people take magical events for granted.[19] Because of this, many Latin American writers and, later, critics decried magical realism for its exoticization of the region and its peoples.[20] At the same time, other scholars have highlighted a decolonial element to magical-realist literature by emphasizing its rejection of Western epistemologies.[21] Moraga wrote *Heroes and Saints* a few years before the major breaches with magical realism took on prominence in Latin American literary studies. Throughout the play, she exploits the mode's emancipatory potential through Cerezita: the bodiless, cyborg head whose very presence evokes both SF and magical realism. Her hybrid subjectivity creates a deconstructive aesthetic that is especially well-suited for decrying the necroliberal policies that have damaged her town.

Clearly, ne(cr)oliberalism posed significant problems to Greater Mexico even prior to NAFTA. Most historians agree that Miguel de la Madrid (1982–1988)—the president who oversaw the General Agreement on Trade and Tariffs (GATT)—laid the groundwork for the passage of NAFTA and Mexico's further integration into the neoliberal order.[22] Of course, capitalism and trade liberalization were not new in the 1980s, either; the market-based policies of Miguel Alemán (1940–1946) had laid the groundwork for the eventual transition to neoliberalism nearly a half century earlier. Moraga and del Toro were thus intimately familiar with the dehumanizing potential of unfettered capitalism long before 1994. In a similar vein, most scholars agree that the United States became a full-fledged neoliberal economy with rise of the "populist conservatism of Ronald Reagan" during the 1980s.[23] Of course, the transition had begun in the 1970s or even the late 1960s, and California, where Reagan served as governor from 1967 to 1975 and the state in which Moraga sets her play, provided the neoliberal blueprint that the rest of the nation (and world) would follow.[24] Indeed, Julie Guthman notes that California's agricultural sector was a significant site of contention during the neoliberal expansion.[25] The deregulation of the agricultural industry had serious repercussions for migrant workers. Mexican, Mexican American, and Chicano field hands saw their legal protections drop significantly throughout the state as businesses began engaging in aggressive agricultural practices—particularly the (over)use of carcinogenic pesticides—that poisoned local grounds and waterways and created serious health epidemics.[26] Due to their legal status, many Mexican fieldworkers had limited legal recourse; this, in turn, exacerbated a necroliberal context that coded migrant farmworkers as an exploitable and even expendable *zoē* whose very lives could be sacrificed in the name of capitalist accumulation. These new realities sit at the heart of *Heroes and Saints*, a play that decries the conditions that plagued migrant workers throughout California and the United States.

## THE CYBORG VIRGIN AND CHILDHOOD CANCER IN CHERRÍE MORAGA'S *HEROES AND SAINTS*

Originally staged in 1992, Cherríe Moraga's *Heroes and Saints* won numerous awards in its first year.[27] This commercial success in no way undermined the critical and resistant nature of the play. The cancer cluster in the fictitious town of McGlaughlin resonated with similar conditions in McFarland, California, a real-world San Joaquin Valley town of fewer than ten thousand where thirteen children were diagnosed with cancer from 1978 to 1988.[28] César Chávez and Dolores Huerta spoke out against the crisis and produced a documentary, *The Wrath of Grapes* (1986), that showed graphic examples of birth defects and childhood cancer cases that had resulted from the irresponsible disposal of arsenic-rich pesticides.[29] Moraga credited this film with inspiring *Heroes and Saints* both because it encouraged her to explore the ecological crises of the San Joaquin Valley and because it tells the story of a boy who was born without arms or legs as a result of his mother's exposure to pesticides during her pregnancy.[30] The boy's condition perturbed Moraga so much that she felt compelled to include it in her play. Just as the limbless boy's physicality drew attention to the necroliberal violence waged against agricultural field hands, Cerezita's bodilessness denaturalizes the conditions that have cast profit maximization as a state of exception that justifies the destruction of Mexican and Chicanx bodies. Cerezita leverages her secular sanctity and her cyborg condition in order to carry out meaningful robo-sacer resistance that challenges the necroliberal status quo.

Indeed, Cerezita's bodiless, cyborg head plays a central role in creating a resistant aesthetic that builds on SF and magical-real tropes. Moraga emphasizes Cerezita's liberatory potential in the opening stage directions:

> CEREZITA is a head of human dimension, but one who possesses such dignity of bearing and classical Indian beauty she can, at times, assume nearly religious proportions. [. . .] This image, however, should be contrasted with the very real "humanness" she exhibits on a daily functioning level. Her mobility and its limits are critical aspects of her character. For most of the play, CEREZITA is positioned on a rolling, tablelike platform, which will be referred to as her "raite" (ride). It is automated by a button she operates with her chin.[31]

Several critics have recognized the play's magical-real aesthetic; indeed, the idea of a living, bodiless head functions especially well in that mode.[32] Moraga's ties to SF are perhaps less immediately apparent, but the referent of an apocalyptic health crisis stemming from corporate greed and Cerezita's robo-sacer condition establishes clear parallels with dystopian literature and other brands of SF. The play's cyborg dynamic is especially interesting when we consider the fact that Moraga is one of only a handful of authors that Haraway engages directly in her Cyborg Manifesto. For Haraway, "Moraga's writing, her superb literacy, is presented in her poetry as the same kind of violation as Malinche's mastery of the conqueror's language—a violation, an illegitimate production, that allows survival."[33] While the theorist refers specifically to Moraga's *Loving in the War Years* (1983), her words could apply just as easily to *Heroes and Saints*. What is more, Haraway's quote explains Cerezita's subversive articulation of both cyborg subjectivity and secular sainthood.

Throughout the play, Cerezita's bodiless head becomes the vicarious face of the women and children who have suffered the most due to unsafe farming practices in the San Joaquin Valley.[34] The bodiless head has a long history in the Chicano, Chicana, and Chicanx imaginary that extends back to the Olmecas.[35] Ever since Luis Valdez staged *The Shrunken Head of Pancho Villa* in 1967, it has taken on a revolutionary value as well.[36] Cerezita's presence lays bare the stakes and the reach of Moraga's radical politics, which aim for nothing less than the emancipation of migrant workers, particularly women, throughout the United States.[37] Given this fact, it is especially important to tease out the nature of Cerezita's robo-sacer resistance. The migrant girl's deformity reflects the inequitable relationship of Anglo Americans and Mexican Americans to farming technology; Cerezita's bodiless condition is the result of her mother's exposure to toxic chemicals during her pregnancy. Her dependence on her raite for any semblance of autonomy associates her with cyborg identity.[38] Of course, this subjectivity ultimately reflects the traumas of ecological injustice rather than the wonders of technoscience.[39] Viewed in a vacuum, Cerezita's cyborg condition is insufficient in and of itself to catalyze revolutionary acts; this fact rings clear when her mother, Dolores, takes the girl's remote and imprisons her in place.[40] While the cybernetic condition created by her raite plays a key role in constructing Cerezita's ambiguous corporeality, Cerezita only succeeds in softening her mother after fully appropriating the image of the Virgin of Guadalupe near the play's end.

Given Cerezita's articulations of both technological hybridity and the holy, it becomes useful to view her as a cyborg Virgin: a figure that draws its revolutionary potential from both technological and mythic sources. I have previously identified cyborg Virgin figures in the mid-century Mexican context who had "a secular salvatory potential."[41] The case of Cerezita shows that this phenomenon appears within communities separated by time, geography, and even nation-state boundaries. Ever since Haraway famously asserted that she would "rather be a cyborg than a goddess," people have tended to view posthumanism in conflict with ecofeminism, which is the intellectual feminist movement that most favored the construction of goddess figures.[42] Nevertheless, critics like Nina Lykke argue that, despite a tendency to revert to "the artefactual" (cyborg) and "the natural" (goddess) respectively, "both [goddesses and cyborgs] challenge the ways in which the modern scientific world-view is rooted in a long tradition that casts the non-human in the role of a mere object and exploitable resource for the human."[43] Lykke's argument takes on greater urgency within the context of this play, where necroliberal interests and biopolitical divisions cast Cerezita and her community as expendable. No figure in the Greater-Mexican religious imaginary more aptly answers Lykke's call for "cybergoddesses" than the cyborg Virgin.[44] The Virgin of Guadalupe's ties to pre-Columbian, Mesoamerican goddesses transformed her into the nations' most popular saint.[45] Viewed in this light, Cerezita's cyborg Virgin sits at the juncture between posthumanism and ecofeminism.

Cerezita's conflation of cyborgian and ecofeminist traits not only challenges the dehumanizing ideologies of runaway capitalism; it also calls the town's inhabitants to political action. Her subversive performance as a cyborg Virgin emphasizes the nationalist potential of Guadalupism—though Cerezita's Chicana/x nation will clearly "accommodate corporeal variation"—while largely downplaying the figure's demand for traditional values.[46] One of the play's earliest scenes shows how Cerezita leverages her robo-sacer status for broad critiques. She sits upon her raite in front of the window and watches as a ewe nurses her lambs. She muses, "the sheep drink the same water we do from troughs outside my window. Today it is an orange-yellow color. The mothers dip their heads into the long rusty buckets and drink and drink while their babies deform inside them. Innocent, they sleep inside the same poison water and are born broken like me, their lamb limbs curling under them."[47] While perhaps overly didactic, this scene underscores a shared biopolitical marginality between Cerezita and farm animals, both of whom belong to a disposable class of life. Cerezita stands in as a synecdoche for the Mexican, Mexican American, and Chicanx populations at large, and as such she severely criticizes environmentally racist farming techniques in the United States. While Cerezita obviously benefits from medical care where the lambs will not, she clearly does not enjoy the same access to preventive protections as do people born in more well-to-do parts of the state.

Cerezita's cyborg status accentuates and challenges the institutionalization of her bare life by highlighting how society views her health as less valuable than that of rich, white people who live far from McGlaughlin. This backdrop leads Arden Elizabeth Thomas to view *Heroes and Saints* as a denunciation of "environmental racism, in which people of color are disproportionately affected by environmental hazards in places where they live, work, and play."[48] María J. Durán builds on Thomas's argument by identifying a systemic use of "slow violence," a term that refers to "environmental degradation that manifests as occluded forms, occurring gradually across time and space," throughout the play.[49] The notion of slow violence suggests a necroliberal logic where childhood cancer and birth deformities are the deadly price that agricultural companies willingly pay to increase profits. The pediatric deaths are structural rather than personal; the victims are *homines sacri* whose lives and health do not figure into decisions about profit maximization. The play's denunciations take on greater urgency when we realize that Moraga deliberately used the performance to speak out against the real-world case of McFarland, where state and industry leaders refused to revise farming techniques despite mounting evidence that unsafe agricultural practices had created cancer clusters in migrant communities.

The actions of state and industry leaders in addressing the cancer clusters in McFarland evinced a desire to maintain the economic status quo rather than improve public health. For example, the state of California sponsored studies that questioned the ties between environmental degradation and negative health results in rural areas. An especially salient example of this scholarship came from Peggy Reynolds, a scientist from the California Department of Health who argued that the statistically significant increases in cancer cases in McFarland had formed arbitrarily.[50] The researchers noted that McFarland's waterways had more arsenic than those of other parts of the state, particularly those in whiter and urban areas. Even so, the researchers asserted that this known carcinogen could not account for the high cases of cancer. They based these assertions on a problematic quantitative study that looked at other agricultural communities that, they claimed, had similar amounts of arsenic in the ground and water but a "normal" number of cases of childhood cancer.[51] Certainly, Reynolds et al. noted that they had made several suppositions that may have skewed their statistical analyses, but they remained adamant that the elevated level of arsenic in the town's water had not contributed to the cancer cluster. Reynolds and another team doubled down on this assertion in a later study. They found an increase in child leukemia in areas that used the pesticide propargite, but they refrained from calling for greater environmental restrictions because they claimed they saw no "dose-response trend over categories of increasing pesticide use."[52] As such, the contamination of rural waterways continued largely unabated, and agricultural executives continued to earn significant profits on the backs of a migrant-worker population that bore the brunt of the negative health-related externalities of these practices.

The aforementioned studies largely ignored the stories of the children who had taken ill. In order to cast doubt on assertions that under-regulated farming practices had disproportionately affected poor children of color, they kept these victims as invisible as possible. These studies' rhetorical strategy reflected how they used the reigning biopolitical framework to justify their necroliberal ends: by referring to cancer cases as numbers, they depersonalized their findings and downplayed the human cost. As state-sponsored researchers produced studies that concluded that wealthy stakeholders were not at fault for these invisible children's diseases, business executives could appear invested in resolving the public health crisis even as they maintained a status quo that was killing many of the most vulnerable members of society. From a biopolitical standpoint, it ultimately did not matter if the state had enabled the cancer outbreaks or if McFarland had just been an unfortunate hotbed of arbitrary cancer cases: the state strove to exonerate itself by exploiting a perpetual state of exception—the need for agricultural production—to cast migrant workers and children as *homines sacri*. Mexican, Mexican American, and Chicanx bodies thus became disposable entities that the state's economic stakeholders were willing to exploit—and even kill—to expand their markets. As Carolina L. Balazs et al. note, this largely remains the case today; elevated levels of arsenic continue to plague the waterways of majority-Latinx communities both in the San Joaquin Valley and throughout the United States.[53]

Given a historical context where "officials deny responsibility, official investigations are fruitless, and the industrial and the agricultural lobby in the state capital has too much power," Moraga's play became all the more urgent.[54] She employs performance techniques meant to denaturalize the dehumanization of the victims by making characters with cancer visible to the audience.[55] The biopolitical divisions of McGlaughlin are perhaps more explicit and exaggerated than what one would find in its real-life counterpart of McFarland, but this only serves to underscore problems that plague Mexican and Chicanx communities in the real-world United States. Throughout the play, the sound of crop-dusters testifies to the necroliberal logic that allows the agricultural industry to treat crops at the expense of Mexican and Chicanx farmworkers.[56] When agricultural companies face resistance, they turn to police helicopters and even live-ammo firearms to keep migrant farm workers in line. The play thus posits access to science and technology as one of the key factors to maintaining the necroliberal system in place. Those in power enjoy the benefits of modernity while shouldering little cost; Mexican and Chicanx fieldhands bear its burdens while reaping few benefits.

As the curtain rises, a group of children dressed in traditional *calavera* (Mexican skull) masks carries a small cross to a cornfield and crucifies a recently deceased child.[57] We learn that this is not an isolated event when a reporter named Anna Perez addresses an implied camera—really the audience—and states, "McGlaughlin is commonly believed to be in a cancer cluster area, where a disproportionate number of children have been diagnosed with cancer in the last few years. [. . .] One of the most alarming recent events which has brought sudden public attention to the McGlaughlin situation has been a series of . . . crucifixions, performed in what seems to be a kind of ritualized protest against the dying of McGlaughlin children."[58] It is telling that Anna Perez finds the crucifixions more disconcerting than the fact that these children have died in the first place. Indeed, Durán argues that the reporter "erroneously focuses on the form of the protest itself rather than on the cruelty and injustice that the children are protesting."[59] Nevertheless, Anna Perez's performance contributes to what Linda Margarita Greenberg calls a "pedagogy of crucifixion" that "teaches the audience [though not necessarily the characters] to re-read the dead as corporate murder rather than private loss, as active *sacrifice* rather than victimhood."[60] The dead children's evocation of Christ highlights their sacrificial potential and denaturalizes their expendability. Most Christian religions hold Christ's crucifixion to be the greatest of all sacrificial acts; the Bible teaches that this death purifies all of humanity and makes it possible to return to God. By appropriating Christological imageries and ascribing them to these children, Moraga denounces constructs of power that have interpellated them into bare life and *zoē*. The local activist Amparo draws attention to this when she states, "if you put the children in the ground, the world forgets about them. Who's goin tu [sic] see them, buried in the dirt?"[61] While government officials claim to oppose the crucifixions on a humanitarian level—these acts are "cruel"—Amparo's words suggest that this opposition more probably stems from the fact that these acts threaten the necroliberal business model. By challenging migrant children's *homo sacer* status, a condition that agricultural companies have exploited for decades in an attempt to build laws that favor their industry over children's rights, these crucifixions have the potential to revolutionize the current modes of production and hurt the pocketbooks of agriculture executives.[62]

For a public familiar with the McFarland crisis, these crucified bodies represent those anonymous children who died of cancer during the 1980s. The play thus uses fiction to bring about a reckoning of sorts for those sectors of Californian society that contributed to the McFarland cancer cluster. William Acree asserts "that the theatre can function as a purveyor of justice, as a space where trials take place, and as a means to come to terms" with injustice.[63] While he refers specifically to the post-dictatorial theatre of the Southern Cone, his argument sheds light on the theatre's potential to hold vicarious trials in any society where the legal apparatus has failed to mete out justice. *Heroes and Saints* provides proxy bodies to stand in for the real-life victims of McFarland, thus encouraging its audience to recognize what happened and take the necessary steps to resist similar events in the future. Of course, Moraga aims to do more than simply provide a surrogate set of bodies and individuals for audiences to identify with in order to mourn. One of the most dangerous potentials of Acree's trial of theatre is that it often produces feelings of catharsis and closure that may frustrate the performance's overall revolutionary potential. Such an effect would run counter to Moraga's goals in writing this play, which has its roots in the highly activist Teatro Campesino movement of the 1960s.[64] Clearly, Moraga aimed for this work to resonate with viewers and contribute to discussions that would catalyze meaningful change regarding environmental racism in agricultural communities.

The playwright uses her cyborg Virgin protagonist to avoid a cathartic end and to call her audience to political action. Cerezita's cybernetic head commands a combination of pity and reverence that she exploits when persuading others—whether characters of the play or even members of the audience—to join her cause. Moraga teases Cerezita's potential at the beginning of the play when Juan arrives at her home and asks Dolores if she would like him to "hear [Cerezita's] confession."[65] The mother replies "what sins could a girl like her have, Padre? She was born this way. Es una santa. We should pray to her, I think."[66] While probably not meant to disconcert the priest, this suggestion alludes to the tension inherent to Cerezita's performance. The cyborg Virgin trope necessarily draws much of its discursive power from the images of traditional Catholicism. At the same time, because Cerezita's cyborg Virgin performance operates within a secular plane, her performance necessarily toes a precarious line between popular and traditional beliefs on the one hand and blasphemy on the other. Indeed, despite her association with the sacred, Cerezita constantly calls religious figures and dogmas into question. We see this most explicitly during her first conversation with Juan:

Juan: Can you turn around? I'd like to talk to you face to face.
Cerezita: You're wasting your time, Padre. I have no use for God.
Juan: You don't believe?
Cerezita: I don't care.[67]

In affirming her own agnosticism, Cerezita raises the possibility of using traditionally religious symbolic forms, such as the Virgin of Guadalupe, in innovative ways. Her cyborg articulation of the Virgin takes advantage of the figure's knack for uniting Mexican and Chicanx communities while at the same time sidestepping questions of faith or an afterlife. This is not to say that she speaks against the value of religion; rather, the veracity of a specific faith lies beyond her concern.

Throughout the play, the institution of the Catholic Church—as opposed to popular faith—serves to thwart revolutionary desire. For example, Juan's affinity for liberation theology makes him into an ally of the people of McGlaughlin, but it also highlights his marginality both within the Church and within state and national politics. At one point we hear a news anchor on the radio report the assassination of several leftist clerics in El Salvador.[68] This dialogue serves first and foremost to frame the health crisis in McGlaughlin within movements for greater social justice throughout Latin America. Héctor Calderón notes that Moraga frequently criticized "the timidity of Chicano literature during conservative times."[69] In including this reference Moraga expresses solidarity with Latin American liberation movements and identifies a shared plight between migrant workers and people from south of the US border.[70] At the same time, this report also highlights Juan's own expendability within McGlaughlin. As a man of the cloth, he enjoys greater privilege than do others, but his advantages will dissolve if he uses his position to advocate too hard for social change. Juan's condition reverberates with the play's historical referent: Pope John Paul II arrived in Nicaragua in 1983 and publicly censured Ernesto Cardenal, a Catholic priest and poet who had joined the *Sandinista* government as minister of culture. Part of the rebuke reflected the recent amendments to the Code of Canon Law that prohibited priests from holding political office. Nevertheless, the very public nature of this action made it clear that liberation theology was not consistent with this pope's vision for the Church.[71] Pope Francis would later revoke all disciplinary actions against Cardenal in 2019, but *Heroes and Saints* takes place in a climate where Juan's political leanings could mark him as apostate and even expendable.[72] His internal struggle between a desire for social activism and his commitment to his faith underscores the fact that he cannot authentically follow both paths.

The second act shows Cerezita transform Juan and many other characters into unashamed activists. She uses her cyborg Virgin performance to replace the traditional (conservative) imageries of the institutional Church with new ones that advocate for the secularly holy cause of social justice. She achieves this with Juan in a scene where she appropriates the image of the Virgin while at the same time bending the figure in ways that traditional Catholics would undoubtedly view as profane. Cerezita makes plans to crucify her unnamed niece with Juan and the town's children shortly after the baby dies. The conversation between the cyborg Virgin and the priest starts with a political focus, but it soon takes on a sexual dynamic. Cerezita says, "I want to taste you, Juan."[73] After sharing an awkward kiss, the priest drops his pants and moves behind her, where he essentially makes love to Cerezita's raite while she begs for him to come around to the front so that she can participate in oral sex.[74] This scene complicates Greenberg's assertion that, "in performing as la Virgen de Guadalupe, Cerezita enacts a saintliness that sacrifices her private self and sexuality [. . .] and must lay those desires to the side in order to become la Virgen for the communal good."[75] Given that Juan's true conversion to the cause occurs only after this sexual encounter, it would appear more likely that this articulation of cyborg Virgin subjectivity achieves its resistant status precisely through a heavy focus on female, nonheteronormative, and nonreproductive sexuality.[76] One could argue that Moraga's emphasis on the value of pleasure casts Juan in a negative light because he flees the home after an awkward climax that leaves Cerezita unsatisfied.[77] That said, this scene also "explores the intersections of sexuality and culture and how these intersections can be used to create powerful subjectivity."[78] Indeed, this segment of the play underscores the deep ties between sexual liberation and environmental justice in Moraga's thought.

The sex act between the priest and cyborg Virgin reasserts the Virgin of Guadalupe's historical ties to Coatlicue and other pre-Columbian fertility and Earth goddesses.[79] The fact that Cerezita draws her power from evoking this pantheon of Indigenous deities differentiates her from mid-century Mexican cyborg Virgins whose resistant potential "comes from their adherence to traditional performativity."[80] As she uses her raite to give, and perhaps experience, the pleasures of the flesh, Cerezita transforms the signification of the Virgin of Guadalupe not only for Juan and herself, but also for the audience. Cerezita transforms herself into a sexualized Virgin prior to converting wayward participants to her cause. As such, the play fits within a tradition of Chicana feminist literature that "refuse[s] the objectification imposed by gender roles and racial and economic exploitation."[81] This scene also speaks to Moraga's own focus on embodiment in both her literary production and her activism. As she explained in an interview with the *Yale Daily News*, "you cannot have a movement without bodies, without people interacting physically, without them meeting in groups and working ideas out face-to-face. [. . .] There has to be embodied action."[82] The embodied action occurs on at least two levels here: Cerezita's (cybernetic) embodiment of the secularly sacred repurposes the Guadalupan image in a way that will no longer inhibit people like Juan from political action. In so doing, she helps the priest to assume a more proactive role that will eventually result in mass protests against the necroliberal financial interests that inundate McGlaughlin.

This retooled cyborg Virgin has a similar effect on Dolores after Cerezita cuts her hair and dresses up like the Virgin of Guadalupe.[83] Dolores has not let her daughter leave the home throughout the play in part to guard her sexuality.[84] In so doing, she has kept her daughter from forming meaningful relationships with people outside her family and made it impossible for her to live the Agambian good life. Beyond hurting Cerezita's social and political life, Dolores has also made it difficult for her daughter to speak out about the McGlaughlin health crisis and other causes that she cares about. As such, Cerezita must first confront the realities within her own community that marginalize female and disabled voices before she can take on Big Agriculture. She achieves this by tapping into her cyborg Virgin status and producing secular sainthood by "blend[ing] popular and orthodox spirituality."[85] Indeed, her mother later worships her rather than the portrait of the Virgin of Guadalupe that hangs on the wall. Cerezita convinces her mother to let her leave the home and participate in her niece's funeral. Yvonne Yarbro-Bejarano argues that, if Cerezita wishes to be a hero that she "must become the saint that her mother wants her to be."[86] That said, Cerezita also demonstrates a great deal of agency by transforming the very imaginary of female sainthood from one of self-renunciation and motherhood into one of social engagement. Indeed, Maria Alicia C. Garza argues that "the melding of the Virgen de Guadalupe and Cerezita is a necessary strategy [. . .] to work through and around institutionalized Catholicism since it no longer is a source of hope for the community."[87] This resignification of the Virgin allows Cerezita to catalyze the "paradigm shift" that allows Dolores to view the hardships of her own life through the lens of social justice rather than religion.[88]

Cerezita remains powerfully redemptive until the end of the play. Similar to the Virgin of Guadalupe, she holds the potential to call people—especially those of Mexican and Mesoamerican descent—to action. Joanna L. Mitchell views Cerezita's performance of the Virgin as a "ploy."[89] Nevertheless,

I would argue that she has more precisely achieved secular sainthood by tapping into the Virgin's greater discursive potential through a sexualized cyborg performance: no longer merely the Virgin, she is also a cyborg and Coatlicue, the goddess of birth and death. This fact rings particularly clearly at the end of the play when she and Juan take Cerezita's deceased niece to the field and crucify her on live television while a stunned Anna Perez and her camera operator look on. When the sharpshooters kill Cerezita in front of this audience, they underscore the degree to which power players in McGlaughlin have employed necroliberal policies to impose their biopolitical hegemony. The scene may seem unbelievable to some viewers, but it draws on the stories of activists like Rene Lopez who was publicly assassinated in Fresno in 1983 for standing up to Sikkema Dairy and voting to receive representation from the UFW union.[90] Nevertheless, the snipers have miscalculated the effects of Cerezita's robo-sacer activism; indeed, they play into her articulation of Coatlicue by killing her and laying the foundation for McGlaughlin's metaphorical rebirth. This fact becomes especially clear when Cerezita's brother shouts "burn the fields!"[91] All of the town's inhabitants—and even Anna Perez, who has previously acted more as a "transcultural mediator" than an ally—set fire to the grapevines.[92]

As the curtain falls, it becomes clear that Cerezita has had to sacrifice herself in order to topple the rigid biopolitical structures in McGlaughlin that have allowed the cancer cluster to continue unabated.[93] Patricia Solis Ybarra alludes to this point when she observes that *Heroes and Saints* "sets the tone for an ongoing consideration of death and how the community puts it to use in its protest of their living conditions."[94] There are certainly problems associated with playing to an imaginary of "virgin sacrifices," but the fact remains that, as a cyborg Virgin, Cerezita is ideally placed to assert the sanctity of her life by allowing herself to be killed in a way that denaturalizes the constructs of migrant *zoē* that permeate her town.[95] In proving both her sanctity and her right to life, Cerezita destabilizes the foundation upon which agricultural executives have built their necroliberal empire. The cyborg Virgin's influence extends beyond the grave. She later haunts the stage in *Watsonville*, a sequel to *Heroes and Saints* that stars Dolores and Juan, who has apparently survived the shooting at the end of *Heroes and Saints*. Cerezita is no longer alive, but her influence continues through both of these characters who have left their indecisiveness behind and become socially engaged activists. The cyborg Virgin's death ultimately brings about a greater societal good by catalyzing a rebellion of workers. Moraga was not the only Greater-Mexican cultural producer of the 1990s to challenge the necroliberal markets of death by asserting the sanctity of killable life. In the pages that follow, I discuss how Guillermo del Toro's *Cronos* also fuses sacred and cybernetic imageries to interrogate Mexico's place in a rapidly globalizing world order.

## SANCTIFYING THE NAFTA RESISTANCE IN GUILLERMO DEL TORO'S *CRONOS*

Few pre-NAFTA films interrogate how the combination of so-called free trade and technological development contribute to a necroliberal order more completely than Guillermo del Toro's *Cronos* (1993).[96] "A low-budget prototype of what [would] become the auteurist brand" of the Oscar Award–winning director, *Cronos* has achieved canonical status in Mexican cinema.[97] The young director filmed this, his first full-length production, in 1992, but he released it in December of 1993.[98] This date only added to the film's critique because it coincided almost perfectly with Mexico's "integration" into the so-called modern economy through NAFTA, which went into effect on January 1, 1994. Given this fact, it should come as no surprise that the theme of necroliberal expansion bubbles just beneath the movie's surface.[99] The film officially takes place in 1997, and del Toro highlights the globalized and cosmopolitan nature of this near-future Mexico City by showing written discourse in a multitude of languages.[100] The film also begins with a score of tango music that draws attention to the Argentine citizenship of the protagonist, Jesús Gris (Federico Luppi). This opening sequence may lead many first-time viewers to wonder where the story actually takes place. Del Toro finally answers this question with a close-up of Jesús's Mexico City license plate. Several critics note that *Cronos* does not directly engage Mexican identity per se.[101] Rather, del Toro focuses on the servile relationship of a very heterogenous Global South—which includes people from countries throughout Latin America—to the Global North.[102] Beatriz Trigo argues that del Toro employed a cosmopolitan cast to attract broader audiences.[103] Her assertion makes sense, but we should also note that the director's focus on so many disparate voices also furthers his case for solidarity against the encroachment of necroliberal capitalism by showing how widespread the destruction of the impending economic order has become. Jesús becomes a new type of robo-sacer actor who uses the tools of necroliberal capitalism—particularly the Cronos Device—against his American oppressors. His resistance transforms him into a Christological cyborg who opposes the neocolonial and necroliberal forces that threaten his family and, by extension, his nation.

Despite the film's competent engagement of the key issues facing early-1990s Mexico, del Toro struggled to secure funding, and his movie was only released in six theaters in Mexico City.[104] This reflected the stigmatization of horror and SF in the national cinema.[105] Nevertheless, it was precisely through these aesthetics that del Toro questioned the wisdom of NAFTA.[106] Del Toro emphasizes the necroliberal backdrop during the opening moments of the film. A male voiceover narrates: "In 1536, fleeing from the Spanish Inquisition, the alchemist Umberto Fulcanelli embarked from Veracruz, Mexico. Appointed official watchmaker to the viceroy, Fulcanelli was determined to perfect an invention that would provide him with the key to eternal life. He was to name it the Cronos Device." Veracruz has historically functioned as the locus of foreign intervention and imperialism in the country: Hernán Cortés arrived in present-day Mexico through that route in 1519, and the United States occupied it in 1847 and 1914.[107] Stacy Rusnak asserts that this beginning highlights Mexico's so-called inferiority complex that has resulted from its dual colonization by Spain and, later, the United States.[108] The Cronos Device and the ensuing monster come to symbolize the structures of power that have ravaged the country and drained it of its labor and resources ever since the colonial period and into the neoliberal era.[109] Mabel Moraña drives this point home when she asserts that the Cronos Device lays bare a "biopolitical apparatus that traverses time, cultures, and cultural spaces" where human blood "oils the gears of capitalism at the expense of life itself."[110] Because Fulcanelli kills Mexicans in order to further extend his own life, we can conclude that he views them as killable *homines sacri*. A. Davies notes that, unlike Dracula—a foreign and ethnic Other from the global periphery who threatens to infect the metropolitan center—Fulcanelli's Cronos Monster represents a dangerous colonizing force that invades the periphery from the center.[111]

It would be an overstatement to claim that Fulcanelli and the other vampiric beings in the film live truly "good" lives. Del Toro emphasizes the grotesque nature of the vampire condition both through his unsympathetic depiction of Western imperialists and through Jesús's suffering and rejection. Edward King and Joanna Page assert that, "against fantasies of technologically redesigned transhuman subjects, the film asserts the posthuman figure of the vampire to evoke 'the ruin of the body' violently dispossessed of subjectivity by the alienating forces of capital."[112] The film self-consciously engages in a twentieth-century, late-capitalist corollary to Karl Marx's assertion that "capital is dead labour, that, vampire-like, only lives by sucking living labour."[113] John Kraniauskas has contributed perhaps the most systematic article to date about how *Cronos* uses the vampire figure to denounce the neoliberalization of Mexico and Latin America.[114] As he argues, del Toro warns against any free trade agreement because these will inevitably justify

Mexican death and suffering in the name of macroeconomic indicators that will enrich the few. What is more, the film provides a space for theorizing the nature of necroliberalism by asserting that, far from a side effect, the systemic destruction of "third-world" life (read: *zoē*) has become the central focus of late capitalism.

Del Toro further ties his production to traditional Hollywood vampire films when the nondiegetic narrator announces that Fulcanelli's reign of terror abruptly ended after four centuries when he died in a fire in 1937. The heat and smoke did not kill him; rather, he perished from a wound to the heart. The director then pans through Fulcanelli's mansion and cuts to a high-angle shot of several bowls that capture the blood of one of Fulcanelli's human victims. The narrator says that officials auctioned off Fulcanelli's belongings and claims that no one found his mysterious device. Nevertheless, the camera rests on a baroque angel—which the audience realizes will eventually reach the film's true protagonist—and the ominous music indicates that the Cronos Device remains hidden in that location. This section plays with the Gothic tradition that has served as the bedrock of popular Hollywood and world vampire cinema, though it imbues the tradition with a Mexican twist.[115] As Adriana Gordillo notes, "the baroque and the Gothic share similar qualities; however, only the former has taken a strong foothold in Latin American cultural landscape."[116] In creating this baroque device, then, del Toro communicates a type of Mexican Gothic to his viewers.[117] Several scholars have highlighted the Cronos Device's subversive potential; Justo Planas Cabrejo, for example, views the device through Freud's *unheimlich*, a reading that emphasizes how the device can denaturalize familiar structures of power, while others have highlighted how it straddles the line between technoscience and religion.[118] Fulcanelli's device entraps a cockroach inside of a clocklike mechanism. When the user straps it on their body, the contraption "bites" them and injects them with rejuvenating blood. Geoffrey Kantaris argues that the device itself is an oppressive cyborg construct that enslaves an insect by fusing its body with gears and metal.[119] Del Toro thus produces a Gothic mode through baroque art on the one hand and constructs the robo-sacer and Christological potential of his main protagonist on the other.

When Jesús first finds the Cronos Device in his shop, he polishes it with Aurora; however, he accidentally activates it and the contraption bites his hand. Del Toro captures this scene with a grotesque closeup that shows several mechanical, arthropodic legs penetrating Jesús's skin. The effects of the bite transform him into a posthuman being who, ironically, loses many of his ties to humanity even as he grows in power (see fig. 1.1).[120] Jesús's first exposure to the machine reflects a common initiatory trope that holds the first sexual penetration to be both painful and pleasurable.[121] The shock of this first encounter does not deter the shopkeeper from returning to the device on multiple occasions; indeed, in an especially fascinating variation of Haraway's assertion of "pleasurably tight couplings" between flesh and metal, Jesús soon becomes addicted to the Cronos Device's effects.[122] This fact comes into focus if we follow the lead of Robin Murray and Joseph Heumann and read the golden Cronos Device as a fertility symbol.[123] In order to keep it working, Jesús will have to consume blood. He recognizes his unquenchable thirst in a scene that takes place shortly after his first bite. He drinks gallons of water from the refrigerator to no avail; del Toro then rests the camera's gaze on a plate of raw meat. His use of color is such that the steak "begins to glow and turn even more blood red."[124] We do not see Jesús consume the blood, but the director implies that Jesús quenches his thirst through this means.

The Cronos Monster proves especially difficult to classify; while critics agree that the creature dialogues with the traditional vampires of Hollywood cinema and Anglo literature, they disagree on how, or even if, it diverges from that mold. Francisco de León signals the Cronos Monster as the first cinematic modern vampire because its propagation depends on technology, while Dolores Tierney reads Jesús as a "postcolonial vampire, resistant to the colonization of the (national) body."[125] Dale Hudson refers to the Cronos monster and other vampiric figures from del Toro's oeuvre as a "new [strain] of vampires, facilitated by globalization."[126] These readings certainly help to explain del Toro's portrayal of a progressive monster who both allegorically and literally overthrows the system of oppression, but they also insist on framing the protagonist through the vampire lens. Other recent scholarship has signaled great tensions between the Cronos Monster and traditional vampires.[127] Ignacio M. Sánchez Prado sidesteps the question of whether or not the Cronos Monster is a vampire and instead critiques the overuse of European theorizations of the vampire in analyses of the film.[128] As the aforementioned critics make clear, any discussion of Jesús's resistant potential must recognize the vampiric qualities that he embodies. That said, in many ways the most compelling aspects of his character emerge through the ways that he is *not* a vampire. Deborah Shaw, for example, views Jesús as a sympathetic Frankenstein's monster.[129] This characterization casts him as a victim of Fulcanelli's mad science rather than as a necroliberal parasite. Given the scholarship that equates Frankenstein with posthumanism, Shaw's reading suggests that Jesús's resistant potential stems at least in part from his transgressive robo-sacer identity.[130]

The most obvious distinction between the Cronos Monster and more

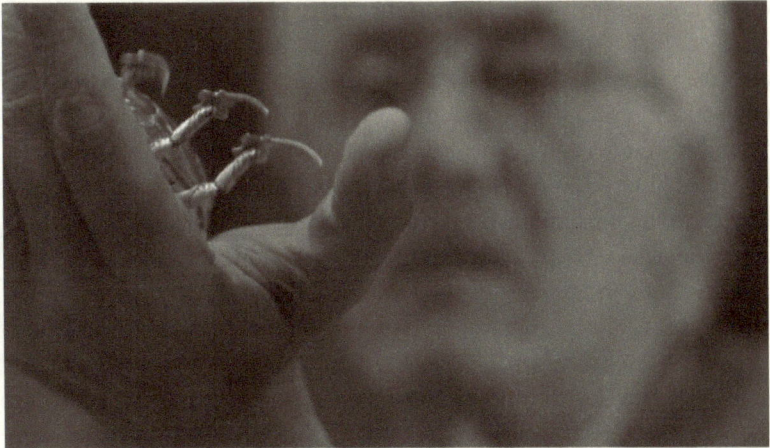

**FIGURE 1.1** Still from *Cronos*. The Cronos Device prepares to penetrate Jesús Gris's skin, thus transforming him into a vampiric, cyborg monster.

traditional vampires is the means of infection, which is alchemical rather than mystical. The intimate relationship between Jesús and the Cronos Device suggests that we may gain a deeper understanding of his resistant potential by viewing him through the lens of cyborg theory. Such an approach is not entirely new; Eljaiek-Rodríguez, for example, refers to Jesús as a "hybrid vampire."[131] For her part, A. Davies argues in passing that "the Cronos device posits the vampire as cyborg through a mutual dependence on the device and of the vampire on each other."[132] Rather than explore avenues of cybernetic resistance, however, A. Davies remains fixated primarily on Jesús's vampiric qualities. Kantaris discusses the film from the vantage point of cyborg theory in an attempt to make sense of the multiple palimpsests that place historical imageries alongside the modern. Somewhat surprisingly, he only identifies two cyborgs: the insect in the Cronos Device, and Dieter de la Guardia, whose multiple surgeries have rendered him dependent on medical technologies for carrying out the most basic corporeal functions.[133] Laurence Davies follows Kantaris's lead when he asserts that *Cronos* imagines a cyborg condition that is "nothing like the engine of liberation that Haraway envisages."[134] However, he bases this argument on the insect that lives within the Cronos Device while ignoring the cyborgian nature of Jesús Gris. The prospect of robo-sacer resistance becomes much more compelling when we view Jesús in this light as well. Ultimately, this character's articulation of cyborg subjectivity facilitates his resistant behavior. It never lifts him out of legal and economic bare life in a biopolitical sense, but it allows him to defeat his oppressors and leave a more just society for his community after his own death.

Jesús's first resistant act is to refuse to give the Cronos Device to Dieter after the robber baron summons him to his factory. As the character most obviously aligned with transnational capitalism and (neo)colonialism, Dieter represents an obvious villain. Shaw notes that del Toro originally imagined him as a Nazi hiding out in Mexico, but his American financier—who ended up not funding the project—had demanded that the film include American characters.[135] Dieter thus represents numerous types of transnational villains and the necroliberal potential of the incipient global order. That said, it would be imprecise to view him or his nephew, Ángel, as figures of NAFTA-era capitalism. As Sánchez Prado convincingly argues, Dieter more neatly invokes the mid-twentieth-century capitalists who championed the Mexican Miracle (Milagro Mexicano), a three-decade period of macroeconomic growth in the country that emphasized trade liberalization and a market-based economy from 1954 to 1970.[136] Indeed, Sánchez Prado further speculates that Dieter has probably controlled his ailing company for at least forty-five years.[137] This is not to say that del Toro does not use the de la Guardias to critique the *idea* of NAFTA; indeed, Shaw argues that "the effects [of NAFTA] are prefigured through the relationship between Gris and the de la Guardias."[138] Rather, because the filming and release predated the expansion of maquiladoras, the displacement of agricultural workers, and the *zapatista* uprising, it would have been impossible for the director to build on the central social and economic issues that beset the country after NAFTA's passage. Instead, the Mexican Miracle was the principal model of liberal capitalist expansion within Mexico during the filming. In aligning his protagonists with pre-NAFTA capitalism, del Toro focuses on an underlying philosophical critique of ne(cr)oliberalism that does not get lost in the details of post-NAFTA turbulence. As the existence of the Cronos Device shows, transnational flows of labor, bodies, technology, and goods have long favored US (and European) actors while signaling Mexican peoples and cultures as expendable.

Dieter's self-assured narcissism facilitates his interpellation of Mexicans and Latin Americans into *zoē*. Beyond believing that his wealth and nationality give him the right to the Cronos Device, he also views Jesús as, in the words of A. Davies, "matter out of place."[139] Indeed, Dieter believes that the shopkeeper's third-world status should deny him the right to wield the contraption. Of course, as Sánchez Prado reminds us, the elder de la Guardia has no convincing claims of ownership to the device, either. Unlike the inventor Fulcanelli, Dieter "is no more than a capitalist who seeks to exploit the benefits of the gadget for his own survival, a consumer of a technology that does not belong to him" (es tan sólo un capitalista que busca explotar los beneficios del artilugio para su propia supervivencia, un consumidor de una tecnología que no le pertenece).[140] Despite having read Fulcanelli's writings multiple times, Dieter's own ignorance of the device's alchemical nature rings clear when he notices that the Cronos Device has pierced Jesús's hand. In a reaction that alludes to something beyond jealousy, he calls the shopkeeper an "imbecile." The elder de la Guardia covets the device, and the fact that he will need to drink human blood does not bother him. Numerous scholars recognize a type of vampiric performativity to Dieter's character for precisely this reason.[141] According to Tierney, vampire subjectivity entails more than the physical urge to drink blood; it also denotes a necroliberal desire to kill and drain Mexico and Mexicans.[142] At the same time, Dieter apparently does not know that the device can bite unwitting victims, like Jesús, as well. Indeed, one could convincingly argue that Jesús owes his Christological cyborg state in no small part to the fact that he has discovered his powers by accident. As such, the Cronos Device has inadvertently created a resistant robo-sacer actor who threatens the necroliberal logic upon which Dieter depends.

Jesús's particular case of cyborg resistance comes from the way it intertwines alchemy and technoscience with religion. Mabel Moraña asserts that "*Cronos* is based in the syncretism of Christian and secular elements and incorporates Gothic features in order to represent the vampire myth in the Latin American periphery, a space historically marked by the effects of colonialism."[143] At the same time, Brad O'Brien asserts that Jesús seeks refuge from *both* the Christian God and the device because they leave him oppressed and unfulfilled.[144] His resistance to necroliberalism and religion shows how subversive articulations of technological hybridity *and* religious dogma can undermine structures of domination. Jesús's ties to the holy highlight his breaches with traditional vampires more than perhaps anything else. Ever since at least the publication of *Dracula*, literary and filmic vampires have functioned as Antichrists due to their bloodlust and their vulnerability to Catholic sacraments.[145] Del Toro never juxtaposes Jesús with crosses or holy water, but he does show that his protagonist cannot bear sunlight. Crucially, Javier Martín Párraga views this "more as an allergic reaction than as a moral punishment" (más como una reacción de tipo alérgico que como un castigo de corte moral).[146] Jesús may share many characteristics with vampires, but he also subverts those constructs that would cast him as either an Antichrist or a life-force-sucking capitalist. His destabilizing nature thus stems from a secular holiness that emerges precisely from how he performs his demonic condition. As Doug Jones—an actor who has played multiple monsters in del Toro's films—explains, del Toro's oeuvre focuses more on *how* characters use their power than whether or not their power is inherently evil.[147] Jesús may crave human blood, but he also refuses to kill and he ultimately sacrifices himself for his people. The refusal to drain people's blood produces an asceticism that further aligns the protagonist with Christ and atonement: his body degrades, but his grotesque suffering signals him as a secular savior.

One of the scenes that most emphatically shows Jesús's robo-sacer secular sanctity occurs when he celebrates the upcoming new year with his family and a group of Argentine expats in Mexico City.[148] When he sits down to eat, he smells a man's nosebleed. Overcome by a desire to feed, he stalks the partygoer to the bathroom. Del Toro teases his audience as he taps into tropes of the vampire genre that seem to foreshadow an imminent kill. Nevertheless, this Christological cyborg only wishes to discreetly drink the man's blood from the countertop. When another bathroom goer frustrates this plan by washing the blood down the drain, Jesús licks a few small drops of blood from the bathroom floor in a disconcertingly voyeuristic shot (see fig. 1.2).[149] Jesús's ability to resist killing the bleeding man sanctifies him at a personal level. Nevertheless, he has yet to seriously challenge the necroliberal system that continues to encourage the consumption and commodification of Mexican and third-world bodies. What is more, colonizing forces within and beyond Mexico continue to relegate him to killable, *homo sacer* status.

Del Toro highlights Jesús's continued biopolitical subservience when Ángel abruptly enters the bathroom and kicks him in the face. The director follows this jarring scene by cutting to a celebration where everyone except for the worried Aurora and Mercedes counts down the seconds to the new year. The director then cuts to a cliff and pans to Jesús's car, which Ángel eventually pushes off the edge with its unconscious owner inside. Ángel does this in part because he hopes that Dieter will stop insisting that he find the Cronos Device if the shopkeeper is dead. Significantly, Ángel "kills" Gris in the wee hours of the morning on New Year's Day. Beyond an abstract celebration of "new birth and new beginnings," the New Year's celebration here refers to the literal advent of NAFTA.[150] Certainly, the film explicitly takes place in December of 1997 and early January of 1998.[151] That said, given the film's release in December 1993, less than a month before NAFTA would go into effect, the significance of the New Year's celebration takes on greater discursive weight. Ángel's murderous actions invoke a biopolitical framework that continues to cast third-world people as killable *homines sacri* in spite of—or perhaps because of—Mexico's greater integration into

**FIGURE 1.2** Still from *Cronos*. Jesús Gris refuses to kill and instead licks drops of blood off the bathroom floor.

the necroliberal world economy.

Jesús's continued bare life shines through from a critical reading of the film's negative space. For example, it seems strange that the police never investigate his death. One could surmise that they figure that he died in a drunk driving accident, but Ángel's actions should raise suspicions. His troubled history with the shopkeeper is no secret, yet Ángel goes to the funeral and touches the cadaver to guarantee that he has indeed died. Ángel ostensibly does this to complete Dieter's orders, but he also gloats over his kill in front of several witnesses. He later visits a crematorium where he verifies seeing Jesús moments before his casket is lifted into an incinerator (the resurrected Jesús has escaped unnoticed). The complete lack of interest from law enforcement stems from the fact that they, too, view Gris's life (and death) as unworthy of their time. If Agamben is correct that *homines sacri* can be killed but never murdered, then it becomes clear that the police choose not to look into Gris's demise precisely because they believe that, even if he was killed, his fate does not merit a law-enforcement response. What is perhaps most surprising is that a simple autopsy would show that he had no alcohol in his system, and it may even indicate that Ángel beat him prior to the crash. The lackluster investigation may reflect the fact that Gris is an Argentine national—indeed, Mexico has a long history of xenophobia toward immigrants—or it could allude to police incompetence in general.[152] It may also reflect the political and economic influence of the de la Guardia family in suppressing the investigation. Just as likely, of course, it could reflect a confluence of these issues.

Clearly, Jesús Gris exists beyond the protection of the law. His robo-sacer condition would seem to refer to the sacred role that his killable body plays in upholding the necroliberal logic of late capitalism, but his resurrection cements his ties to the holy within a Christian tradition. S. T. Joshi argues that *Cronos* "is, in a way, a perverted retelling of the death and resurrection of Jesus Christ."[153] He correctly observes the film's adaptation of the traditional story of Christ's ministry and resurrection. However, I would stop short of calling Jesús Gris "perverted" because del Toro does not use this character to create an anti-Christian discourse.[154] Rather, similar to Christ during his forty-day fast, Jesús Gris learns that he has a mission to complete, and he foregoes unholy temptations in order to accomplish it. Significantly, he only becomes truly resistant when Dieter and later Ángel place Aurora's life in danger. Left to his own devices it is entirely possible that he would hide in his granddaughter's toy box and slowly waste away. Jesús's final (successful) act of robo-sacer resistance comes about, ironically enough, because Dieter has refused to teach him how to properly use the Cronos Device. He visits the robber baron in secret after his resurrection and complains that his body has fallen apart. It is here where Dieter attempts to stab Jesús through the heart after Jesús begs for an escape from his vampiric state, and Aurora intervenes by hitting Dieter on the head and knocking him out.

As the duo prepares to leave, del Toro pans back to Dieter, whose blood leaks across the floor. Overcome by thirst, Jesús drinks from his antagonist's neck while Aurora silently looks on. This scene lends greater credence to Tierney's reading of Jesús as a postcolonial vampire, and it shows an allegorical inversion from the Marxist vampire trope; indeed, the lower-class individual consumes the lifeblood of the capitalist. The combination of eerie, nondiegetic music and a low-angle closeup paradoxically casts his condition as both monstrous and very human. The scene also shows one of the first cases of robo-sacer resistance in the film; rather than share the Cronos Device with a man who would use it to extend his pitiful existence by devouring Mexicans, Jesús drains the colonizer of his life force, thus metaphorically reingesting the labor that Dieter has stolen. Del Toro emphasizes a secular holiness in Gris by signaling him as the only one capable of truly resisting and reversing the de la Guardia family legacy. His secularly holy cyborg condition allows him to overthrow the capitalistic Dieter de la Guardia where others could not. Perhaps in an attempt to circumvent any readings that would associate Gris's actions with murder, del Toro does not permit his protagonist to kill Dieter. Rather, Ángel unexpectedly arrives and breaks his uncle's neck while, unbeknownst to him, Jesús and Aurora look on. Rodríguez-Hernández and Schaefer correctly read Ángel's act as one of "launder[ing]" Dieter's wealth so that he can use it for "other, more personally satisfying [...] causes" (like a nose job), but they ignore how the biopolitical implications of this murder differ from those when he "killed" Jesús a few days prior.[155] Because he cannot relegate Dieter to killable bare life, Ángel's actions will cause him serious legal trouble if he cannot frame someone else. It is largely for this reason that he tries to kill the Grises when he sees them; given their troubled history with Dieter, he could easily blame them. Ángel chases the duo to the roof of the factory and taunts Jesús, telling him that he will kill Aurora. Jesús responds by hurtling his antagonist and himself multiple stories to the ground.

Speaking on his violent altercations with both of the de la Guardias, Tierney asserts that "Jesús's sympathetic nature means that spectators want to see him drink the blood of the predatory US capitalist de la Guardia and pull the violent (though not unsympathetic) Ángel to his death."[156] She is certainly correct about the generic expectations of the audience, but we must also note that these actions would be unacceptable except under extenuating circumstances. This state of exception differs in key ways from that which interpellates the *zoē* into *homines sacri*. Instead, it represents a problematic articulation of what Agamben calls "*iustitium*," or a moment where the "the law stands still."[157] Agamben discusses this term as it refers to creating the conditions through which the state can extralegally kill its own citizens, some of whom may not even be *homines sacri*.[158] These scenes go even further and imagine the conditions through which robo-sacer heroes from marginalized communities can justifiably kill those who belong to the supposed *bios*. The film's state of exception emerges precisely at the juncture of transnational wealth and state power that have come together to bar people like Jesús from political power and even safety. Far from *homines sacri*—beings whose extralegal killings uphold and maintain the logic of sovereignty—the de la Guardias represent the source of necroliberal power that marginal actors must bring down through robo-sacer resistance. Gris's act of killing Ángel creates an allegorical rupture that will potentially reimagine a more just and inclusive future. Even when Jesús's acts of violence are justifiable, however, these skirmishes have only compounded his bloodlust. It will be harder to practice restraint later on.

Because Jesús can never undo his own violent deeds, his very act of saving Aurora has corrupted him and transformed him into a potential killer. This fact becomes especially clear when he fights the urge to drink Aurora's blood after his revival. Only after she says "grandpa" (abuelo), her only dialogue in the entire film, does he regain self-control and allow her to live.[159] Waldron argues that Gris "refuses to sacrifice the blood of his own people, of his own youth, simply to keep himself, the older, alive."[160]

As a true robo-sacer champion, Gris ends up favoring "blood-love" over "bloodlust," and he sacrifices himself for the betterment of his community.[161] Of course, the fact that he has even considered taking his granddaughter's life causes trauma not only for himself but for Aurora as well.[162] When Gris realizes that the desire to feed will one day overcome him, he destroys the Cronos Device. This act both liberates the insect from its centuries of slavery—though its liberation comes through death—and frees Gris from a nascent colonial drive that has budded within him. The threat that Gris could become a new colonizer rings especially clear when we recognize *Cronos*'s indebtedness to Mexploitation and lucha libre cinema. Del Toro explicitly signals his indebtedness to this genre of cinema during the scene in the mortuary when he films a poster of Blue Demon, the luchador-turned-actor who, along with El Santo, served as that genre's greatest star. As I have argued previously, the masked-wrestler champions of this cinema played heroes who fought off the agents of external imperialism, but their characters also validated projects of internal colonialism.[163] Simone Weil argues that revolutionary figures rarely tend to do more than "drive out one team of oppressors and replace them with another."[164] Viewed against this backdrop, Gris's self-renunciation and resignation to death becomes especially noteworthy. In refusing to become a metaphorical colonizer, Gris cements his Christological role. He has sacrificed himself and carried out these corrupting, resistant acts so that others, like Aurora, will not have to.

Del Toro closes the film by cutting to a high-angle shot that captures an arthropodic Jesús lying on his bed and covered in insect skin while his wife and granddaughter mourn. The shot fades to a bright white that alludes to the grandfather's salvation. Persephone Braham asserts that this end "insists on the legitimacy—*and even sanctity*—of the vampire hero."[165] Sánchez Prado argues that Jesús has to die because "any survival of the ghosts of the past would raise the question of their role in the present."[166] Shaw takes a different approach when she argues, "in an inverse working of the messianic story, his [Jesús's] sacrifice results in a rejection of immortality and an embrace of death."[167] By destroying the Cronos Device, Jesús Gris transforms himself into a secular savior: he has allegorically liberated Mexico from the oppressive onslaught of transnational capital and he has protected Aurora, and everyone else, from having to taint themselves in the process of liberation. What is more, he has shown great personal valor in refusing to embrace the colonialist and necroliberal drives that tempt him. He is precisely the champion that Mexico needs as it embarks on a neoliberalizing project that will commodify so many aspects of Mexican being. At the same time, del Toro espouses a fatalistic, though not necessarily pessimistic, approach to robo-sacer resistance. Robo-sacer activism has provided a potent tool for action by helping Jesús combat the institutional power of the de la Guardia family. However, it seems that a benevolent robo-sacer actor must ultimately sacrifice himself to topple the necroliberal order. Jesús Gris thus serves as a sacrificial lamb precisely because he gives up his life after establishing a form of normalcy.

## CONCLUSION

As this chapter has shown, the confluence of secular sanctity and cyborg subjectivity in *Cronos* and *Heroes and Saints* denaturalizes constructs of *homo sacer* expendability by casting robo-sacer actors as members of the global and national *bios*. Both fictions build on a dystopian context to critique the expansion of neoliberalism by highlighting the devastating effects of unfettered capitalism of past eras. Perhaps the most interesting insight that this comparison has provided is that posthumanist criticisms of the necroliberal order predated NAFTA by several years. Intellectuals and cultural producers recognized ne(cr)oliberal globalization's potential to dehumanize Mexican and Chicanx communities long before 1994. The secular sanctity of Jesús and Cerezita proves especially interesting because both characters refashion the religious symbols of the hegemony and use them toward a resistant end. As they do this, they create a spiritual mestizaje that mirrors the ambiguous, deconstructive hybridity of the SF cyborg. In the end, both works provide innovative critiques of the necroliberal order by fusing elements of SF with magical realism (*Heroes and Saints*) and Gothic horror (*Cronos*). The Christological cyborg and the cyborg Virgin so effectively challenge the economic status quo because their compounded hybridity, which engages the technological, the generic, and the religious, resists classification and thus opens a space to negate the necroliberal status quo.

One of the thematic issues that most closely aligns these works is that they imagine Greater-Mexican protagonists who experience a relative lack of access to the benefits of technology. This, in turn, casts them as technologically bare *homines sacri*. In *Heroes and Saints*, agricultural companies willingly sacrifice the lives of their workers to produce more crops, but they do not kill for the sake of killing. In the case of *Cronos*, Fulcanelli and Dieter actively seek to shed and consume Mexican blood, but they do so to feed their own quests for immortality. In both cases, the destruction of *homo sacer* bodies continues to occur within a biopolitical paradigm because it primarily occurs to uplift the *bios*.[168] That said, some post-NAFTA Mexican and Chicanx SF authors from the same decade imagined dystopian worlds where the destruction and consumption of the *zoē* formed an end in and of itself. In these fictions, people voyeuristically watch *homo sacer* bodies fall apart from the effects of physical and economic violence. Not surprisingly, technology plays a central role in capturing and disseminating these images to audiences in these cyberpunk worlds. The next chapter discusses Pepe Rojo's "Ruido gris" (1996) and Ernest Hogan's *Smoking Mirror Blues* (2001). Both narratives engage an especially pernicious necroliberal order that celebrates and promotes the killing of the *zoē* in order to further the profits of media companies. Under such circumstances, the nature and methodology of robo-sacer resistance becomes especially uncertain.

CHAPTER 2

# Existing in the Necroliberal Order Online

Robo-Sacer Subjectivity
in Pepe Rojo's "Ruido gris" and
Ernest Hogan's *Smoking Mirror Blues*

A young man undergoes an elective surgery to connect his eyes and voice to the mediasphere so that he can become an "ocular reporter." In this capacity, he documents the suicides, kidnappings, robberies, and terrorist attacks that plague his city. He suffers depression as he becomes increasingly enmeshed in the commercialization of death, but he has few avenues for escape because his employer effectively owns his body. In another, unrelated case, a Mexico City woman invents the god simulator, a chip that uses artificial intelligence to render different gods and upload them to the internet. When her Chicano lover, Beto, pirates the algorithm, he uses it to reanimate Tezcatlipoca, the Aztec god of mischief. Upon coming to life, this deity takes over Beto's body and uses it to conquer not only cyberspace, but also the physical world. These two episodes, coming from Pepe Rojo's "Ruido gris" (1996) and Ernest Hogan's *Smoking Mirror Blues* (2001) respectively, respond to both the implementation of NAFTA and the technological advancement that characterized the 1990s and early 2000s in Mexico and the United States. The narratives imagine the mediasphere and cyberspace as a neoliberal and neocolonialist entity that devalues human life by subordinating it to the logic of the market. Indeed, the mediasphere becomes a space from which those in power can cast anyone as killable—or at least exploitable—*zoē*. Because the characters of these narratives live in a hypermodern world, they cannot break away from the cybernetic context that they inhabit. They try to resist through subversive articulations of technology, but they ultimately cannot conceive of a way to transcend the necroliberal order.

Both "Ruido gris" and *Smoking Mirror Blues* occupy privileged positions within their respective SF traditions. Rojo published "Ruido gris" at a key moment in the history of Mexican SF; it was not until the 1980s that governmental bodies recognized the genre's value in the national letters.[1] The story has enjoyed an influential, though modest, distribution precisely because it won the Kalpa award for best Mexican SF story in 1996. Rojo greatly expanded the text's reach when he posted it online after disagreements with his publisher.[2] The story's readership was expansive enough that Andrea L. Bell and Yolanda Molina-Gavilán chose to include it under the title of "Gray Noise" in their anthology of translated Iberoamerican SF texts, *Cosmos Latinos: An Anthology of Science Fiction from Latin America and Spain*. This translation cemented Rojo's prominent place in Mexican and Latin American SF by making his story accessible to English-speaking academics around the world. As for Hogan, many people refer to him as the "father of Chicano science fiction."[3] In a 2020 interview, Hogan said with self-deprecating humor that he had earned this title only because of his age, though he also acknowledged that he was the first Chicano(a/x) author to make a career out of writing SF specifically.[4] *Smoking Mirror Blues* was Hogan's third novel, and he published it after receiving significant praise for both *Cortez on Jupiter* (1990) and *High Aztech* (1992). The cultural impact of the novel rings clear as we consider Hogan's continued relevance twenty years later. As his success so powerfully confirmed, Chicanx authors could write culturally authentic texts that appealed to a broad audience.

Despite the clear importance of these authors in their respective Greater-Mexican literary communities, scholars have paid them only scant attention. Hogan's marginalization in Chicanx literary studies has ironically resulted in large part from his commercial success. In building a career out of writing SF, he necessarily published popular narratives that proponents of so-called high literature either ignored or met with disdain. For Rojo, the lack of recognition probably reflects an overall stigmatization of SF within both Latin American literary studies and the region's publishing industries that only recently has begun to abate.[5] These two authors make for an interesting comparison for several reasons. As contemporaries, they wrote and continue to write during the same time period. Because of this, they have confronted similar conditions albeit from opposite sides of the US-Mexico border. The fact that both authors imagine dystopian, necroliberal markets of death highlights how technological and economic development had produced dire biopolitical ramifications among both Mexican and Chicanx communities.

Brief plot descriptions will facilitate our discussion.

"Ruido gris" tells the story of a young, unnamed narrator who has undergone a surgery to become an "ocular reporter": someone who has had a camera inserted into his eye so that everything he sees becomes the property of the media company Rojo Digital. The narrative begins with the protagonist recounting his experiences filming people as they commit suicide by leaping from buildings. Immediately thereafter, the narrative cuts to an experience where the protagonist has to report on a shootout at a crime scene. He learns that some people have kidnapped a child. Following the altercation, he interviews a police officer. A criminal leaps from a closet and shoots the officer in the face. Elated about the spectacular footage, the company pays the narrator a large commission. Much to his employer's chagrin, the protagonist refuses to work for several days afterward because he does not urgently need funds. One day, he goes out again and witnesses a terrorist attack at a mall. He sees the perpetrators plant a bomb, and then he notices several security guards draw near to the explosive. When he opens his mouth to alert them, the producers contact him through his earpiece and tell him not to interfere but to prepare himself to produce spectacular footage of the imminent explosion. His masterful shot captures the deaths of the security guards and the destruction of the store. His conscience starts to weigh on him as he realizes that he played a major role in the security guards' deaths. The story finishes as he contemplates a possible suicide. The ambiguous ending leaves us unsure if the narrator goes through with it or not.

Hogan creates a dizzying, postmodern aesthetic through a frenetic and fragmented text that, on average, shifts narrators two times per page. The many storylines include, but are not limited to, the following: Beto uses the god simulator chip to bring Tezcatlipoca to life in cyberspace. The AI entity possesses Beto, who is high and in a trance. This creates two parallel iterations of the god of mischief: Tezcatlipoca, the entity that inhabits the mediasphere, and Smokey Espejo, the version of Tezcatlipoca that exists in Beto's brain. After growing frustrated with an inability to immediately sync information between themselves, the duo decides to get a chip implanted in Beto's brain that allows for near-instantaneous communication between Smokey Espejo and cyberspace. A group of monotheistic (probably Christian) extremists called the Earth Angels seeks the god simulator because they wish to conjure the One True God in cyberspace. They try to steal the chip from Xóchitl, the Mexico City engineer who invented the chip (Beto had seduced her and pirated the program in order to simulate Tezcatlipoca). Xóchitl flees to Los Angeles in search of Beto. Beto's ex-girlfriend, Phoebe, falls in love with Smokey Espejo, who keeps her by his side because he realizes that her mere presence inhibits Beto's mental will and thus facilitates Smokey Espejo's continued dominance in that body. Two mediasphere security guards, Zobop and Tan Tien, try to capture Tezcatlipoca in cyberspace. They set a trap that uses Tezcaltipoca's hedonism against him by conjuring an image that puts Tezcatlipoca in bed with the African loa Erzule and Marilyn, an irreverent syncretic fusion of the Virgin Mary with Marilyn Monroe.[6] While Tezcatlipoca engages in a threesome with these goddesses in a cyberspace hallucination, the security officers push him out of Beto's mind and into a prison for AI beings. As the novel ends, however, it appears that Tezcatlipoca has escaped from his prison, and Beto starts to act possessed again.

Both of these narratives employ a cyberpunk referent to engage many of the key questions that abounded among Mexican and Chicanx thinkers at the turn of the twenty-first century. "Ruido gris" clearly fits the cyberpunk mold through its pessimistic representations of a technologically advanced yet culturally and spiritually bankrupt city. *Smoking Mirror Blues* proves a bit more difficult to define: some scholars refer to Hogan's fiction as postcyberpunk due to its relative optimism and playfulness, while others place it more squarely in the field of cyberpunk proper.[7] In any event the influence of cyberpunk rings clear in both narratives. For example, both texts use dystopia to critique the negative political and economic effects of the runaway technological development that coincided with the implementation of NAFTA.[8] Most studies of cyberpunk have centered on the Anglo-American context, though there have been a few notable works on the genre's role in Latin America as well. Brown and Ginway, for example, argue that Latin America's colonized condition has led the region's authors to imagine clunkier technology and greater authoritarianism than what one would find in English-language examples of the genre.[9] On the one hand, their assessment rings less clear in the fictions of Rojo and Hogan, both of which imagine sleek new technologies that inhabit Greater-Mexican spaces. On the other hand, however, the narratives embody Brown and Ginway's characterization by directly engaging a necroliberal authoritarianism that casts death as more profitable than life.

Building precisely on the political and even postcolonial nature of Hogan's novel, Josh Rios observes certain ties to Afrofuturism.[10] Indeed, *Smoking Mirror Blues* fuses SF, religious, subaltern, and nonheteronormative discourses into a posthuman pastiche.[11] The ties to Afrofuturism are perhaps less obvious in "Ruido gris," but the story clearly engages notions of technological domination as it imagines how those in power use technology to consume the very lives of the residents of the city that they oppress. The Afrofuturist lens provides valuable insights to my discussion of the necroliberal condition in each narrative. Regarding the necropolitics inherent to Afrofuturist literature and thought, Achilles Mbembe argues that "the Self always rediscovers its own form in the Other's gaze, albeit in an inverted form." As a result, attempts at deconstructive renderings of the coloniality of power frequently "become simple self-contemplation, [...] simple hyperbole of the Self."[12] Mbembe's observation gets at the heart of both "Ruido gris" and *Smoking Mirror Blues*, where attempts at robo-sacer resistance either backfire or fail to overthrow oppressive structures of power. Both Rojo and Hogan imagine a cybernetic world where online activism provides the potential for marginalized people to make their voices heard. Nevertheless, as Mbembe argues, "nothing guarantees direct access to speech."[13] As my reading of these narratives suggests, even when they act autonomously, robo-sacer subjects rarely set the terms for how others will view and interpret their resistant actions. Both their activism and their attempts to engage in political speech inadvertently create further necropolitical spectacle.

In both narratives, technology and late capitalism come together to produce a dehumanizing state of exception that monetizes human suffering and even death. Certainly, the works engage in fruitful dialogue with Donna Haraway and Chela Sandoval by imagining ways that cyborg activism can initiate the politization of the *zoē*. That said, Rojo and Hogan lack the aforementioned scholars' optimism. Both fictions reverberate with very real concerns about the emerging "digital divide" that facilitated the Global North's continued domination of the Global South during the 1990s and the 2000s.[14] Popular discourses in the United States continued to code Mexico as technologically bare—and its inhabitants as *zoē*—even as the country integrated into the global economy. Similar conditions of technological bareness existed among Mexican American and Chicanx communities in the United States.[15] Viewed against this backdrop, it is only natural that Rojo and Hogan would view geographically uneven technological development as inextricable from the neoliberal (and necroliberal) project.[16]

"Ruido gris" and *Smoking Mirror Blues* prove especially remarkable when viewed alongside the generally positive reception that NAFTA received from both the business and academic communities in the early to mid 1990s.[17] Rojo and Hogan remain decidedly critical both of the necroliberal order and of the ways business interests leverage technology to exploit Mexican and Chicanx lives. In both narratives, the expansion of technology has created new means of exploitation that continue to cast members of the so-called *zoē* as technologically bare while rich, privileged actors reaffirm their *bios* by flaunting their technological hegemony. In each of these fictions, necroliberal society has evolved to use the televisual technologies of the mediasphere—and particularly televisual technologies—to create a landscape that can dehumanize any individual without warning. Vested business interests create a uniquely robo-sacer context by interpellating any and all victims of violence—most of whom supposedly belonged to the *bios*—into expoloitable *zoē*. Indeed, the fictional media corporations gleefully broadcast the deaths of everyday citizens to increase their ratings. The authors allude to the potential for robo-sacer resistance, but they express reservations about the possibility of overcoming the necroliberal order. For Rojo, subversive acts in the integrated circuit cannot bring about structural change because they will never transcend the individual level. What is more, media companies appropriate resistant acts to their own necroliberal ends by sensationalizing them and projecting them on television screens across the city and nation. Hogan presents Tezcatlipoca as an AI actor whose delusions of deistic grandeur allow him to foment a revolution in both cyberspace and the physical world. Instead of demanding a more democratic order, he simply installs himself as the new incarnation of what remains a necroliberal and oppressive order.[18] In "Ruido gris," media companies like Rojo Digital have created cyborg reporters whose sole purpose is to capture the violent deaths that occur every day throughout their city. The nature of the work alienates the narrator, but he can find no meaningful avenue for resistance at a systemic level.

### CONSUMING DEATH IN PEPE ROJO'S "RUIDO GRIS"

"Ruido gris" imagines a world where the technological infrastructure of an ever-connected world devalues the human experience. Throughout the story, Pepe Rojo underscores the marginalization not only of his unnamed protagonist but of all of the inhabitants of his dystopian city. The residents feel alienated from their work and their very lives because the necroliberal order has commercialized the most intimate aspects of their existence through television technologies.[19] The story emphasizes the marginalization of the ocular reporters, characters who lose their free will after signing on with a news conglomerate. The bodies and minds of these cyborg individuals become the property of the media companies that finance their operations.[20] Similar to the people he films, the narrator is the product of a deeply cybernetic necroliberalism that has reduced every human being to an exploitable body.[21] The narrator's company views him as an expendable *homo sacer*, but his performance denaturalizes those constructs that facilitate his relegation to bare life. In so doing, he also critiques the efficiency models that characterized the neoliberal shift of the 1990s that had devastated so many sectors of Mexican society. The story also shows how the prevalence of information throughout the city interpellates any resident—especially those who suffer—into the raw material for sensationalist reports. The story questions how people can resist global capitalism when its omnipresence both in the physical world and the mediasphere constantly devalues human life. Rojo ultimately provides more questions than answers, but his story advocates for a methodology of the oppressed where people avoid using technology in a dehumanizing way even when society pushes them to marginalize those weaker than themselves. Individuals who disconnect from the integrated circuit can live meaningful lives, but their deliberate self-ostracization from political discourse dooms them to a perpetual state of apolitical *zoē*.

The story's quality is undeniable, but its value extends beyond aesthetic considerations because it engages the most important debates surrounding technological development and the advent of neoliberalism that permeated 1990s Mexican society. Throughout the story we see how the protagonist's cyborg identity subjects him to the demands of a brutally efficient neoliberalism that alienates him from himself. Rojo's rejection of neoliberalism takes on greater significance when we consider the fact that "Ruido gris" was published two years after the implementation of NAFTA, which had opened Mexican markets to foreign investment and thus revolutionized the economy. It is important to note that the principal oppressor in "Ruido gris" is neither the government nor foreign businesses, but a market-based economy where media corporations exploit both their workers and their audiences for profit.[22] This reflects the historical reality that the transition to neoliberalism was especially aggressive and notable in the Mexican media. Shortly after the implementation of NAFTA, several television stations, particularly TV Azteca, emerged to challenge the hegemony of Telemundo.[23] On the one hand, this had the democratizing effect of reducing the influence of the alliance between the PRI and Televisa and allowing diverging opinions to appear on the air.[24] On the other hand, this neoliberalization meant that television channels had to compete with each other for viewers. It was for this reason that TV Azteca released the program *Ciudad desnuda* (1995–1997), effectively a televisual tabloid that reported in a sensationalized manner on the kidnappings, robberies, and murders that happened daily in Mexico City.[25] While controversial, *Ciudad desnuda* scored solid ratings against Televisa, especially in difficult time slots.[26]

As it documented the lives (and deaths) of real people from Mexico City, TV Azteca participated in the massmediation of society.[27] According to Nery Córdova, massmediation has played a "transcendental role in the incorporation of diverse social groups into public life, the market, competition, and the spectacle that all this entails" (el papel trascendente para la incorporación de diversos grupos sociales hacia la vida pública, el mercado, la competencia y el espectáculo que todo ello conlleva).[28] The case of *Ciudad desnuda* challenges this assertion to some degree. Given that it achieved its successes through the promise that "blood will flow" (escurrirá sangre), this program interpellated all of the inhabitants of Mexico City into a class of potential *zoē* that unregulated entertainment companies could exploit to improve their ratings.[29] Far from facilitating the inclusion of its audience into public and political life, which corresponds to the *bios*, this program validated a necroliberal condition that affirmed the expendability, of everyone. Agamben explains that "the realm of bare life—which is originally situated at the margins of the political order—gradually begins to coincide with the political real, and exclusion and inclusion, outside and inside, *bios* and *zoē*, right and fact, enter into a zone of irreducible indistinction."[30] These words can help us to understand the situation in mid-1990s Mexico, where the imposition of NAFTA represented a state of exception in and of itself. Under these circumstances, television companies could cast anyone, including the dead, as an exploitable, *homo sacer* body. What is more, they frequently did so when they determined that such behavior would increase ratings and profits.

For Agamben, the sanctity of the *homo sacer* resides in the fact that "the production of bare life is the originary activity of sovereignty."[31] As biopolitical states and businesses sort people into *bios* and *zoē*—and especially when they identify the exceptional circumstances that would justify the killing (though not the murder) of the *homo sacer*—they also define the terms of their own existence. Given that privatization would necessarily marginalize the less-privileged sectors of society, this was precisely the situation that 1990s Mexico confronted when Rojo wrote this story.[32] Beyond capitalizing on the suffering of the people of Mexico City, programs like *Ciudad desnuda* created a sort of Andersonian "imagined community." The constant representations of Mexican bare life institutionalized a new, necroliberal social hierarchy that constantly cast Mexico City residents as exploitable bodies whose value extended no further than their ability to make money for investors. People throughout the city would contribute to television companies' bottom line either by consuming their products (and crucially, commercials) or by becoming the product that these companies peddled.

Stephen C. Tobin argues convincingly that Pepe Rojo based Rojo Digital—the fictional news program to which the ocular reporter of "Ruido gris" contributes—on the true case of *Ciudad desnuda*.[33] This affirmation validates Bell and Molina-Gavilán's reading of the story as "an indictment of sensationalist media and society's macabre voyeurism."[34] The story thus provides a fruitful space from which to theorize robo-sacer resistance. Certainly, the omnipresence of television screens—rather than internet connection—more precisely imagines a "televisual" (instead of a truly cybernetic) society.[35] Nevertheless, the prevalence of television viewers throughout the city becomes "a symbolic amalgam of the half-human, half-consumption-automatons citizens have become."[36] Beyond transforming its audience members into exploitable bare life, the story's media corporation also dehumanizes its reporters by forcing them to risk their lives in order to produce increasingly spectacular, generally uninformative footage.[37]

The dehumanization of reporters is most visible through SECLE, a new disease that affects those who have too much contact with electronic apparatuses. Héctor Fernández L'Hoeste observes certain similarities between SECLE and cancer, but the most explicit parallel is with the cases of AIDS and the ensuing homophobia that plagued Mexico during the 1990s.[38] Indeed, a type of mediaphobia abounds in the narrator's city; the noncyborg majority rejects ocular reporters because they fear possible contagion even though that would be impossible given that SECLE is not communicable. The protagonist's cyborg condition thus denies him any degree of human contact and contributes to his sense of isolation.[39] One especially unnerving aspect about this story is that the media corporation continues to produce ocular reporters even though it knows that many of them will die from SECLE. The city's poor continue to undergo surgeries to become ocular reporters because they have no other option, and the media companies happily consume their *zoē* in their never-ending quest for higher ratings. García captures the level of commercialization of the lives of these cyborg reporters when he explains that they "have a certain labor life that comes to expire after a determined amount of time" (tienen cierta vida laboral que llega a caducar a determinado tiempo).[40] In the end, the company does not worry about the lives and deaths of its workers because it can replace them. The city's poor represent an inexhaustible supply of labor that the company can constantly consume. Shafer confirms that "it is not the technology per se that dehumanizes the narrator, but the neoliberal apparatus that employs such technology for mass consumption."⁴¹ In the end, technology is but a tool that the corporation employs in its quest to increase its ratings and maximize profit.

Rojo emphasizes that the corporation views its employees more as machines than as people throughout the story. Indeed, the company trains its ocular reporters to suppress their natural, human impulses with the end of achieving more spectacular footage. One fascinating example of this tendency appears at the beginning of the story when the protagonist reports on a nearby shooting. Noting that there are still hostilities, he repeats the following training in his mind:

> When it is impossible to set up an external camera to situate the action, the reporter should obtain a few establishing shots—"long shots"—to ensure that the space in which the action takes place is logical to the viewers. Reporters should prepare fixed shots first, and only later, when there is action, can they use motion shots.⁴²

These instructions appear throughout the story, and they generally remind the narrator to subordinate his natural drives for self-preservation and altruism to the interests of an entertainment corporation. Beyond interrupting the narration, every rendition of the story that I have seen creates a robotic aesthetic by using a font that simulates the text one would see on a digital clock. We can thus read these instructions as a type of programming that transforms ocular reporters into robotic, cyborg employees. The text emphasizes that the corporation does not care if its employees report on current events in an ethical and professional manner; rather, these workers must entertain through sensational stories and filming techniques. The commercialization of human beings—both of reporters and of the subjects of a given report—sits at the heart of these robotic instructions. Far from potentially liberating, the cyborg condition of this protagonist binds him violently to the necroliberal order. We see the extent to which his training has colored his work when he interviews a police officer after the shooting. He suddenly narrates, "the next thing I register—*and I suppose it's gonna be pretty spectacular since my shot was a close-up of his face*—is a flash of light and his face exploding into pieces of blood and flesh."⁴³ His only complaint is not that he just saw a man die or even that his own life was in danger. Rather, he laments the fact that he lacks the external microphones necessary for capturing the sound of the explosion. Luckily, he believes that the sound engineers at his company will add that for dramatic effect.

This problematic reaction underscores the necroliberal nature of the protagonist's work. The reporter has just witnessed a murder, yet his first concern is not for the victim but how to improve his audience's experience in viewing this violent death. The ambiguity of the narration leaves the reader wondering if the protagonist could have warned the officer; indeed, he incapacitates the shooter immediately afterward. The narrator's indifference toward death underscores the fact that, in this city, human life has been reduced to mere merchandise sold on national television screens. Ginway captures the necroliberal logic of the protagonist's work when she writes, "the fact that the society appears to perpetuate itself through the deaths of human bodies becomes a grotesque image of the abject combining consumption and death."[44] Rather than offer his condolences to the fallen officer and his family, the ocular reporter instead criticizes the policeman for his "carelessness." In an internal monologue, he asserts that "it's always good to criticize institutions. It raises the ratings."[45] His desire to manufacture a crisis rather than participate in any type of mourning reflects a necroliberal logic in which "ratings and fame stand above human dignity and safety."[46] The narrator's cynicism proves uncomfortable, but it also reflects the yellow press that abounded in 1990s Mexico and remains in place well into the twenty-first century.[47] As Fernández L'Hoeste notes, "Rojo's story documents a transition in the sensibilities of the modern era, according to which news coverage has abandoned its responsibility to provide information in favor of entertainment" (el cuento de Rojo documenta una transición en la sensibilidad de la era moderna, según la cual el cubrimiento noticioso ha devenido en entretenimiento, dejando a un lado su responsabilidad de información).[48] Viewed in this light, we can never know for certain if the fallen officer committed an error or not. The narrator has only raised doubts about this action to entertain through scandal. The ocular reporter thus dehumanizes the very people he covers in his attempts to sell his reports.

According to Fernández L'Hoeste, the narrator's alienation increases each time he commercializes the suffering of others rather than treat them like the human beings they truly are.[49] Indeed, the narrator decides to resist at the very moments when he enjoys his greatest professional successes precisely because these leave him especially unsatisfied with his life. His cyborg anatomy interrupts his attempt to resist in public because the corporation could begin transmitting his recordings live at any moment. If he were to see a car crash or an armed robbery, for example, the company would appropriate those images and place them on the air. Far from Haraway's "pleasurably tight couplings" between flesh and metal, then, his bionic eye, in the words of Ginway, "warns [us] of the addictive need for news by the public and those who are sacrificed to feed it."⁵⁰ The prosthetic extensions of the narrator disturb him and underscore his institutionalized bare life by stripping him of any vestige of privacy. It is precisely for this reason that the narrator does not leave his home nor transmit anything for several weeks following the shooting: he knows that the company will never transmit boring projections of his tile floor.⁵¹ Crucially, the narrator does not take this time off out of an altruistic desire to resist alone. Rather, he stays home after the airing of particularly successful stories because he has sufficient money to subsist for a few days. Once he gets hungry or needs to pay rent, he returns to his job. The narrator's lack of ambition evinces the disgust that he feels toward a profession that reduces human beings to the funds they can generate for the media corporation. He proclaims that he would like to rip out his right eye "by the roots" to remove the camera he holds inside, but he knows that such an action would be useless because the media company would sue him and he would have to recuperate any and all money lost to his employer.⁵²

He returns to the job only after running out of money, and within a few minutes he witnesses a terrorist attack at a department store. He sees two security agents approach a bomb. As he narrates,

> I'm about to shout at them to get away when I hear a voice in my ear. "Where the fuck are you? [¿Donde chingados estás?⁵³] Straighten out the shot, show us something we can broadcast. Are you in the store?" I slowly correct the shot, steadying my head in a slow pan while I notice the red indicator light switch on in my eyes. I manage to spot the two security guards in the candy section. I force myself not to blink, and the bomb explodes.⁵⁴

The company loves the footage, but the narrator leaves with desperate feelings of guilt. In another internal monologue, he muses, "Today I crossed a line. I don't know and I don't care if I killed the security guards. It's one thing to report on stuff that happens and another thing to make what happens more spectacular."⁵⁵ From this point forward, the unnamed protagonist begins to reject the robotic aspects of his being in an attempt to recapture his humanity. He affirms, "I don't want to think about anything. My whole body aches."⁵⁶ While this pain clearly results from having survived a violent explosion, the narrator's emphasis on his body reminds us of the division between flesh and metal: if a necroliberal society has demanded his inaction before the security guards' deaths, his body—the organic part of him that includes both his brain and mind—feels remorse and guilt. In this moment, he recognizes that, beyond relegating ocular reporters to *zoē*, the necroliberal order also views the city's millions of inhabitants—most of whom have never inserted cameras and microphones into their bodies—as expendable. The simple act of living in this cyberpunk society dehumanizes all of the city's residents because people constantly consume the deaths of their neighbors. Disgusted, the narrator fantasizes ways to disconnect himself from the integrated circuit, but the only feasible way to do this is through suicide.

The necroliberal project is so deeply entrenched in this society that the unnamed narrator cannot disarticulate himself from it even when he imagines its rupture. Numerous theorists have proclaimed that "it is easier to imagine the end of the world than the end of capitalism."[57] This story suggests that it is also easier for people to contemplate their own end than to consider an alternative to a systemic market of death. Suicide represents, at best, an individualist escape that leaves the institutions and tools of domination completely intact. From the story's earliest moments, the narrator has identified suicide news reports as the junk food that keeps Rojo Digital afloat. Videos of people hurtling themselves from rooftops saturate the mediasphere, and ocular reporters can earn enough money to maintain themselves for two days if they film one live.[58] This fact underscores a problematic reproduction of the means of (media) production in the city.[59] The suicides result from a dehumanizing commercialization whose reach is so great that many people—including the narrator—view death as their only escape. Nevertheless, media corporations exploit suicide victims even at the moment of their demise; violent deaths generate viewers and money. The companies never admit their own role in the suicide epidemic, but they disseminate these acts on live television while at the same time alienating the city's inhabitants from their lives. In so doing, they reproduce the means of production in an Althusserian sense: far from a coincidence, the company's suicide broadcasts perpetuate a necroliberal system that ensures similar stories (and footage) in the future. The media corporation thus signals all members of society as potential *homines sacri*; indeed, the fascination with especially gory footage only serves to further dehumanize the dead.

The narrator is so enmeshed in this necroliberal discourse that he imagines the staging that he would devise to film his own suicide. He would install cameras in several locations, he would begin to transmit, "someone would criticize me for thinking that rooftop terraces were news, until they received the signals from the other cameras and realized what I was about to do."[60] The original Spanish rendering creates greater ambiguity; unlike Bell's translation, the narrator switches tenses stating "until they [. . .] realized what I am going to do" (hasta que [. . .] se dieran cuenta de lo que voy a hacer).[61] As such, it is never certain whether the protagonist kills himself or not. Whatever the case, he knows that, in this moment, the producers will cease to chastise him and that they will instead broadcast his grisly fate. He will show up on television screens across the country as people flip channels in search of something interesting to watch. The necroliberal contagion becomes especially evident when we realize that the narrator plans to escape his life of alienation by feeding the very industry that has drained him of his will to live in the first place. He could, after all, opt for an isolated death where the company would be unable to commodify his suicide, but he prefers a spectacular death that will draw spectators. The fact that even the most alienated people choose to end their lives on television underscores the great successes of Rojo's necroliberal society. In many ways, the narrator will have produced his most successful story when he captures his own death. Certainly, he will finally have his own fifteen minutes of fame post mortem. Far from producing a rupture with the necroliberal order, this death, fantasized or real, will do little more than convert him into the most recent suicide of many. He would (or will) appear across television screens throughout the country for a few minutes, consumed by millions, until another event captures their interest. The protagonist may view suicide as a way to achieve personal relief, but the fact that he will leave the dehumanizing system intact is also by design. Given that he lives in a context that commodifies every aspect of his humanity, the narrator cannot imagine a way to legitimize his death and escape the necroliberal system that would separate him from the unbridled capitalism that has created his death drive in the first place.

The story's conclusion validates, to a certain extent, Frederic Jameson's assertion that "cyberpunk is not really apocalyptic" because it enjoys its own excesses.[62] Rojo presents a pessimistic society where necroliberalism has penetrated even the daily lives of the residents of the city. Nevertheless, the author refuses to imagine a revolutionary act that would topple the hypercapitalist system that has marginalized his protagonist and those people on whom he reports. The story ultimately treats robo-sacer resistance as an individual's ability to overcome the machinist elements of their being in favor of the human. The narrator generally achieves this in the days following a successful report because he can satisfy his physical needs without carrying out further exploitation. Even in his most resistant moments, then, this protagonist has to act within a necroliberal model. These circumstances explain his plans to commodify his own suicide: even as he recognizes how rampant capitalism has dehumanized his life and those of others, the notion of structural change seems so alien that he never even considers it. As such, suicide represents the reporter's only escape. Nevertheless, his death will not stop the cybernetic, necroliberal order from continuing to exploit those who live in the city.

"Ruido gris" ends with the same pessimism that has permeated the entire story. In this dystopian future, human beings have been reduced to mere bodies whose value is inextricably tied to their ability to generate and/or spend money in a dehumanizing, cybernetic, necroliberal order. Death represents the only escape from this world because there is no way to modify the economy or societal values. Televisual discourses continue to relegate all of the cities' inhabitants to *zoē* even after individual activists speak out against a society where human suffering becomes a source of spectacle. Rojo's vision of a near-future cyberpunk world was one of many that emerged in the late 1990s and early 2000s. Indeed, Ernest Hogan's novel, *Smoking Mirror Blues* invites an interesting dialogue with this story precisely because he imagines a heavily connected world as well. Similar to Rojo, Hogan imagines a context where technology and commerce have become fully integrated in a postmodern necroliberal order. Beyond depicting a necroliberal order that takes voyeuristic pleasure in the deaths of expendable individuals, Hogan also imagines ways that people from throughout Greater Mexico enter and annex cyberspace for their own ends. That said, the liberatory potential of Hogan's mediasphere remains up for debate given that the most successful acts of subversion largely reinscribe a necroliberal order on a new context.

## TAKING OVER THE NECROLIBERAL MEDIASPHERE IN ERNEST HOGAN'S *SMOKING MIRROR BLUES*

*Smoking Mirror Blues*'s frenetic narrative invites numerous readings, but in this section I will focus primarily on how the AI Tezcatlipoca uses the mediasphere to conquer the very civilizations—Hispanic and Anglo—that most directly destroyed and consumed the pre-Columbian peoples and cultures of the Americas. The god's digital performance sits at the heart of his robosacer actions. Throughout the novel, Hogan posits the mediasphere as a highly democratic space where a confluence of voices produces a postmodern pastiche of discourses. Daoine S. Bachran argues that the novel advocates for a greater visibility of Chicanx voices in the media.[63] At the same time, she also notes that Tezcatlipoca's tricksterization of the mediasphere produces acritical, problematic representations of race and especially gender and (female) sexuality that ultimately undermines the liberatory potential of the novel.[64] Indeed, if we read this novel as a prequel to *High Aztech*, a possibility that seems reasonable given that pre-Columbian religions have surpassed Christianity as the world's most popular faith in that novel, then it would appear that Tezcatlipoca ultimately establishes himself at the center of a new cybernetic, physical, and even spiritual order. Viewed against this backdrop, Tezcatlipoca's successes result from his ability to use the flaws of the current system to his advantage. Rather than install a just world order, the pre-Columbian deity does little more than install himself as the new hegemon in a world that remains doggedly necroliberal.

The extent of the markets of death in this near-future society shine through in the novel's first pages when we learn of Dead Daze, a play on words involving the homophones "days" and "daze." Dead Daze is, of course, a postmodern, transcultural reimagining of the traditional Mexican Day of the Dead. The event has become a citywide rave that combines elements of both the Day of the Dead and Halloween while also featuring deadly riots, popular music, and powerful new drugs like Fun. Dead Daze epitomizes the means through which this postmodern world commercializes different ethnic characteristics to the point of changing them beyond recognition. The festival's very name alludes to a necroliberal nature that does not exist in the pre-Columbian, Mexican, and Chicanx versions of the celebration. People from around the world flock to the city to see the brazen acts of violence up close. The novel begins as the US president addresses the citizens of his country in an attempt to exploit the necroliberal market while simultaneously avoiding liability for the inevitable loss of life:

> Not just as your President, but as someone who cares about you, I strongly recommend that you don't go out into the streets to celebrate Dead Daze this year. The SoCal medianets will provide excellent coverage for all festivities that you can watch from the safety of your own home. You wouldn't want to get caught in any riots like there were last year.
> 
> But, if you do find yourself out celebrating this upcoming Dead Daze, please, try to behave yourself, and cooperate with the National Guard and your local police.[65]

Instead of seeking out those people who do not deserve to live, necroliberal actors in the novel seek ways to commericialize the loss of human life for their own financial gain. Of course, a necroliberal society cannot exist without at least tacit approval from the political system. The president's exhortation that the people not go out during Dead Daze comes across as nothing more than a half measure. His promise that reporters will broadcast everything, for example, acknowledges the fact that many people *will* celebrate, and some will even die: there would be nothing to report on if everyone remained indoors and no one were hurt. Similar to "Ruido gris," the omnipresence of mediasphere cameras interpellates everyone in the city into exploitable bodies whose deaths may serve to get media companies the publicity they crave.

This same necroliberal logic facilitates Tezcatlipoca's ascension. Shortly after possessing Beto, for example, Smokey Espejo leaves his host's home and joins the Dead Daze festival. A feared leader of the Olvidadoid gang threatens him for wearing clothes from the previous year: in this dystopian future, textile corporations finance gangs who force people to buy new, stylish clothing each year or face violent consequences. Smokey Espejo immediately kills the gangster in front of hundreds of witnesses and reporter drones. A news producer cries out, "Did you get it? In closeup? Great! Of all the sumato luck! I can't chingow believe this! It's great! We caught a SoCal citizen exercising his legal right to kill a registered gangster in self-defense! Every network on the planet will want it!"[66] The media company relishes the footage because it will sell exceptionally well. Instead of facing legal action, Smokey Espejo receives praise not only from those who are physically present, but from audiences throughout the world. This particular scene underscores multiple levels of the necroliberal order in Hogan's fictitious Los Angeles. Bachran argues that "as gangs gain corporate sponsorship, they remain illegal, allowing the creation and destruction of gang members to provide money for corporations."[67] Her argument underscores the biopolitical conditions that continue to mark so many Chicanx youths as expendable criminals in Hogan's dystopian Los Angeles. After Smokey Espejo kills the gangster, for example, the AI Tezcatlipoca in the mediasphere contacts the victim's corporate sponsors and convinces them to contract Smokey Espejo as the replacement leader of the Olvidadoid gang.[68] In a move that demonstrates the company's desire for profits over any loyalty to its workers, the company immediately agrees. Shortly thereafter, Smokey Espejo puts together a band and prepares a concert that he will broadcast across the mediasphere to celebrate the final day of Dead Daze. The song, "Smoking Mirror Blues," will hypnotize audiences the world over and allow Tezcatlipoca to possess millions of people at once.

Throughout the novel, Hogan posits technology as a dangerous tool that humans and AI beings can exploit for their own necroliberal ends. Nevertheless, Elsa del Campo Ramírez asserts that the novel "is not so much concerned with establishing judgment on the ways technological advances can be used for immoral purposes as it is with pondering the role that technology plays in our lives."[69] Beyond showing how media corporations use their technology to cast others as killable, Hogan also imagines how an AI god could use these same innovations to assert his own biopolitical supremacy as a god. As the aforementioned scene makes clear, Tezcatlipoca's claims to superiority directly reflect his ability to cast others as killable *homines sacri* and then act accordingly. As he kills with impunity, he draws attention to his own greatness. In an Agambian sense, his desire to kill without remorse plays a key role in establishing him as a sort of digital hegemon. Indeed, his act of killing facilitates his rise precisely because it places him on a separate plane from everyone else. People come to accept Smokey Espejo precisely due to his collaboration with Tezcatlipoca, who takes advantage of the mediasphere's postmodern diversity fetish to market his pre-Columbian order to the masses.

The troubled relationship between technological development and cultural pastiche is key to understanding the novel's "chicanonautico" discourse.[70] Hogan thus signals mestizaje—a term that has been key to both Chicanx and Mexican thought for more than a century—as a major focus of his work.[71] That said, far beyond a relatively limited mixture between Spaniards and Amerindians, Hogan's mestizaje refers to an exaggeratedly cosmopolitan context that puts people from numerous racial and ethnic categories in cross-cultural communion. More problematically, the novel celebrates racial fusion through a voyeuristic treatment of interracial sexuality and racialized plastic surgeries, both of which it describes in objectifying, consumerist terms. Del Campo Ramírez observes the problematic discourse when she asserts that, throughout the novel, "a particular ethnic category is not at all related to notions of tradition, behavior, history, or any other social parameter, but simply to physical appearance."[72] Whether deliberately or not, the novel's focus on miscegenation sits at the heart of its contradictory nature. On the one hand, as Lysa Rivera notes, Hogan's aesthetic creates a space where "multiculturalism and cultural syncretism" can freely exist.[73] In this way, he deconstructs the divisions between hegemonic and subaltern discourses and provides a space from which the subaltern can articulate themselves equally. On the other hand, however, these allusions to mestizaje play a central role in producing a "protonationalist" discourse in his narrative.[74] This allusion to nationalism would suggest that, rather than aim for cross-cultural understanding, Tezcatlipoca ultimately plans to establish a new pre-Columbian hegemony in place of the Anglo-American, Mexican, and Chicanx ones that currently define life in the historical lands of the Aztecs.

Hogan does not imagine a unified, Greater-Mexican order. Rather, he depicts several loosely connected communities of Mexican descent whose very division is part and parcel to their understanding of one another. The text suggests that, on its own, mestizaje will never provide the discursive tools necessary for uniting the different Mexican nations—Mexican (mestizo), Chicanx, and Indigenous (particularly pre-Columbian and Aztec)—under a single umbrella. Hogan's skepticism about the possibility of a reconciliation between mestizo and Indigenous cultures separates him from many prominent Chicana/x voices.[75] Indeed, the novel posits that a curious form of cooperative competition characterizes the interactions throughout Greater Mexico.[76] Much of the racial hybridization depicted in the novel reverberates with the official mestizaje of postrevolutionary Mexican society that aimed to "deindianize" the country by emphasizing ties to Europe.[77] The imaginary of the colonizing mestizo is especially obvious in the case of Beto, a character who is both misogynistic and essentialist in his depictions of race.

The text makes clear Beto's problematic attitudes through his decision to simulate a trickster god rather than a more mature one like Quetzalcoatl. As Carl G. Jung reminds us, "physical appetites dominate" a trickster's actions.[78] Beyond casting Tezcatlipoca as a trickster, we should also recognize that Beto himself exhibits trickster traits as he uplifts himself above his female and Indigenous Greater-Mexican counterparts.[79] The Chicano programmer's disrespect toward other members of the community rings clear when he Orientalizes pre-Columbian religious practices while conjuring this Aztec deity.[80] Beyond deliberately choosing to perform this ritual on Dead Daze—a festival that is itself a problematic appropriation of pre-Columbian festivities—the programmer also attempts to recreate pre-Columbian rites across physical and digital space. He places an obsidian mirror on his computer monitor, beats drums, plays a song that repeats the name of Tezcatlipoca on loop, and smokes Fun.[81] This possibly offensive, postmodern ritual reverberates surprisingly well with other Chicanx literary depictions of pre-Columbian ceremonies, albeit with a cybernetic twist. As Anzaldúa writes, "The Mexican Indians made mirrors of volcanic glass known as obsidian. Seers would gaze into a mirror until they fell into a trance. Within the black, glossy surface, they saw clouds of smoke which would part to reveal a vision concerning the future of the tribe and the will of the gods."[82] Hogan depicts a similar condition when he writes, "Beto slipped from an almost-hypnotic state to a hypnotic state."[83] Tezcatlipoca takes over the programmer's body at precisely this moment.

In the end, Tezcatlipoca's possession of this character represents a case of posthuman, cyborg resistance where an oppressed individual—the recently simulated, Indigenous Tezcatlipoca in this case—uses the integrated circuit in subversive ways to overcome their oppressors, Beto in this case. Far from committed to the emancipation of his people, the Chicano programmer embodies the vices of toxic machismo that Chicana/x theorists have long decried.[84] Beto's misogyny, coupled with his Orientalization of pre-Columbian cultural forms, comes to associate him with those attitudes that have facilitated both the Conquest and the continued marginalization of Amerindians and women in the Mexican and Chicanx contexts.[85] Viewed in this light Tezcatlipoca's possession of the programmer represents an act of justice. The trickster god subdues and recolonizes the mestizo macho's body and consciousness prior to his own ascension. Similar to Haraway's cyborg, Tezcatlipoca displaces his "inessential" creator and inserts himself into the physical world through his physical avatar, Smokey Espejo.[86] Tezcatlipoca finds numerous uses for his possessed creator's body in his quest for money, notoriety, and power. That said, the deity does little to advocate for women and Indigenous cultures.

Tezcatlipoca's trickster tendencies facilitate his triumph in the mediasphere, though his success highlights the limits of robo-sacer resistance in bringing about a more democratic world. The god of mischief prospers in a postmodern context where numerous voices abound and truth is relative. Hogan emphasizes this fact through the playful prose that accompanies Tezcatlipoca's awakening: "the god found this new existence confusing; so with his trickster's curiosity, he reached out through the nanochip, through Beto's computer, into the mediasphere for the information he needed about this strange new world he had entered, and how he could go about being a trickster-warrior god in it. He was delighted."[87] Tezcatlipoca quickly learns that money is the key to power, and he goes about earning it for himself. His willingness to base his authority on riches rather than an intrinsic supremacy sets him apart from the One True God, an AI simulation of a monotheistic deity, probably the Christian God, who self-destructs after losing faith in himself shortly after being uploaded to the mediasphere.[88] Tezcatlipoca's godliness is more biopolitical than theological. In referring to himself as a god, he explicitly casts his existence as an extreme form of *bios* that relegates everyone else to relative bare life and *zoē*. The trickster god's power emanates from his ability to cause chaos by interrupting the machinations of the hegemonic order. On the one hand, the novel reflects the internet's ability to reach countless people and create polyspatial movements and solidarity. On the other hand, however, Tezcatlipoca's unorganized, polyspatial actions make it difficult for him to establish and articulate objectives beyond simple disorder. Even so, Tezcatlipoca establishes a cybernetic Aztlán through his charismatic spontaneity.

The notion of a cybernetic Aztlán is, of course, problematic. Aztlán refers to the territory from which the Aztecs are said to have originated—generally understood to be the contemporary US Southwest—that sits to the north of present-day Mexico City.[89] That said, Rafael Pérez-Torres notes that, in contemporary discourse, Aztlán "functions as an empty signifier" that Chicanx thinkers and activists have exploited in different ways.[90] Aztlán thus becomes any place where people of Mexican descent in the United States specifically—and perhaps Greater Mexico more generally—can come together to resist US, Anglo-Saxon xenophobia.[91] Chicana feminists have invoked the term to imagine a resistant space from which to oppose both Anglo-Saxon discrimination and gender-based violence from Chicano men.[92] Viewed against this backdrop, Hogan's invocation of a cybernetic Aztlán seems quite natural. The physical spaces of the novel take place in the mythic ancestral lands of the Aztecs and the Mexica, with narrative fragments occurring in Mexico City, Phoenix, and Los Angeles. Nevertheless, Tezcatlipoca cannot reconquer these territories until he takes over the mediasphere. Hogan imagines a context where both cyber and physical space have grown more cosmopolitan, but the legacy of colonialism remains intact. As Tezcatlipoca exploits the diversity of the mediasphere, he entices people of numerous races and cultures away from the colonizing ideals of Europe and into a pre-Columbian fold that casts him as a member not only of the *bios* but of deity as well. Tezcatlipoca interpellates everyone else into *zoē*, but the Dead Daze participants still flock toward him due to his charisma. In this way, Tezcatlipoca (re)conquers a (cyber)space that previously belonged to his oppressors, both Anglo-Saxon and mestizo, and makes it pre-Columbian.

Many of the most ethically questionable elements of Tezcatlipoca's robosacer project center on the difficulty of coordinating events between the mediasphere and the physical world. When he possesses Beto, for example, the trickster god creates two distinct yet paradoxically identical entities: Tezcatlipoca, the AI worm that roams the mediasphere, and Smokey Espejo—a Spanglish translation of Tezcatlipoca's name in Nahuatl—who has conquered Beto's body. This duality reflects the most up-to-date questions about embodiment and knowledge while at the same time creating an irreverent simulacrum of Christian theology. Smokey Espejo and Tezcatlipoca become both one and separate beings in a way that mirrors the Trinity. The trickster god thus uses his possession of Beto to challenge these tenets of Christianity while at the same time exalting himself as a leader in the cosmological realm. The use of Spanglish in naming Tezcatlipoca's physical manifestation stands as an example par excellence of the heterotopia and cultural fusion that occurs throughout the novel.[93] At one level, it highlights the border crossing and code-switching that characterizes Chicanx identity and representations of mestizaje in academic and creative works.[94] At a deeper level, however, it also shows an ostensibly Indigenous character who appropriates the languages of the two great European conquering cultures that have imposed their cultures on the historic Aztlán. In appropriating Beto's body, the trickster god reenacts a form of settler colonialism that has historically stripped Indigenous peoples of their ancestral lands. Of course, in this case, the Indigenous actor takes back his heritage from a person of European/mestizo descent. Smokey Espejo thus deconstructs the myth of the Hispanic mestizo as the true heir of pre-Columbian society. As such, he undermines one of the key doctrines of twentieth-century Mexican and Chicanx thought that facilitated projects of internal colonialism throughout Mexico on the one hand, while producing exclusionary forms of Chicanismo during the Chicano Movement on the other.[95] After denaturalizing the hegemony of the European peoples and cultures that inhabit Aztlán, Smokey Espejo and Tezcatlipoca collaborate to (re)conquer their homeland both technologically and culturally.

Tezcatlipoca and Smokey Espejo have to explore strategies that will allow them to maintain constant communication. At first, Smokey Espejo uses Beto's cellphone to go online and inform Tezcatlipoca of events in physical space. The delay proves burdensome for both, and the duo decides to undergo a surgery that will connect Smokey Espejo/Beto's brain directly to the mediasphere. This scene dialogues masterfully with Haraway's notion of "pleasurably tight couplings" between the organic and the inorganic.[96] Smokey Espejo and Tezcatlipoca experience a type of ecstasy when they finally achieve communion between the mediasphere and physical space. They notice that they lose a few microseconds in their communications, but they rejoice because they no longer have to maintain a clunky communication through Beto's cellphone.[97] According to Hayles, in a network society, "embodiment [. . .] takes the form of extended cognition, in which human agency and thought are enmeshed within larger networks that extend beyond the desktop computer into the environment."[98] In undergoing this surgery, Smokey Espejo and Tezcatlipoca merge their previously fragmented consciousnesses to the point that Tezcatlipoca/Smokey Espejo has completely fused his/their presence in both cyberspace and physical space. From this point forward, the two incarnations of the trickster-deity can coordinate their Reconquista of the Hispanic and Anglo cultures. Nevertheless, we should also note the biopolitical ramifications of this scene: Tezcatlipoca and Smokey Espejo install an implant in Beto's brain without their host's permission. In so doing, they further conquer Beto's body and trample on any notion of free will. Hogan plays out an interesting confrontation within Beto's brain where his mind confronts the AI being that has taken over his body. Beto says, "you're nothing but an AI simulation!"[99] Smokey/Tezcatlipoca responds that he is indeed a god, and he orders Beto to bow before him.

This confrontation highlights the tensions inherent to the posthumanist deconstruction of the brain/mind divide in a way that showcases Tezcatlipoca's necroliberal motivation. The scene dialogues especially well with Hayles's theorization of a "technological unconscious"—as opposed to a Freudian unconscious—that continually "automatize[s]" human beings as they grow ever closer to their technology.[100] The scene also speaks directly to the greatest fears surrounding free will in an information age. The cognitive battle centers on the desires of both Beto and the AI parasite to control his body and inhabit physical space. Tezcatlipoca is willing to kill Beto's mind and become the new owner of his host's physical body. Hayles observes that posthumanism "shares with its predecessor [liberal humanism] an emphasis on cognition rather than embodiment."[101] As such, the idea that Tezcatlipoca could kill a person's conscious and then appropriate the body sits precisely at the juncture between the posthuman and liberal-human understandings of embodiment and information. The novel ultimately casts information and the body as two separate entities whose logic is so intertwined that we cannot comprehend one without the other. For example, Hogan narrates the battle between Beto and Tezcatlipoca in physical terms despite the fact that it happens in Beto's brain: "Beto couldn't move. He didn't have a body anymore. He was just a skeleton, and his skull was his still-living brain."[102] In taking over Beto's body, Tezcatlipoca effectively erases and kills his antagonist's mind while keeping the brain and body alive and ready for possession. Tezcatlipoca believes that he must sacrifice Beto prior to his own ascension. In this way, the Aztec trickster deity highlights a similar logic between the necroliberal markets of death and pre-Columbian religions, both of which call for victims who, like the Agambian *homo sacer*, must be killed so that the reigning structures of power can remain intact.

Throughout the novel, it appears that Beto has no hope of regaining control of his mind and body. Nevertheless, the cybersecurity officers Tan Tien and Zobop as well as Xóchitl attempt to free him by using Tezcatlipoca's trickster nature against him. They hack into Smokey Espejo's brain moments before his concert and create the illusion that Tezcatlipoca is in bed with Erzule and Marilyn.[103] They manage to cut the trickster god off from the mediasphere and imprison him, thus freeing Beto from this AI possession. The scene underscores the shortcomings of Tezcatlipoca's trickster strategies. He has created a great deal of mayhem, but he has struggled to identify and carry out any sort of real strategy because he follows his desires and appetites rather than showing the discipline necessary to achieve clear objectives. He has done an exemplary job of fomenting polyspatial solidarity, but he cannot yet translate that into political gains. If Tezcatlipoca's trickster nature undermines his ability to plan, it also makes it difficult to keep him imprisoned. The Aztec god of mischief soon finds a way to escape from his cybernetic cage. In yet another scene that questions the distinction between the physical and the virtual, he eats the metaphorical walls that bind him and reenters the mediasphere.[104] The novel finishes with the following short paragraphs:

> In his cell in the University of California at Cucamonga Medical Center's psychiatric wing, Beto chanted, "I am Quetzalcoatl. I am Quetzalcoatl . . ."
> And the laughter of Tezcatlipoca crackled throughout the mediasphere.[105]

Despite everyone's attempts to contain Tezcatlipoca, Beto appears to remain a (re)conquered body, and the Aztec god of mischief continues to plan the triumphant return not only of his religion but also of his culture.

This conclusion also suggests that, beyond breaking out of his confines, the god has also resurrected his brother Quetzalcoatl, a much more disciplined deity. As he confronts the necroliberal world of Hogan's near-future novel, Tezcatlipoca realizes that Quetzalcoatl would be better suited to installing a new order both in the mediasphere and in physical space.[106] Viewed in this light, Quetzalcoatl's cybernetic return seems to fulfill those Indigenous prophecies that predicted his Messianic return and the subsequent liberation of the Indigenous peoples of the Americas, a millenarian prospect that thinkers like Enrique Florescano associate with a Christian—rather than Mesoamerican—imaginary.[107] Together, the duo of Tezcatlipoca and Quetzalcoatl will carry out a mischievously spontaneous yet coldly calculated offensive that will eventually reinstate pre-Columbian greatness. While this will be wonderful for the two AI deities, it will not mark an improvement for the humans who will continue to live in a necroliberal world. Far from using his robo-sacer resistance to bring about greater freedom, Tezcatlipoca has sought only to enrich himself; even his decision to resurrect Quetzalcoatl reflects his own self-interest.

## CONCLUSION

This chapter has shown how Mexican and Chicanx cyberpunk engaged a 1990s and early 2000s society that grew increasingly depersonalized as technological and economic changes shook the foundations of the countries of North America. Both Ernest Hogan's *Smoking Mirror Blues* and Pepe Rojo's "Ruido gris" provide bleak perspectives on the potential for robo-sacer resistance to usher in a new era of liberty and human rights. The narratives imagine near-future worlds where the interconnectedness of the mediasphere creates incentives that relegate people to *zoē*. Perhaps the most terrifying similarity between the two narratives is that, in both cases, private media companies exploit the deaths of individuals in order to increase their ratings and profitability. The markets of death are so powerful that even those who, like the protagonist in "Ruido gris," would like to resist end up validating the necroliberal order in their moment of rupture. Even successful cases of robo-sacer resistance, like that of Tezcatlipoca, do little more than turn the tables and install a new necroliberal hegemon. Both narratives challenge Haraway's notion of a resistant cyborg in favor of a more sinister entity. These cyberpunk narratives were not alone in their criticism of the economies of death that plagued Mexico and the United States following the passage of NAFTA. Many literary and cultural producers expressed concern with the oppressive labor practices that disproportionately cast Mexican and Chicanx bodies as expendable components of a global economy of production. The following chapter discusses two works: Alex Rivera's *Sleep Dealer* and Rosaura Sánchez and Beatrice Pita's *Lunar Braceros 2125–2148*. Similar to "Ruido gris" and *Smoking Mirror Blues*, these works engage with the idea that so-called free trade has created a necroliberal market of death. Nevertheless, where Rojo and Hogan focus primarily on the consumption of dead bodies, these later works imagine worlds where the economic and political apparatus feeds on the labor of racialized bodies to the point that they break down and can no longer survive.

# Part II. NAFTA after the Transition

Expendable Life in a Necroliberal Age (2006–2018)

CHAPTER 3
# Hacking the *Bios*
Disposable Braceros and Bare Life in Alex Rivera's *Sleep Dealer* and Rosaura Sánchez and Beatrice Pita's *Lunar Braceros 2125–2148*

Shortly after the passage of NAFTA in 1994, the Peruvian-American artist and filmmaker Alex Rivera created Cybracero Systems, a mock corporate website that advertised a supposedly new technology in which Mexican workers would use the internet to export their labor to robots in the United States.[1] According to the website, "Cybracero Systems was created with one objective in mind: to get all the work our society needs done, while eliminating the actual workers and all the difficulties that workers imply: health benefits, housing, IRS, INS, union conflicts, cultural and language differences etc." Rivera aimed primarily to highlight the tension between nationalist hostility to immigrants and the neoliberal dependence on cheap, migrant labor in the United States.[2] Nevertheless, he was shocked when he started to receive inquiries from interested parties soliciting his services.[3] In 1997, Rivera added a mockumentary, "Why Cybraceros?," to this project.[4] Through these media he critiqued both Operation Gatekeeper, a mid-1990s initiative meant to curb immigration through San Diego, and the Bracero program (1942–1964), in which thousands of Mexicans entered the United States for agricultural work and were exposed to unethical labor practices.[5] In the short film, which plays like a five-minute contribution on a cable news program, a female narrator states, "As the American workforce grows increasingly sophisticated, it is [. . .] harder to find the hand labor willing to do these grueling [agricultural] tasks." She then segues to a discussion of cybraceros, people who live and work in Mexico while controlling robots that carry out agricultural tasks in the United States.[6] Her report creates rigid biopolitical divisions that cast Mexican workers as exploitable *zoē* whose bare existence means they do not deserve the same labor protections as US citizens.

In this chapter, I discuss two dystopian works of borderlands SF that reverberate with the conditions that Rivera established in the early days of his Cybracero Project. I begin with a study of Rivera's feature film *Sleep Dealer* (2008), and I follow with Rosaura Sánchez and Beatrice Pita's coauthored novella, *Lunar Braceros 2125–2148* (2009). Beyond being important US-Latinx literary and cultural producers, Rivera, Sánchez, and Pita have also dedicated much of their lives to immigrant rights.[7] Their real-world experience in activist circles informs how they theorize robo-sacer resistance and contributes to both works' inclusion in the canon of Chicanxfuturist literature and film.[8] These fictions imagine an ever-expanding capitalism that has spread across cyber and physical space, enriching itself by draining disposable workers of their labor and energy. Both novella and film focus on futuristic braceros who face the same problems—lack of pay, unsafe working conditions, and systemic bias and racism—that plagued bracero workers in the mid-twentieth century United States.[9] Holders of capital police their biopolitical privilege by institutionalizing a digital divide that favors their continued dominance. Interestingly enough, their commitment to enforcing technological divisions in society ultimately holds the seeds for robo-sacer resistance: if *bios* and biopower reside in technological superiority, then the hacktivist heroes of both works realize that they have to tap into global networks, often through illicit means, if they wish to assert their right to life. *Sleep Dealer* and *Lunar Braceros* thus converge in promoting hacking as a powerful means of resistance that allows the oppressed to undermine necroliberal flows of capital and information.

Brief plot summaries will help explain how the director and the authors imagine technology's role in dehumanizing the oppressed and facilitating robo-sacer resistance. *Sleep Dealer* depicts Memo Cruz (Luis Fernando Peña), a young peasant from Santa Ana del Río, Oaxaca. Prior to his birth, a foreign corporation, Del Rio Water, dammed the local river and began charging for its use.[10] The company produces *Drones!*, a reality show that follows US-based pilots who plug into the internet and merge their nervous systems with unmanned bombers so that they can take out actors who threaten the company's financial interests. Memo takes up a hobby of hacking conversations and accidentally breaches the water company's military line. The next day, the corporation sends drones to destroy Memo's home on live TV. The pilot, Rudy (Jacob Vargas), blows up the house and kills Memo's father, Miguel. Memo leaves Santa Ana for Tijuana where he becomes a node worker at an *infomaquila*, or a factory where workers plug into the internet and control robots in the United States. Commonly referred to as sleep dealers, these factories transform workers into zombie-like beings who exist in a dreamlike state. The dangers of this work come into focus when Memo meets people who have gone blind from the job. Memo meets Luz (Leonor Varela), a female node worker and digital journalist, on a bus. Luz sells the story of their interaction through a blogging platform called TruNode. Rudy buys her story and requests more information. Luz seeks Memo out, forms a relationship with him, and slowly learns about his past. Memo eventually realizes that Luz has sold his information and leaves her. Rudy goes to Tijuana, finds Memo, and offers to blow up the Santa Ana dam. Memo reunites with Luz, and the trio breaks into Memo's place of employment. Rudy plugs into the internet and blows up the dam. The protagonists go into hiding.

*Lunar Braceros* is a fragmentary novella that consists of different voices, stored on nanochips, who speak to Pedro, a young boy who was born and raised in exile in the Andean city of Chinganaza, Perú. The United States has fractured; the strongest country in the Americas is Cali-Texas, a nation-state that includes what used to be the Southwestern United States and several northern Mexican states. The Cali-Texas government has aligned itself entirely with corporate interests: it sends citizens who fail to pay rent for any reason—including temporary unemployment—to reservations where they provide free labor for the economy. No one can leave the reservation without first receiving sponsorship from someone with the funds necessary to ensure that they will no longer be a public charge. Lydia, the novella's principal narrator and Pedro's biological mother, is born on the Fresno reservation (FresRes). Her knack for science and technology earns her a scholarship and the possibility for a lucrative career that may free her parents from the reservation. Instead, she demonstrates against the reservation and lands in prison. She eventually accepts a position as a Teco—or a technician at a waste management facility on the moon—both because she wants to travel to outer space and because it will shorten her sentence. She and her partner, Frank, soon learn that their employer kills workers who finish their contracts; this practice allows the company to send larger shipments of mined lunar resources to earth. The team mutinies and escapes. Lydia hacks the corporate operation systems and opens a window to mount a counteroffensive. They hijack a spaceship and return to earth. They land in Tierra del Fuego, Chile, before finally taking refuge in Chinganaza.

Several critics have situated both the novella and the film within a body of so-called "farmworker" SF. Sarah D. Wald, for example, argues that the novella and film "position migrant farm labor at the nexus of social and environmental injustice."[11] That said, as Curtis Marez points out, these works "retrospectively sound the death knell for prior moments of agribusiness futurism by narrating near and distant futures where technology has not replaced workers but expanded their exploitation."[12] Sánchez, Pita, and Rivera depict Mexican and third-world bodies as inexhaustible sources of labor whose existence on the opposite side of an arbitrary border—a wall in *Sleep Dealer*, a barbed-wire fence in *Lunar Braceros*—means that corporations can exploit them to the point of death.[13] Workers who cannot bear the brutal working conditions lose their jobs to others who can.[14] Both works document the creation of a commodified *zoē* class whose principal value comes not from an intrinsic humanity but from the funds that they generate. Within the necroliberal logic of *Sleep Dealer* and *Lunar Braceros*, workers' deaths represent the (apparently reasonable) price of development. In Agambian terms, the institutionalized state of exception is the omnipresent quest to increase profits, and private industry and the state can work *homo sacer* laborers to death to achieve this end. The robo-sacer lens proves especially useful when engaging these fictions precisely because powerful nations exploit a technological divide to maintain their power.

Rivera, Sánchez, and Pita may concur about the necroliberal potential of a dystopian late capitalism to dehumanize large swathes of the population, but the political economies that they imagine—and particularly their understanding of national borders—differ in key ways. The very existence of Cali-Texas alludes to a New World Order where national boundaries have dissolved in favor of economic ties. Rather than disappear, borders become internal, and those unfortunate enough to live on reservations find themselves interpellated as *homines sacri*.[15] For his part, Rivera symbolizes Mexican, Latin American, and third-world bare life through countless shots of a militarized border wall between San Diego and Tijuana that separates the Global North from the Global South.[16] The film shows how, even in an age of internet connectivity, a person's geographical location contributes to their relative privilege. This stands in stark contrast to *Lunar Braceros*, where, rather than exploit foreign workers, Cali-Texas simply takes advantage of its frequent recessions to enslave its own citizens. Despite these differences, the dystopian visions of both *Sleep Dealer* and *Lunar Braceros* converge in the belief that hegemonic forces exercise necropower against exploitable classes. The treatment of poor Mexican and Chicanx populations in both fictions underscores a condition where a "growing gap between high-tech and low-tech means of war" sits at the heart of the Global North's domination of the Global South.[17] As Achille Mbembe notes, the resulting "war machines" of such orders function primarily to satisfy the demands of global capital, particularly the demands of (neo)colonial extractivism.[18] Rivera and Sánchez and Pita further concur that the high-tech war machines of their fictions allow global corporations to kill laborers or drain them to the point of breaking without fear of legal repercussions.

Both fictions signal the digital divide as prerequisite to the Global North's ability to separate *bios* from *zoē* and thus exercise necropower. The third-world, colonized hacker thus emerges as one of the few figures capable of resisting the dystopian status quo. It is instructive to view both the film and the novella alongside the discourses of hacktivism that came about in the mid- to late 1990s. An exact definition of *hacktivism* remains elusive, but at its core, the term refers to "the (sometimes) clandestine use of computer hacking to help advance political causes."[19] Mexican and Chicanx activists pioneered the practice and theory of certain brands of hacktivism in the aftermath of the implementation of NAFTA and the Zapatista Rebellion in the mid-1990s.[20] Indeed, Ricardo Domínguez's Electronic Disturbance Theater (EDT) (discussed in the introduction of this book) made news worldwide as a polyspatial collection of activists coordinated attacks on specific webpages at predetermined times with the goal of crashing the servers. Both *Sleep Dealer* and *Lunar Braceros* take inspiration from EDT as they consider hacktivism's potential for creating polyspatial solidarity. The ties to Ricardo Domínguez ring clear in both works: at the beginning of *Sleep Dealer*, Memo reads a book called *Hackear para principiantes* (*Hacking for Dummies*) by one R. Domínguez.[21] Sánchez and Pita have been colleagues of the hacktivist pioneer at the University of California at San Diego for years. The protagonists of both works breach neocolonial servers in order to extend a political voice to the *zoē*. As such, the works identify hackers as the ideal cyborg actor for, in the words of Chela Sandoval, "develop[ing] technologies to 'see from below.'"[22] The hackers of both works sidestep one of Donna Haraway's greatest concerns with cyborg activism, which is that "to see from below is neither easily learned nor unproblematic, even if 'we' [a term that could apply to cyborgs, intellectuals, or both] 'naturally' inhabit the great underground terrain of situated knowledges."[23] Because cybraceros and lunar braceros already exist from below, they do not have to learn a new point of view. Rather, they can focus on infiltrating the "integrated circuit" and effecting revolutionary change.[24] As multiple actors converge at the same place in virtual—or even physical—space, they produce a communion of sorts that allows them to crash the necroliberal interests of the moneyed class.

Writing specifically on *Sleep Dealer*, Hernán Manuel García asserts a postcyberpunk "aesthetics of hope" (estética de esperanza), which he describes as "a metaphor that helps to question notions of third-world work and identity in the information age" (una metáfora que ayuda a cuestionar nociones de trabajo e identidad en la era de la información desde el Tercer Mundo).[25] García's appraisal of the film is perhaps overly optimistic, but it proves useful in highlighting the potential of hacking and robo-sacer resistance to establish a more just society. He does not discuss *Lunar Braceros* directly, but his words apply equally to the novella. Even in the face of systemic oppression, the protagonists of both works continue to demand their rights, and they do so through the discursive tools at their disposal. Neither of these works' aesthetics of hope emerges from an unequivocal, cathartic victory against necroliberal capitalism; instead, they "close with openings, positing futurity, or the pressing but unfulfilled desire for a future."[26] These fictions celebrate a certain tenacity in the human spirit that pushes people to continuously speak out in the name of social justice and equality from generation to generation. Robo-sacer resistance thus comes to represent the newest methodology of the oppressed.

One of the most interesting components of subaltern resistance in both works is that Rivera, Sánchez, and Pita imagine a Pan–Latin American alliance as crucial to effecting meaningful resistance. Jennifer M. Lozano refers to this community as a "transborder Latinx 'connection' through technology" that will resist the attempts by white US citizens to impose their societal values throughout the hemisphere.[27] Indeed, both fictions fetishize Indigenous cultures from Mesoamerica and the Andes as the ideal counterpoint to a North American, necroliberal hegemony.[28] At the same time, Thea Pitman and Claire Taylor implicitly recognize a degree of competition between US-Latinx communities and Latin Americans from beyond the United States. As the critics argue, *Sleep Dealer* is set in a world "that makes it possible to render *virtual* brown-bodied and explicitly Latin American—rather than domestic Latinx—workers as a cheap, efficient, pleasant and even attractive solution" that US employers can exploit.[29] They do not discuss *Lunar Braceros* directly, but their argument proves useful to our discussion of the novella as well. Sánchez and Pita imagine a similar dichotomy, albeit through the inverse situation: cheap, Cali-Texan Latinx workers power their country's industry from the reservations while Indigenous communities in South America—though not those of the historical United States and Mexico—enjoy a degree of autonomy.

At the same time, both fictions ultimately heed the call of Gloria Anzaldúa to build a greater solidarity between US-Latinx and Latin American communities throughout the world.[30] We see the potential for such collaboration when the lunar braceros seek refuge in South America, where they can live beyond the reach of Cali-Texas. Pan–Latin Americanism is even more pronounced in *Sleep Dealer*, which owes its very production to collaboration between US-Latinx and Latin American artists. Technically a joint US-Mexico production, the criticism is fairly divided as to how to classify it. English-language scholarship from US-based academics as well as scholars of American studies throughout the world tends to emphasize the film's US-Latinx status.[31] Spanish-language scholarship—particularly that from Latin America and Spain—tends to situate the film as Mexican.[32] Still other theorists categorize the film as a hybrid or transnational production.[33] Sophia A. McClennen encapsulates this position when she posits it as a US film "shot using runaway [read cheap, foreign] labor."[34] In the end, the film is a transnational production with elements that reverberate with US-Latinx studies, Mexican studies, and border studies.

## BARE LIFE AND CYBORG LABOR BEYOND THE BORDER IN ALEX RIVERA'S *SLEEP DEALER*

*Sleep Dealer* imagines the dehumanizing potential of a near-future economy fueled by cybraceros who can export their labor, but not their bodies, to the United States. Throughout the film, Rivera depicts "new forms of control that validate the needs of the privileged at the expense of those who may need access to resources most."[35] Shots of physical space show a militarized concrete wall that formalizes constructs of Mexican bare life through the violent separation of countries. Even within Mexico, the divisions between urban and rural (particularly Indigenous) communities remain heavily guarded.[36] Cyberspace itself becomes a collection of interconnected borders that divide and alienate people, machines, and information along racialized and geopolitical lines. Rivera deftly situates his audiences on the different sides of this multiplicity of borders by focalizing his story through "three cyborg-bodied 'node workers'": a Mexican cybracero who works construction in the United States (Memo), a Chicano drone pilot (Rudy), and a South American blogger who has immigrated to Tijuana (Luz).[37] In so doing, Rivera underscores key similarities and differences between these characters' lived experiences and how these have influenced their biopolitical privilege.[38] Ultimately, the polyspatial solidarity that emerges among these protagonists culminates in collective action against Del Rio Water. As Rudy's drone strike shows, marginal beings acquire significant power when they come together against their necroliberal overlords through technology.

Given its provocative subject matter, it should come as no surprise that the film has inspired a great deal of scholarly attention. Most studies center on Marxist critiques of the dehumanization of labor.[39] Arturo Vargas, for example, claims that the movie is "a commentary and interrogation of the postapocalyptic consequences of unbridled neoliberalism" (es en su esencia comentario e interrogación de las consecuencias posapcalípticas del neoliberalismo desenfrenado).[40] This quote directly signals the necroliberal backdrop against which Rivera films the entire production. Fabio Chee views the film's dystopian setting as the logical result of US policies that, for decades, have failed to normalize the presence of immigrant bodies.[41] Several scholars have focused on the ecological cost of Del Rio Water's actions in the fictitious Santa Ana.[42] Others, like Micah K. Donohue, situate *Sleep Dealer* within the relatively new field of the "cybergothic."[43] For his part, Curtis Marez argues that Rivera reappropriates the story of the "migrant worker narrative" from George Lucas's *Star Wars* and returns it to its US-Latinx roots.[44] Sarah Ann Wells casts the film as a work of borderlands SF that distinguishes itself from other veins of SF because "division is not between upper and lower worlds but *across* spaces whose interdependence is as pronounced as their inequalities."[45] Clearly *Sleep Dealer* has secured a place of import within the pandemonium of Mexican, Latin American, and US-Latinx film studies.

Nevertheless, the most pertinent studies to this chapter deal specifically with the intersection of technology and the Agambian state of exception. Javier Duran, for example, argues that *Sleep Dealer* "depicts the ultimate biometric state and its ensuing virtual borders as the logical developments of current global capital technocratic efforts."[46] Duran elucidates how this border creates an exceptional state that withholds privilege from the so-called *zoē*; nevertheless, he elides the possibility for the oppressed to use technology to resist.[47] Hernán García diverges from this reading by positing Memo as a picaresque hacker who follows several mentors and learns to use technology toward subversive ends.[48] B. V. Olguín challenges both, arguing that the film posits liberation as "accessible only through the complete rejection of modern machines and postmodern technologies."[49] These three critics reach antithetical conclusions about Rivera's understanding of the revolutionary potential of cyborg subjectivity. Duran ignores any questions of emancipation; Olguín shares Duran's pessimism, but he suggests that liberation can occur if people return to a more "natural" setting; García argues that technology becomes liberatory through hacking. My own theorization of robo-sacer subjectivity helps reconcile these competing arguments. Technology—at least as understood in the film—certainly creates and establishes a biometric border that dehumanizes those who live on the periphery; indeed, Memo remains expendable even after (or perhaps because) he connects his body to the global economy.[50] Nevertheless, he,

**FIGURE 3.1** Still from *Sleep Dealer*. An automated gun points at Memo and his father as they attempt to buy water from the dammed-up river.

Rudy, and Luz acquire revolutionary potential by engaging in subversive hacktivities that undermine the status quo.

The heavy-handed allegorical nature of the film led to mixed reviews upon release, but this element facilitates Rivera's sophisticated critique.[51] In an unpublished paper, J. Jesse Ramírez argues that, for Rivera, "the freedom of America [the United States] becomes a farce without the freedom of *América* [Latin and Latinx America]."[52] The first case of America's technological domination of *América* occurs at the beginning of the film. Memo and his father hike through a dry riverbed to buy water from a dammed corporate compound that belongs to Del Rio Water.[53] Throughout this sequence, Rivera employs high-angle longshots and occasional close-ups that emphasize his protagonists' marginalization. When they reach the dam, Rivera employs high-angle close-ups from the point of view of an automated machine gun that threatens to kill Memo and Miguel if they do not pay a toll (see fig 3.1). The gun addresses them first in English and then in Spanish, a fact that suggests that the corporation does not trust Mexican employees to look out for corporate interests.[54] As these film techniques so masterfully demonstrate, the current structures of global capital do not extend *bios* to Memo or Miguel; rather, they reduce them to mere bodies whose value goes no further than the level to which Del Rio Water can exploit them for financial gain. The majority of the film shows how Memo and his family face constant dehumanization in a depersonalized world where technology extracts wealth, and even humanity (*bios*), from the poor.

In this fictitious future, Mexico's technological deficit to the United States creates conditions where US corporations enjoy de facto sovereignty in the country. Del Rio Water dehumanizes and intimidates the people of Santa Ana through a televisual monopoly that allows it to air programs like *Drones!*, a live show where drone pilots in the United States execute suspected so-called aqua terrorists, people who demand access to their own water. The show's premise—"blow the hell out of the bad guys"—depends on the extralegal, *homo sacer* status of political dissidents whom it kills without due process. What is more, it exacerbates a similar televisual market of death to those explored in Chapter 2 by exploiting human deaths for profit. The program draws to mind the Bush-era military doctrine of pre-emption, though it also alludes to a troubling trend where the military has delegated certain responsibilities to private contractors.[55] As Michael Martínez-Raguso argues, *Drones!* "becomes a parody that very effectively represents the process of normalization of the [Agambian] exception."[56] The program's success causes peasants like Memo's brother, David (Tenoch Huerta), who is an avid fan, to affirm Del Rio Water's right to kill those who seek access to their own natural resources.[57] As Memo's brother watches this program, he "delight[s]" in the spectacle of *homo sacer* deaths, thus uncritically accepting the targets' guilt.[58] In this way, David participates in a type of Andersonian "imagined community" that leads oppressed, third-world subjects to collude with transnational capital against natural allies and even themselves.[59]

Drone technology further institutionalizes third-world *zoē* by keeping attackers and victims on different sides of the border. Because the executioners pilot their aircraft from a base in San Diego, they rarely see the people they kill. Within this context, drone warfare becomes a type of videogame that absolves the killer of any wrongdoing.[60] This lack of contact between the victim and the victimizer makes drone warfare especially brutal, both in the film and in real life. Within the context of the movie, the commonplace nature of drone warfare produces what McKenzie Wark refers to as "Gamespace," or a post-digital Symbolic Order.[61] In Santa Ana, Gamespace rules stipulate that local peasants acquiesce to the economic and military demands of Del Rio Water. What is perhaps most chilling about this construct is that the "Game" structures the lives of everyone in Santa Ana—and by extension the entire Third World—despite the fact that none of these will ever pilot a military-grade drone. The inhabitants of Santa Ana have learned through programs like *Drones!* that any act of perceived resistance will mark them as "aqua terrorists" and turn them into military targets. These conditions transform all of the inhabitants of Santa Ana into killable robo-sacer subjects as the technologized state of exception limits their agency. Most of these people never explore the resistant potential of their cyborgian condition, but their very hybridity still imbues them with the ability to expose the fissures that run rampant within the dominant ideology.

Memo inadvertently codes himself and his family as aqua terrorists when he breaks the rules of Gamespace and hacks into conversations around the world in an effort to experience something beyond his home. This scene challenges the characterization of Martínez-Raguso, who argues that the "immaterial" nature of online activity allows node workers "to cross an impermeable border."[62] Instead, Rivera shows cyberspace to be a highly physical collection of interconnected borders across which machines communicate. The film illustrates the existence of these cyberborders, and the dangers of illicitly crossing them, through parallel edits that follow radio and digital signals from one cyberborder to another. Memo places his headphones over his ears, and the footage crosscuts to a satellite that receives signals from his computer and transmits data back to him. Such a conception places the film directly in Hayles's understanding of posthuman society, where the instantaneous flow of information between different bodies (silicon, organic, etc.) represents the most important characteristic that separates the human from the posthuman.[63] This potential to send forbidden signals between bodies is what makes cyborg resistance—and particularly hacking—so subversive. Beyond adding to the suspense, Rivera's use of film conventions like parallel editing also posits a heavily policed cyberborder in a way that would be difficult to express through other media. Even as people stay grounded in physical space, their influence reaches across numerous cyberborders at the same time.

As the film makes clear, Del Rio Water should not view Memo's inadvertent breach of a military line as a threat. Far from seeking to overthrow the necroliberal order, Memo primarily uses technology for what Iskandar Zulkarnain would call a voyeuristic "thrill."[64] If we define cyber resistance as physical beings who move within virtual space to subvert physical actors on the other side of a cyberborder, then Memo has done nothing of the sort. Nevertheless, his breach of a military line defies the cyberborder and places his home on the *Drones!* hit-list. Rather than engage in costly litigation that could exonerate Memo and his family, the company designates the Cruz home as an aqua terrorist stronghold, which automatically justifies the use of lethal force. Agamben can further elucidate the surprising absence of judicial review as he notes that one defining characteristic of the historical *homo sacer* of the Roman Empire was that "the person whom anyone could kill with impunity was nevertheless not to be put to death according to ritual practices."[65] Because a trial in a court is a civil ritual, it is categorically denied

**FIGURE 3.2** Still from *Sleep Dealer*. Having survived the initial strike, Miguel Cruz crawls out of his home and stares at the drone that will take his life. Rudy has to see the humanity of the man he will kill.

to *homines sacri* like suspected aqua terrorists. If a person acts suspiciously, the company takes immediate action to make an example of them.

The only remarkable aspect of this frighteningly routine military action is that the drone pilot, Rudy, fails to kill Miguel when he blows up the house. Instead, Memo's father crawls outside with serious injuries. Rivera crosscuts between both sides of the cyberborder throughout this scene; Miguel stares at the drone that will kill him while the pilot hesitates. No longer alienated from the people he kills for his job, Rudy suddenly peers beyond the symbolic order of Gamespace and into the Lacanian real, where he can no longer deny Miguel's humanity (see fig. 3.2).[66] Ana María Manzanas Calvo views this altercation through a biopolitical lens that places US-Latinx populations in tension with Latin Americans: "Rudy successfully becomes another version of the *homo incorporatus* that seems to exist at the expense of creating new versions of *homo sacer* such as Memo's father."[67] Viewed in this light, Rudy has chosen to assimilate to the US imperialist project at the expense of his own culture and heritage. Cordelia E. Barrera, however, argues that this scene forces Rudy to confront his "desconocimientos," a term she borrows from Anzaldúa that refers to "a position in which one's reality is so overwhelming that he or she chooses to ignore it."[68] After killing Miguel—which he only does after receiving multiple orders to fire—Rudy suffers a type of PTSD that forces him to confront the fact that he has taken human lives.[69] He thus comes to question the validity of the system upon which he has based his personal and professional identities.

Rudy's reluctance to follow repeated orders to kill suggests that even militaristic technology can evoke feelings of compassion when it puts people in communion with each other. In another scene, Rudy carries out a similar strike on aqua terrorists in Colombia, but he feels no remorse because he does not see the suffering, helpless bodies that he destroys. The murder of Miguel Cruz weighs heavily on his conscience because of the personal connection his drone established prior to the kill. The pilot's feelings of guilt come not from abstract statistics regarding *homo sacer* casualties but from the intimate connection he establishes with his victim. The scene of Miguel's death suggests that, while necessary to constructing a necroliberal corporate Gamespace, technology and cyborg subjectivity also hold the keys to deconstructing notions of Mexican bare life. Rudy's existential crisis stretches the conventional understandings of posthuman theory, where cyborg resistance generally occurs as technologized bodies articulate themselves in ways that force society to reconfigure the reigning body politics.[70] In Rudy's case, the cyborg is the agent, not the object, of oppression. Cyborg identity remains at the core of his newfound search for justice; however, this is because technology has forced him to recognize the humanity of those whose lives he previously viewed as expendable. Rudy comes to question not only Miguel's guilt but the very distinction of aqua terrorist that transforms people into *homines sacri*.[71] Significantly, he does not eschew technology, but embraces it as the most effective means of resisting the deadly flow of global capital.

The film may equate technology with oppression, but this is because the integrated circuit already rests in the hands of the powerful. It is for this reason that Barrera argues that "the antagonist here is not technology, unchecked industrial development, or even the environmental damage that the passage of NAFTA in 1992 brought to the borderlands"; instead, it is "the erasure of poor, marginalized communities via dehumanizing labor practices."[72] It is for this reason that Rivera compares and implicitly evaluates the forms of resistance that different characters employ. Memo and Rudy follow the rules of the game and become node workers by connecting their bodies to the global economy. Miguel, however, dedicates himself to his milpa and other physical—rather than virtual—labor. At the film's beginning, both Rudy and Memo view this disconnected life as self-defeating. Experiencing technological sophistication as a Foucauldian "technology of the self" that pushes them to articulate their subjectivity through the systems of knowing that they inherit from their oppressors, these cyborg characters believe that successful resistance must take a form that the oppressors can understand.[73]

Viewed in this light, the film suggests that peripheral communities must modernize in the image of their necroliberal colonizers if they wish to earn a seat at the proverbial table. Of course, US stakeholders do not wish to extend such a platform to those they oppress; as such, they perpetuate Mexican and Latin American bare life by making sure that the region's access to technology remains incomplete. The resulting technological inequity between countries lends credence to Agamben's thought by reflecting a globalized biopolitics that favors rich, Anglo-American, US citizens over their Greater-Mexican counterparts. Because they exist outside of the main innovative sectors, countries like Mexico become coded as technologically bare.[74] At the same time, the film itself finds value in the strategies of both Memo and Rudy on the one hand and Miguel on the other. Hacktivist attacks on corporate interests will get the oppressors' attention in a way that a commitment to subsistence agriculture alone will not. That said, if marginalized communities want to search for meaning after emancipating themselves, they must tap into the cultural memory of their ancestors.[75] By the film's end, Memo learns that his communion with the past provides him necessary tools for counteracting the alienation of global connectivity.

Node technology represents one of the most contradictory phenomena of the entire film. It opens new avenues for wealth accumulation, but it also serves to mark workers as expendable. Carolina Rueda gets at the tension that nodes create when she argues that they "generate feelings of strangeness and/or rejection, but can also symbolize the presence of an unknown epistemic order leading to the possession of privilege."[76] The tension between privilege and marginalization sits at the heart of the film's treatment of robo-sacer resistance. Node work improves people's financial situations, but it also commodifies them "on a cellular level" and produces long-term bodily harm.[77] Nevertheless, it also endows people with the ability to connect across the border walls that divide the physical world. Viewed in this light, the film's cyborg protagonists come to employ what Sandoval calls a "middle voice" that is "transformative of itself and its own situation while also being acted upon."[78] Transnational companies view node workers as expendable bodies whom they can drain.[79] Nevertheless, cyborg status can also give node workers a "transformative" and revolutionary potential by facilitating participation in a cybernetic community that resists the necroliberal order. Memo cannot become a node worker on his own in Santa Ana; instead, he has to migrate to Tijuana.

Tijuana's relative position of privilege when compared to Santa Ana reflects real-life systems of internal borders that exist within Mexico. Ever since the mid-twentieth century—and particularly in the years since the passage of NAFTA—US corporations have built factories called maquiladoras in Mexican border cities to take advantage of the lax labor laws.[80] Just as the promise of node work lures Memo away from Santa Ana del Río in *Sleep Dealer*, the presence of work in maquiladoras in real-world Mexican border cities has attracted millions of Mexican workers from the south and the interior. The arrival of this "foreign" (fuereño) working class has led to the creation of rigid social hierarchies that exclude migrants.[81] Rivera's near-future Mexico exists under similar conditions.[82] Indeed, an internal system of borders separates Indigenous peasants from mestizo city-dwellers.[83] Similar to Del Rio Water, the Mexican state also views its rural citizens as a threatening *zoē*; as such, it carefully monitors their movement. As Memo travels to Tijuana, his bus becomes an exceptional site that delivers him to an urban center where he will be able to connect to the integrated circuit through node work. Nevertheless, this does not mean he will automatically experience emancipation. Instead, his bare life rings clear shortly after his arrival when he settles in an abandoned shack that lacks electricity and running water.[84]

Memo soon learns that he will have to solicit the service of a black-market vendor called a *coyotec* if he wishes to become a node worker. The dangers that these figures pose serve as an obvious allegory for the present-day use of shady coyotes who charge hefty prices to traffic migrants to the United States.[85] The real-life Mexican state tolerates coyotes despite their infamous disregard for human rights because it covets the remittances that workers will send home.[86] The decision to allow coyotes (or *coyotecs*) to circulate freely throughout the country, then, represents one of many cases where transnational flows of capital increase corruption in the receiving country.[87] Both in the film and in real life, the potential for (particularly Indigenous) migrants to earn a foreign income takes precedence over the state's obligation to ensure its citizens' safety. One could thus argue that Indigenous Mexicans are *homines sacri* in their own country.[88] At the same time, the *coyotecs* of Rivera's film differ from twentieth- and twenty-first-century Mexican coyotes in that they do not take their clients across a physical border. Rather, they provide prosthetics that allow poor laborers who cannot afford the costly procedure in a safe environment to, in the words of Memo, connect their nervous systems to the global economy.[89] The state chooses not to regulate the industry, thus allowing *coyotecs* to carry out risky procedures on prospective node workers due to the macroeconomic gains that these workers will produce. Rivera emphasizes the dangers that *coyotecs* represent when one lures Memo to an abandoned building, beats him, and steals his money. Luckily for Memo, Luz, a *coyotec* herself, seeks him out the following day because she wants to sell a follow-up story to her buyer. She carries out the procedure and warns him, "sometimes you control the machine, and sometimes the machine controls you." This warning highlights the dehumanizing potential of cyborg subjectivity throughout the film, a fact that transnational corporations constantly exploit when dealing with him and other node workers.[90]

Upon accepting work at Cybraceros SA de CV, Memo becomes little more than a metaphorical battery that drains its labor across the border.[91] In a wink at both Marx's vampire and Eduardo Galeano's *Las venas abiertas de América Latina* (1971), node-worker bodies break down over time as they export their life force across the cyber and physical border.[92] Cybraceros may earn more than they would in the fields, but they remain expendable bodies that exist near the bottom of the biopolitical hierarchy. In one scene, Memo's coworker convulses following a power surge. Memo and his manager carry him away, and the film implies that the character dies. Even so, the plant maintains normal operations.[93] In another scene, Memo sees the reflection of the robot that he controls on the window of the skyscraper he is building. The shot discursively signals him as more machine than human and plays an integral role in fomenting his eventual rebellion.[94] As Manzanas Calvo notes, Memo's employer disposes of any elements that may humanize its workers.[95] In so doing, it further institutionalizes Mexican *zoē* while emphasizing the relative position of power afforded to holders of global capital in the United States.

The Global North's desire to consume the life force of Latin American communities in the Global South leads to the monetization of even the most intimate of human relationships.[96] We see this most clearly through Luz, who develops a romantic relationship with Memo in order to learn more about his history so that she can sell it on TruNode. Ande Davis decries Luz's actions for the "capitalist and colonialist attitude it embodies."[97] Luz's behavior is especially problematic given the film's critique of neocolonial structures of power.[98] That said, several critics, and even Rivera himself, proclaim that Luz dedicates her blog to social justice causes.[99] China Medel takes these apologetic arguments the furthest by asserting that TruNode creates a "biopolitics of memory" that challenges the state of exception that programs like *Drones!* inscribe on third-world bodies.[100] Nevertheless, TruNode's business model depends on both the commodification of Indigenous peasants like Memo and the subjugation and borderline enslavement of its bloggers. TruNode knows when Luz tries to lie, omit, or embellish her stories, and it forces her to tell only the "truth"; as such, it coerces her into sharing details that she would otherwise omit.[101] At the same time, Luz decides to impinge on the privacy of Indigenous people throughout the country when she sells their stories without first consulting them. The manipulative nature of her work rises to the fore when she secretly uploads stories even after embarking on a romance with Memo. When she asks him personal questions when they go on dates, we cannot know if she does so for personal connection or financial gain.

We see the lengths to which Luz will go to decipher the mysteries of her lover's past (in order to later sell them to her anonymous client) when she suggests that they plug their nodes into each other as they make love "in order to see each other" (para podernos ver). Luz tells Memo that the nodes will intensify their sexual experience by allowing them to break through the barriers that separate their bodies and peer into one another's minds. This romantic idea takes on an ominous tone given her desire to sell his story. The film presents cybersex as a means through which partners can intensify their connection and transcend language. Bodies become organic borders that lovers circumvent, sending thoughts—represented as images rather than words—through nodes and cables. The following sequence consists of several dissolves that create a montage that moves between the eerily robotic movement of their bare bodies and the images they send. The bodies and memories become one as Rivera blurs the point where one ends and another begins. Numerous critics view this scene as an optimistic approach to sexual liberation.[102] At the same time, such studies ignore the ways that Luz appears to take advantage of Memo.[103] Node sex allows Luz to hack her lover's brain by penetrating him and experiencing his life for herself. As Raúl Rodríguez-Hernández and Claudia Schaefer point out, she has struggled to tell Memo's story precisely because she has been unable to relate to his lived experience.[104] Nevertheless, Memo shares images of his village and what appears to be an explosion—although it may be a filmic representation of a synapse—that seems to refer to the strike that killed his father. As such, she uses the nodes to finally see and feel for herself what he has gone through.

The film remains silent on whether Luz uses Memo's memories in any of the reports she sends Rudy. Nevertheless, she sends one final story following this exquisitely intimate experience. In so doing, she fulfills her function as a "lubricant"—itself a sexually suggestive term—for the solidarity that will later form among Rudy, Memo, and herself.[105] Given that TruNode will not allow her to omit details that she finds too personal, it would appear almost certain that Rudy views the very personal images that Memo has sent her of his own life during node sex. Clearly, this late-capitalist cyber world has depersonalized the most intimate of human relationships, reducing them to mere business transactions. In another context, the lovers' sexual and cybernetic union could represent the sublime fusion of both mind and body.[106]

In this case, however, their bare bodies become a grotesque metaphor for both characters' *zoē*. As Alfredo Suppia and Igor Oliveira note, "the dystopia of *Sleep Dealer* speculates about a drastic collision between the public and private spheres in favor of capital" (a distopia de *Sleep Dealer* especula sobre uma drástica colisão entre as esferas pública e privada em favor do capital).[107] Memo's bare life becomes public spectacle as Luz sells his thoughts and emotions against his will, while TruNode has coerced Luz to sell secrets about her significant other, thus alienating her from her own sexuality.[108]

The danger of selling Memo's stories to an unknown buyer manifests itself when Rudy crosses into Tijuana and finds Memo at a restaurant that he often frequents following his shift. Rudy could not know where to find him if Luz had not uploaded this information via TruNode. At first, Memo flees in terror, but he eventually realizes that Rudy wants to redeem himself for having taken Miguel's life. Ever the hacker, Memo suggests that they "repurpose the nodes" to free Santa Ana from Del Rio Water.[109] As Fiona Jeffries notes, Rivera imagines a digital world that is "participatory, decentralized, and diffuse."[110] US corporations have used this decentralization to their advantage by tailoring cyberspace to import labor while blocking undesirable bodies from entering the country. However, nodes provide the possibility for human connection and radical democracy through hacktivist movements like the dam strike. Memo, Rudy, and Luz undergo several disappointingly easy reconciliations after meeting up, and they soon agree to join each other in Pan–Latin American solidarity against global capitalism. In this way they finally move beyond the "intra-racial yet imperial dynamic" that has existed among them so that they can stand united against the US necroliberal order.[111] Interestingly enough, it is only through Luz's morally dubious blog publications that the trio has converged in Tijuana with the goal of engaging in polystpatial resistance and political activism against the Santa Ana dam.[112]

The trio enters Memo's place of employment, where Rudy hacks into the network and claims that he has been called to an emergency operation. In so doing, he, Memo, and Luz "subvert the limits of the hegemonic network."[113] Equally important, these characters assert their "joint kinship," a term that, according to Chela Sandoval, refers to "those who share [...] lines of affinity."[114] García notes that Rivera's editing produces a montage that expresses a polytemporal—and, I would add, polyspatial—solidarity through a magical-real aesthetic.[115] Rivera drives home the notion of polyspatiality when Memo places a videocall to his family and his brother shows him that the river has returned; clearly people from multiple places take joy in the strike. As Rivera makes clear, the most successful robo-sacer hacktions will occur as people from across the Mexican (and Latin American) nations come together to halt the necroliberal onslaught of US late capitalism. The drone strike seems to come right out of Haraway's cyborg myth, where cyborgs, as the bastard product of the military industrial complex, act against their creators in favor of social justice. Labor and space may remain racialized, and perhaps the exploited continue to be interpellated into *zoē*, but the trio proves it is possible to use the system against itself.

At the same time, it is difficult to view the dam strike as truly revolutionary. In taking out this target, Rudy has removed a limb of oppression, but not the root. Militarized corporate interests remain in foreign lands, and transnational corporations continue to use technology to interpellate third-world people into bare life. More troubling still, the characters may be unable to carry out similar acts in the future because they are forced into exile from the integrated circuit, which reads people's biometric information before letting them connect. Sharada Balachandran Orihuela and Andrew Carl Hageman argue that these characters' "mode of resistance too readily operates within the structures of power and control it is meant to resist."[116] At the same time, Manuel F. Medina asserts that the film presents a case where "good triumphs over evil" (el bien triunfa sobre el mal).[117] Neither argument is particularly satisfying. One is left wondering what type of resistance Orihuela and Hageman would find acceptable, while Medina's assertion seems overly optimistic. The tension, and even slippage, between failure and success, and the question of how to treat the strike on the dam, are palpable as the film ends. Rudy can never return to the United States; indeed, he "symbolically assumes Memo's [previous] life" when he disconnects from the network and moves south where the US military will not find him.[118] B. V. Olguín criticizes this ending because, rather than effect systemic change, the trio carries out only "one act of revenge."[119] At the same time, Marissa K. López muses that the dam strike may spur future resistance.[120] The trio has clearly shown that a small group can make a sizable impact against global capitalism, but they will need more voices from diverse locations to effect systemic change throughout the world.

Robo-sacer resistance has yet to meet its full potential by the time the film ends. Rivera emphasizes the border's continued exceptional status by closing with a high-angle shot of Memo's recently planted cornfield which sits parallel to a no-man's-land between the Mexican and US border fences (see fig. 3.3). On the one hand, the protagonist's crops look insignificant next to the armored wall. On the other hand, he and Luz challenge imperial constructs of third-world *zoē* by defiantly positing the milpa and subsistence agriculture as a re-existing, decolonial path for Mexican modernity.[121]

**FIGURE 3.3** Still from *Sleep Dealer*. Even after the successful attack on the dam, the US-Mexico border remains heavily policed, with fences being erected in both countries.

The scene reverberates with Camilla Fojas's observation that "*Sleep Dealer* does not erase the past to showcase the future but brings these two temporalities together, foregrounding a vital critique of the fiction of modern notions of linear progress."[122] In returning to the milpa, Memo emphasizes his willingness to exist in a future that emulates Indigenous practices and ways of knowing. At the same time, he understands that he must "connect" and resist when called to do so. He does not specify whether this is a metaphorical connection to his past or a hacktivist connection to the integrated circuit, but a focus on both the natural world and cybernetics will sit at the heart of his future hacktions.[123] Robo-sacer resistance entails tenacity. Memo and his friends have carried out their impressive attack, but now they must regroup, find like-minded allies, and continue the struggle. Only then can they succeed in building a viable alternative to the necroliberal society that they currently inhabit. Interestingly enough, Rosaura Sánchez and Beatrice Pita imagine a similar condition in *Lunar Braceros 2125–2148*, a novella whose narration tells of a group of rebels that regroup in the Indigenous city of Chinganaza prior to waging war on the Cali-Texas reservation system.

### HACKING IN SPACE: *LUNAR BRACEROS*

Similar to *Sleep Dealer*, *Lunar Braceros 2125–2148* focuses significant attention on how necroliberal forces weaponize technology to institutionalize reslifer and lunar-bracero *zoē*.[124] The notion of resistance also takes on greater significance as this "future history" progresses.[125] Numerous critics have noted the novella's critique of "labor exploitation, racism, sexism, and military domination."[126] As the authors denaturalize historical programs and institutions like the reservation system and carceral farmworking by setting them in the distant future, they provide a SF rendering of many of the all-too-familiar cultural battles of the twentieth and twenty-first centuries.[127] The depiction of Lydia—an intellectual hacker who constantly uses her skills to illicitly access data from Cali-Texas and corporate servers—becomes especially interesting precisely for this reason. In positing a Chicana hacker as the ideal protagonist for resisting this futuristic necroliberal order, the authors implore their readers to consider the potential of robo-sacer resistance to bring about cultural revolution. At the same time, the authors emphasize that hacktions in cyberspace only bring about systemic change when they coincide with physical acts in the real world.

The authors depict their dystopian future as the logical result of present-day and historical acts of imperialism and racism within the United States.[128] The New Imperial Order (NIO)—a corporatist consortia of private interests—colludes to accrue ever-more capital for the rich few while excluding the vast majority of world citizens from economic opportunity. The establishment of a reservation system for the poor and unemployed, most of whom are people of color, produces a type of internal colonialism where "the border is relocated inside of the country."[129] In this context, traditional notions of citizenship imbue people with few, if any, rights. Rather, a person's value arises from their net worth. Not surprisingly, Indigenous people and immigrants find themselves especially marginalized. Because of this, Joy Ann Sánchez-Taylor asserts a shared, colonized experience among Indigenous and diasporic communities in the novella.[130] These conditions ultimately produce what Brittany Henry calls a "decolonial methodology" that comes explicitly into focus as we interrogate the hacktivism of the novella's Indigenous and diasporic characters.[131]

The very form of Lydia's narration highlights the novella's understanding of robo-sacer potential. Lydia refashions the nanotext—a technology that Cali-Texas engineers have created to "break the last chain in cultural (and class) remembrance"—to contest her discursive and physical erasure.[132] José Roberto Flores uses this fact to celebrate the novella's differentiation from "other dystopian texts that advocate for the total rejection of technology" (otros textos distópicos que abogan por el rechazo completo de la tecnología).[133] Certainly, the embrace of technology is measured. Runaway development has facilitated the ecological destruction of the planet and aided in the oppression of people throughout the world. Nevertheless, within the context of the novel, successful resistance depends on the transgressive use of technology.¹³⁴ As Lydia's activism shows, when placed in the right hands, technology can become a tool for preserving the environment and advocating for greater social justice. This assertion challenges Marissa K. López's claim that the authors "discount" cybernetics and biotechnology "in favor of an unwavering faith in the superiority of the unadulterated human body."¹³⁵ The novella clearly explores the tension between the human and the posthuman (or transhuman), but it also imagines a deep interconnection between cyberspace and physical space: successful activists maintain a presence in both.¹³⁶

The question of embodiment and cybernetics rings particularly clearly through the illustrations of Mario A. Chacón that appear throughout the book. The cover art depicts a human skeleton—probably Lydia—wearing a spacesuit while floating between earth and the moon (see fig. 3.4). Chacón builds on a rich history of skeleton artwork that undermines the construction of Mexican, Mexican-American, and Chicanx bodies as expendable.¹³⁷ Indeed, few images embody bare life more than skeletons, themselves the bare remnants of a former human organism. At the same time, Chacón transposes these bare-bone images to a dystopian context where skeleton protagonists also embody cyborg subjectivity and robo-sacer resistance. As Sandoval explains, the transgressive potential of the cyborg body comes not from technology alone but from the hybridization of competing and contradictory worldviews. She further argues that the use of hacking, prosthetics, and so forth constitutes the cyborg "skills" that make up "the methodology of the oppressed."¹³⁸ Sandoval's argument proves especially useful when discussing Chacón's illustrations. At a definitional level, the cover art identifies Lydia as a cyborg by emphasizing her spacesuit. We should bear in mind that the term cybernetic organism (cyborg) entered the scientific lexicon in 1960 when Manfred E. Clynes and Nathan S. Kline theorized it as a means of achieving space travel.¹³⁹ As the image reminds us, this cyborg status certainly has an oppressive component: the state happily risks lunar bracero lives because it views them as killable *homines sacri* who carry out necessary but dangerous industrial functions.¹⁴⁰ Nevertheless, these tools of domination can also become weapons of resistance when employed in projects of emancipation. Indeed, when coupled with skillful hacking, this spacesuit-clad Chicana skeleton will leverage her robo-sacer potential to undermine the financial interests of powerholders in Cali-Texas.

In the aggregate, these illustrations suggest that the so-called *zoē* can only reach their revolutionary potential through robo-sacer resistance. This rings especially clearly in the following episode from Lydia's childhood: "my brother [Ricardo] and I had bikes and we enjoyed riding them to the edge

**FIGURE 3.4** Cover art from *Lunar Braceros* shows a cyborg skeleton after a successful revolt in space. Illustration by Mario A. Chacón

of the Reservation, which was surrounded by razor wire that also separates one complex from another."¹⁴¹ An earlier illustration on page 17 refers to this scene: two skeleton children park atop their bicycles in front of that same barbed-wired barrier; a watchtower with armed guards sits in the background (see fig. 3.5). According to Manzanas Calvo and Barba Guerrero, "the image of mobility [. . .] is arrested by the barbed wire that seems to sever the wheels of their bikes."¹⁴² In both its textual and visual rendering, the FresRes embodies a dystopian future totalitarianism that fits Agamben's theorization of an order "defined as the establishment, by means of a state of exception, [. . .] that allows for the physical elimination not only of political adversaries but of entire categories of citizens who for some reason cannot be integrated into the political system."¹⁴³ As true *homines sacri*, the inhabitants of the FresRes remain beyond political discourse due to their own poverty or to that of their parents. Chacón's illustration highlights the unethical nature of an inherited, childhood *zoē* through its depiction of child skeletons whose fleshless bodies symbolize their separation from political discourse and economic opportunity. Unlike the empowered cyborg skeleton who graces the book's cover, bare, skeletal children lack the strength, skills, and expertise to resist. Much of their overall impotence reflects their inability to engage in robo-sacer resistance; even if we employ a deliberately expansive definition of cyborg condition that would extend cyborg subjectivity to a person riding a bike, this would not provide the children with a resistant, hacktivist methodology.[144]

As these children will learn soon enough, even an aptitude in STEM often proves insufficient to escaping the reservations. Ricardo finishes his degree and earns enough money to free his parents, but his experience is rare. Most of the time, a reslifer's education simply "results in ever more specialized forms of labour exploitation."[145] This is certainly the case with Lydia, who joins the anarcho Maquis—a radical political group dedicated to toppling the reservation system—while in college. Throughout the novella, she vacillates between digital hacktions and collective action in physical space. In her earliest recorded act of civil disobedience, she and a group of students hold a barbecue outside of the FresRes. They cut a hole in the barbed-wire fence and share their food with the people who live inside. She ends up in prison with a long sentence after a short trial. The state ostensibly punishes Lydia for the vandalistic act of cutting the barbed-wire fence, but it truly imprisons her because, for that fleeting moment, she empowered her fellow reslifers to stand against the reservation system. In attempting to recuperate a political voice both for herself and for the reservation at large, her acts have challenged the necroliberal and biopolitical logic upon which Cali-Texas bases its authority. As Michel Foucault would say, "it is the crime that seems nothing but a shadow hovering about the criminal, a shadow that must be drawn aside in order to reveal the only thing that is now of importance, the criminal."[146] In physically separating Lydia from society at large, Cali-Texas attempts to remove her from political discourse.

Nevertheless, the novella shows how twenty-second-century technologies challenge some of the assumptions of the nineteenth- and twentieth-century prison system that Foucault theorizes. In a world where internet connectivity allows people to communicate across borders and barriers, all it takes is a skilled hacker to use technology to secure the *zoē*'s political voice. L. Rivera gets at this point when she argues that the oppressed characters of the novella employ Sandoval's "cyborg skills" in order to "contest, survive, and transform the experiences of cultural dislocation, labor exploitation, and diaspora."[147] While in prison, Lydia becomes a robo-sacer activist by leveraging her "high-tech training" into opportunities to work on different computer systems at the prison and (illicitly) access sensitive data.[148] Lydia's hacktivism quickly becomes polyspatial as she captures and disseminates key intelligence to her comrades in arms who remain outside of the jail. For example, she learns through this means that Juan Gómez, the

**FIGURE 3.5** Internal illustration from *Lunar Braceros* depicting children as skeletons as they ride bikes on the Fresno Reservation. Illustration by Mario A. Chacón

leader of her anarcho-Maquis cell, tipped off Cali-Texas officials about their manifestation at the FresRes and landed her in prison.[149] After acquiring this information, she sends a coded message to her comrades, who coordinate Juan's assassination.[150]

Sánchez and Pita explore the synergy between hacktivism and embodied resistance even more explicitly when Lydia travels to the moon. Her work consists of processing nonrecyclable goods, radioactive waste, carcinogens, and other types of garbage from earth. As such, it "link[s] waste control and population control as part of the same discussion for the new state capitalism of the twenty-second century."[151] The authors tout this waste regime as the logical culmination of imperial US dumping that has plagued Native American, Mexican, and Mexican American communities for decades.[152] It is for this reason that María Herrera-Sobek situates the text within a body of literary and cultural production dating back to the Chicano Movement that views ecological justice as a key component of Chicanx rights.[153] The Cali-Texas necroliberal drive extends further than simply placing its employees in hazardous environments, though this ultimately results in Lydia and Frank's sterility.[154] Rather, after careful cost/benefit analyses, company executives decide to kill all lunar braceros—both Tecos and miners—rather than pay for their return voyage to earth.[155]

Sánchez and Pita (re)introduce the concept of robo-sacer resistance precisely when Lydia and Frank accidentally discover the remains of Frank's brother, Peter—whose team had finished their contracts a few months prior—in some discarded waste capsules.[156] They conceal their discovery from Bob Cortés, the chief surveillance officer, by turning off their coms links; if their employer suspects they know anything, it will exterminate them.[157] Viewed in this light, Lydia's hacking and technological prowess proves key to creating the conditions through which she and Frank can circumvent corporate surveillance and educate their coworkers without Houston's knowledge.[158] Beyond a tool for promoting interconnectedness and polyspatiality, technology also provides the means to control the flow of information. Lydia's grandmother has taught her since childhood that, for any activist to succeed, "controlling communication is fundamental."[159] Because of this, the hacker protagonist breaches and disrupts corporate surveillance on the lunar base. In this way, she controls the communication and organizes meetings in physical space beyond the snooping ears of her employer. When Bob leaves the base to attend to administrative duties, she gathers his discarded hardware and makes a rogue surveillance system that allows her to access the security mainframe and see all that he sees.[160] She also occasionally simulates power surges to temporarily shut all transmissions down and facilitate short meetings. Given the novella's commitment to solidarity, it should come as no surprise that the Tecos decide to coordinate their escape plan with a nearby mining crew. When the lunar braceros are finally ready to act, they turn off all surveillance, confront Bob, and tie him up. They later find him convulsing in his office: the corporation has inserted a chip into his brain that forces him to transmit security updates every few hours. The Tecos remove the chip and transmit a message to Houston saying that all is well; in so doing, they maintain control of all communications. They also give Bob an ultimatum: join their cause or die.

This episode epitomizes the problematic relationship among Bob and the Tecos. The lunar braceros despise him for sending previous tech teams to their deaths, but the novella casts him as a victim of the same necroliberal apparatus that interpellates everyone else as *homines sacri*. Given that Bob is Latino, and probably Chicano, the text clearly does not communicate an unexamined pro-Chicanx discourse. Throughout the novella, Lydia mentions numerous revolutionary movements—particularly Indigenous rights movements in the twentieth and twenty-first centuries—yet she remains silent on the Chicano Movement (El Movimiento).[161] This omission is especially telling when we realize that the physical territory of the authoritarian, Cali-Texan state corresponds almost perfectly with that of the mythic region of Aztlán.[162] Indeed, R. Hudson asserts that Sánchez and Pita forward a narrative in which El Movimiento was (and perhaps remains) "complicit with the ongoing oppression of Chicanxs and Latinxs more broadly in the United States."[163] From the earliest moments, the novella questions Aztlán's liberatory, utopian potential and instead posits a necroliberal, and even fascist, underbelly to the discourse.[164] Ylce Irizarry notes that "an attention to solely race simplifies the novel's crisis."[165] While the center of power remains Anglocentric, Cali-Texas (itself a dystopian articulation of Aztlán) facilitates rather than resists a necroliberal order.[166] People of color—including Latinx people—remain disproportionately on the periphery due to a relative lack of socioeconomic privilege.[167]

Bob functions as the site of the novella's critiques of Chicanismo.[168] His first name is an Anglicization of the Spanish-language name Roberto, while his last name equates him with Mexico's misogynistic conquistador Hernán Cortés. As such, he embodies the mestizo (male) ideal that has aimed to erase rather than embrace the Indigenous heritage of Mexican (and Chicanx) society for centuries.[169] Bob's affiliation with the more exclusionary iterations of Chicanismo becomes especially clear when we consider the fact that Lydia's team comprises people whose identities—Chicana, lesbian, Asian-Chicanx, Filipino, African-American, and Afro-Latino—correspond with groups that were "alienated by the UFW [United Farm Workers Union]" which "refus[ed] to extend liberation to other people of color."[170] Lydia's allies thus come to embody different communities that compose Anzaldúa's mestiza/[x] consciousness. The novella asserts that one of the most dangerous antagonists of robo-sacer Chicana/x hacktivism is Bob and, by extension, the exclusionary tendencies of El Movimiento. When the Tecos give him a chance to explain his actions, he tells them that he became the only survivor of the first three companies through mere good fortune: the corporation granted his request for an extension after his first tour on the moon. When he accidentally learned what had happened to his team, the corporation forced him to collaborate with their necroliberal project and "always be at their beck and call."[171]

Bob's willingness to go along with the murderous project of his employer means he will never engage in robo-sacer resistance. Nevertheless, his position as a surveillance officer showcases the intimate ties between technology and domination. One especially troubling sequence shows Bob use the communications system to manipulate his employees. In a scene that takes place shortly after Frank and Lydia discover the bodies of the previous team, the couple appears to see Frank's brother, Peter, through their dashboard while driving across the lunar surface. Instead of wearing a spacesuit, however, he has on "a t-shirt, jeans, and sandals."[172] Lydia turns off her coms system and the image disappears. After proving that it was a technological mirage, she whispers "someone's messing with our minds."[173] The text never explains Bob's motivation for transmitting this image. One could argue that he does this to alert Lydia and Frank about Peter's fate. Given their interaction with him after their return, however, such a reading seems unlikely. Instead, Lydia's characterization of the digital mirage as "a form of torture" seems more probable.[174] While Bob has the tools at his disposal to bring together the Tecos and explain their shared plight, he opts instead for relative safety in exile on the moon. As he later admits, "I am their spy and as time has passed I have come to enjoy my position and the power it gives me over the newbies, despite my knowing that I will never leave this place."[175] Bob provides an interesting foil to Lydia and her brand of hacktivist, Chicanx solidarity. Rather than resist, he gives in and becomes an informant against his natural allies because this will make him a little bit safer. Lydia understands his motivation, but she rejects it and refers to him as a "prick."[176] Interestingly, Bob defects to the Tecos when he realizes they can return him home. The novella's message rings clear: Chicanx liberation—and, indeed, that of the oppressed throughout the world—cannot occur in a racist, machista context. That said, Chicanx activists of all stripes can and should unite with their natural allies under inclusive banners.

The value of broad solidarity and hacktivism rings especially clearly during the insurrection at the mining camp. Olguín asserts that the uprising "becomes linked to other coordinated actions against capitalists and their agents; the rebellion is designed not just to escape the alienating servitude of moon labor, but as a class war waged by subalterns against the forces buttressing capitalism."[177] The successful battle showcases how Lydia's hacking has facilitated the successful revolt; the lunar braceros seize the building without suffering any losses precisely because they exploit the element of surprise. That said, this section of the novella poses serious ethical questions for activists and hacktivists. After taking over the base, the lunar braceros decide to have a trial for the officials who have killed their predecessors. If Agamben is correct that trials are civil rituals reserved for the *bios*, then it would appear that these lunar braceros have refused to give in to the temptation to cast their oppressors as automatically killable."[178] That said, this may be commitment in name only since the verdicts are essentially predetermined. Indeed, while the jury deliberates, an unidentified character poisons the corporate leaders. When the jury returns, their enemies have already died. This execution, while understandable, undermines the attempt at civil society that they have ostensibly sought to uphold. As Lydia explains, "nobody appeared to be shocked by the sight of the 14 'sleeping' diners, nor did anyone ask what had happened or who had done it or anything of that kind. The only question seemed to be, 'what's next?'"[179] Certainly, these executions are punitive, and one could argue that they fit under the rubric of self-defense. Nevertheless, the fact remains that the lunar braceros clearly view this as an act of killing and not murder. Crucially, the shuttle pilots do not suffer the same gruesome fate as their counterparts.

A cynical read suggests that the lunar braceros value the pilots' lives not because of their innocence or their intrinsic *bios*, but because they need the pilots to fly them home. That they would act in such a transactional way at the very moment when they contest their own bare life is especially problematic. They oppose the necroliberal logic of a society that would kill them, yet they engage in biopolitical cost/benefit analyses that value certain lives over others based on their productive potential. They treat the pilots as prisoners until they finally land in Tierra del Fuego, Chile, far beyond the reach of the Cali-Texas government. We see another articulation of robo-sacer activism when the Tecos return to earth and hold a rushed press conference where they denounce the human rights violations carried out against lunar braceros on the moon.[180] Here the Tecos leverage communications technology to their advantage: their visibility means that Cali-Texas cannot send assassins without provoking an international scandal. Tellingly, the lunar braceros leave out the detail that they executed corporate officials because such an admission could weaken needed international sympathy for their case.[181] Their strategy works; the lunar braceros receive asylum, and Cali-Texas cannot overtly punish them. As the story loses prominence, however, different members of the crew die in mysterious ways.

Fearing that Cali-Texas spies may kill them next, the survivors flee to Chinganaza, one of the few political, economic, and ecological refuges from the necroliberal Cali-Texan hegemony. Upon arriving, they integrate into an Indigenous community built on collectivist values.[182] Olguín argues that the novella embraces "a Marxist XicanIndi@ paradigm that resists naïve agrarian utopias bequeathed to SFF [science fiction and fantasy] by Thomas More's [. . .] *Utopia*."[183] The presence of this utopia in physical space challenges Manzanas Calvo and Benito's assertion that "national borderlines [...] seem unimportant" in the novella.[184] Clearly, physical distance from the Cali-Texas border has permitted this and a few other autonomous regions to flourish in relative prosperity. That said, this futuristic Chinganaza upholds the critics' deeper point: "the line of separation between the chosen and the disposable [...] needs to be carefully watched and maintained."[185] One explanation for the city's continued existence is that global society has determined that this Indigenous community lacks any ties to modernity. As such, Cali-Texas has no reason to expend valuable resources to incorporate it into a global order. Rather, it allows the town to continue to exist as a de-facto reservation beyond global discourse.

The Indigenous community in Chinganaza is highly traditional in its relationship to the earth and the land, but it is also technologically advanced. The settlement thus appears to enjoy the best of both the natural and the cybernetic worlds. Nevertheless, its remoteness creates a prison of sorts for Lydia and her companions, all of whom eventually return to Cali-Texas to resist the reservation system. This drive reflects the novella's advocacy for collective action in physical space rather than simply seeking refuge. As Henry points out, refugeeism would reverberate with "a settler colonial logic of removal, location, and replacement."[186] Henry's characterization is certainly problematic in that it equates refugees with settler colonialists, but she elucidates much of the thinking behind Lydia's decision to leave Pedro and return to Cali-Texas. As Lydia explains in one nanotext, "only participation in collective action ever gave me a sense of freedom."[187] Rather than read Lydia's decision to leave as a mother's abandonment of her child, it seems more appropriate to follow the lead of Ulibarri, who emphasizes how the novella queers the concept of family and weds it with radical labor politics.[188] Far from abandoned, Pedro has an entire village of trusted parents.[189] What is more, Lydia remains present through her nanotexts, which ultimately lead Pedro to Cali-Texas as well, where he either finds her or continues her struggle.

This open ending leads Ulibarri to assert that the overthrow of the oppressive Cali-Texas regime "remains purely speculative and can never be fully imagined within the novella."[190] Lydia and her comrades desire a world free from bare life and worker expendability, but their efforts prove more preparatory than decisive. Robo-sacer activism has provided opportunities to short-circuit Cali-Texan power, but the subversive use of technology is insufficient when left to its own devices. As Lydia proclaims in her penultimate nanotext to Pedro, "It's time for a new strategy. [...] Perhaps it's time for a new version of the old urban guerrilla tactics that were declared defunct two centuries ago."¹⁹¹ Robo-sacer discourse will remain key to recruiting and to carrying out strategic acts, but the reslifers will need to supplement these hacktions with armed uprising. Some may argue that this ending alludes to the ultimate impotence of robo-sacer activism. Such a reading, however, fails to account for the ways that Lydia's hacking has challenged an authoritarian regime. Furthermore, it would appear that one of her greatest achievements has been that of using nanotexts to inspire the future generation, symbolized by Pedro, to remain committed to an emancipatory cause.

## CONCLUSION

In the end, both *Sleep Dealer* and *Lunar Braceros 2125–2148* share a nuanced view of technology and power in contemporary society. The hegemony uses its technological privilege to imbue itself with the technological good life while relegating those of the developing world (or the reservations) to a technologically bare, expendable existence. In both cases, hackers seek to breach the necroliberal center of power and manipulate social conditions to their own advantage. We see this when Rudy destroys the Santa Ana dam and when Lydia masterminds a lunar revolt by circumventing the surveillance systems of the Cali-Texas corporation. That said, robo-sacer resistance poses serious questions as well: while it provides a powerful tool for denaturalizing the most egregious cases where the Global North exercises necropower, it generally fails to remove the root causes of oppression. Rather, it catalyzes movements that will, hopefully, bring about systemic change in the future. The fictions deal with the limited success of their protagonists in similar ways: Memo, Rudy, Luz, and Lydia follow up their hacktions by adopting Indigenous lifestyles outside of the integrated circuit, but they vow to enter again. Ultimately, the full potential of robo-sacer resistance remains untapped as each fiction ends. Nevertheless, the optimistic reader or viewer recognizes how Alex Rivera, Rosaura Sánchez, and Beatrice Pita view hacktivism as a powerful tool for counteracting the dehumanization of Mexican and Chicanx laborers who far too often have been interpellated into *zoē* and *homo sacer* status. Of course, one of the most poignant examples of human disposability in the age of NAFTA is the plague of feminicide that has scourged the maquiladora industry of Ciudad Juárez. In the following chapter, I discuss how Mexican authors, playwrights, and filmmakers theorize the roll of technology in creating and resisting the "femi(ni)cide machine."

CHAPTER 4

# Robo-Sacer Resistance and Feminicide

Gabriela Damián Miravete's "Soñarán en el jardín" and Carlos Carrera and Sabina Berman's *Backyard/El traspatio*

A policewoman named Blanca Bravo struggles to investigate the serial murders of working-class women in 1990s Ciudad Juárez, but a combination of political, law-enforcement, and financial interests hamper her work at every turn. At the same time, a young girl named Juana migrates to Juárez to labor in the maquiladoras. Her work proffers her a newfound independence, but it ultimately leads to her violent rape and murder at the hands of a former romantic partner and a trio of feminicidal men. In another work, an elderly woman named Marisela creates and maintains holograms that evoke different *desaparecidas*—women disappeared and murdered as a result of patriarchal violence—who tell their stories at a museum.[1] While her activism has stopped further cases of feminicide from occurring, the woman struggles over the ethics of representation. The state wishes to use these holograms to trumpet its supposed successes in curtailing feminicide, but Marisela wishes to use these technologies to bring the dead back to life. These episodes, taken from Sabina Berman's (2005) and Carlos Carrera's (2009) *Backyard/El traspatio* and Gabriela Damián Miravete's "Soñarán en el jardín" (2018) represent very different beliefs surrounding the ethics of representing the desaparecidas. Where "Soñarán en el jardín" holds that one should not use the stories of feminicide victims for personal gain, *Backyard/El traspatio* is a popular-cinema production that engages the stories of the desaparecidas through a thriller/slasher mode in an attempt to leverage the Juárez murders toward a strong box-office performance.

Unlike the other chapters in this book, this one does not include a Chicanx literary or cultural product. This does not reflect a lack of interest in feminicide on the US side of the border. Deep ties exist between Mexican and Chicana/x activists who stand together against feminicide both in Juárez and throughout Greater Mexico.[2] Numerous Chicanx thinkers have engaged feminicide both critically and artistically, framing it as a borderlands issue that transcends the Mexican context.[3] While certainly a Mexican production—it represented that country in the Oscars in 2009—*Backyard/ El traspatio* situates the Juárez feminicides through a transnational lens.[4] Its filming in both El Paso and Juárez, coupled with the conscious decision to hire US-Latino actors like Jimmy Smits, underscores the movie's transnational, borderlands production and appeal. These elements may not make *Backyard/El traspatio* a Chicanx or US-Latinex film, but they do trouble the distinction among Mexican, Chicanx, and US-Latinx cultural production, particularly in the borderlands. In many ways, for example, *Backyard/El traspatio* shares more in common with Gregory Nava's Hollywood thriller *Bordertown* (2007) than with other popular Mexican movies.[5] In the end, I juxtapose *Backyard/El traspatio* with "Soñarán en el jardín" for several reasons: firstly, the comparison facilitates a discussion of feminicide both in the context of 1990s- and 2000s-era Ciudad Juárez and throughout Mexico; secondly, Berman and Damián Miravete imagine strategies for robo-sacer resistance that go beyond simply associating modernity and the technologization of the border with necroliberal projects of death. Both works view wireless technology as a tool that feminist activists can use to promote polyspatial resistance that effects change in the physical world.

The fictions studied here posit technology as a means through which women and their allies can commune against a corrupt order that facilitates feminicide. The works anticipate major popular movements like #NiUnaMás, #SiMeMatan, and #MiPrimerAcoso, which have provided women with a platform to speak out against feminicide and demonstrate throughout Mexico and the world.[6] We see this particularly clearly in "Soñarán en el jardín," where Marisela's story reads like those of the #MiPrimerAcoso tweets where women would "[narrate] an account of being verbally assaulted or ogled in public at a young age or being touched inappropriately by a family member, classmate, or family friend."[7] In this way, the story highlights the quotidian sexism that women throughout Mexico face. As the story insists, the normalization of these types of gender violence lays the groundwork for permitting feminicide on a grand scale.

These fictions prescribe mass, polyspatial resistance as a means through which women and their allies can change sexist practices and attitudes at a systemic level.

Brief plot descriptions will facilitate the discussion.

*Backyard/El traspatio* cuts between two parallel stories that follow a pair of charismatic female characters: Blanca Bravo (Ana de la Reguera), a newly arrived police officer tasked with investigating the feminicides, and Juana (Asur Zagada), a newly arrived migrant from southern Mexico who seeks employment at the maquiladoras.[8] These two characters are cousins in Berman's screenplay, but they are not related in Carrera's film.[9] Blanca discovers murdered women throughout the film, and she follows a handful of leads that evoke different theories that abounded throughout the 1990s regarding the identity and motive(s) of the Juárez killer(s). She eventually identifies Mickey Santos (Jimmy Smits)—a businessman from El Paso who runs multiple clubs in Juárez—as a prime suspect. Juana embodies the profile of the stereotypical feminicide victim in Juárez: young, single, Indigenous migrant, and maquiladora worker.[10] She goes to one of Mickey Santos's clubs and meets Cutberto (Iván Cortés), a Oaxacan migrant who also works in the revolutionized borderlands economy. They consummate their budding romance by making love, and the following day Cutberto sees her at a club dancing with another man. He berates her in public, and three local men—referred to as the norteños in Berman's screenplay—restrain him, telling him that he should punish Juana's infidelity later. They give him a date-rape drug to incapacitate her. He takes her to the norteños' home, where he rapes her. The film follows a predictable sequence from here: the norteños tell Cutberto to "share" Juana with them; they load her into a van where they rape her, and then they force Cutberto at gunpoint to suffocate her with a plastic bag. Berman's screenplay and Carrera's film follow different trajectories after Juana's murder, and I discuss both of these at length at the end of my discussion of the film.

"Soñarán en el jardín" centers on Marisela, a ninety-four-year-old caretaker who has spent the majority of her life attempting to rebirth feminicide victims through holographic avatars. These "silhouettes" take on the physical and mental characteristics of the women they represent. She bases them on the photographs, social media posts, and written correspondence that they produced during their lives. In this fictional future, school-age children go on field trips to Marisela's garden, where they interact with these holograms and learn of the lives stolen by feminicide. Despite having curtailed the murder of women through her technological endeavors and a collaboration of sorts with the state, the caretaker remains bitter. She recognizes that her garden has played a key role in immunizing Mexican men against their violent machismo, but she resents the fact that this has only occurred through a dehumanizing spectacle of silhouettes who continue to lack agency.[11] The story provides a profound discussion on the ethics of representation. On the one hand, all of the characters concur about the potential of the holograms to curtail future acts of feminicidal violence. On the other hand, however, the state continues to focus on the deaths—rather than the lives—of these desaparecidas by viewing them solely through the lens of sacrifice. As the text makes clear, Marisela and the state operate under contradictory ethical and biopolitical imperatives: the caretaker wishes to use the holograms to return life to the desaparecidas, while the state views the silhouettes as immunological agents that cure men of their feminicidal tendencies.

The dystopian elements of "Soñarán en el jardín" become clear once the text exposes the fissures that emerge in officialist utopian discourses in light of Marisela's dreams of resurrecting the dead.[12] The dystopian elements of *Backyard/El traspatio* prove less obvious given its setting in the mid-1990s, approximately fifteen years prior to 2009, the year when it was filmed. Of course, the film also refers to the 2000s through several references to over a decade of violence against women that would not have fit in the official, mid-1990s setting. Nevertheless, the film's dystopian nature comes to the fore when we situate it within a body of cultural production that, according to Jean Franco, "depict[s] Ciudad Juárez as a premonitory sign of what is to come."[13] Certainly, this does not mean that feminicide originated in Juárez before spreading across the country. Rather, the brutal murders in the border city laid bare the dystopian, patriarchal reality that women throughout Mexico and the borderlands had confronted for decades or more. The specter of Juárez also haunts "Soñarán en el jardín" despite the fact that Damián Miravete sets the story in central Mexico. While she moves her story from that border city, her female characters have to endure unbalanced gender dynamics in the workplace due to the precarity of their financial situations.

Each of the aforementioned fictions identifies the necroliberal order as the dystopian cause of rampant feminicide throughout Mexico. The texts resonate precisely because they speak to a real-world referent where women, particularly those of the lower classes, have turned up missing while traveling to and from work.[14] A significant body of evidence underscores the deep ties between the burgeoning neoliberal economy and the increase of feminicide in Juárez. Numerous experts note that the vast majority of victims arrived in Juárez from out of state in search of work at the maquiladoras.[15] Essentially transnational sweatshops, most scholars agree that maquiladoras became significantly more integrated into the national economy with the advent of NAFTA.[16] The maquiladoras have a long history of race-, gender-, and sex-based discrimination.[17] As such, it is perhaps unsurprising that they played an outsized role in the feminicide cases that shook Ciudad Juárez during the 1990s and 2000s.[18] Sergio González Rodríguez approaches the maquiladora industry and the Juárez femicides through the posthuman lens, theorizing a "femicide machine" (máquina del feminicidio) that systematizes the murder of women. As he argues, within the maquiladora economy, "the individual [. . .] becomes a prosthesis, a kind of cyborg working beneath the most vertical form of command pittance."[19] Women workers thus become cogs in a neo-Fordian machine that devalues them, casting them as killable and exchangeable precisely because of the crucial economic role that they play in society.[20] The necroliberal logic runs perniciously deep: the promise of employment and economic autonomy draws lower-class women to these dangerous jobs.[21] Nevertheless, their employers refuse to invest in worker safety because they can simply hire new employees if their current workers die.[22]

Berman, Carrera, and Damián Miravete present the murder of women in Mexico as a systemic practice where public and private actors prove incompetent at best or complicit at worst. The murders thus go beyond "femicide"—which Diana E. H. Russell and Roberta H. Harmes define as the murder of women for being women—and become "feminicide," a term that refers specifically to the gender- and sex-based murder of women within a legal, political, and social context that facilitates impunity.[23] The terms *femicide* and *feminicide* share similar, intertwined etymologies. The latter term comes from the Spanish *feminicidio*, which is, in turn, a Spanish-language rendering of the English femicide. The term *feminicidio* gained traction (in Spanish) throughout Mexico during the 1990s to describe the Juárez murders.[24] During the 2000s and into the early 2010s, translators generally rendered the term *feminicidio* as *femicide* in English. By 2010, thinkers like Rosa-Linda Fregoso and Cynthia Bejarano had expressed a preference for the term *feminicide* because it allowed for a deeper interrogation of the misogynistic roots of the murder of women in the Mexican context than did the more generic *femicide*.[25] This terminology proves especially important in Mexico, where ineffectual state responses facilitate the continued murder of women.[26] Berman, Carrera, and Damián Miravete recognize the formidable conditions that hinder those attempts to resist structural feminicide.

At their best, these fictions function as activist works not only by theorizing forms of resistance within their narratives but by raising awareness and catalyzing real-world movements against the structural conditions that continue to facilitate the murder of women in Juárez and throughout Mexico. At their worst, however, these fictions exploit the deaths of the desaparecidas for financial, and even ne(cr)oliberal, gain. In no place is this clearer than with the representation of dead and broken female bodies. Mabel Moraña notes that "the process of social incorporation of the corpse is, for the most part, ideological and discursive" (el proceso de incorporación social del cadáver es, en gran medida, ideológico y discursivo).[27] Her observation highlights the differences between Carrera's film—and to a lesser extent Berman's screenplay—and Damián Miravete's story. *Backyard/El traspatio* depicts dead bodies in a way that discursively holds the desaparecidas responsible for their own deaths.[28] For its part, "Soñarán en el jardín" attempts to imagine ways to restore the body after it has disappeared. In denaturalizing the conditions that facilitate feminicide, these works advocate for women's inclusion in the *bios*. Both Berman and Damián Miravete imagine contexts where determined women and their allies create metaphorical—and even real—armies through electronic mobilizations against a capitalist class that continues to code them as disposable. I will begin my discussion with *Backyard/El traspatio*, a film that lays bare the necroliberal policies that view women workers as exposable commodities rather than human beings.

### REMEMBERING OR EXPLOITING THE DEAD?
### A SLASHER AESTHETIC IN *BACKYARD/EL TRASPATIO*

Written by Sabina Berman and filmed by Carlos Carrera, *Backyard/El traspatio* is a fictionalized account of the feminicides that plagued Ciudad Juárez after the establishment of the booming maquiladora economy that coincided with the negotiation and implementation of NAFTA in the early 1990s. The movie takes several cues from a body of documentaries about the desaparecidas, but it is also a commercial suspense film.[29] Berman's careful research led her to interview the families of numerous victims as she strove to write her screenplay in a way that would "accurately" represent the plight of the desaparecidas.[30] Perhaps for this reason, the movie includes many of the key players who inhabited the national imagination at the height of the Juárez feminicides: transnational maquiladoras and their owners; female workers from southern (largely Indigenous) Mexican states; international human rights organizations; and ineffectual and/or corrupt police, local, and state governments. Of course, the film's fictionalized nature provides space for creative liberty that allows Berman and Carrera to put faces on the criminals, victims, and government officials whose lives intertwine with one another in a city plagued by gender violence. That said, several key differences between the screenplay and the feature film evince slightly different cinematographic projects. Carrera produces a genre film that exploits the dead by presenting feminicide through a slasher aesthetic that negates the possibility of movement politics. Berman's screenplay engages elements of the slasher as well, but she also explores the potential of robo-sacer resistance in a more optimistic way. Both versions of *Backyard/El traspatio* attempt to balance commercial demands with an activist project, but they enjoy differing degrees of success. Where Berman negotiates the ethically difficult terrain in a way that allows her to theorize forms of resistance, Carrera ultimately upholds traditionalist values that undermine the resistant project that the film purports to espouse.

The film's commercial focus undermines its resistant potential by unethically exploiting the deaths of the desaparecidas for profit. As Alicia Vargas Amésquita argues, the film reproduces the "social practices inherent to the context that it attempts to denounce" (prácticas sociales inherentes al contexto que pretende denunciar).[31] Indeed, the production follows all-too-closely what Ignacio M. Sánchez Prado calls patterns of "exotic violence" and "neoliberal fear," a "configuration of an imaginary [of Mexico] that simultaneously appeals to the worldview held by the privileged groups that benefit from the region's neoliberalism and to the voluntaristic politics of the progressive and pseudo-progressive sectors of Western intelligentsia."[32] Not surprisingly, productions of this sort often blame the desaparecidas for their own deaths because they have supposedly not taken adequate precautions or because they have embraced their sexuality and enticed serial rapists to attack them.[33] We see this in *Backyard/El traspatio*, a film that most critics classify as a thriller.[34] My own reading of the film through the slasher lens builds on this previous scholarship; indeed, slasher films have historically sat at the threshold between thriller and horror.

Unlike traditional horror films, slashers do not necessarily have to take place in a fantastic world (though they certainly can). Rather, they tend to center on "sexually disturbed" individuals who take out their rage on sexually liberated women.[35] While such films ostensibly communicate traditional norms regarding gender and sexuality, they also are products of a more sexually open society. They take voyeuristic pleasure in the taboo while at the same time upholding conservative social norms. On the one hand, the genre notoriously kills off young female characters who engage in premarital and/or extramarital sex.[36] On the other hand, however, the moviegoers themselves watch sex acts that "[encroach] vigorously on the pornographic."[37] In this way, the genre paradoxically upholds conservative sexual norms even as it allows viewers to consume highly sexualized material. These generic elements resonate with *Backyard/El traspatio*, where the implementation of NAFTA has produced societal changes that have upended traditional approaches to gender roles and sexuality, thus apparently resulting in a wave of feminicides.[38]

The decision to model *Backyard/El traspatio*—particularly Carrera's version—after the slasher proves especially problematic in light of the genre's voyeuristic representations of femicide and feminicide.[39] Violence against women frequently occurs in these films as a means to punish women whose lifestyles challenge conservative social mores.[40] This holds true in *Backyard/El traspatio*, where a violent containment of female sexual autonomy undergirds the feminicidal logic throughout. Elizabeth Villalobos underscores this dynamic when she notes that the film posits "the restoration through violence of the order established by the patriarchal power of the nation-state" (la restauración a través de la violencia del orden establecido por el poder patriarchal del Estado-nacional).[41] One wonders throughout the movie if the depictions of bare corpses communicate disgust with the continued relegation of women to killable, bare life, or if they represent winks at the slasher genre.[42] *Backyard/El traspatio* certainly differs from traditional slashers in many ways. For example, the production does not easily fit John Kenneth Muir's observation that, in slashers, "the killer is usually distinguished visually from the more homogenous victim pool by his or her manner of dress. [. . .] To some extent, the slasher-movie villain is also distinguished by his or her monstrous weapon."[43] The killer(s) in *Backyard/El traspatio* prove(s) more communal. Speaking on borderlands television, Héctor Domínguez-Ruvalcaba notes that "the predatory sexual attack is an omnipresent form of killing whose monstrous image is embodied by a man who abuses women."[44] The film emphasizes how numerous men become killers of women, often with distinct motives.[45] That said, each of the killers in the film exhibits sexual rage and a penchant for low-tech weapons (particularly plastic bags) that they use to commit and flaunt their gruesome murders. These slasher elements accentuate the conservative undertones regarding gender and sex that permeate the production.

The film casts the advent of NAFTA as the principal contributor to the increased rate of feminicide because it has revolutionized the gendered nature of the home economy on the one hand while casting women workers as expendable on the other. In this way, it reverberates with the observation of Kara M. Kvaran that slashers tend to be set in times and places plagued by economic hardship.[46] Throughout the movie, the dehumanizing effect of maquiladora work serves less as a critique of the industry than as a filmic device to signify the perils facing Juana and other women. Unlike traditional slashers, where a small group of friends and frenemies face off against a killer, rampant neoliberalization in this film has integrated female workers (as a bloc) into the local economy, thus paradoxically empowering them *and* coding them as expendable bodies whom factories can easily replace. Nina Namaste argues that, within the film, "women's value in the global economy is purely an economic one; their worth is calculated in dollars, cents, costs and profits, and thus, their worth as human beings is not even considered."[47] These women—almost exclusively Indigenous immigrants from southern Mexico—come to function as an apolitical *zoē* who are interpellated into bare life precisely because they carry out the necessary labor to fuel the global economy. We see this with Juana, whose disposability stems from her status as an (interchangeable) piece of a transnational machine of production. Sayak Valencia and Sonia Herrera Sánchez note that "the discursive technologies of the *maquilas* contribute to the production of working women as rubbish [. . .], objectified like pieces on the assembly line."[48] Similar to other female maquiladora workers in Juárez, Juana becomes a cyborg subject: her body fuses with the means of production, which alienates her from the product of her labor.[49] This cybernetic fusion between worker and machine allows her to earn her own money for the first time. Berman makes a point to emphasize that Juana breaks away from the patriarchal grip of her father as she gains greater independence; Carrera makes the point more implicitly by showing her in an all-female household.

Juana's cyborg identity as a maquiladora worker may provide her with a wage and disposable income, but it also interpellates her as a robot who carries out mechanical labor. As Anna Kingsley observes, "Juárez's capital-driven setting might proffer independence, but it does not value human life."[50] When Juana asks her cousin Márgara for a break on her first day, her cousin scolds her, saying, "Hold on. Don't lose the rhythm. I'll cover you, but don't lose the rhythm. Keep going and when I say now, let me in. NOW!" (Pérate. No pierdas el ritmo. Yo te suplo pero no pierdas el ritmo. Tú síguele y cuando te diga ya me dejas pasar. YA).[51] Márgara tells Juana that she can take only one ten-minute break per nine-hour shift.[52] Clearly, the workers' synchronization with the machine and the production line matters more than their health (see fig. 4.1).[53] That the maquiladora employs a labor model that would be illegal in the United States—its principal export market—is neither ironic nor surprising. Rather, it emphasizes the historical reality of a post-NAFTA society where lax labor laws make Mexican-produced goods competitive in the United States and Canada.[54] This same dehumanization ultimately interpellates maquiladora workers into killable, bare life. Stuart A. Day notes that, in the film, "trafficking in women is the same as trafficking in merchandise"; as such, neoliberal flows reduce women to mere goods or producers of goods.[55] This, of course, underscores what Emily Hind refers to as an "exceptional state of exception" in Juárez, where corruption, smuggling, and extralegal activities have coexisted alongside supposedly legitimate industries for centuries.[56]

The interplay between legal and illegal business rings especially clear in a scene where an American lobbyist meets with the governor of Chihuahua to express opposition to any plan that would require maquiladoras to invest in secure transportation for their workers.[57] This scene, of course, reflects real-world cases where maquiladoras have resisted pressure to take even small steps to ensure the safety of their workers.[58] In the film, the lobbyist patronizingly explains that Mexican employees earn $1.15 USD per hour, while Chinese workers cost $1.00 USD per hour.[59] Faced with the ultimatum that the companies will leave if they have to ensure employee safety traveling to and from work, the governor acquiesces. His decision emphasizes the precarity of women laborers in this filmic representation of Ciudad Juárez.[60] The governor's decision not to invest in the security of Juárez's maquiladora workers underscores the necroliberal logics that he espouses. Rather than take responsibility for women's safety, he shifts the blame, claiming that killers target women based on how they dress or the makeup that they wear.[61] In reducing what is clearly a structural problem to the individual level, the state applies a ne(cr)oliberal logic that leads it to focus solely on profits while absolving itself of the human costs associated with economic development.

The reduction of systemic issues to the individual level rings especially clearly when the maquiladora requires Juana to take a pregnancy test prior to accepting work. The companies refuse to invest in their employees' safety, but they take great interest in controlling their sex lives. The doctor gives Juana birth control pills, warning her to speak with him prior to engaging in sex because she will lose her job if she becomes pregnant. The company's health policy reflects actual, though exaggerated, policies that maquiladoras communicated to their workers during the 1990s; women had to take pregnancy tests prior to being hired, and, if they became pregnant, their employers would refuse to make even minor accommodations.[62] Many view this scene as a testament to the exploitation of maquiladora employees, both real and fictitious.[63] Nevertheless, this scene also represents a clear case where the film's invocation of traditional sexual norms undermines its attempts to critique the maquiladora industry, which has long denied any responsibility in the proliferation of systemic feminicide. The film certainly denounces

**FIGURE 4.1** Still from *Backyard/El traspatio*. Juana begins her job at a maquiladora, where she will become a cog in the machine of production.

those companies that police the private lives of their employees, but it also casts women's sexuality as professionally and physically dangerous. In so doing, the film ultimately shifts blame to the victims, suggesting that they have brought their deaths upon themselves. Neoliberalism continues to lie at the heart of the murder of women, but rather than reflecting a result of impoverishment that forces women to commute at dangerous hours, the culprit now becomes independent women whose newly acquired disposable income makes them more sexually active. Following this logic, the breach with traditional sexual mores leaves them more vulnerable to sexual violence and feminicide.

A close reading of the circumstances surrounding Juana's murder, for example, identifies her newfound sexual liberation as the principal cause of her rape and death. Anna Costanza Baldry and Maria José Magalhães assert that the very logic of slasher films "distort[s] the interpretation of the crime" of femicide (and, one could add, feminicide) by imposing a misogynistic morality that reframes the audience's perceptions of the crime.[64] Vargas Amésquita notes how this phenomenon plays out in *Backyard/El traspatio* when she asserts that the film "justifies the aggressions" (justifica las agresiones) against Juana precisely because she has "lost" her traditional values.[65] Vargas Amésquita may overstate her argument, but the film clearly insinuates that Juana would have remained alive had she not cheated on her boyfriend.[66] This fact rings all the more clearly in light of the grotesque sympathy with which Carrera's film—and to a lesser extent Berman's screenplay—treats Cutberto's character. While he has kidnapped and raped his ex-girlfriend, the aggrieved boyfriend had never planned to kill her, and he cries when the norteños force him at gunpoint to murder her. What is more, they throw him unceremoniously out of the car shortly after disposing of Juana's body, and he later claims that he, too, was kidnapped. When juxtaposed with the murderous norteños, Carrera seems to at least partially absolve Cutberto of drugging, raping, and kidnapping his ex-girlfriend.[67] Indeed, Lydia Huerta Moreno muses that many moviegoers may even sympathize with him.[68] Even after the film ends, Carrera portrays the Oaxacan migrant more as an unwitting accomplice than as a cold-blooded killer.[69] On the one hand, Juana's death at the hands of Cutberto speaks to the reality of domestic violence, a principal cause of feminicide that differs from that imagined by media accounts of the Juárez desaparecidas.[70] On the other hand, in depicting Cutberto in a relatively positive light, the film places much of the blame for Juana's murder on the victim herself.

Beyond the discursive connotations, the slasher aesthetic surrounding Juana's death proves ethically problematic from a stylistic standpoint. Rape and feminicide would figure as thematic issues in any film about the desaparecidas. That said, the film makes a spectacle out of Juana's death by reducing it to the demands of the genre. Similar to murder victims in other slashers, *Backyard/El traspatio* juxtaposes Juana's death with a sexual encounter.[71] Slasher killers usually do not engage in the sex acts themselves, but they *do* punish their victims for embracing their sexuality. The norteños and Cutberto kill Juana precisely because her sexual autonomy offends their misogynistic attitudes. Carrera highlights the rape to create what Clover calls the "shock" aesthetic, an element that produces the spectacle inherent to the genre.[72] The scene's gruesome nature rivals the most sadistic scenes from any slasher in large part because it stands in to represent the murders that have plagued Juárez in real life. Referring to this scene, Day asserts that "Berman has exhumed the real," a fact that leads him to imbue the representation of Juana's murder with resistant potential.[73] Kingsley views the scene as "justifiable [. . .], albeit somewhat gratuitous."[74] Focusing on the camera angles, she notes that Carrera does not film the attack from the perspective of the aggressors; rather, he cuts between a mortified Cutberto and a dying Juana.[75] These cinematographic elements lead her to view the scene not as "pornographic spectacle" but as "moral realism."[76] Clearly, the film attempts to denounce the horrors of feminicide. Nevertheless, in creating this spectacle out of real-world feminicides, the movie codes the desaparecidas as exploitable bodies. In so doing, it at least implicitly invokes a body of borderlands television and film that frames sexual violence as a result of a "general decadence of values" or "a crisis of patriarchal principles."[77] Because of this, it appears that the film includes Juana's harrowing death not to achieve activist ends so much as to represent the "exotic violence" that producers deemed necessary for securing large audiences.[78]

The scene's ethical ambiguity rings all the more clearly when the murderers throw Juana's naked body from the van. On the one hand, the shot underscores Sonia Herrera Sánchez's argument that Juana "ceases to be a woman, a person, and becomes a body" ([deja] de ser una mujer, una persona, para convertirse en un cuerpo).[79] The idea that this charismatic character is now just another (forgotten) desaparecida repulses the viewer. At the same time, however, her nude body evokes the slasher aesthetic that fetishizes the sexualized bodies of the dead. Given that Juana represents real-world victims of feminicide, this fetishization proves especially unethical. The question as to whether this scene will foment greater mobilization against feminicide remains unanswered, though it seems unlikely. Hind argues that "*Backyard* illustrates the problem of the *homo sacer* without inventing an alternative" (*Backyard* retrata la problemática del *homo sacer* sin inventar alternativa).[80] Her assertion rings particularly true in the case of Carrera; indeed, the director largely ignores Berman's exploration of robo-sacer resistance in her screenplay in favor of a more explicitly slasher model. The balance of this chapter will compare Berman's discussion of possible avenues for robo-sacer resistance with Carrera's decision to opt for a cathartic conclusion that ignores the possibility of robo-sacer mobilization.

### ROBO-SACER RESISTANCE AND THE SLASHER AESTHETIC: CARRERA'S FILM VERSUS BERMAN'S SCREENPLAY

Both Berman and Carrera posit vigilantism—particularly the torture and extrajudicial killing of murderers—as a viable reaction to ineffectual state responses to feminicide. Berman depicts extralegal violence when Blanca shoots Cutberto in his extremities following the murder of Juana (her cousin in this version). Perhaps as a result of the sympathetic light through which Carrera depicts him, Blanca does not shoot Cutberto in the film, though she does shoot the wall behind him. That said, in Carrera's film she and another police officer ambush and kill Mickey Santos after he kidnaps a teenage girl. The violence against both of these feminicidal actors has led to some misgivings among critics. Namaste argues that "in using unethical methods [Blanca] perpetuates the highly patriarchal, ineffectual, and gender-based behaviors of her profession."[81] Sánchez Prado views the film more positively, suggesting that Blanca "contest[s] neoliberal ideals from within."[82] Interestingly enough, his assertions would suggest that resistance against neoliberalism "from within" can entail working outside the law. Blanca's extralegal shootings in both Berman's playscript and Carrera's film suggest an oppositional biopolitics to those of the necroliberal Juárez where she works. The feminicide machine may code women as killable, but Blanca views the exceptional threat as the permissive, necroliberal order that refuses to hold men accountable when they murder women. The killers themselves become a variation of that Agambian life that does not deserve to live.[83] That said, Berman and Carrera handle their critiques in different ways. Berman's screenplay uses the shooting of Cutberto and its aftermath to theorize radio's potential to foment robo-sacer resistance. For his part, Carrera frames the extralegal killing of Mickey Santos through the genre of the slasher, thus producing a cathartic ending that largely ignores the need for movement politics.

Given that the movie takes place before most Mexicans had access to the internet, radio represents the most democratic technology available to the masses. It reaches large (generally local) audiences, and it contributes to local political and cultural discourse. Radio has long played an integral role in constructing and disseminating official narratives in Mexico, but it has also provided a space from which people have resisted state overreach.[84] What is more, the technology has provided platforms from which marginalized, particularly Indigenous, communities have challenged officialist narratives.[85] Both versions of the film highlight the work of Víctor Peralta (Joaquín Cosío), a radio broadcaster who calls out the rampant corruption that has facilitated the Juárez feminicides.[86] The second scene of both the film and the screenplay depicts Peralta as he settles into his chair and pontificates on the structural problems facing his city:

> Peralta: Juárez was never a nice place. But we can't deny that it's only gotten worse. We got the maquiladoras because of our low wages. Rural women came and keep coming to work in the maquiladoras. The narcos brought their violence so they could cross into the United States from here. [...] Prostitution took off. And in the end, to crown the disaster, the murder of women became commonplace. Juárez is a nice little backyard between two entryways: the US and Mexico City. I use this brief history as an ode to the new dead woman with a K on her tooth.

> Peralta: Así provincial chula nunca fue Juárez. Pero ni qué alegar que ahora sí se nos sobrecomplicó. Llegaron las maquiladoras por la mano de obra barata. Llegaron y siguen llegando las pueblerinas a trabajar en la maquila. Llegaron los narcos y su violencia, a cruzar por aquí la frontera hacia los United. [...]

*Llegó la prostitución. Y al final, para coronar el desmadre, llegaron las muertas. Bonito traspatio de dos entradas es Juárez: de los United y de México. Valga este breviario como pésame a la nueva muerta con K en el diente.*[87]

Through this preamble, Peralta conditions his listeners (diegetic) and viewers (the audience of the film) to seek out the ties between the rapid neoliberalization of the US-Mexico border region on the one hand, and the increased violence against women on the other. Similar to the chorus of the ancient Greek theatre, he serves as a moralistic conscience who calls our attention to the injustices that plague his city.

Unlike the traditional chorus, which remains outside the narrative, however, Peralta takes on a substantive role by forging a friendship with Blanca and taking concrete actions that advance the film. Indeed, Peralta soon becomes one of the few characters that Blanca trusts.[88] On numerous occasions, she shares evidence with him rather than with her co-workers, a fact that underscores her lack of confidence in her colleagues, most of whom accept bribes.[89] Her alliance with Peralta ensures that the people of Juárez can cite actual facts—which they have learned by listening to the radio— to undermine official narratives on feminicide. In this way, the radio host produces an analog form of polyspatial resistance. His radio transmissions thus produce what Marshal McLuhan calls an "extension of the human nervous system that is matched only by speech itself."[90] As such, his discourse comes to reverberate with the posthuman. After all, Hayles builds on McLuhan when she asserts that posthuman being emerges as a result of the free flow of information across, between, and among bodies.[91] Peralta facilitates precisely this transfer of information and knowledge across different subjects throughout Juárez by pontificating on the air. Peralta's listeners may lack the ability to communicate one with another on his show, but they *can* follow his lead and manifest in physical space. His show becomes the site through which numerous individual stories come together, testifying of a shared trauma that the city's residents could not acknowledge without his aid. Indeed, the current reading of McLuhan suggests that the broadcaster creates new synaptic connections across a city that would otherwise remain segregated along geographic, cultural, and class-based lines. Furthermore, his decidedly masculine testimony challenges even the gendered divisions that have normalized the brutal murder of women in the city.[92]

The potential for radio-based resistance to challenge politics as usual rises to the fore in Berman's screenplay when the governor arrives in Ciudad Juárez shortly after Blanca shoots Cutberto. The broadcaster turns to the airwaves and proclaims, "Glory to God in the highest. The governor of Chihuahua visits us today. Officially, he comes to attend a dinner with the Association of Maquiladores. [. . .] Unofficially, he comes to retire the Juárez Chief of Police and appoint another. And of course, to imprison officer Blanca Bravo, who shot a poor, helpless murderer at point-blank range" (Aleluya Dios en las Alturas. El Gobernador de Chihuahua nos visita hoy. Oficialmente viene a una cena con la Asociación de Maquiladores. [. . .] Extraoficialmente viene a jubilar al Comandante del Policía de Juárez y nombrar nuevo Comandante. Y por supuesto a encarcelar a la policía Blanca Bravo, que baleó a quemarropa a un pobrecito asesino).[93] Peralta does not endorse police brutality when he minimizes Cutberto's extralegal shooting. Rather, he expresses disgust with a social order where, in the words of Valencia and Herrera Sánchez, "*habeas corpus* is a male-exclusive privilege" that explicitly does not pertain to desaparecidas like Juana.[94] As Peralta insinuates, the fact that government leaders care more about Cutberto than Juana encapsulates official uninterest in solving the Juárez murders. Berman's text seems to validate such a reading when the governor expresses greater rage about Blanca's actions than about the rampant cases of feminicide throughout the city. The governor's criticisms of Blanca downplay Cutberto's role in Juana's harrowing murder. Given the circumstances of mass impunity, Peralta's voice reminds viewers—both implicit and explicit—that Blanca has punished Juana's killer herself because she does not trust the legal system to do anything. The government's focus on punishing her instead of Cutberto—an admitted accomplice to a harrowing murder—exposes the insignificance of female lives in the eyes of state leaders.

In Berman's screenplay, Blanca and the governor suddenly hear numerous cars honking outside the building as they argue. The governor's assistant explains that Peralta has called on local residents to demonstrate against the decision to punish Blanca. In shooting Cutberto, the officer has taken the law into her own hands and fulfilled a fantasy that the silenced masses have harbored for years. She has become a local heroine as Peralta has discussed her deeds on the air. In a testament to McLuhan's theorization of radio's ability to create a metaphorical nervous system, Blanca's story has almost certainly traveled throughout the city by word of mouth as people have heard of her acts on the radio and shared them with others. Through Peralta's interventions, then, people from across the city have communed in solidarity against a political establishment that remains impervious to the murder of women. Beyond shaming state and local political leaders, the demonstration also threatens the transnational maquiladora industry. Given that the governor has staked his political legitimacy not on the protection of female workers lives but on the continued expansion of a capitalistic order, he refuses to give in to the protestors at this time, proclaiming, "'the people' don't tell me what to do. A hundred people, two hundred people, a thousand people making noise: they are nothing. [. . .] There are millions in the silent majority" (a mí no me manda 'la gente.' Cien gentes, doscientas gentes, mil gentes haciendo ruido: no son nada. [. . .] Los calladitos, son millones).[95] The governor wishes to ignore these popular demonstrations because he has ascended to power by currying the favor of transnational corporations and capital, which has a greater say in local politics than do his voters.

That said, the governor's actions belie his words. As Peralta has grown the city's collective nervous system, he has built an "echo chamber" that has invalidated previous political calculations regarding the city's balance of power.[96] In so doing, his radio show has diluted the governor's so-called silent majority by inundating the airwaves with facts that undermine official proclamations. He has long told the stories of the desaparecidas and the incompetent state response. As the so-called silent majority has come in contact with facts that undermine official narratives, they have soured on their elected leaders. The governor implicitly concedes the extent of Peralta's influence when he orders the Comandante to block the streets surrounding his meeting with the Asociación de Maquiladores because he does not want local protesters to undermine his carefully choreographed image of competency and control.[97] As this scene demonstrates, the people of Juárez—the vast majority of whom reject the recent surge in violence—have significant, if untapped, political potential. If they follow Peralta's lead, they may reshape the political and economic landscape of their city. The movement remains in its infancy as the screenplay ends, but the possibility of resistance through technology continues in place. Berman emphasizes the (admittedly limited) successes of the Peralta-led movement at the close of her screenplay, which calls for a series of parallel edits that show different characters as they continue with their lives. Peralta's voiceover narrates in the background. We learn that Blanca keeps her badge. The protest has frustrated the governor's attempts to fire Blanca cleanly. Nevertheless, he ensures that she will no longer investigate feminicides in Juárez by securing her transfer to Yucatán.

The shooting of Cutberto and its aftermath catalyzes a series of events that allow Berman to theorize the potential (and limits) of robo-sacer resistance in combatting feminicide. Peralta's popular movement calls out the incompetent government response, but it cannot end feminicide through protests alone. One could argue that, because Berman aims to enlist her viewers to action through distancing rather than catharsis, she cannot depict a triumphalist robo-sacer action in her screenplay.[98] Furthermore, the film's grounding in the historical feminicides of the 1990s means that she cannot wander too far from the source material. In the end, Berman attempts to call her viewers to action by signaling the *potential* of polyspatial, robo-sacer resistance in decrying the political and economic conditions that facilitate the systemic murder of women. In this way, Berman's screenplay itself aims to employ technology to push its viewers to action. By showing a partially successful movement in her film, the author avoids the pitfalls of catharsis and—at least in theory—foments political action. Unlike Berman, Carrera chooses not to explore robo-sacer resistance and instead opts to produce a popular commercial film. Not surprisingly, the slasher once again provides useful tools for analyzing this conclusion. Rather than explore the potential for robo-sacer resistance through depictions of rallies on Blanca's behalf, he unambiguously casts the policewoman as the film's Final Girl. The Final Girl, of course, is a common trope in slasher cinema where a female protagonist defeats the killer at movie's end.[99] Indeed, many of the most commented aspects of Carrera's film speak directly to the construction of Blanca as a Final Girl.

For example, de la Reguera's "androgynous" performance has drawn significant attention from film critics.[100] This observation reverberates with a significant body of work on slashers that identifies "androgynous" —or "boyish" —performativity as a defining trait among most Final Girls.[101] Such performances leave these heroines' feminine sexuality unexplored, thus coding them as "worthy" of defeating the killer. This rings especially true for Blanca, who dresses in pants (never a dress), rejects overtly feminine hairstyles, and avoids makeup throughout the film. The character's apparent asexuality proves particularly notable given that de la Reguera's most famed roles up to this point included sexy parts in commercial melodramas.[102] Even as the character eschews makeup, her presence on the screen harks to her sex appeal through a presence of absence.[103] Viewed in this light, Blanca's grooming habits further evince an asexuality that distinguishes her from those who end up dead in the desert, a fact that underscores the tension between androgyny and sexualization that proves so key to the Final Girl trope.[104] Hind argues that the film forwards an imaginary of "de-feminization" and "de-sexualization" where female activists against feminicide give little thought to their physical appearance.[105] Such an aesthetic fits the generic expectations of popular (particularly slasher) cinema, but it ignores the existence of real-world, anti-feminicide female activists, the vast majority of whom wear makeup and dress in normatively feminine ways.[106] Beyond reflecting fantasy rather than reality, then, this representation also

**FIGURE 4.2** Still from *Backyard/El traspatio*. Blanca enters a long, dark corridor in a shot that calls to mind the devices of slasher cinema.

insinuates that victims of feminicide bear at least some of the blame for their own murders.

The ties between Blanca and the Final Girl trope do not end with her relative asexuality. Similar to Final Girls in slasher films more generally, Blanca constantly comes face-to-face with the mangled corpses of feminicide victims.[107] In one scene, for example, Blanca discovers an underground freezer in the desert where the murderers keep the bodies of the women they kill. In a wink at the genre, where the protagonists always go into dark hallways on their own, she decides to enter without calling for backup (see fig. 4.2).[108] This scene appears in both Berman's screenplay and Carrera's film, but the version takes on a more explicitly slasher feel in the latter. The music and cinematography suggest that someone will leap out at any moment. Carrera even includes a jump scene when he cuts to brief shots of the nude bodies of dead desaparecidas before cutting back to the police officer. The problematic nature of this shot rises to the fore when we realize that the bodies are not actually there. Rather, Blanca has simply imagined how this industrial freezer must have looked a few weeks ago before an array of women were dumped in the desert following an extended period in a freezer. This scene replicates the slasher's "rapid alteration between registers—between something like 'real' horror on the one hand and camp, self-parodying horror on the other."[109] Certainly, the film does not play these mutilations for comic effect, but its irreverent use of this jump scene shocks the audience and satisfies the generic expectations of the viewers. As Blanca comes face-to-face with the horrors that women face in her city, she prepares herself for her ultimate confrontation with Mickey Santos.

The film justifies Blanca's extrajudicial killing of Santos by reminding audiences that he will simply bribe his way out of prison if she arrests him.[110] As such, Blanca must work outside the law to curb the exceptional threat that Mickey Santos poses to the women of Juárez. The film may hold the desaparecidas accountable for not taking the necessary precautions to remain alive, but it also casts men who kill women as an evil that Blanca must root out. In their reading of this scene, Dana A. Meredith and Luis Alberto Rodríguez Cortés assert that, "probably obeying the dictates of the thriller genre, Santos's death avenges his victims and offers audiences the possibility of catharsis. Such cathartic closure, however, dulls the sense of urgency needed to push viewers to action."[111] The current discussion only further emphasizes their point. As Clover notes, audiences come to identify with the Final Girl so completely by the film's end that they "become if not the killer of the killer then the agent of his expulsion from the narrative vision."[112] Viewed in this light, both Blanca *and* the audience resolve the Juárez feminicides when they kill Santos together.[113] Moviegoers thus leave the screening absolved of any need to intervene in the real world; they have done enough vicariously through Blanca. Ultimately, Carrera remains silent about technology's potential for mobilizing against the root causes of feminicide. Instead, he provides a fantasy where an officer can restore order by killing a villain in those cases where the institutions tasked with maintaining civil society have failed. One could argue that Carrera never aimed to call his viewers to action; instead, he built on popular genres to dress a commercial film up as activist while at the same time marketing the deaths of the desaparecidas by telling their stories through the slasher mode.

We should certainly note that Berman's screenplay plays up Blanca's role as the Final Girl as well. In some ways her text does so more explicitly than Carrera's film: the screenplay narrates a chase sequence where Santos bribes the Comandante to tell him where he can find Blanca. He then attempts to kidnap, torture, rape, and murder her. His sadistic machinations prove his undoing, however, as she ultimately kills him and escapes. Berman's Blanca fits within a tradition of Final Girls who "kill the killer on their own, without help from the outside."[114] At the same time, Berman's more explicit depiction of a Final Girl chase scene allows her to distinguish her protagonist more fully from the corrupt dealings that characterize Mickey Santos's extrajudicial killing in Carrera's film. In the screenplay Blanca acts in self-defense when a murderer attempts to kill her in a sadistic game of cat-and-mouse. If any exceptional state exists that would justify the taking of human life, then this type of self-defense most certainly would qualify. Clearly, Berman also builds on the thriller and slasher modes. That said, in exploring the potential for robo-sacer resistance, Berman moves beyond the limitations of the genre and identifies a way to (hopefully) engage her audience and promote further action from them at the conclusion of her screenplay.

In the end, both Berman and Carrera face the significant dilemma regarding whether or not someone can ethically represent the Juárez feminicides through fiction and, particularly, commercial cinema. Both do a laudable job of highlighting the ties between a rapidly ne(cr)oliberalizing economy and the relegation of women—especially migrant Indigenous workers in the maquiladora industry—to killable bare life. That said, the screenplay and the motion picture employ very different strategies for theorizing how to resist the ever-expanding markets of death. Berman's screenplay navigates this difficult representational terrain by foregrounding the possibility for mass resistance through radio-based polyspatial organization. In showing a successful manifestation, Berman ties Juana's death to a deeper discussion of resistance more generally. That said, it remains an open question as to whether this is enough given that she also insinuates that Juana has brought her death on herself by cheating on Cutberto. For his part, Carrera largely ignores questions of resistance on screen, focusing instead on violent scenes showing mutilated bodies and gruesome murders. The director may believe that, in leaving little to the imagination, he will turn people against similar violence in the real world. Nevertheless, his most shocking scenes ultimately conform to the generic expectations of the slasher. In so doing, he not only blames the desaparecidas for their deaths, but he also undermines the film's resistant potential. Instead, he ends up with a commercial film that complains about contemporary feminicidal violence without providing a means to mobilize its viewers against the continued murder of women. This discussion surrounding the ethics of representation in *Backyard/El traspatio* leads us to "Soñarán en el jardín," a story that remains skeptical of those who would use the stories of the desaparecidas for financial gain.

### REMEMBERING VERSUS REVIVING: AN ETHICS OF REPRESENTATION IN "SOÑARÁN EN EL JARDÍN"

Set in a near-future, supposedly enlightened Mexico, Gabriela Damián Miravete's "Soñarán en el jardín" imagines a 2079 context where female activists have used technology—particularly social media and holographic avatars of the dead—to shake the state out of its complacency and force it to take concrete steps to curtail feminicide. Given the recent turn toward engaging contemporary issues from a fantastic mode, it should come as no surprise that Damián Miravete would engage the topic of feminicide through SF.¹¹⁵ The author alludes to the Juárez murders throughout, but she also emphasizes the fact that feminicide occurs in all parts country.¹¹⁶ In this way, the story extends Nuala Finnegan's observation that "*feminicidios* manage to be about Mexico's past and present at the same time."¹¹⁷ Given the story's subject matter, it would appear that the topic of feminicide engages the future as well. "Soñarán en el jardín" has enjoyed significant success; it was the first Mexican short story to win the annual Otherwise (formerly Tiptree) Award at the 2018 session of WisCon, an annual feminist SF and fantasy convention held in Madison, Wisconsin.¹¹⁸ The judges lauded the story's interrogation of the continued marginalization of women both in Mexico and throughout the world. As they proclaimed, "by offering a possible look into the future, far from giving the sense of a closed chapter, the story itself is a device of memory preservation, a call to action, and a fine example of science fiction as a tool for feminist exploration and social change."¹¹⁹ These words capture one level of the story's resonance, but they ignore the central conflicts that undergird the story. Far from celebratory, "Soñarán en el jardín" highlights the fissures that continue to exist in this near future between activists who wish to resurrect the dead through new technologies, and an amoral state that uses the silhouettes for self-serving purposes.

The idea that one can overcome death through technology reverberates with post- and transhumanist thought. Hans Moravec, for example, argues that human beings will eventually achieve an individual immortality of sorts by creating simulations of the mind and inserting them into computers.¹²⁰ N. Katherine Hayles notes the comfort that such possibilities provide for a species preoccupied with overcoming death.¹²¹ Marisela's holograms bring a certain level of nuance to previous theorizations of transhumanist immortality. Where Hayles and Moravec privilege information flows in their interrogation of the (post)human condition and technological immortality, Damián Miravete foregrounds the continued centrality of the body. Indeed, in her story, corporeality becomes both the object and subject through which we can understand the humanity of the desaparecidas.¹²² The idea that Marisela must resurrect the dead through a careful reconstruction of the body based on photographs and a digital trail rather than through a careful decoding of the brain proves especially tantalizing in a philosophical sense. As Moravec notes, any attempt to cheat death through technology would produce such drastic corporeal changes that humans would essentially become different beings. The changes would be so radical that "personal death as we know it differs from this inevitability only in its relative abruptness."¹²³ Marisela's strategy differs from that of Moravec: she reconstructs the victims' humanity by uploading memories from archival sources—rather than the brain—into the avatars. She still lacks the technology to bring them fully to life as the story ends, but she sits on the cusp of achieving this goal.[124] Unfortunately, she does not receive financial or moral support from the state in her attempts to resurrect the dead. Instead, those in power try to use the garden for solely immunological ends.

State projects prove especially noteworthy in light of Gareth Williams's observation of the "precarious" relationship among "sovereign exceptionality, immunity, the law, and collective life" in Mexican letters and culture.[125] One could argue that the state's commitment to curtailing the murder of women reflects not a desire for justice per se, but its drive to maintain legitimacy. Cecilia Eudave follows in this vein when she asserts that the state "appropriates" the garden and uses it in a didactic means in order to wash its hands of previous negligence.[126] Indeed, the state only comes to express interest in curtailing feminicide *after* Marisela's successful activism through technology. Even then, it focuses primariliy on lauding itself for its successes. Far from eliminating the existence of a state of exception within Mexican politics, Marisela's robo-sacer resistance changes the emergency from continued capitalist expansion, which necessarily entails the loss of women's lives, and instead makes feminicide itself into the exceptional threat to state sovereignty.[127] Faced with this new threat to its legitimacy, the state opts to undermine constructs of female expendability by co-opting Marisela's work. Ironically, these very actions cast the silhouettes themselves as a new type of *homo sacer*: immunizing agents whose deaths prove prerequisite to the state's ability to establish legitimacy and sovereignty in 2079. This, of course, occurs because the state hinges its legitimacy on its ability to prevent *new* cases of feminicide from occurring. It needs the victims of the late-twentieth and early twenty-first centuries to remain dead so that it can highlight its own successes in ending feminicide in 2079.

The desire to protect the *bios* through immunological programs does not necessarily signal the state as benign. As Williams notes, "democratic autoimmunity is a name for the techniques that the social body establishes in order to immunize itself (and therefore save itself) from the disorder and violence it itself installs and perpetuates, while at the same time sustaining societal differentiations and separations that are deemed to be necessary for the stratification and partition of wealth and privilege."[128] Williams's theorizations of Mexican immunization differ from those in other contexts in several key ways. Roberto Esposito's immunization paradigm, for example, conceptualizes a process through which the state prioritizes the individual (*immunitas*) by inoculating each individual citizen against the excesses of an apparently dangerous community.[129] That said, Williams views Mexican immunization as an often-violent process where modernity "has been predicated on the permanent application of state power in the construction of social order, rather than on the self-limitation of state power via a legal system guaranteeing individual rights and limiting public power."[130] Such a characterization proves especially useful to the current study because it shows how immunization and the Agambian state of exception coexist alongside one another in the creation of state policy. As the story makes clear, the silhouettes provide the inoculation that children—particularly boys—must metaphorically ingest in order to overcome their destructive tendencies.[131] Where Marisela wishes to instill life in her silhouettes by imbuing them with memory and subjectivity, the state wishes only to capitalize on the garden's spectral potential to instill cultural memory of past atrocities in order to (unfairly) take credit for the fact that such violence no longer occurs.

The spectral nature of the silhouettes alludes to the slippage that Teresa López-Pellisa identifies between posthumanism and the ghostly body, though the current discussion of holograms expands beyond her work.[132] The grounding of the silhouettes within the posthuman draws attention to these holograms' overall resistant potential, which Marisela and the state use in different ways. The holograms function as what Jacques Derrida calls revenants, or "one who returns."[133] They are, after all, echoes of the past whose very existence in the present draws us forever back to the losses of previous generations. This produces what Derrida refers to as hauntology: a play on words that, in English, combines the terms *haunt* and *ontology* to signify "ontology, theology, positive or negative onto-theology."[134] Avery Gordon asserts that haunting evokes an emotive response that allows societies to process their "desaparecido[a]s" in a way that transcends logic and gets at truths that would remain otherwise hidden.[135] We see this clearly within recent Mexican literary and cultural production, where the presence of spectral beings facilitates a communion of sorts between living and dead that "catalyzes an individual memory that usually becomes collective" (cataliza una memoria individual que se suele volver colectiva).[136] An example of this occurs in the story, when a school-aged boy named Tomasito interacts with one of the holograms:

"Are you a ghost?"
"No. I'm a memory. Like a photograph."
"Like a video of before?"
"Yes, exactly that. Thomas, do you have grandparents?"[137]

This dialogue becomes especially interesting in a Derridean sense; while the hologram denies being a ghost, she clearly identifies herself as a revenant and specter through her invocation of words like "memory" and "photograph," both of which speak directly to spectrality and hauntology.[138]

The immunological potential of this spectral encounter rings clear when Tomasito receives a painful, though not unbearable, shock after he attempts to touch the silhouette without receiving her consent. His teacher says, "You don't even know her yet. Greet her, tell her your name first." From here, we learn that the park has recently added "unpleasant" stings to the silhouettes so that the children will interact with them as they would with real, flesh-and-bone people. Marisela suggests that this is to learn a lesson, though the text remains vague as to what that lesson should be. On the one hand, it could be that boys and men should respect boundaries and receive permission before touching girls and women.[139] After all, as Sergio González Rodríguez notes, "violence against women represents, unfortunately, the foundation of feminicide" (la violencia contra las mujeres representa, por desgracia, el fundamento del feminicidio).[140] On the other hand, however, the principal lesson seems to be that one cannot touch the dead because they lack bodies. Regardless of the exact interpretation, this scene becomes especially uncomfortable in light of Sayak Valencia's observation that, in neoliberal society, "we lose our *property rights to our own bodies*."[141] The park and the state own the rights to these holograms despite the fact that they represent real people who died decades earlier. It may use shock features to teach children how to interact with other people, but it also appropriates these bodies for its own immunological ends. This strategy proves effective from an immunological perspective: Tomasito may live in 2079, but through this specter, he experiences a sense of loss that remains palpable well into the early decades of the twenty-first century.

The near-future setting proves especially pertinent to the story in light of David E. Johnson's observation that "the logic of temporal delay informs the culture of feminicide."[142] Indeed, the fragmented narrative consists of two primary storylines that emphasize how feminicide has morphed over time in this fictional Mexico. The first fragment, narrated in the future tense, tells of the ninety-four-year-old Marisela, who sits in a garden with her holograms during a preschool field trip and speaks with a male schoolteacher. The second one, narrated in the past tense, tells of Marisela's youth and her experience growing up in a violently machista society in the 2000s and 2010s. The future-tense narration accentuates the spectral nature of the narrative by positing the elderly Marisela as a figure from ages past whose lived experience reaches back to days outside of what one would generally call living memory. The intercalated fragments in the past prove almost testimonial as they tell of a culture of misogyny that fosters a climate where feminicide exists. Carol Clark D'Lugo notes that Mexico has a long history of fragmented narratives, primarily novels, through which authors "lay bare the building blocks of their 'construction,'" both literary and social.[143] This holds particularly true in "Soñarán en el jardín," where the fragmented storyline represents a society broken by murderous machismo on the one hand and Marisela's desperate attempts to resurrect the dead and curtail feminicide through her holographic memory project on the other.

Marisela represents an entire generation of women in Mexico marked by the trauma of day-to-day sexual violence, a fact that the text communicates through an array of flashbacks. As a young, prepubescent child, for example, her uncle enters her bedroom and masturbates while leering at her; as a teenager, her boss corners her at a shoe store and demands sex; she enters a professional workplace at the Gran Compañía de Telecomunicaciones (a thinly veiled reference to TelMex) where she learns that executives fire women who struggle with technology. The story asserts that casual and professional misogyny lays the foundation for a world where feminicide becomes endemic. Given her company's predisposition to fire women who struggle with technology—which reflects real-world, structural barriers to female education in the country—the young Marisela and other women like her must enroll in as many classes as possible.[144] Simply passing her courses will not be enough; instead, she has to earn top marks. She succeeds, but many women from poorer backgrounds do not. In one of the more obvious allusions to the feminicides of 1990s- and 2000s-era Juárez, Marisela's classmate, Dulce, is kidnapped, disappeared, and murdered while commuting to a job that she depends on to pay for her weekend classes. In Dulce's case, an assortment of sexist attitudes and what Elvia R. Arriola calls "corporate indifference" conspire to create the conditions of her eventual murder.[145] If she did not have to navigate the intersections of gender, class, and likely race, Dulce would almost certainly have remained alive. This murder marks Marisela's social awakening; while she has long recognized sexism, she can no longer remain silent. She befriends Las Argüenderas, a group of teenage girls who had been friends with Dulce, and together they explore collective action by using social media and other platforms to identify and publicly shame abusive boyfriends, parents, and male executives.

The inclusion of Las Argüenderas places the story squarely within the sphere of robo-sacer activism. Regarding the transformative nature of technology in conceptualizing and combatting gender violence in Mexico, Cristina Rivera Garza asserts that "most people who acknowledge violence against women have generally accepted that rapists and killers are deranged men from the working classes or unhinged men from organized crime ranks, but the names that the Mexican #MeToo movement aired in public belonged to well-known figures from prominent backgrounds or well educated men—authors, publishers, curators—the public was not used to fearing."[146] Real-world activists have thus taken advantage of the democratic nature of the internet to challenge old ways of framing gender violence. In so doing, they have drawn attention to the structural factors that allow men—particularly those who are rich and respected—to carry out differing degrees of violence on women with impunity. Such structural conditions have long facilitated feminicide. Viewed in this light, women from #MeToo and #NiUnaMás have used digital platforms to contest those who would interpellate women into *homo sacer* status. These movements, which occurred more-or-less concurrently with the writing and publication of this story, shed light on the role of technology in resisting feminicide.

The story theorizes the interplay between an online presence and meaningful resistance in physical space. When the narrator says that the Argüenderas "grew until they formed an army made of women of all ages who went where their presence was missing," she alludes to the polyspatial nature of resistance, where people from around the world can interface in a single online space.[147] Of course, Damián Miravete's economy of words—a key attribute of the genre of short fiction—impedes her from fleshing out the exact nature of this hybrid resistance. We cannot be sure, for example, if they shame abusive men primarily online, or if they do so in physical space. Regardless, the story implies a digital component to their actions. Las Argüenderas assert the type of joint kinship among women—and women of color—that cyborg theorists like Donna Haraway and Chela Sandoval have long championed as key components of any "methodology of the oppressed."[148] Their collective action catalyzes a tectonic shift within the country that challenges the reigning biopolitics, thus making it impossible for the state to continue to allow men to abuse women. One key component of these initial movements has been an online presence that has facilitated the flow of information among women and permitted them to act in solidarity.

Throughout the story, the most obvious example of robo-sacer resistance comes from Marisela, who learns to use lasers at her work and then employs them to create holograms that testify of the senseless violence of feminicide. In recuperating the records of the desaparecidas and putting them into holographic, embodied beings, the caretaker brings together thousands of individual memories that become part of an archival repository that toes the line between living and dead. The narrator notes the ambitious nature of Marisela's project: "Every one of the murdered women, with her body and her name, would be replicated in a three-dimensional hologram using testimonies and materials provided by their relatives, friends and, above all, the information recovered from their personal email accounts and social media: photographs, videos, letters, conversations... everything would be used to recreate in the most precise way their voices, their movements, their reactions; to, in some way, *bring them back to life*" (emphasis in original). Unlike a significant body of fictional literature that eschews modernity and any attempts to bring the cadaver to life through technology, "Soñarán en el jardín" views the technological resurrection of the dead as a positive potentiality of modernity.[149] Indeed, Damián Miravete interfaces with the posthuman referent in numerous ways. First of all, she alludes to Donna Haraway's cyborg myth, where a specifically female actor uses technological skills learned at the mercy of the patriarchy to undermine gender-based oppression.[150] After all, while not cyborgs, the holograms come about due to Marisela's work at the Gran Compañía de Telecomunicaciones, a company whose actions seem at least complicit with Dulce's death.[151]

The caretaker's idea of using these projections to give new life to the desaparecidas underscores Rosi Braidotti's observation that "Life/*zoe* can be a threatening force as well as a generative one."[152] The museum becomes a space of necrowriting, a term that Rivera Garza defines as "forms of textual output that seek to shake off the dominion of what-is-one's own."[153] For Rivera Garza, necrowritings represent a "poetics of disappropriation" through their opposition to necropolitical, and, one could argue, necroliberal, practices.[154] Marisela strives to achieve precisely this end through her creations. In the early days, her work takes on a testimonial nature by calling out state indifference to the murder of women. This, of course, speaks to the real-world Mexican context where, despite an ever-increasing number of murdered women, very few cases of feminicide are investigated under that rubric, and fewer still—around two percent—end in conviction.[155] Viewed against this backdrop, Marisela's museum becomes a place to draw attention both to the lives lost and to the failures of an ineffectual state. In sharing the intimate details of the lives of the desaparecidas, Marisela highlights their humanity. Far from expendable, they become fully human people who have suffered wrongdoing at the hands of their killers and of a state that has refused to protect them. These necrowritings transform society by forcing the state to focus on defending women or lose its mandate to govern. Even this, however, proves insufficient for Marisela, who wishes above all else to restore life to the dead through technology.

As she uses artificial intelligence to bring to life the memories of the dead, Marisela creates silhouettes that exist beyond Agambian notions of *bios*, *zoē*, and *homo sacer*. Instead, they become liminal figures that toe the line between life and death, presence and absence.[156] As such they become living in their death. Writing on the conditions of "living dead" (zombies) and "undead" (vampires), M. Elizabeth Ginway argues that, "as creatures that combine the living and the dead, on the borderline between binaries, they often represent a sense of collective and personal trauma."[157] Her observation applies equally to the holograms. While not exactly alive, these projections, reverberate with Carolyn Wolfenzon's theorizations of ghosts within Mexico that "symbolize unresolved historical and political problems and give voice to the marginalized" (simboliza[n] problemas históricos y políticos no resueltos y le[s] da[n] una voz a los marginados).[158] As these spectral figures draw their audience's attention to the shared trauma of gender violence, they become simulacra of reality. Yet, as they interact with living beings, they take on what Umberto Eco calls a "hyperreal" nature where "the sign aims to become the thing, to abolish the distinction of the reference."[159] As this occurs, the simulacra of the dead become problematically more "real" than the women on whom they are modeled.[160] Marisela's struggle to transform her holograms from living-dead projections into living entities constitutes a central component of the story. She faces two primary roadblocks in her attempts to achieve this. At a practical level, the technology remains elusive, though recent advances suggest it will soon exist. More importantly, however, the state depends on the hyperreal, spectral nature of the silhouettes to validate its self-congratulatory claims to have ended feminicide.

The disagreements between Marisela and the state about how to use the garden stem from their contradictory opinions regarding the desirability of a hyperreality that emphasizes collective trauma at the expense of individual justice. As the narrator explains, "the State decided that the memorial should serve an additional function to earn the right to permanence. It would serve as an educational space against violence." The statist project entails the standardization of the artificial intelligence algorithm of the silhouettes that further eliminates the individuality of each spectral voice. The holograms become a homogenous group of avatars with similar dialogue consisting of announcements that they are dead. Where Marisela wishes to affirm the *bios* of the desaparecidas by bringing each individual to life, the state prefers to emphasize the number of women who died through less personable dialogues. The fissures between Marisela and the state become clearest regarding the the proper role of the desaparecidas in

2079 Mexican society. Given that it depends on the spectral effects of an undead entity—and not an actual living organism—to make its critique, the state does not support the idea of restoring life to the dead. Marisela, however, adopts a different view where she can tell the stories of the dead while at the same time attempting to resurrect murdered individuals. Marisela does not oppose the immunological goal of ending feminicide. Indeed, she has spearheaded the very movements that have ended it in the first place. Rather, she expresses frustration with the state's uninterest in reviving the dead. Viewed in this light, Damián Miravete's narrative shows how projects of autoimmunity lead the state to emphasize the sacrifice of the desaparecidas rather than to seek ways to grant them life.

This is not to say that the state views the holograms and desaparecidas as killable *homo sacer* subjects. The very act of building this museum speaks to the state's commitment to denaturalizing previous constructs of female expendability. In supporting the museum, it inscribes the desaparecidas into the very fabric of political (un)life by telling their stories in an attempt to curtail feminicide and, incidentally, maintain legitimacy before the population. Unlike a traditional revenant that functions as "a trace that evidences the ruptures in hegemonic discourse," the silhouettes represent spectral imageries that the hegemony has incorporated into the official discourse.[161] As such, they become that sort of discourse that, in the words of Rivera Garza, "define themselves as critiques" despite largely reinscribing themselves within the hegemony.[162] From a statist perspective, Marisela's dream of rebirthing the dead does not represent a desirable end. If successful, she could conceivably undermine the immunological thrust of current state projects. By highlighting the lives lost, the state casts the desaparecidas as wronged members of a national *bios*. These women have sacrificed their own lives—something that would be impossible if they were homines sacri—so that a new generation of women can experience *bios* in peace. At the same time, however, in creating a museum, the state necessarily commodifies the dead, stripping them of their individuality and agency.[163] We should note, for example, that the story makes no mention of any attempts by the state to punish the perpetrators of feminicide despite the fact that a demand for justice lies at the heart of spectral theory and discourse.[164] Instead, the state appropriates the silhouettes to an immunological role that puts them at odds with Marisela's dream of restoring stolen life to the holographic bodies.

A cynical reading would hold that the state opposes any attempt to resurrect the dead through technology because it needs the silhouettes to remain revenants: memories of the past forever trapped in the present. If they become living entities that interact with and evolve in the present, then they might lose their spectral nature and thus their testimonial value. Certainly, the state's contributions to curtailing feminicide prove laudable: one of the principal readings of the story centers precisely on the fact that Marisela and the state have together improved conditions in this late-twenty-first-century Mexico to the point that feminicide no longer exists.[165] That said, my focus on statist projects of immunization underscores the amoral motivations behind the state's actions.[166] As such, we can better identify how the state consciously redirects Marisela's push to resurrect the desaparecidas. The caretaker's frustration with statist narratives rings particularly clear when the preschool teacher comments to Marisela that "at least the deaths of all those women were good for something." She responds, "It's one thing to voluntarily give your life for a cause and it's another to be killed for it. Which would you like more? That your life had been good 'for something' or to have lived?" The disagreement enunciated here has nothing to do with divergences on policy. The caretaker takes solace in the fact that feminicide has abated throughout the country, and she supports the use of these spectral holograms to decry the wrongs of past times. Nevertheless, she bristles at the idea that these murders are somehow less atrocious given the utilitarian end that the victims' stories have achieved. As Oswaldo Estrada makes clear, "nothing justifies their deaths, not even future learning or the transcendence of history" (nada justifica sus muertes, ni siquiera el aprendizaje futuro o la trascendencia histórica).[167] The caretaker understands the value of her work in reducing gender violence throughout the country, but she wishes she could do more.

The story ends with a brief description of Marisela's work after the garden closes for the day. Rather than simply shutting down the system, she has programmed the silhouettes to sleep, thus creating the illusion that the desparecidas remain alive. At this point Marisela still lacks the necessary technology to permit her holograms to dream. Nevertheless, she reveals her great ambition: "during the day they will be heroines, silhouettes, memories, they will say that they are dead, but the nights will be theirs. They will construct what was taken from them. In the garden they will dream of their future." Through such an act, the silhouettes will continue to play their immunological role even as they enjoy a life of sorts that allows them to be more than mere revenants meant to guilt men into respecting women. Marisela will make her holograms dream of her own accord because she will receive no support from the state, which concerns itself only with immunization. Justice may lie beyond the state's purview, but it remains front-and-center for Marisela, who will continue to labor to bring about her vision until she breathes her final breath. In setting aside the night for these women to live, Marisela strikes a tenuous balance between supporting a necessary immunological campaign on the one hand and respecting the individuality and lives of the dead on the other. In this way, she can protect the social body against the systemic evils of feminicide even as she provides a space for the murdered to live again. More than revenants who remain frozen in the past even as they linger into the present, Marisela's holographic silhouettes will one day become agents in their own right. The caretaker's desire to recreate the lives of the dead proves valuable both in identifying an ethics of representation within the story and in opening questions about how to best represent the desaprecidas in the real world.

## CONCLUSION

In the end, Sabina Berman, Carlos Carrera, and Gabriela Damián Miravete provide valuable discussions about the relationships among technology, the body, and feminicide in Mexico. Each of the works sheds light on González Rodríguez's notion of a femicide machine by viewing necroliberal technology as a dehumanizing tool that interpellates women into bare life. That said, Berman and Damián Miravete also imagine means through which activists can take advantage of different technologies: radio, social media, or even holograms, to denaturalize statist (in)actions. Certainly, both works recognize that people cannot end feminicide by simply using technology. Nor do they claim that revolution will come easily. Rather, they end with protagonists who remain committed to doing more to tear down the structures that make feminicide so common. Blanca ends up on the other side of the country, unable to investigate further cases, while Marisela seeks a way to truly restore the lives of the dead. Of course, the biggest hurdle that the caretaker faces is a state that continues to take advantage of the dead to further its own legitimacy. In this way, the story poses valuable questions about *Backyard/El traspatio*. One could argue that, similar to the fictional state in "Soñarán en el jardín," Carrera, and (perhaps) Berman exploit the stories of the dead to produce a commercial film. Certainly, my reading of the production through the slasher lens underscores the problematic, traditionalist discourses that manifest themselves throughout. Even as *Backyard/El traspatio*—particularly Carrera's film version—indicts NAFTA and the necroliberal order, it also represents a type of neoliberal, commercial cinema that seeks to make money by exoticizing the experiences of the desaparecidas. In the end, each of the fictions studied above calls for change, but they do so with varying degrees of success and ethical justification. In the following chapter, I discuss the transnational drug trade, another manifestation of the necroliberal order that has devastated Mexican and Chicanx communities.

CHAPTER 5

# Guns, Narcos, and Low-Tech Cyborgs

Magical Realism, SF, and the Posthuman in Julio Hernández Cordón's *Cómprame un revólver* and Rudolfo Anaya's ChupaCabra Trilogy

Perhaps no industry embodies the necroliberal drive in twenty-first century Mexican and US society more than the illicit drug trade.[1] The juxtaposition of the lavish lifestyles of drug capos with the grisly murders of police, rival gang members, and disloyal subordinates lays bare the extent to which economic strength coincides with a dominion over life and death. Drug violence has captured the popular imagination on both sides of the border; indeed, narcos have assumed a heroic persona in much Mexican cultural production due to a supposedly heroic, rebellious nature.[2] Rafael Acosta argues that these narratives produce and normalize structures of violence by tapping into mythic structures that "produc[e] real effects" in those around them.[3] Oswaldo Zavala asserts that narco literary and cultural production aids in the construction of an Agambian state of exception that enables the prolonged, unwinnable offensives of the drug war that the state would otherwise be unable to justify.[4] The state frequently engages in violence that results in collateral damage, a fact that has led numerous Mexican citizens to distrust official channels at least as much as drug traffickers.[5] The state plays a controversial role in the US context as well, where, for decades, drug policy has served as a mask for legislation targeting Black and Chicanx communities.[6] Viewed against this backdrop, it should come as no surprise that Mexican and Chicanx literary and cultural production often critiques not only drug capos, but also the state, both Mexican and US, for its role in perpetuating violence. In the pages that follow, I discuss Rudolfo Anaya's ChupaCabra trilogy and Julio Hernández Cordón's film *Cómprame un revólver*. Both the author and the director use a magical-real mode and an SF referent to imagine armed resistance as a robo-sacer act that the oppressed can employ against organized crime and a complicit state.

We can learn a great deal by comparing the depictions of the drug war in a Mexican film to that in a Chicanx trilogy of novels. The dynamics of the illicit narcotics trade differ greatly in each case, but the experiences of both of these Greater-Mexican populations intertwine in many ways. A brief history will highlight key similarities and differences in how Mexican and Chicanx communities have traditionally experienced the conflict.

The term "war on drugs" entered the US lexicon in 1971, when President Richard Nixon proclaimed an "all-out offensive" on drug abuse, which he framed as an existential national emergency.[7] In the speech, he called for the increased policing of domestic communities that, not coincidentally, opposed him politically. The journalist Dan Baum recently detailed a conversation he had with John Ehrlichman, Nixon's assistant to the president for Domestic Affairs, in which the bureaucrat stated:

> The Nixon campaign in 1968, and the Nixon White House after that, had two enemies: the antiwar left and black people. [...] We knew we couldn't make it illegal to be either against the war or black, but by getting the public to associate the hippies with marijuana and blacks with heroin, and then criminalizing both heavily, we could disrupt those communities. We could arrest their leaders, raid their homes, break up their meetings, and vilify them night after night on the evening news. Did we know we were lying about the drugs? Of course we did.[8]

While Nixon couched his opposition to drugs in moral and health-based terms, a biopolitical imperative lurked in the background from the beginning. Ehrlichman did not mention Chicanx activists directly, but western states had a long history of criminalizing drugs to crack down on Mexican and Chicanx communities.[9] Rudolfo Anaya engages the anti-Chicanx thrust of US drug policy in his ChupaCabra trilogy, where drug usage signals the inhabitants of East Los Angeles as *homines sacri*.

Beyond using drug policy as a justification to police domestic populations, Nixon and his successors also exploited drug usage in the United States as a perpetual state of exception that would justify interventions in Mexico and throughout the hemisphere.[10] George W. Grayson, for example, notes that the Nixon administration pressured the Mexican government to support several initiatives aimed at curtailing the transport of controlled substances into the United States in the early 1970s.[11] It did not take long for Latin American leaders to learn that they would have to crack down on drug trafficking within their own borders if they wished to curry favor with US administrations. It is from this context that we must consider the decision of Mexican president Felipe Calderón to declare the Operativo Conjunto Michoacán (Joint Operation Michoacán) on December 11, 2006. The initiative "gave permission to the country's armed forces to unilaterally carry out missions related to public security and combat DTOs [drug trafficking organizations]."[12] Coming on the heels of his hotly contested electoral victory—despite allegations, fair or not, of rampant fraud—many viewed this and later offensives as an attempt by the president to shore up the legitimacy of his sexenio, both domestically and internationally.[13] This strategy seems to have worked: in declaring war on organized crime, Calderón gained the support of the administrations of both George W. Bush and Barack Obama.[14] The Mexican president also unleashed a state of exception that resulted in the emergence of "necropolises" in numerous cities across the country that had enjoyed decades of peace before the intervention.[15] National and international observers soon began to question whether Calderón's Mexico had become a failed state.[16]

In bringing together the work of Anaya and Hernández Cordón, this chapter highlights the biopolitical conditions that have resulted from US drug prohibition on both sides of the border. Both Hernández Cordón and Anaya situate their fictions within dystopian contexts grounded firmly in what R. Guy Emerson refers to as the contemporary "death world."[17] The dystopian quality of *Cómprame un revólver* rings particularly clearly given its setting in a dismal near future.[18] Anaya engages dystopia by framing vice as a spiritual malady that results throughout the US Southwest when the region's Chicanx and Native American inhabitants forget their mestiza/x heritage and become unworthy of the utopian promise of Aztlán. Both sets of fictions focalize their stories through characters from the cultural periphery: Rosa in Anaya's novels, Huck in Hernández Cordón's film. Anaya focuses primarily on drug abuse and over-policing in Chicanx communities. For his part, Hernández Cordón imagines a world where organized crime has supplanted the Mexican government. In both cases, the illicit drug trade represents a necroliberal industry that reproduces itself and accumulates capital through death. Viewed in this light, despite coming from different Greater-Mexican communities, both the author and the director interrogate the potential for armed, robo-sacer resistance to contest the biopolitics of the drug war. In both cases, this robo-sacer activism depends on an armed resistance that appropriates the logic of militarization against both the drug cartels and the complicit (or absent) state.

Brief summaries of the film and trilogy will facilitate our discussion.

Hernández Cordón's *Cómprame un revólver* tells the story of a dystopian, near-future northern Mexico. The government has fallen, and competing cartels vie for control of large swathes of territory. All economic activities filter through organized crime. The film centers on Huck, a young girl who lives with her drug-addict father, Rogelio, who maintains a baseball field for the local cartel. Huck's mother died as a result of feminicide, an apparent result of the expansion of cartel sovereignty that has drastically lowered the female population. Rogelio constantly chains Huck in place so that no one will kidnap her. He also makes her cross-dress as a boy by cutting her hair and giving her a mask to wear in public. One night, he unchains her and she plays outside with a trio of orphans called the Lost Boys. One of these, Ángel, lost his hand when the local crime boss cut it off. An armed narco catches wind of the children's presence and investigates. Rogelio saves the children by strangling the narco to death. Other members of the cartel capture Rogelio and bring him before the boss, who also happens to be the deceased man's cousin. The boss interrogates Rogelio, but the father denies having killed anyone. The boss enters Rogelio's camper where Huck is hiding under the bed covers. The boss removes their mask to reveal themself as a trans individual; their gender fluidity leaves an impression of wonder on Huck, who watches, unnoticed, from the bed. The boss leaves the camper and orders Rogelio's execution. The sicarios fire multiple rounds. The bullets ricochet off of the tree that sits directly behind him, but none of them so much as graze Rogelio despite the fact that multiple gunmen have shot at him with automatic weapons from point-blank range. Noting Rogelio's luck, the boss orders him to attend their birthday party the following night with his daughter and a band. At the party, an armed group—perhaps members of a rival cartel, statist forces, or anti-cartel rebels—opens fire, killing or imprisoning all of the attendees except for Huck and the boss, both of whom hide in ice coolers. The boss becomes a parental figure to Huck, and they promise to allow her to dress like a cisgender girl. The boss gives Huck a pistol and teaches her how to use it. They then give Huck the gun to keep watch while they sleep. The Lost Boys appear on the riverbank and tell Huck that it was the boss who cut off Ángel's arm. Huck then shoots the boss in the head while they sleep and rejoins her friends.

Anaya builds *Curse of the ChupaCabra* (*Curse*), *ChupaCabra and the Roswell UFO* (*Roswell UFO*), and *ChupaCabra Meets Billy the Kid* (*Billy the Kid*) around Rosa Medina, a fictional assistant professor of English at Cal State, Los Angeles.[19] When she isn't teaching, she volunteers at a center for at-risk Chicanx and Native American youths who struggle to overcome drug addiction. In *Curse*, she and a graduate student named José travel to Lago Negro, a fictional town near Puerto Vallarta, to investigate supposed ChupaCabra attacks. She soon learns that the local drug cartel has hired a man named Malorio to order his ChupaCabra to kill and terrorize anyone who interferes with cartel interests.[20] Malorio places the curse of the ChupaCabra on Rosa, telling her that the monster will follow her wherever she goes, wreaking havoc in her life and in the lives of her loved ones. Shortly thereafter, the creature kills José. Rosa returns to the United States and explains what happened to Detective Dill of the LAPD. Unbeknownst to her, Dill works with the cartel. After an altercation with the ChupaCabra in LA, she decides to flee to her family in New Mexico. She meets a Navajo shaman and healer named Uncle Billy who does a ceremony to protect her against the curse of the ChupaCabra. She then visits her friend, a Catholic priest named Father Larry, who gives her an old pachuco switchblade with a crucifix engraved on the handle that will help her to "cut away the evil."[21] When she learns that the cartel plans to release the ChupaCabra on the streets of Los Angeles, she travels to Lago Negro to stop them. She discovers that the cartel plans to transport the monster on a cruise ship, so she buys a pass and boards the ship. In the climactic scene, the ChupaCabra escapes from its cage and kills El Jefe, Malorio, and Dill, all of whom try to save themselves by firing impotently at the monster. When the ChupaCabra turns its attention on Rosa, she brandishes her mystical knife, and it cowers away. The boat sinks and the ChupaCabra drowns.

*Roswell UFO* and *Billy the Kid* are more traditionally SF than *Curse*. In *Roswell UFO*, Rosa discovers that a clandestine US agency called C-Force has created alien/ChupaCabra hybrids. One of these, a creature named Saytir, has taken over the US government, the international drug trade, and several other lucrative enterprises. Rosa learns that Ed, an acquaintance from high school, has hacked a government mainframe and stolen a copy of the ChupaCabra genome. Rather than destroy the information, he has placed it on a CD that he has hidden in the Old Santa Rosa Chapel. After the duo finds the CD, Rosa's friend Nadine drops her off at a local library with a woman named Marcy. Nadine promises Rosa that Saytir cannot enter the library because it is a sanctuary. At the end of the novel, Rosa travels with Marcy to a spot in Roswell. Aliens arrive and take Marcy on board; Rosa returns to the town, where Nadine drives an explosive-laden car into C-Force headquarters, thus destroying the lab and everything (and everyone?) inside.

In *Billy the Kid*, Rosa is struggling to write a novel about Billy the Kid when she receives an instant message from Marcy, who is still living on the

UFO. Marcy informs Rosa that Saytir is still alive and that he wants her flash drive.[22] Marcy offers to send Rosa back in time so that she can meet the real Billy the Kid and tell his true story. Throughout the novel, Rosa interacts with the marginalized peoples of New Mexico and tells their stories of oppression before the law. At the same time, she must dodge Saytir and several HIMITs (weaker ChupaCabra/alien hybrid creatures), all of whom have pursued her through a wormhole to Billy the Kid's time. In one scene Josefita Chávez, a fierce outlaw and general of the Lincoln County War, asks Rosa to write the story of the Mexicanos and Mexicanas of nineteenth-century New Mexico Territory. She gives Rosa a pistol to protect herself. Rosa hides in a small home during the Battle of Lincoln. When the home catches fire, Saytir arrives and confronts her. She shoots him and escapes. She later learns that Saytir is growing weaker because he lacks the genetic information on her flash drive, and, as a result, he can no longer hurt her. When Billy the Kid dies, Rosa buries the flash drive with him. She returns home through the wormhole ready to write of the true Billy the Kid and to notify the FBI that C-Force has taken over much of the US government and the international drug trade.

Entrapped within a biopolitical framework that writes them off as killable, both Huck and Rosa use firearms and other weapons not only to protect themselves, but to assert their right to *bios*. In this way, the fictions reverberate with the observation of Sophie Esch that "the firearm appears as a prosthetic for citizenship, a means for people to affirm themselves as political and social subjects."[23] Under these circumstances, "the firearm becomes a means to be seen or heard."[24] In other words, Esch theorizes the firearm, and perhaps other weapons, as a tool through which members of the *zoē* can forcefully achieve a political voice. The critic thus invites us to imagine the armed women of these fictions as cyborg activists, a fact that would code their acts as robo-sacer resistance. Indeed, these female protagonists become low-tech cyborgs: people who depend on relatively simple machines like guns or enchanted knives to achieve a political voice.[25] Firearms thus provide the necessary preconditions to *bios* because they ensure that marginal voices are heard. Within the context of a festering war between the state and organized crime, the protagonists of these fictions choose to replicate the violence of their oppressors to resist. These conditions draw to mind Donna Haraway's words: "for us [women and cyborgs], in imagination and in other practice, machines can be prosthetic devices, intimate components, friendly selves."[26] It may go against the grain to associate firearms with Haraway's notion of "friendly selves," but the act of armed resistance reverberates with her understanding of cyborg resistance as the subversive refashioning of technologies of oppression—guns were a key technology that facilitated the conquest, after all—toward liberatory causes.[27]

At the same time, both works express reservations about the use of weapons to assert an individual or communitarian *bios*. As Agamben notes, the very act of engaging in warfare discursively converts people on all sides of a given conflict into expendable animals as they enter a metaphorical slaughterhouse.[28] Hernández Cordón shows this most poignantly through cinematographic techniques that align each character with bare life. Anaya, on the other hand, proves more difficult to place. He views armed conflict as empowering when weapons become spiritual prostheses that connect the individual who wields it to their broader community. Indeed, by communing with other actors of the traditional Aztlán, Rosa interfaces with a utopian potential that breaks the dystopian, drug-infested present. Both the author and the director tie the liberatory nature of armed resistance to their differing representations of the fantastic. Their works broach SF through their representation of dystopia, aliens, and time travel. Nevertheless, both men ground their respective texts more firmly within the realm of magical realism. In Hernández Cordón's case, magical-real phenomena accentuate cases of quotidian violence that relegate characters to *zoē*. In Anaya's trilogy, however, the magical-real discourse stands in direct opposition to the necroliberal, dystopian aesthetics of the drug war and state-sponsored overreach.

Magical realism has fallen out of vogue among Latin Americanists in recent decades in large part because it has led to reductive approaches both to the region's literary and cultural production and to its inhabitants. Often problematically tied to local, non-Western (read: Indigenous and African) cosmologies where people supposedly accept irrational, and even magical, events as unremarkable or quotidian, many have charged that the mode Others—rather than champions—marginal communities in Latin America.[29] Furthermore, the traditional emphasis on magical realism in Latin American literature reflected the expectations of international consumers more so than any intrinsic Latin American literary style.[30] Jorge Volpi asserts that magical realism has only recently faded into the background of the region's literary and cultural scene as "new exoticisms" (nuevos exoticismos), like narco literature, take its place.[31] Viewed against this backdrop, one could charge that both Hernández Cordón and Anaya produce works that play to multiple stereotypes of Latin American literary and cultural production: not only do they engage the subject of narcos, but they do so through a magical-real mode. There is certainly merit to such an assertion, but it ignores how the authors fuse magical realism with SF and dystopia to innovate a new aesthetic that moves beyond that of previous generations in Latin America.[32]

Interestingly enough, while the ChupaCabra trilogy and *Cómprame un revólver* both employ a magical-real mode, they do so in oppositional ways. Christopher Warnes divides magical realism into two camps: faith-based and irreverent. The former "often [. . .] call[s] upon the reader to suspend rational empirical judgements about the way things are in favour of an expanded order of reality. Frequently, [. . .] it does this in order to recuperate a non-western cultural world view."[33] This is the vein of magical realism that has led to criticism among Latin American writers and critics, and it fits the conditions of Anaya's trilogy especially well. Rosa, for example, achieves communion with her mestiza/x roots in large part by validating and participating in Native American traditions and popular Catholicism. At the same time, Hernández Cordón never mentions Indigenous or mestizo cosmologies. Instead, he engages in a type of "irreverent" magical realism that aims to denaturalize the necroliberal conditions of the drug war by "elevat[ing] the non-real to the status of the real in order to cast the epistemological status of both into doubt."[34] The director achieves this end by juxtaposing scenes of quotidian violence with surreal and magical-real imageries that confuse the viewer's understanding of what constitutes reality and what does not.

Each of these fictions also interfaces with very different wings of SF. Neither one employs a cyberpunk aesthetic, but their works do fit within an expanded definition of the genre. The ChupaCabra in *Curse* is more of a fantastic manifestation than a SF creation. However, the following novels depict Saytir, who is a SF/fantastic monster, along with aliens and time travel, all of which fit more cleanly under the SF rubric. For its part, *Cómprame un revólver* follows the tropes of dystopian and postapocalyptic fiction in a way that remains true to the setting in Mexico. Ricardo Bedoya Wilson underscores this fact when he argues that "the specific and recognizable referent of a country overcome by institutionalized crime does not block the film from aligning with the generic codes of postapocalyptic fiction" (las referencias específicas y reconocibles de un país asolado por el crimen institucionalizado no impiden que el relato se afilie a los códigos genéricos de la ficción postapocalíptica).[35] That said, Hernández Cordón's postapocalyptic SF referent emphasizes the technological stagnation that has resulted from a drug war that has decimated civil society. He limits his representations of digital technology to an old computer in Rogelio's trailer and a smartphone that a sicario uses to flirt with a significant other. Throughout the film, powerful actors carry out acts of quotidian violence that both institutionalize the cartel's de facto sovereignty and make it impossible to produce and distribute new technological devices. Continued cruelty has thus brought about a technological dark age where the niceties of modern culture, like access to running water and dependable electricity, have largely disappeared.

## QUOTIDIAN VIOLENCE, MAGICAL REALISM, AND ROBO-SACER RESISTANCE IN JULIO HERNÁNDEZ CORDÓN'S *CÓMPRAME UN REVÓLVER*

Clearly, the interplay between a magical-real mode and a cyborgian system of violence sits at the heart of *Cómprame un revólver*. If one of the hallmarks of magical realism is the quotidian nature of magic in daily life, then it is worth noting that Hernández Cordón depicts a world of quotidian violence where acts of cruelty have become mundane due to their everyday nature.[36] The film embodies the aesthetics of slower cinema, which, according to Olivia Cosentino, "taps into slow cinema's characteristic use of a static, observational camera and long takes, while its engagement with the quotidian nature of violence cites slow cinema's obsession with the minutiae of the everyday."[37] This aesthetic can be difficult to watch for many reasons, a fact that almost certainly contributed to the film's struggles both to draw large audiences to theaters and to appear on streaming platforms.[38] Nevertheless, it has enjoyed significant critical praise due to its powerful social commentary. The director casts each character as a grotesque manifestation of bare life in a way that interrogates the institutionalized state of exception that gives narcos dominion over life and death. In this dystopian context, access to firearms produces a type of low-tech cyborg identity that allows the *zoē* to resist—and, far too often, carry out—acts of quotidian violence. That said, when marginalized characters resort to violence, they reproduce the structures of domination that have interpellated them into bare life in the first place.

Referring to himself as a Mesoamerican filmmaker, Hernández Cordón has Mexican, Guatemalan, and US citizenship.[39] Aiming to build a cinematography that is appropriate for the context from which he films, he has cultivated an auteurist brand centered on low-budget productions that reflect the poverty of the nations where he films.[40] One of the most recognizable traits of his movies is the casting of amateur actors and children to highlight the traumas of war in daily life.[41] The director has leveraged this style to secure international funding by appealing to the attitudes of international audiences surrounding Latin American culture and cinema.[42]

Few phenomena inform his work more directly than the biopolitical and necropolitical divisions of contemporary society.[43] Indeed, the continued killability of racial, ethnic, and sexual minorities serves as a centerpiece of his cinematic production.[44] While the director uses aesthetic strategies to advocate for social justice throughout his cinema, the progressive nature of his films—particularly the inclusion of nonheteronormative sexualities—has hurt his marketability with Guatemalan audiences.[45] That said, he has a steady and loyal following in Mexico and throughout Western Europe and North America.[46] Viewed in this light, it would make sense that Hernández Cordón would film a project on the Mexican border: a film set in that country would be more likely to find viewers. That said, he stays true to his overarching style in *Cómprame un revólver* as he envisions the Mexican drug war in large part through the lenses of gender and trauma.

Similar to many of his previous projects, which focus on the collective reaction—particularly among Indigenous populations—to the state-sponsored genocide of Guatemala, *Cómprame un revólver* highlights the effects of institutionalized violence on individuals and communities.[47] That said, the Mexican context requires a slightly different generic approach. Within his Central American cinema, "there is no future, and when it is represented, the past is a stinging wound that provokes only one reaction: more violence" (carece de futuro, y el pasado, cuando se representa, es una herida punzante que provoca una sola reacción: más violencia).[48] Set in the context of the Mexican drug war, *Cómprame un revólver* approaches past, present, and future somewhat differently. Rather than invoke cultural memory, he employs speculative strategies to project contemporary traumas into a dystopian future where an unchecked conflict will continue to take a toll on Mexican citizens for decades to come.

Hernández Cordón highlights the quotidian nature of drug violence from the film's earliest moments by depicting the Lost Boys locked in small cages. The children ultimately escape, and the following day they play with Huck, who notices that her friend Ángel no longer has a hand. The boy reveals that the narcos cut it off and says that he wishes for nothing more than to find and hold his lost hand again. The matter-of-fact way in which he recounts his trauma, coupled with his friends' inability to understand or fully empathize with him contributes to what Cortés calls an "aesthetics of indifference" that permeates Hernández Cordón's cinema.[49] When one of the Lost Boys asks Ángel why he wants to see his dead, useless extremity, the injured child simply explains, "You don't get it. Sometimes I feel my hand open or closed." (Tú no sabes nada. A veces siento que tengo la mano abierta o cerrada).[50] Ángel lacks the language to explain his desire to reunite with his missing body part, but his lamentation speaks directly to the film's posthuman referent by highlighting and challenging the deconstruction between the self and the body. N. Katherine Hayles alludes to this deconstruction when she refers to the body as the "original prosthesis."[51] Such a characterization casts the body as a "container of the putative self" that exists in the mind.[52] The film also underscores the distinction between the body—a Platonic form of sorts that functions as an imaginary of what a proper body should look like—and embodiment, or the actual act of having and inhabiting a body that ultimately fails to uphold the platonic ideal.[53] Following his dismemberment, Ángel suffers alienation from his own body, a prosthetic he has long viewed as an inseparable component of his self. Spatially separated from his dead limb, his psychological connection to it grows all the deeper as he grieves its loss.

The posthuman referent proves especially useful because it casts Ángel as an anti-cyborg whose technologically and legally bare existence has relegated him to bare life and *zoē*. Linda F. Hogle refers to the so-called natural body as a "self-regulating organism," a definition that allows her to classify people with donor organs as a class of cyborg.[54] Ángel, of course, represents the opposite case: rather than a person surviving due to donated organs, he is an amputee who lost his hand—part of the prosthesis of the self—against his will. If Haraway is correct that cyborg figures can transcend, or at least contest, Foucauldian biopolitics, then it would appear that anti-cyborg subjectivity could do the opposite.[55] Indeed, the brutal nature of his amputation, coupled with the refusal to allow him to grieve the loss of his limb, serves to cast Ángel as a disposable *homo sacer* who lacks access to firearms or other "prostheses of citizenship."[56] He thus remains on the periphery and exposed to violence. Indeed, Ángel only receives his hand at the end of the film after Huck executes the boss. In reuniting with his decomposing limb, he transcends, albeit imperfectly, the self/other divide between the severed limb and his body. In so doing, he reasserts his humanity at a psychological level. Of course, the fact that the film ends a few short minutes afterward underscores the fact that a true resolution never arrives.

Far from advocating a cathartic ending—"happy" or "sad"—Hernández Cordón seems more interested in producing a film that, similar to Brechtian political theatre, denaturalizes the violent status quo and calls spectators to action. For Brecht, catharsis undermines political action because it entails a restoration of order; even "sad" endings produce a degree of closure that would stop the public from engaging in political debate after viewing a production. Indeed, the thinker asserts that cathartic, melodramatic theater causes people "to stare rather than see, [. . .] listen rather than hear."[57]

Hernández Cordón avoids such acritical viewings through a "slow and challenging" aesthetic where "the spectator experiences disruptive emotions, which are difficult to express."[58] We see this clearly in *Cómprame un revólver*, where the film's grotesque imageries of mutilated children and quotidian violence stifle any pretense of melodramatic catharsis. Instead, viewers must contemplate the institutionalized *zoē* not only of Huck and the Lost Boys, but that of her father and, perhaps, even of the narcos who terrorize them. The director uses this backdrop to explore the alienation that results among those who grow up and live in a context of unmitigated, quotidian violence. In a truly Brechtian fashion, the film's aesthetics denaturalize the institutionalized *zoē* of the main characters through brutal scenes that emphasize the different strategies of dehumanization that run rampant throughout. Far from a flaw, then, the lack of loveable protagonists reflects a conscious creative decision that draws attention to the conditions that perpetuate misery in this dystopia.

In Hernández Cordón's fictitious Mexico, drug cartels have sacrificed riches and fame in order to satisfy an ever-increasing drive to kill and exert power over life and death. Gone are the lavish mansions and fancy pickup trucks that appear in so many narco films. Instead, capital and riches provide the means through which crime bosses come to function as local sovereigns. The film thus reverberates with the work of Sayak Valencia, who argues that the "*parallel State*, represented by national and international criminals[,] reshapes biopolitics itself and uses necropolitical practices to seize, preserve, and capitalize on the power to *inflict death*."[59] The director's dystopian setting simply postulates a future moment when the "absent state" (Estado ausente) has abdicated its sovereignty and ceded biopower and even necropower to organized crime.[60] One could argue that the film's setting—particularly the idea that drug violence poses an existential threat to Mexican sovereignty—ultimately aligns it with statist discourses that have, according to several scholars, constructed the narco in order to create a perpetual state of exception that justifies state violence where it would otherwise not be permissible.[61] Of course, the Mexican state has a long history of overselling the threat that drug cartels pose to society at large. As Luis Astorga notes, while organized crime has long challenged the sovereignty of state and local governments, it has never posed an existential threat to the federal government's overall claims to sovereignty.[62] In focusing his critique on drug traffickers rather than the necroliberal system that has allowed them to coalesce into powerful cartels in the first place, the film privileges the individual level of analysis over the (trans)national. Resistance comes to mean little more than one individual standing up to another, often through armed violence.

**FIGURE 5.1** Still from *Cómprame un revólver*. A man at bat in a baseball game with an assault rifle strapped to his back.

We see this especially clearly with the narcos who play on the baseball field that Rogelio maintains. Even in leisure, they carry their weapons. Several shots show men swinging their bats with their assault rifles strapped to their backs (see fig. 5.1). At one level, Hernández Cordón uses these weapons as discursive shorthand to signal the men in the park as narcos; as Esch notes, the firearm functions as the "artifact that most clearly identifies one as participating in the [narcotics] business."[63] That said, beyond mere props aimed at calling to mind a phallocentric, violent masculinity, these weapons also attest to the deadly potential that drug traffickers exhibit even when not engaging in criminal activity.[64] The presence of armed baseball players highlights the liminal status of the ballfield and, by extension, that of Rogelio and Huck. Agamben asserts that "the state of exception is not a special kind of law (like the law of war); rather, insofar as it is a suspension of the juridical order itself, it defines law's threshold or limit concept."[65] The sovereign narco community keeps Rogelio alive because he provides a valuable service by keeping the ballfield in good condition. Officially unaffiliated with the cartel, Rogelio interacts with its members both as a professional who maintains their leisurely activities and as an avid consumer; indeed, the narcos pay him for his services not in money but in drugs. Even as Rogelio carries out certain economic functions for the cartel members, they frequently assert their biopolitical superiority by excluding him from their activities and reminding him at all times that they can kill him if he ever becomes a nuisance.

Huck faces even more marginalization than her father due to the omnipresence of feminicidal violence. In this dystopian future, the expansion of drug cartels has resulted in the disappearance of almost all women, including Huck's mother. As such, the film promotes the popular, if flawed, notion that drug traffickers and organized crime carry out the majority of murders against women in the country.[66] Rogelio strives to protect his apparently cisgender daughter from feminicide by forcing her to perform masculinity in public. We see this most clearly in his decision to call her Huck, a boy's name that he uses in an attempt to hide her biological sex from potential killers. If David E. Johnson is correct that a common strategy of anti-feminicide activism is to proclaim the names of victims to assert the humanity of the dead, then Rogelio's use of a boy's name for his daughter produces a dehumanizing alienation.[67] In order to continue to live she has to suppress her name and her gender identity and live an unauthentic existence. The forced cross-dressing thus produces a poignant form of misgendering, which is a pervasive form of violence that abounds in contemporary society.[68] Given the specifics of Huck's gender performance, her embodiment of masculinity proves neither resistant nor empowering. Rather, she performs an alien gender identity due to the constant threat of feminicide.

Given her constant exposure to acts of dehumanization, it should come as no surprise that Huck grows hardened to quotidian violence and cruelty. She never explicitly asks for a gun or a revolver, but she hangs drawings of handguns on the walls of her father's camper. Similar to revolutionary actors throughout Latin America, she views firearms as a prosthesis of citizenship. If the firearm has become "a menacing repurposed tool for and trope of sexual violence," then female characters like Huck come to believe that they cannot resist without making their own voices heard by further repurposing these weapons to a resistant end.[69] Indeed, the petition at the heart of the film's very title, *Cómprame un revólver* (*Buy Me a Gun*), represents the girl's desire for her own prosthesis of citizenship that she can use to seize a political voice and thus enter the *bios*. Hernández Cordón drives home this desire for armed self-defense through shots of Huck and the Lost Boys as they—similar to the Lost Boys of *Peter Pan*—test catapults and other impressive, low-tech weapons that they have built to fight not pirates but narcos. The children may believe that sophisticated weaponry will set them free, but the film proves less optimistic.

Hernández Cordón's magical-real aesthetic suggests that violent resistance will only validate the structures of power that already abound. The director introduces the magical-real dynamic in the movie's second scene when a voiceover of Huck narrates, "Everything that is told in this movie is real. Luck is also real, and so are lucky men. They pass it down to their daughters, who pass it down too, and so on. [. . .] I'm sure that my dad is a lucky man. Otherwise, how could he survive in a place as violent as this?" (todo lo que se encuentra en esta película es real. La suerte es real, y hay hombres con suerte. Y estos hombres les heredan su suerte a sus hijas y esas hijas a sus hijas o a sus hijos. [. . .] Estoy segura que mi papá tiene suerte.

O si no, ¿como sobrevivirías un lugar bronco?) Her narration adheres to Warnes's observation that magical realism "treats the supernatural as if it were a perfectly acceptable and understandable aspect of everyday life."[70] At first glance, Huck's words seem like those of an unreliable, childish narrator who adores her father.[71] That said, the magical-real components of the film come to transcend childish perceptions in subsequent scenes that juxtapose quotidian violence with irrational, magical-real aesthetics. Far from a source of liberation, the magical-real mode places Huck on a path that will strip her of her innocence and initiate her into a cycle of quotidian violence.

The first magical-real sequence of the film happens when the boss orders Rogelio's execution, and no bullets graze his body (some appear to have gone through him without leaving a mark). Seeing that Rogelio has indeed benefitted from supernatural luck, the boss orders him to attend their birthday party. As they explain, "I want some of your luck for my birthday" (quiero tu misma suerte para mi cumpleaños). The magical-real mode provides an invaluable framework for analyzing the scene. The drug lord decides not to kill Rogelio due to a hazily defined notion of luck. While irrational, none of the characters question the decision. What is more, the boss makes it clear that they are not saving Rogelio's life out of mercy but out of self-interest: the boss wants Rogelio's luck for themselves. This act reverberates with Warnes's depiction of irreverent magical realism, where "truth claims of causality are seen as contingent on consensus, founded in language, and driven by discourse rather than reality itself."[72] The characters ascribe Rogelio's survival to magic despite the fact that they cannot know for certain that they are correct. What is more, rather than trouble themselves with questions about how or why he survived, they try to channel magical fortune toward themselves.

Hernández Cordón further foregrounds the magical-real referent during this same scene when Huck sees the boss remove their mask, thus revealing locks of long hair styled in a normatively feminine manner. For Kim Sasser, one of the telltale signs of magical-real literature (and, one could add, film) is that "fantastical events are described in a deadpan manner or, inversely, when ordinary objects such as ice are described as wondrous."[73] Huck's wonder at the boss's embodiment of gender fluidity—especially when juxtaposed with the "deadpan" treatment of Rogelio's survival at his execution—clearly reverberates with this trait of magical realism. At the same time, this depiction of a nonbinary boss contributes to those attitudes that have identified trans and gender-fluid people as national threats since at least the Porfiriato.[74] As they oversee an effectively sovereign cartel, the boss becomes the dominant figure in an order that has overthrown civil society and facilitated feminicide. As such, the boss comes across as a traitor against other people with marginalized gender identities because they oversee a necroliberal, patriarchal order.

Hernández Cordón's brand of magical realism differs from most examples of postcolonial Latin American magical realism, where magic provides an avenue for resistance against oppressive regimes.[75] We see this clearly in the case of Rogelio, who has to take Huck to the boss's birthday party after surviving his execution. The simple act of taking her to the party proves perilous. Indeed, this segment of the film interfaces more directly with the feminicidal referent than does any other. They travel in a car with Rogelio's band and stop at a checkpoint where armed sicarios take Huck, who is masked and dressed like a boy, from the car. She screams offscreen and a narco exclaims, "it's a girl!" (es niña). Hernández Cordón does not show how the narcos discover Huck's biological sex, but her scream alludes to probable sexual violence; indeed, the director shows the narcos frisking the men at that moment. The narcos initially refuse to return her to her father. On the one hand, their action highlights the biopolitical context: because the men at the checkpoint embody Valencia's parallel state, they can exercise dominion over life and death with impunity. If the narcos wish to satisfy their own sexual fantasies on Huck's body, then they can do so because she belongs to an unprotected, *homo sacer* class. That said, their actions also reverberate with the necroliberal context: the narcos' actions draw to mind those of drug cartels in cities like Ciudad Júarez who have long contributed to feminicide by trafficking women and girls as prostitutes.[76] The only reason that Huck survives is that her driver tells the armed narcos that the boss themself has requested Huck's presence at their birthday party. The criminals realize that they must do as the boss commands or face their own unceremonious executions. Rather than a strict binary of *bios* and *zoē*, then, the film suggests that each character enjoys varying degrees of power and privilege based on myriad factors. The violence does not abate after this encounter: a sicario kills the Colombian driver in order to free up a seat in the car to the party, brushing his action off by saying that nobody cares about Colombians; a rival gang opens fire on the party killing almost everyone, and Huck survives after her father hides her in a cooler.[77]

The director follows the massacre scene with another round of magical-real, and even surrealist, aesthetics by fading to white and employing ominous music. From there, he cuts to Huck, who exits the cooler and walks across a desert floor littered with corpses. Rather than have the actors portray their dead characters, however, Hernández Cordón uses two-dimensional paper cutouts (see fig. 5.2). Coupled with the eerie music, these

**FIGURE 5.2** Still from *Cómprame un revólver*. Huck stands among numerous victims from the shooting. Their flattened corpses look more like cardboard cutouts than human bodies, a fact that plays to the magical-real aesthetic.

images transpose Huck to a magical-real plane; at the same time, these abstract corpses denaturalize quotidian violence by highlighting the absurdity of a world where cruelty is mundane. As is common in magical-real fiction, Huck does not marvel at the unnatural corpses that surround her. Rather, she searches for her father. Sasser notes that both surrealism and magical realism use "eccentric juxtapositions in order to critique reason from within the empire."[78] Her argument applies particularly well to this scene, where the solitary child stands in a field of death afraid and alone. Huck ultimately finds Rogelio being dragged by a truck, and her father knocks her unconscious to stop her from following him to his certain death. She later awakens to see that he has given her his lucky tooth, which she hugs reverently, as if entrusting herself to its care. The lucky charm seems to work. Moments later, she finds Ángel's hand. The juxtaposition of this tactile, three-dimensional limb with the two-dimensional bodies on the ground highlights the slippage between the realist and magical-real modes. Shortly after retrieving her friend's hand, Huck discovers the boss. Given that they are the only adult survivor of the attack, it would appear that Rogelio's luck has momentarily rubbed off on this character as well.

Throughout the rest of the film, the boss functions as a parental figure of sorts who attempts to inculcate Huck with their biopolitical attitudes. When they see that Huck carries Ángel's hand, for example, they tell her that the boy is a "rata" (thief/rat), a term that implicitly justifies his dismemberment by aligning him with bare life and *zoē*. Only after teaching Huck to distinguish between *bios* and *zoē* does the boss show Huck how to handle, load, and fire a handgun. Far from a prosthesis for (subaltern) citizenship, the Capo views the weapon as a tool for policing any attempts to threaten their hegemony. The scene where Huck kills the boss marks the moment that the girl becomes a resistant robo-sacer actor. In using the gun against the character that entrusted her with it in the first place, she brings out the cyborg's "unfaithful" potential against illegitimate parental figures.[79] The killing also invites us to extend Esch's theorization of the firearm as a prosthesis of citizenship.[80] Not only does the gun become an extension of Huck, but the girl becomes a prosthetic extension of Ángel as well as the rest of the Lost Boys. If effective citizenship demands a person's (or group's) ability to make their voice heard, then Huck's handgun has aided in that effort. That said, while the boss's death represents a change in the face of oppression, the assassination has done little to resolve those threats that the children will continue to confront well into the future. In killing the boss, the young girl has not ushered in an era of freedom and peace; rather, she has chosen to participate in a society of violence.

The film closes with Huck narrating that she and the lost boys will put together plans to rescue her father, whom she believes remains alive and imprisoned. She still has a few shots left in her handgun, and her friends have their slingshots and booby traps. Together, they will stand against the incursion of organized crime. This ending alludes to a possible cyborgian utopia (or dystopia) that reverberates with Haraway's rejection of the "model of the organic family."[81] Rather than align herself with adult caregivers, Huck has integrated into a makeshift family with the Lost Boys. That said, necroliberal drug violence remains as strong as ever. The children will depend on a combination of luck and weapons to fight for a better future, but their ultimate victory may never come into fruition. In the end, Hernández Cordón's fusion of speculative fiction with magical realism produces a remarkable methodology for interrogating several aspects of the drug war. His vision for the future remains bleak, but hope persists. Hernández Cordón fuses magical realism and speculative fiction in a way that rejects catharsis and, hopefully, inspires the audience to become more politically engaged. Certainly, Hernández Cordón is not the only person to fuse SF, dystopia, and magical realism to interrogate the nature of biopolitics and necroliberalism in the drug war. Rudolfo Anaya places these modes in dialogue in his ChupaCabra trilogy as well. That said, he produces a more readerly text that aims for a cathartic experience. If Hernández Cordón views a bleak future where violence simply begets more violence, Anaya envisions a world where a magical-real connection to one's roots produces the spiritual fortitude necessary to overcome the necroliberal effects of the drug war.

## MESTIZAJE, WEAPONS, AND WRITING IN RUDOLFO ANAYA'S CHUPACABRA TRILOGY

Rudolfo Anaya's influence spans across Chicanx literature, with many critics hailing him as the tradition's "founding father."[82] Most follow the lead of Manuel Broncano, who situates the author's narrative at the intersection of "Modernism, Social Realism, Magic Realism, and Postmodernism."[83] Anaya adds another level to this characterization with his ChupaCabra trilogy by articulating a dystopian SF narrative through a magical-real mode. All three novels posit robo-sacer resistance as a means through which marginalized actors can assert their humanity before an oppressive political class. Across the trilogy, Rosa learns that she can only stand against an array of ChupaCabras, drug cartels, and corrupt government agencies by asserting and validating her mestiza/x heritage through a spiritual communion with the marginalized peoples—particularly Hispanic Mexicans and Native Americans—of the US-Mexico border region.[84] Rosa's subaltern allies consist of Chicanx addicts (and former addicts), Indigenous people, and even nineteenth-century New Mexican *Hispanos* and *Hispanas*.[85] Together, these groups engage in what Andrea J. Pitts refers to as "insurrectionist ethics and agency" where "identity-related claims play a role within practices of resistance."[86] Indeed, as Rosa builds communion with these groups, they protect her through enchanted talismans: her crucifix, her knife, and, in *Billy the Kid*, the pistol of the female rough rider, Josefita Chávez. Rosa repays her debt to these communities by giving them a voice through writing.

Rosa seeks to foment a mystical cyborg subjectivity that can erode divisions between individuals and bring them together as a single, interethnic collective. The crucifix, knife, and pistol come to function as agents of what Chela Sandoval calls "radical mestizaje," which reconciles Haraway's cyborg with Anzaldúa's mestiza by asserting both theoretical traditions as "methodolog[ies] that [run] parallel" to one another.[87] The talismans, while by no means technologically advanced, reverberate with Joanna Zylinska's theorization of the prosthesis as the "articulation of the slippage between the self and its others."[88] They thus produce a type of cyborg subjectivity that facilitates communion between marginalized people across time and even space. Anzaldúa, Haraway, and Sandoval prove key to my reading of the ChupaCabra trilogy because they provide a vocabulary for tracking cyborg subjectivity and mestiza/x discourse across the novels. As such, they prove necessary to tracking Anaya's understanding of Chicanx resistance in light of the ever-expanding drug war in Mexico and the United States. In the pages that follow, I show how Rosa develops a radical mestiza/x consciousness to combat the illicit drug trade, shady US government agencies, and ChupaCabras. I begin with a close reading of *Curse*, and I finish with a discussion of *Billy the Kid*. Across all of these novels, Rosa becomes the site through which the people of the borderlands can interface one with another and promote a more just society. Indeed, she stands against an array of economies of death—ranging from nineteenth-century US expansionism to the contemporary drug war—that have subordinated Chicanx and Hispano/a interests to those of the region's Anglo populations for centuries.

Rosa's role in healing her community proves especially interesting as we consider the thought of Anzaldúa, who traces drug abuse to a form of machismo that, she claims, results from the "racial shame" that manifests itself among Chicano men who deny their mestiza/x heritage.[89] Her theorization may not account for drug abuse among those who are not Chicano men, whether Chicana/x or people of different ethnic groups, but it allows her to assert ties between drug abuse and a toxic masculinity that has historically caused significant harm within her community. Not surprisingly, Anzaldúa posits mestiza(/x) consciousness as the means to overcome these vices; after all, a communion with one's roots can eradicate racial shame.[90] In the trilogy, Rosa strives to help Chicanx recovering drug addicts adopt a practice of radical mestizaje to overcome their chemical dependency and uplift their people. All three novels discuss her volunteer work at a clinic for inner-city youths struggling to overcome addiction. Beyond simply helping individuals overcome self-destructive behaviors, Rosa also embarks on an investigative journey to identify those actors who deliberately dehumanize Chicanx and Mexican people and communities in an attempt to increase their profits in the illicit drug trade.

That said, at the beginning of *Curse*, Rosa struggles to connect with oppressed and marginalized communities. Her life in California, where she has accepted a tenure-track position as a professor of Chicano literature at Cal State, Los Angeles, has broken her connection to the mestiza/x landscape and to the peoples of New Mexico.[91] This fact offers fresh insight into Enrique Lamadrid's observation that Anaya's literature is "in constant dialogue with nuevomexicano and Chicano cultural tradition."[92] While the critic places the Nuevomexicanx and Californian Chicanx experiences under a common umbrella, he also notes that these are not identical. In both contexts, the "colonization of the Americas ha[s] caused amnesia about the ancient peoples of the New World in relation to mestizo identity."[93] That said, the invisibility of Indigenous and (mestizo) Mexican contributions to local history is more pronounced in California due to its history of expansion and settler colonization.[94] William A. Calvo-Quirós argues that

*Curse*'s setting "normalizes the Chicana/o experience as an integral part of the American Southwest, particularly California."[95] The critic is probably correct that Anaya sets that novel (mostly) in California to engage Chicanx communities beyond his home state. That said, the author continues to privilege New Mexico as the spiritual center of Aztlán.[96]

Despite engaging such interesting subject matter, *Curse*—along with the rest of the trilogy—has received scant attention from the academic community. The few who have mentioned it have tended to cast it as children's literature implicitly less worthy of scholarly attention than other titles.[97] William A. Calvo-Quirós, one of the few to study *Curse* in depth, argues that the novel "exposes the effects that greed and drug trafficking have had on the Chicana/o community."[98] In this way, *Curse* embodies Anaya's commitment to a "political stance" that typified his work from the 1980s forward.[99] Throughout the trilogy, Anaya uses the ChupaCabra to produce a mythopoesis, a common trope in his literature that allows him to, in the words of Lamadrid, "[interpret] and mediat[e] the contradictions in the everyday historical experience for the people."[100] Of course, the ChupaCabra—which metonymically represents the drug trade—stands in opposition to a multiethnic mestiza/x communion. Anaya's ChupaCabra is a creative reimagining of the *chupacabras*, a monster that first entered the global imagination after alleged sightings in Puerto Rico in 1995. The creature quickly became a popular urban legend as Puerto Rican farmers reported grisly attacks where it had drained livestock, particularly goats, of their bodily fluids.[101] The word *chupacabras* literally means goatsucker in English. It did not take long for sightings to spread to Mexico, South America, and the US-Mexico borderlands.[102] The vampiric impulses of the *chupacabras*, coupled with its emergence during the initial phases of the neoliberal shift in mid-1990s Latin America, led many to associate it with the negative macroeconomic and microeconomic effects of globalization.[103] When Mexico experienced runaway inflation shortly after the implementation of NAFTA, for example, socially engaged artists began illustrating the monster to resemble the former president Carlos Salinas de Gortari. In this way, they discursively turned this proponent of NAFTA into a "chupatodo" (sucker of everything).[104]

Anaya follows in the footsteps of his Mexican counterparts, adapting the folk monster to the necroliberal context of the war on drugs. His decision to use a vampiric monster to critique necroliberal markets makes sense given his previous work, which conceives of the Chicanx nation as an internal colony that functions to ensure the economic well-being of (particularly Anglo) Americans.[105] Such characterizations reverberate with Karl Marx's theorization of capital as a vampiric, labor-sucking entity.[106] That said, in *Curse*, Anaya amends the vampiric nature of his monster to reflect the contemporary, twenty-first-century context. For example, rather than profit off of Chicanx labor, the ChupaCabra and the cartel prey upon these communities' consumption of addictive substances. Throughout *Curse*, Anaya refers to both the ChupaCabra and illicit drugs as "monster[s] that destroy brains."[107] In so doing, his creation reverberates with Mabel Moraña's observation that "the *chupacabras* expresses a lack of confidence in the efficiency and objectives associated with modernizing projects, along with the ideas of progress."[108] Indeed, if we conceive of the illicit drug market as one of the purest manifestations of the ne(cr)oliberal drive, then we realize that progress and modernity have created the tools through which government policies and organized crime have dehumanized Mexican and Chicanx communities for decades.[109]

Anaya establishes the dehumanizing potential of the ChupaCabra—and that of the illicit drugs that the monster symbolizes—in an early scene of the novel where Rosa and her friend Herminio perform an autopsy on a goat that had recently died in a ChupaCabra attack. They find two small holes at the base of the animal's skull that appear at first glance to evoke traditional associations of the *chupacabras* with vampires. When they open the skull, however, the animal's liquified gray matter leaks out, a fact that leads Rosa to exclaim, "ChupaCabra is not drinking the blood of animals; the monster destroys their brains."[110] The biopolitical ramifications of their discovery take on greater significance in light of Giorgio Agamben's association of the "detach[ment] from any brain activity" with *zoē*.[111] Anaya emphasizes this through José and Chuco, two Chicano characters who, similar to the goat, die after a ChupaCabra punctures their skulls and scrambles their brains. The fact that they die similarly to a domesticated animal meant for slaughter emphasizes their bare life. Anaya drives this point home when Rosa asks the crooked Detective Dill if he finds it odd that an autopsy revealed that José's brains were "fried."[112] The officer replies, "Not really. Your homeboys use crack. It burns their brains. Meth does the same. So does sniffing paint. After a while you see them wandering on the streets. Till they drop."[113] When Rosa counters that José did not do drugs, Dill shows her criminal files that include arrests for possession when José was in high school. The detective then says that Chuco had ties to a gang throughout his life. Given both men's histories, Dill refuses to investigate further.

Clearly, these Chicanx characters' associations with drugs dehumanize them and bar them from equal protection under the law. The ChupaCabra/alien hybrid villain Saytir makes this point in *Billy the Kid* when, reflecting on Chuco's death, he proclaims, "we feed dope to the young so we can control them!"[114] Once he creates a *homo sacer* class ineligible for protection under the law, the villain can exploit them for further gain. These conditions suggest that transnational actors in government and organized crime have conspired together in a quest to profit on the back of Chicanx suffering.[115] It is for this reason that Calvo-Quirós argues that "creating a consciousness about the reality of the Chupacabras [and, by extension, the drug epidemic], as experienced by the community, is an essential part of the project of emancipation proposed by Anaya in his novel."[116] Such knowledge can only occur through writing that explores the numerous factors that have led to drug abuse within Mexican and Chicanx communities on the one hand while exposing those who exploit these communities for gain on the other.

Rosa fortifies her connection to her roots when she returns home to New Mexico and meets the Navajo shaman Uncle Billy. Given Anaya's fascination with Carl Jung, it should come as no surprise that the author uses shamanic characters to "explore the dynamics between individual and collective identities."[117] In *Curse*, Uncle Billy helps Rosa to forge a meaningful connection with her Native American ancestry in order to confront the issues—both ChupaCabras and organized crime—of the present. Davis-Undiano observes that, in Anaya's detective literature (a genre to which *Curse* clearly belongs), Chicanx sleuths "can be effective as a detective only when [they learn] to view [their] li[ves] as existing against the backdrop of the complex cultural history that is the Americas."[118] Indeed, Rosa experiences what Flys Junquera terms "epiphany of the landscape" as she interacts with the Uncle Billy.[119] The shaman tells her that the ChupaCabra is an ancient shapeshifter whom he can ward off with traditional rituals. When she has to leave Uncle Billy's care, the young professor gives him her crucifix and asks that he bless it. This scene fits within a larger current in Anaya's narrative that celebrates "a tapestry of spiritual beliefs that draws on Catholicism as well as Indigenous spiritual practices."[120] The crucifix comes to symbolize the syncretic drive that typified Anaya's own approach to religion, which focused on borrowing spiritual archetypes from multiple sources.[121] After bequeathing it to Uncle Billy, her cross ceases to be a mere symbol of her Catholic beliefs and becomes a prosthetic extension of herself that remains with the Navajo peoples of New Mexico. If the crucifix represents a part of Rosa that stays behind, then the pachuco switchblade that she receives from Father Larry becomes a prosthetic extension of her mestiza/x community that accompanies her as she leaves to investigate cartel and ChupaCabra activities.

Even so, Rosa still lacks the power to ward off the ChupaCabra when she first discovers it encaged on the cruise ship. The creature rams against the bars that hold it, and Rosa flees to her room, where she tries to sleep. She dreams of Uncle Billy "praying over [her cross] and thus sending her protection."[122] From the dream, the shaman chants, "I will pull the witch objects out of your soul. You will become a warrior woman. You are in harmony with nature *and your community*. You are a warrior for the people."[123] This scene invokes other novels by Anaya where characters learn to commune with Native American cultures and cosmologies—and thus tap into their mestiza/x consciousness—through dreams.[124] At this moment, Uncle Billy cures Rosa of her "*susto*," a term that Christina Garcia Lopez defines as "soul fright, a spiritual ailment in which the soul (or part of it) is frightened out of the body following trauma."[125] Rosa's susto, of course, refers to the curse that Malorio has placed upon her at the beginning of the novel. That said, Anaya predicates Rosa's worthiness as a warrior woman on the fact that she has never struggled with addiction. The novel thus exemplifies Rosaura Sánchez's observation that "despite his critical commentary on several social and political issues, [Anaya's] detective novels ultimately deal with spiritual and psychological concerns, placing causality elsewhere."[126] The focus on personal purity deprives *Curse* of the necessary nuance for a systemic critique of the drug trade by centering its analysis of drug usage principally on individuals.

At the same time, Anaya's narrative strategy allows him to highlight the spiritual characteristics that will, in his view, facilitate a Chicanx rejection of illicit drug use. Rosa's apparent virtue and her ties to her community distinguish her from criminals like Dill, El Jefe, and Malorio. The Chicana professor depends on a mystical solidarity with her mestiza/x community to resist ChupaCabra attacks, but her criminal antagonists place their trust in their firearms. An argument between Dill and El Jefe illustrates this point:

> "You smell it, then you have a few seconds before it eats your brains," Jefe said and took a pistol from his holster. "If I see it, I will kill it."
> "Malo said bullets can't kill it." [Dill responded].
> "Bullshit! This will put a hole in it!" [El Jefe retorted]
> "I don't think so. It's got to be something from the church, the natives at Lago Negro said. Maybe a stake in the form of a cross?" [Dill said]
> "You think the maledición [*sic*] is a vampire? Bullshit!" [Malorio said][127]

El Jefe's trust in his guns over superstition leads to his quick demise; Dill and Malorio find his corpse as they search the ship for both Rosa and the ChupaCabra. Shortly thereafter, the monster attacks the duo, slaying both as they discharge their weapons in desperation.[128] The bullets do not harm the ChupaCabra, but they do start a fire by blowing up some oil barrels. Their actions prove the Indigenous people at Lago Negro correct: guns and other weapons cannot contain the ChupaCabra. Rather, spiritual harmony provides the conditions necessary to overcome brain fryers, be they drugs or ChupaCabras. After killing Dill and Malorio, the ChupaCabra charges toward Rosa. The Chicana professor lifts the pachuco switchblade and the monster cowers away. As Anaya explains, "the young woman held a power the beast could not defeat. With a final scream it turned and disappeared into the black smoke."[129] Of course, the power that Rosa bears is not physical but spiritual; she has come to wield it only after communing with her New Mexican past through Uncle Billy's prayer. The ship sinks shortly thereafter, taking the ChupaCabra down with it. The city hails Rosa as a hero after she publishes the story of her experience.

*Curse* imagines a type of mystical cyborg resistance where people can transcend cultural differences and physical distance through prostheses that allow them to resist the onslaught of divisive, necroliberal forces. In so doing, the novel prescribes a fix for a dystopian present where the illicit drug trade has continued to wreak havoc within Chicanx communities for decades. Calvo-Quirós notes that the ChupaCabra ultimately represents more than just the drug trade: "it also includes the creation of policies of subjugation that favor the emergence and perpetuation of oppression and social inequality that allows vulnerability to be normalized."[130] The illicit drug trade and drug traffickers did not come into existence on their own; rather, a complex set of policies, laws, and political leaders have created the conditions under which such actors can thrive.[131] In communing with her mestiza/x heritage through the crucifix and the knife, Rosa develops a strategy for favoring Chicanx and Mexican communities and individuals over the encroachment of necroliberal capital. The Indigenous members of her community proffer her spiritual protections that end up saving her life, and Rosa uses her platform as an academic to amplify subaltern voices through writing, thus integrating Chicanx voices into the political class.

Anaya further foregrounds questions of cybernetics and scientific advancement in *Roswell UFO* and *Billy the Kid*. In *Roswell UFO*, Anaya introduces Saytir, who functions as the principal antagonist in the final two novels. Anaya makes an explicit allusion to cyborg theory early in *Billy the Kid* when Rosa narrates that "Saytir is a new Cyborg. [...] A kind of Terminator, but far more dangerous than the comic book or movie character."[132] Significantly, Anaya only uses the term *cyborg* when referring to this genetically engineered villain. As such, he frames the posthuman as the culmination of the necroliberal drive and thus as something humanity should avoid.

The author himself seems not to view the spiritual cyborg communities of his books as posthuman despite the fact that cyborg theory clearly provides valuable insights to these aspects of the novels. Anaya finishes *Roswell UFO* with an author's note that discusses his concerns with runaway scientific and technological advancement. As he writes, "What if the same science that is being used to cure so many diseases is used for evil purposes? [. . .] As science probes deeper into the life-force and the essence of what makes us human, society must also deal with the ethical questions generated by such advancements."[133] The author does not dismiss the posthuman as fully irredeemable, but he remains pessimistic about the ethical dilemmas that it will unleash. For Anaya, the technological age requires people who are "knowledgeable both in science and the humanities," an assertion that he explores in great detail in *Billy the Kid*, where Rosa's knowledge of New Mexico's past plays a key role in defeating Saytir.[134]

Anaya's skepticism of science has led scholars like Roberto Cantú to assert an "antimodern" modernity in the Chicano author's oeuvre.[135] Cantú convincingly situates him within a rich US tradition dating at least as far back as Thoreau, but Anaya's emphasis on mestizaje also invites us to engage the underexplored ties between his distrust of science and the aesthetic monism of the Mexican philosopher José Vasconcelos.[136] I have previously described Vasconcelos's aesthetic monism as "a symphony of discourses, all of which were subordinated to a metaphysical paradigm."[137] Vasconcelos has come under fire within Mexican studies for the xenophobia and racism inherent to his mestizo ideal.[138] His work has enjoyed a warmer reception in Chicanx studies, especially since the publication of Anzaldúa's *Borderlands/La frontera* in 1987.[139] That said, Latinx scholars like Pitts distance themselves from the racist elements of Vasconcelianism when exploring the thought of Anzaldúa.[140] Anaya avoids the racist overtones of Vasconcelos's work, but similar to the Mexican philosopher, he suggests that science can only facilitate an inclusive mestiza/x paradigm if we subordinate it to humanistic and metaphysical ways of knowing. In these latter two novels, unchecked scientific advancements foster corrupt government and organized crime that grows out of a necroliberal imperative that he imagines in opposition to an Anzaldúan, mestiza/x order. Even as the trilogy becomes more explicitly SF, then, it continues to privilege the mystical cyborg consciousness that emerges among Rosa and other Chicanx and Nuevomexicanx populations as they commune through different prostheses.

In *Billy the Kid*, Rosa builds a comradery of sorts across time—though crucially *not* space—with Billy the Kid and Josefita Chávez against the constant onslaught of necroliberal markets in New Mexico and across the borderlands. The novel takes place almost a century before the War on Drugs and the neoliberal period in the United States, but markets of death have already emerged in Anaya's New Mexico territory. Indeed, Anaya implicitly posits the War on Drugs as the most recent manifestation of necroliberal practices that have plagued the Southwest ever since the United States annexed the territory from Mexico. In order to discuss this novel's balance of magical realism, SF, and historical fiction, we will need to briefly discuss the historical context. Following the US Civil War, eastern-US capitalists flocked to New Mexico. In their search for financial gain, they displaced those Indigenous and *Hispano/a* populations already living there.[141]

In many cases, these settlers broke federal laws; the United States had agreed to recognize the property rights of those who had lived in the territory prior to its annexation.[142] John-Michael Rivera asserts that by the 1870, "Mexican and Native American bodies had now become 'part' of the American republic's body politic, but only by means of assimilation, erasure, or dehumanization."[143] It was from this context that Henry McCarthy, who later adopted the moniker of Billy the Kid, swore to resist the dehumanizing flow of capital. An Irishman, he learned to speak fluent Spanish and quickly integrated into the local *Hispano/a* community, where many knew him as *El Bilito*.[144] Along with many disenfranchised *Hispanos/as*, Billy the Kid formed a posse called the Regulators who vowed to protect *Hispano/a* and Native American rights to the land. Billy the Kid's opposition to expansionist financial interests resulted in a series of skirmishes that culminated in the Lincoln County War, which pitted the Regulators against Sheriff William J. Brady and an array of colonialist agents. The Kid's mobilization against moneyed interests produced a state of exception that cast him and his posse as expendable *homines sacri*. The territory reserved the right to kill him or renege on any legal guarantees made to him in order to ensure the continued economic well-being of newly arrived, white settlers.[145] Perhaps the most egregious case of betrayal occurred when governor Lew Wallace broke a promise to pardon Billy the Kid in return for the outlaw's cooperation during a murder trial.[146] *El Bilito* escaped from prison but killed two police officers in the act. He later died when a group of men ambushed and killed him.

Rosa knows this basic history, but she wishes to tell it from the *Hispano/a* perspective. In a metafictional wink at Anaya's own attempts to reconstruct the positive relationship between *El Bilito* and Nuevomexicanos/as, Rosa pushes back against official and popular histories that have elided *Hispano/a* and Native American accounts despite the fact that their interests undergirded the entire conflict.[147] Most works on Billy the Kid have come through an Anglo-American filter in the form of dime novels that associated both the outlaw and his sympathizers with barbarism.[148] These conditions led Billy the Kid's ally Martin Chavez to lament in 1936 that "we who really knew him [The Kid] know that he was good and had fine qualities. We have not put our impressions of him to print and our silence has been the cause of great injustice to The Kid."[149] This is still largely the case nearly a century later, as Billy the Kid's story—particularly that of his relationship with Native American and *Hispano/a* populations—remains largely untold.[150] Nevertheless, Anaya uses his time-traveling protagonist to finally provide an *Hispano/a* and Chicanx telling of the story of Billy the Kid and the Regulators. The novel emphasizes how the failure to tell this side of Billy the Kid's story has led to the erasure of many key *Hispano/a* participants in the Lincoln County War from the collective memory. This holds especially true in the case of Josefita Chávez, a historical woman who has received scant historiographical and cultural attention despite serving as deputy of the *Hispano* contingent that fought alongside *El Bilito*. The historian Robert Utley mentions her in passing, and his anecdotes paint the portrait of a strong-willed Regulator who fought alongside Billy the Kid as an equal.[151] Nevertheless, most historians ignore her completely, and Hollywood has written her out of most, if not all, of its scripts. Given these facts, Josefita's words to Rosa take on greater significance: "'You write our story! [. . .] We lose our land. The Americanos want land for cattle. Soon all is lost.'"[152] The novel rescues her from relative ignominy, making her known not only to Chicanx readers, but to audiences from all ethnic backgrounds.

A shared drive to resist racial and class-based injustice unites Josefita with Rosa. Indeed, the novel frames the New Mexican *Hispana* as a precursor to Chicana activism, which has morphed and developed from the male-dominated context of the 1960s, to the Chicana feminism of the 1980s, and more recently to the Chicanx focus that had taken hold by the second decade of the twenty-first century. Similar to the Chicanas like Rosa who will emerge in the next century or two, Josefita Chávez confronts a cultural landscape that strives to push her to the periphery. The similarities between these two Southwestern women of Mexican heritage rings particularly clear in light of Angie Chabram-Dernersesian's assertion that Chicana and Mexican American female activists have historically "had to embody themselves as males, [. . .] and dwell only on their racial and/or ethnic oppression."[153] Throughout the novel, Josefita—one of the fiercest defenders of New Mexican property rights—enunciates her politics through ethnic and class-based terms. In so doing, she effectively "throw[s] punches for her race" while largely ignoring questions of gender.[154] In turning to the firearm, riding on horseback, and commanding her troops during the Lincoln County War, Josefita engages in activities traditionally viewed as masculine. Viewed in this light, Josefita's decision to give Rosa a one-shot pistol, with the charge to use it when she needs it most, proves telling.[155] Josefita explicitly predicates her protection on Rosa's willingness to write her story. The two women thus commit to support one another in a form of Mexican American / Chicana/x solidarity.

Rosa ends up using Josefita's pistol during the Battle of Lincoln on July 15, 1878, when Saytir attacks her in a burning home. The ChupaCabra/alien's decision to attack Rosa during this conflict highlights his continuation of the necroliberal practices that manifested themselves in nineteenth-century New Mexico and have continued to target Mexican American and Chicanx communities into the present.[156] Two oppressive forces, Saytir and Sheriff Brady, converge at this precise time and place independently of one another to impose their will on Chicanx, Indigenous *Hispano/a*, and mestiza/x people. Just as Josefita prosthetically accompanies Rosa through this ordeal through her pistol, Rosa joins the Regulators through her laptop, which she uses to compile and narrate the events of the battle. This fact adds extra weight to Saytir's demand that she surrender her computer to him. The ChupaCabra/alien villain needs her flash drive because it holds the only copy of a mapped alien genome. That said, if he takes the computer, Rosa will not finish her novel nor will she recover the voices of *El Bilito*, Josefita, or countless others. Beyond an attack on just the Chicana professor, then, Saytir's demands would condemn New Mexico *Hispanos/as* to further historiographical and cultural marginalization and, by extension, a form of apolitical *zoē*. Rosa refuses Saytir's command, and the monster charges to kill her. Rosa lifts Josefita's pistol and shoots Saytir between the eyes. She does not kill her (nearly) invincible foe, but she deters his attack and escapes.[157]

Given Rosa's comparison of Saytir to the Terminator, it is worth noting that her escape evokes the films of that franchise, where the protagonists temporarily incapacitate their attackers with firearms long enough to get away and resume the fight at a later time.[158] What is more, her survival depends on an almost familial bond, in this case, her ties to Josefita Chávez and other *Hispanos/as*.[159] Similar to the enchanted knife in *Curse*, Josefita's gun represents more than the sum of its parts: it functions as a prosthesis through which Josefita and others like her can defend Rosa without being physically present. Rosa, Josefita, and Billy the Kid symbiotically assist each other to contest the biopolitical divisions that create constructs of expendable life. The outlaws ultimately fail to curtail colonialist expansionism, but they keep Rosa alive and help her to keep the flash drive away from Saytir.

We later learn that their perseverance has taken a powerful toll on Saytir. In a final confrontation, Rosa discovers that the villain's DNA has begun to deteriorate and that he will die if he cannot get hold of the data on her flash drive.[160] After this confrontation, Saytir fades to the background, and Rosa can focus on writing the story of Billy the Kid and those who ride with him.

Rosa's obligation to write grows all the more urgent after Billy the Kid dies. Writing on the historical events that transpired in New Mexico, J. Rivera notes that "implicitly, it is the slaying of the Kid [. . .] that enables Frederick Jackson Turner to argue that the frontier, as a geographical line dividing civilization from savagery, has been closed a little over a decade later."[161] Billy the Kid's death thus symbolically marks the victory of financial interests over Native American and Mexican claims to the land. We see this most clearly following the outlaw's burial, when a *Hispana* woman tells Rosa, "we want to live in peace, but no guns."[162] The character does not condemn the Regulators for defending Mexican and Native American rights, but she expresses an overall exhaustion with armed violence. Left unsaid in this dialogue is the fact that peace—or at least nonviolence—will entail continued Anglo-American expansion and the perpetual subservience of nonwhite bodies. Knowing how New Mexican history will continue, Rosa buries her flash drive with Billy the Kid. The outlaw has dedicated his life to combatting markets of exploitation and death in New Mexico. In death he will guard this piece of evidence so that Rosa can prove the existence of C-Force and denounce it. When she returns home through a time vortex, she realizes that Saytir remains stuck in Billy the Kid's time because he lacks the spiritual knowledge necessary to open a wormhole and return home.[163] The aliens who sent her back have mastered time travel not through their grasp of technology alone, but through their holistic understanding of myth, nature, and the humanities. The New Mexico landscape once again functions as a facilitator of communion; indeed, the novel posits the Pecos Valley as a particularly mythic, haunting space.

Rosa's writing "[creates] sacred space" by giving voice to those who opposed the violent expansionism that followed the US Civil War.[164] Spiritual expertise, rather than technological skills, provides the competency necessary for her to thwart Saytir's plan to control the US government and the drug trade. Having survived her ordeal, Rosa can return to her own time, where she will tell the stories of Billy the Kid, Josefita Chávez, and so many others. In so doing, she will challenge the reigning narratives of bare life and *zoē* of these heroes of New Mexican history. Across the trilogy, Anaya has connected firearms to writing and speaking by positing self-preservation as a prerequisite to speaking. In the scenes where Rosa stands against the ChupaCabra—either the monstrous beast of the first novel or Saytir of the final two—she does so with prostheses that connect her to other subaltern communities that contribute to her mestiza/x heritage. The magical-real union between Rosa and her mestiza/x consciousness serves as a counterbalance to necroliberalism and runaway science. Indeed, the subaltern characters of these novels participate in robo-sacer resistance as they preserve Rosa's life so that she can speak for them. In the end, the Chicana professor's use of letters deconstructs notions of bare life across the centuries and signals the possibility a new, empowering Chicanx subjectivity where the people overcome necroliberal interests like the drug war through spiritual growth.

## CONCLUSION

In the end, both Anaya and Hernández Cordón imagine worlds where marginalized individuals use weapons as prostheses of citizenship to make their voices heard against oppressive sovereigns.[165] Both of the fictions interface with SF through different speculative strategies, but they ultimately fall more squarely within the realm of magical realism. Anaya and Hernández Cordón articulate different forms of magical realism: the former articulates a form of religious magical realism by validating Indigenous spirituality and signaling it as the means through which Chicanx actors can access their mestiza/x heritage. Within this framework, Chicanx actors can overcome drug trafficking and other necroliberal threats through a spiritual communion that purifies them as individuals and foments a community capable of withstanding the encroachment of oppressive regimes. In each of the novels, the author cements his solutions for resisting the drug trade through cathartic endings that posit Rosa's as the definitive example for other Chicanx people to follow. For his part, Hernández Cordón is less interested in calling for communion than he is in calling into question the necroliberal system upon which the drug war depends. He employs an irreverent magical realism that juxtaposes real and irreal images in an attempt to confuse viewers' certainty about what constitutes real and what does not. Coupled with his Brechtian style, this cinematographic strategy ultimately distances viewers and opens the possibility for critical readings. The director emphasizes that Huck's killing of the crime boss has not fundamentally reshaped society by abruptly ending the film immediately after this act. Rather than uplift his child protagonist as an example to emulate, he leaves his audience unsatisfied, thus forcing them to figure out how to resolve the drug crisis on their own.

CONCLUSION
# The Limits of Robo-Sacer Resistance

In the introduction to their edited volume *Data Protection, Homeland Security and the Labor Market*, vol. 1 of *The Politics of Technology in Latin America*, Avery Plaw, Barbara Carvalho Gurgel, and David Ramírez Plascencia argue that the "technological omnipresence [of the twenty-first century] has raised novel legal, ethical, and political issues concerning the relationship between governments and their citizens, especially regarding the contraposition of negative and positive liberties."[1] *Robo Sacer: Necroliberalism and Cyborg Resistance in Mexican and Chicanx Dystopias* has attempted to shed light on some of these issues by interrogating the interface of the body with technology in recent literary and cultural production from Greater Mexico. As the different chapters have shown, this body of work tends to view technology as a key factor in constructing the social relations of the necroliberal order. On the one hand, a person's access to technology—or the lack thereof—plays an integral role in determining their economic role in society. On the other hand, the subversive use of technology provides a powerful means through which marginal actors can denaturalize the dehumanizing status quo. The fictions discussed throughout this book speak to, and in many cases have even anticipated, real-life cases of technology-based oppression and resistance by imagining the confluence of speculative technologies with Mexican and Chicanx bodies. As this book comes to a close, a few areas for further research come to the fore. First, the book's theoretical framework lends itself to future studies on robo-sacer subjectivity in Greater-Mexican, US-Latinx, Latin American, and even world dystopian fiction. Second, this book has provided a valuable framework for theorizing real-world political movements where the interface of the body with technology has played a key, if underappreciated, role.

*Robo Sacer* alludes to the potential for cross-pollination between literary and cultural studies on the one hand and the social sciences on the other. This becomes especially clear as we consider the generic tendencies of dystopian fiction, which, according to Ruth Levitas, "portrays the darkness of the lived moment, the difficulty of finding a way out of a totalizing system."[2] Dystopias often engage their political referent more explicitly than do other types of literary and cultural production for precisely this reason. Furthermore, they often speculate about how authoritarian governments will use new technologies—both real and imagined—to further their grip on power.[3] For this reason, the exact nature of the technologies employed in a given work matters less than their intersection with the political context. Dystopias deal with many of the same issues, albeit often in hyperbolic form, that real-world political activists engage. *Robo Sacer* is not the first book to consider the role of technology in fomenting resistance in Latin America. Claire Taylor and Thea Pitman, for example, have both written extensively on the intersection of online performance and social activism.[4] The critics discuss numerous ways through which different actors have employed technology to contest unjust power differentials between Latin America and the United States. Their insistence on engaging real-world discourse provides a necessary counterpoint to my own fiction-based analyses. At the same time, however, *Robo Sacer*'s theoretical framework highlights new perspectives that may help to center future studies on the intersection of biopolitics and technology. Across their work, Taylor and Pitman express significant criticisms of neoliberalism, for example, but they stop short of theorizing markets of death. As a result, biopolitics remains outside the purview of their particular studies. *Robo Sacer* thus provides a theoretical language that allows us to better gauge the biopolitical and necropolitical ramifications of technologies of domination as articulated in Latin America.

This book provides a useful theoretical framework from which to engage questions of online activism more generally. Again, the focus on how activists must confront biopolitical realities proves especially illuminating. Beyond simply calling out oppressive systems of domination, the literary and cultural production studied throughout this book imagines strategies for using technology to denaturalize the necroliberal state of exception. Activists of all stripes—both fictional and real-life—undertake their projects to challenge some aspect of politics as usual and, crucially, to make their voices heard. In this way, my theorization of robo-sacer resistance as a means to politicize the *zoē* rises to the fore. Hilda Chacón has highlighted several aspects of the expansion of technology, such as "government-driven espionage" and corporate data-mining, that tend to undermine the democratic ideals that online activists espouse.[5] Nevertheless, she also optimistically reminds her readers that online activists can use technology to other, more humanizing ends. The individual studies in Chacón's edited volume speak directly to different strategies through which online activists counteract the oppressive underbelly of modern technology. Sergio Delgado

Moya, for example, discusses Ricardo Domínguez's Transborder Immigrant Tool, a cellphone app from the early 2000s that directed undocumented migrants to sources of potable water as they traversed the unforgiving terrain of the US Southwest while also sending them poems to boost morale.[6] Other chapters from that book discuss strategies for finding a cultural voice through online discourse.[7] When people disseminate popular discourse, they necessarily begin to take on political responsibilities and privileges. In so doing, they achieve a political voice that they can use to more effectively advocate for themselves and others.

Similar to the fictional characters discussed in this book, online activists strive to denaturalize their marginalization and demand a political voice for themselves and their allies. In many cases, they turn to social media to build chains of polyspatial solidarity and stand up to hegemonic actors. I have previously written on the case of United We Dream (UWD), a US-based organization that uses internet and social media to advocate for so-called DREAMers, or people who were born abroad but left their home countries as small children and came of age in the United States.[8] As that case so poignantly demonstrates, immigrant youths, nearly 80 percent of them Mexican citizens, successfully demanded concrete actions from the US state through virtual activism that translated into demonstrations in physical space.[9] On the one hand, youths from this demographic tended to have less access to new technologies than did their citizen peers; on the other hand, however, they successfully leveraged what they had to denaturalize their exclusion from citizenship rights.[10] The case of UWD proves especially instructive because it resulted in the creation of Deferred Action for Childhood Arrivals (DACA). This Obama-era program started under executive order, and it has provided a framework through which people who entered the country without papers as children can, in the words of former president Barack Obama, "come out of the shadows" and work openly.[11] While they have not secured citizenship rights (which include the right to vote), UWD's online presence has translated into actions in physical space that have allowed 1.5-generation immigrants to finally participate in the economy and live relatively normal lives on par with those of their US-citizen counterparts.

DACA's success in resisting repeated attempts by anti-immigration politicians—up to and including former president Donald Trump—to remove it underscores the role that repeated robo-sacer activism has played in ensuring that DREAMers maintain their hard-fought, though narrow, legal privileges.[12] The case of UWD encourages a more in-depth look at similar movements, whether in Mexico, among Latinx and Chicanx activists in the

United States, or people from other countries and communities altogether, where marginalized actors have challenged a biopolitical status quo through online activism that has imbued them with a political voice that they otherwise would never have achieved. Future scholarship about online activism in Latin America and throughout the so-called Third World would benefit from the theorization of robo-sacer identity. When activists use technology to speak out and organize, they create a polyspatial movement that facilitates the critique of oppressive biopolitical conditions that relegate so many to the periphery. Such actions thus represent attempts to literally engage in political discourse, which, by definition, represents an attempt to join the *bios*. Such activism takes on numerous guises. Some people may be content to build comradery among themselves or with another niche community.[13] Others may seek to engage directly with local (or global) political debates that will affect them directly despite the fact that they cannot vote or otherwise advocate for themselves through official, political channels.[14] In any event, the robo-sacer lens provides valuable insight to both the social sciences and to cultural studies.

Of course, *Robo Sacer* sheds light on real-world cases that extend beyond just online activism. Indeed, the book provides a language for gauging the biopolitical underpinnings of an array of new and emerging technologies. For example, it provides a unique angle from which to view the Colombia-based company KiwiBot. Truly a transnational initiative, the company builds autonomous robots in California that it uses to inexpensively deliver food and other goods at several University of California campuses as well as in other select cities and sites throughout the United States.[15] These robots mostly use autonomous driving technology, but they also depend on system operators in Bogotá to ensure that the machines operate properly and safely.[16] Much of the scholarship on the company refers to the engineering feat that these robots represent.[17] Other studies discuss strategies to increase the robots' efficiency through expansions in self-driving technology.[18] With the exception of very few studies, most scholarship tends to ignore the ramifications of these technologies on the future of labor. Even in those cases, the essays tend to focus on automation generally while ignoring the geopolitical ramifications of the company's business model on Latin American workers.[19]

The discussions undertaken in this book push us to consider the biopolitical suppositions that undergird this and other technologies. My discussion of Alex Rivera's *Sleep Dealer* in Chapter 3, for example, calls to mind numerous uncanny similarities between KiwiBot and the fictional corporation Del Rio Water. It would certainly be a stretch to claim that KiwiBot shares the necroliberal vision depicted in Rivera's film. The company does not drain its workers of their life force or protect its investments with a program similar to *Drones!* That said, KiwiBot unquestionably integrates Colombia's relatively lax labor laws into its business model. Furthermore, US consumers still acquire cheap foreign labor while the workers themselves remain abroad. The company's cost of operations in the United States remains competitive precisely because the cost of wages remains artificially depressed as workers from a low-wage country—mostly college students who earn less than $2 USD per hour—provide cheap services remotely to some of the most expensive metropolitan centers in the world.[20] These conditions necessarily bring biopolitical distinctions to the fore as they justify low compensation for workers in one geographical space to provide goods to consumers in another, more expensive part of the world through virtual and robotic technologies. Far from liberatory, technology provides new tools through which privileged parts of the world can profit off the backs of underpaid workers from the Global South. Clearly, scholars must take into consideration the unbalanced relationship between North and South as they theorize and discuss the advent of new technologies.

At its core, this book has sought to interrogate human relations as mediated through modern technology. While I have highlighted some cases where the book's methodology sheds light on real-world cases of technological expansion, *Robo Sacer* has primarily centered on representations of technology in dystopian literary and cultural production from Mexican and Chicanx creators. The fictions that I have discussed focus primarily on how the conflation of technology with the ne(cr)oliberal economy has produced an array of markets of death. That said, the cases where oppressors deliberately kill for the sake of killing prove quite rare; rather, they exploit and drain bodies for their own economic gain. Many of the most common divisions of people and bodies in these fictions occur as technology exacerbates biopolitical divisions in national and transnational contexts that allow the most privileged sectors of society to consume the labor, and thus the life force, of racial, ethnic, and gender Others. *Robo Sacer* thus provides a useful vantagepoint from which to view major economic shifts throughout Latin America by forcing us to always consider the socioeconomic dynamics that exist within the region and throughout the Western Hemisphere. Beyond providing valuable tools for diagnosing the causes of the problem— unequal access to resources being central among them—the robo-sacer lens also suggests a means through which oppressed individuals can resist. This book has highlighted the deep relationship between literature and politics by emphasizing how these two fields intersect one with another.

Of course, in focusing solely on dystopian works that are critical of NAFTA, *Robo Sacer* has, almost by definition, engaged texts that communicate a left-of-center perspective. As such, this book's treatment of robo-sacer resistance, similar to Donna Haraway's theorization of a resistant cyborg, may overestimate the liberatory potential of robo-sacer resistance while downplaying the potential for oppressive forces to appropriate cyborg discourse in ways that buoy the necroliberal status quo. An array of popular texts and films from both the United States and Mexico has emerged in recent years that uses cyborg imageries to appropriate progressive discourses toward reactionary ends. Many of these fictions employ a type of right-wing, dystopian robo-sacer discourse. In these works, protagonists from traditionally privileged communities find themselves relegated to *zoē* and even *homo sacer* status while people from traditionally marginalized communities find themselves suddenly in the role of oppressor. These recent fictions, most of them cinema, tend to frame demographic and cultural change as nefarious processes that strip traditional powerholders, often deliberately, of any sort of political voice. In this way, they reverberate with John Rieder's observation that SF from the colonial center tends to imagine cases where traditional colonizers find themselves at the mercy of new, imperializing threats.[21] Right-wing robo-sacer discourses tend to be especially explicit in identifying immigrants and other marginalized actors as threats to a democratic order. Under such conditions, SF and dystopian fiction tend to lose their liberatory potential and instead buoy those discourses that would justify further violence against marginal groups.

### RIGHT-WING BIOPOLITICS AND THE LIMITS OF ROBO-SACER DISCOURSE: FRANCISCO LARESGOITI'S *2033* AND PIERRE MOREL'S *PEPPERMINT*

The idea that privileged sectors of society could employ the means and tools of robo-sacer resistance—both technological and, crucially, discursive—is not particularly new. Ever since the election of Donald Trump in 2016, progressives and scholars have come to recognize the role of internet in political movements from both the Left and the Right. Jen Schradie, for example, argues that online movements favor conservatives in numerous ways: "not only is technology failing to erase the barriers toward organizing movements, it may be making things worse by creating a digital activism gap. Rather than offering a quick technological fix to repair our broken democracy, the advent of digital activism has simply ended up reproducing, and in some cases intensifying, preexisting power imbalances."[22] In many cases, right-wing digital activists have used online tools to mimic robo-sacer discourse, calling attention to specific grievances in an attempt to paint themselves as the true victims of an increasingly diverse society.

As they depict themselves as the victims of a shifting cultural landscape, politicians from the Right gain cultural currency with their voters while at the same time defanging the discourse of their progressive opponents regarding structural inequality. Such political strategies often neutralize progressive voices and pave the way for conservative candidates to achieve electoral victory. Indeed, one could argue that conservative politics in the United States has come to use digital media to react against progressive ideas, including those surrounding immigrant rights, that have gained cultural currency through online activism.[23] Less research exists on the Mexican case, but the proliferation of anti-progressive discourse, particularly as it relates to immigrant rights and marriage equality, would suggest that the same holds true there.[24] The rise of conservative social media has, in many instances, challenged the gains of robo-sacer activists in the real world. Future research needs to gauge the interrelationship between conservative and progressive media from an array of national contexts. At the moment, most of the attention remains focused on popular movements like #YoSoy132, #NiUnaMás, #BlackLivesMatter, #MeToo, and so forth. Such a bias among scholars toward progressive causes systematically ignores the significant presence and successes of online, conservative activists throughout the world.

Given the presence of anti-progressive forces online in both Mexico and the United States, it should come as no surprise that a great deal of literary and cultural production also appropriates different elements of robo-sacer subjectivity and resistance toward reactionary ends. We thus cannot assume that cyborg imageries automatically become resistant when they juxtapose colonized and/or third-world bodies with technology. One especially salient example of a film that employs a right-wing robo-sacer discourse is Pierre Morel's (2018) *Peppermint*, a film that centers on Riley North (Jennifer Garner), a lower-middle-class white woman from California. This wife and mother loses both her husband and daughter in a drive-by shooting perpetrated by the fictional García Cartel while the family buys peppermint ice-cream at a Christmas carnival. Overcome by grief, Riley trains for five years before returning to downtown Los Angeles to wage a one-woman war on the Mexican and Chicano killers who murdered her family.[25] At first glance, the film exhibits many of the characteristics that appear throughout the dystopian texts I have described in this book. The illicit drug trade has created a necroliberal market that casts people—particularly working-class whites like Riley and her family—as expendable. At first, the grieving mother naïvely trusts the justice system to identify and punish the shooters who killed her family. Her idyllic faith in the system disappears, however, when she comes up against the cartel's army of crooked attorneys, bought-off judges, and dirty cops who work overtime to keep the murderers out of prison. At one point, a lawyer enters her home and tries to bribe her to stay off the witness stand during the trial. She refuses, but her testimony fails to secure a conviction because García has bought off the judge.

Faced with a biopolitical context that favors the rich—transnational, Mexican drug traffickers in this case—over supposedly honest, hardworking, and explicitly white individuals like herself, Riley ultimately engages in an array of robo-sacer activities to avenge the deaths of her family. Similar to Huck in *Cómprame un revólver*, she acquires big guns that she uses to kill the gangsters that plague Los Angeles. Her firearms become a literal prosthesis of citizenship as she uses them to tear down the alliance between the García Cartel and the California law enforcement apparatus that has silenced her voice and made it impossible for her to receive justice for her family. Similar to the protagonists in "Ruido gris" and *Smoking Mirror Blues*, she becomes famous on social media after she kills corrupt judges, crooked cops, and narcos. Like Lydia in *Lunar Braceros*, Riley uses different types of technology, particularly social media and her cellphone, to contact influential reporters. She uses these media to publicly tell her story and explain her motives for killing each of her victims. As such, both she and her supporters come to interpellate her kills into an Agambian "life that does not deserve to live."[26] Because these criminals have used their corrupt control of the system to terrorize the "good" inhabitants of the city, they must be purged. Unlike the works discussed previously in this book, however, *Peppermint* does not advocate for the rights of marginalized communities, particularly those of Mexican and Latin American descent. Rather, the film aims to uplift a supposedly threatened US society against the encroachment of "dangerous" Mexican immigrants, all of whom are apparently violent narcos whose dirty money has given them unparalleled influence in the country.[27] Far from advocating for social justice, the film conflates Mexican and Chicanx identity with criminality. The very presence of these foreign (and foreignized) bodies in the country creates a state of exception that "good," gun-wielding vigilantes like Riley must confront, even if the government and law enforcement refuse to do so.

Throughout the film, the only Spanish-language dialogue occurs in scenes where drug kingpins worship the infamous narco saint La Santa

Muerte (Holy Death / Saint of Death), or when criminals converse among themselves, ostensibly unintelligibly to the audience, as they plan and carry out acts of violence against Riley and other characters.[28] Clearly, the film posits Mexican and Chicanx communities as an un-American threat that must be violently contained, or even expelled, from the country. *Peppermint* lacks originality—indeed, it essentially retells the story of Marvel's *Punisher* from the perspective of a woman—but it embodies a neoliberal cinema built to turn a profit.[29] It earned US$35 million against US$25 million in production costs.[30] Given the financial conditions under which it was produced, the film had to cater to a relatively niche audience that was mostly white and conservative, or at least apprehensive about supposed increases in migration across the US-Mexico border.[31] The anti-Mexican and anti-Chicanx discourse was thus part and parcel of the movie's marketing strategy. In emphasizing this dynamic, the film ensured enough attendance at the box office to overcome the initial production costs. The film's regressive politics were thus a necessary component of the film's overall success. In showing a white woman violently resist an imagined necroliberal world that consumes white bodies while uplifting Mexican and Chicanx criminals, the film participates in contemporary attempts to criminalize Latinx bodies in the United States.

Similar to films released in the United States, Mexican commercial cinema tends to promulgate the overriding politics of its principal paying audiences. Ignacio M. Sánchez Prado asserts that, in recent years, a neoliberal production model has forced filmmakers in the country to cater their movies to the upper-middle-class audiences who can afford to go to the movie theater.[32] As such, Mexican commercial cinema tends to reflect bourgeois values that would meet the prospect of robo-sacer resistance—particularly one that challenges current social hierarchies—with skepticism. This is not to say that these films do not engage with biopolitical, necropolitical, or necroliberal ideas. Rather, similar to their US counterparts, such Mexican films tend to employ these concepts in ways that support a reactionary politics. They generally do this by appropriating the discourses of the Left while at the same time subordinating them to a conservative agenda.

We see this in Francisco Laresgoiti's problematic *2033*, which tells of a dystopian, future Mexico City where a violently irreligious state has produced drugs that make people, particularly those who are religious, look like big-game animals. Members of the governing class consume these substances and then hunt believers for sport, often from helicopters. The film's cinematography heavy-handedly asserts that state power relegates religious people to *zoë* and *homo sacer* status. At the same time, it also posits faith as the only means to overcome the dehumanizing aims of a hypermodern, dystopian nation-state. Throughout the film, only people of faith recognize that the state-fabricated drug Tecpanol converts people into "robots" who blissfully go about their lives carrying out more and more work for the necroliberal interests of the dictatorial regime. The film employs a reading of the Cristero War (1926–1929) that absolves the Catholic Church, and particularly local Mexican clergy, of the significant blame they shouldered for the conflict.[33] In so doing, it communicates a right-wing biopolitics that charges secularists with depriving people of faith, and by extension the nation at large, of their human rights. This position does not stand up to scrutiny, especially when we consider the privileges enjoyed by Christians and particularly Catholics throughout the country. Nevertheless, 2033 uses a visceral straw-man argument to suggest that those who support a secular state also support the systemic murder of people of faith. In so doing, it makes its political commentary by tapping into the anger of Catholic and religious Mexicans, many of whom perceive a decrease in their own privilege—real or not—in a rapidly secularizing and de-Catholicizing country.[34] The film thus employs biopolitical discourses to decry alleged slights against people of faith in a way that aims to frustrate progressive causes like greater secularization within the government.

My brief discussions of both *Peppermint* and *2033* would seem to suggest that robo-sacer resistance is nothing more than an overly optimistic, fanciful ideal. The most pessimistic of us may determine that robo-sacer resistance does little more than provide tools that traditionalist forces can appropriate to their own counterrevolutionary ends. Such a dismissal of the potential for robo-sacer resistance ignores the fact that these reactionary fictions ultimately mimic the liberatory discourses of the oppressed and, crucially, not the other way around. Even when they produce reactionary discourse, such films necessarily underscore the ways cyborg subjectivities can and do interface with the biopolitical status quo. *Peppermint* and *2033* temper an overly optimistic approach to robo-sacer resistance, but they cannot obscure the fact that third-world and marginalized cyborg figures can and do denaturalize internalized hierarchies of power. The very fact that these films react against the progressive potential of robo-sacer discourse testifies to the value of cyborg resistance in overcoming the necroliberal status quo.

Achille Mbembe provides some clues as to why the robo-sacer lens remains a potent discursive tool even in light of those who would appropriate it to oppressive ends. Speaking specifically about Afrofuturism, he asserts that subaltern SF provides strategies for a radicalization of our understanding of humanism by providing a means to transcend the master/

slave dichotomy.[35] The Chicanxfuturist and Mexican speculative fictions discussed throughout *Robo Sacer* do something similar as they articulate Mexican and Chicanx subjectivity beyond a colonialist relationship with the United States and push it into a more authentic realm. Indeed, this book has centered on the generically impure nature of Chicanx and Mexican speculative fictions. While the fictions discussed throughout clearly dialogue with SF, most of them also branch into genres and modes like horror, magical realism, and the Gothic in ways that trouble the demand for pure genre boundaries that abound throughout the North American academy. This impurity sits at the heart of these fictions' resistant potential. As they redefine genres like SF, they open new means to imagine an autochthonous future. The different chapters of this book have highlighted cases where the intersection of SF with other genres has proven key to an individual work's interpretation and to its treatment of the relationship between oppression and resistance. Clearly, scholars of Latin American literary studies would do well to interrogate the interplay among SF and other fantastic genres within the region's literary and cultural production. Such studies will help to identify strategies for denaturalizing racist and colonialist mentalities that continue to haunt contemporary Chicanx, Mexican, and Latin American society. It would be especially valuable to employ the robo-sacer lens from a comparative approach that moves beyond the Latin American context. Such studies would foreground the analytical advantages of the robo-sacer lens by highlighting strategies that progressive voices continue to employ in their quest for greater social justice throughout the world.

The Global North's technological domination of the Global South remains a defining characteristic of the contemporary digital divide and the ensuing necroliberal order. Under these circumstances, many people may feel inclined to disconnect completely from the internet and other increasingly automated modes of production. Nevertheless, such strategies, while tempting, tend to provide nothing more than individualist opportunities to extract oneself, successfully or not, from a mechanized system of domination. As such, they fail to engage the causes of dehumanization in Greater Mexico (and beyond) at their root. Rather than suggest that people simply avoid technology and disconnect from the internet, *Robo Sacer* celebrates the potential for marginalized people—particularly those of Greater Mexico—to use technology in subversive ways to advocate for their own political interests. In the coming years, the role of technology in the production, distribution, and consumption of goods on both sides of the US-Mexico border will only expand. As such, Mexican and Chicanx critiques of the necroliberal order will continue to interrogate the interface of the body with different technologies of production. In this way, Greater-Mexican dystopian fictions will continue to call out the biopolitical assumptions that have enabled a dehumanizing, necroliberal world while at the same time imagining ways to create a more just society.

# Notes

**INTRODUCTION**

1. Tucker Carlson, *Tucker Carlson Tonight*, Fox News, March 23, 2020. Posted to YouTube by Dadakoglu on March 23, 2020, https://www.youtube.com/watch?v=g78VheRUHpY.
2. Walter Benjamin, "On the Concept of History," trans. Dennis Redmond, 2005, Marxists Internet Archive, accessed April 20, 2021, https://www.marxists.org/reference/archive/benjamin/1940/history.htm; Giorgio Agamben, *State of Exception*, trans. Daniel Heller Roazen (Redwood City, CA: Stanford University Press, 2005), 1–6.
3. A number of lawsuits were filed throughout the United States regarding the dangerous conditions that meatpackers faced. See, for example, *Alma v. Noah's Ark*, 4:20-cv-03141, (Lincoln, Neb., 2020), https://www.aclu.org/legal-document/complaint-alma-v-noahs-ark; *Jane Does I, II, III and Friends of Farmworkers, Inc. D/B/A Justice at Work in its Capacity as Employee Representative v. Eugene Scalia, in His Official Capacity as United States Secretary of Labor; Occupational Safety and Health Administration, United States Department of Labor*, 1:02-at-06000-UN (Middle District of Pennsylvannia, 2020), https://www.documentcloud.org/documents/7000971-Doe-v-OSHA.html.
4. Jazmyn T. Moore et al., "Disparities in Incidence of COVID-19 among Underrepresented Racial/Ethnic Groups in Counties Identified as Hotspots during June 5–18, 2020—22 States, February–June 2020," *Morbidity and Mortality Weekly Report* 69, no. 33 (2020): 1123.
5. "Executive Order 13917 of April 28, 2020, Delegating Authority under the Defense Production Act with Respect to Food Supply Chain Resources during the National Emergency Caused by the Outbreak of COVID-19," *Federal Register: The Daily Journal of the United States Government*, April 28, 2020, https://

www.federalregister.gov/documents/2020/05/01/2020-09536/delegating-authority-under-the-defense-production-act-with-respect-to-food-supply-chain-resources.

6. Meatpacking remains an exceptional industry with the Biden administration. As of this writing, the Center for Disease Control continues to allow potentially infected workers to continue laboring in person. See "Meat and Poultry Processors: Interim Guidance from CDC and Occupational Safety and Health Administration," Center for Disease Control (CDC), Feb. 6, 2021. https://www.cdc.gov/coronavirus/2019-ncov/community/organizations/meat-poultry-processing-workers-employers.html.

7. Ryan J. Folely, "Fired Boss at Tyson Iowa Pork Plant says COVID-19 Betting Pool was a 'Morale Boost,'" *USA Today*, Dec. 9, 2020, https://www.usatoday.com/story/news/nation/2020/12/29/fired-waterloo-tyson-manager-says-covid-19-bet-morale-boost/4070995001.

8. Georgeanne M. Artz, "Immigration and Meatpacking in the Midwest," *Choices: The Magazine of Food, Farm, and Resource Issues* 27 no. 2 (2012), https://www.choicesmagazine.org/choices-magazine/theme-articles/immigration-and-agriculture/immigration-and-meatpacking-in-the-midwest-; William H. Frey, *Diversity Explosion: How New Racial Demographics are Remaking America* (Washington, DC: Brookings Institution Press, 2018), 55; Jessica Leibler et al., "*Staphylococcus aureus*: Nasal Carriage among Beefpacking Workers in a Midwestern United States Slaughterhouse," *PLOS One* 11, no. 2 (2016): 4.

9. See Héctor Amaya, *Citizenship Excess: Latinas/os, Media, and the Nation* (New York: New York University Press, 2013), 2.

10. See Michel Foucault, "The Birth of Biopolitics," in *The Essential Foucault*, ed. Paul Rabinow and Nikolas Rose (New York: The New Press, 2003), 202–7.

11. Michel Foucault, *The History of Sexuality*, vol. 1, *An Introduction*, trans. Robert Hurley (New York: Pantheon Books, 1990), 141.

12. See Giorgio Agamben, *Homo Sacer: Sovereign Power and Bare Life*, trans. Daniel Heller-Roazen (Redwood City, CA: Stanford University Press, 1998), 136–43.

13. Agamben, *Homo Sacer*, 80–83.

14. Agamben, *State of Exception*, 1.

15. Agamben, *Homo Sacer*, 12.

16. David S. Dalton and Douglas J. Weatherford, introduction to *Healthcare in Latin America: History, Society, Culture*, eds. David S. Dalton and Douglas J. Weatherford (Gainesville: University of Florida Press, 2022), 1–3.

17. Unless otherwise indicated, all translations are mine. "'El riesgo de coronavirus solo es para los ricos. Los pobres somos inmunes': Las polémicas declaraciones del gobernador del Estado mexicano de Puebla sobre el Covid-19 han tenido como efecto que la prensa local investigue su patrimonio," *La Razón* (Monterrey, NL), Mar. 27, 2020, https://www.larazon.es/internacional/20200327/lu44xqevwjekvme6sio4qhrooi.html.

18. Shashank Bengali, Kate Linthicum, and Victoria Kim, "Los ricos infectaron a los pobres al propagar el coronavirus por el mundo," *Chicago Tribune*, May 12, 2020, https://www.chicagotribune.com/espanol/sns-es-ricos-infectan-pobres-propagan-coronavirus-mundo-20200512-n44ud2ivczclnhyphf3skt2gdq-story.html; Emily Green, "How Mexico is Coping with a Coronavirus Outbreak Partially Imported from Vail, Colorado," *Colorado Public Radio News*, Apr. 2, 2020, https://www.cpr.org/2020/04/01/how-mexico-is-coping-with-a-coronavirus-outbreak-partially-imported-from-vail-colorado.
19. See Brian Hanrahan and Paulina Aroch Fugellie, "Reflections on the Transformation in Mexico," *Journal of Latin American Cultural Studies* 28, no. 1 (2019), 113–37.
20. At the time of this writing, Worldometer (2021) ranks Mexico fourteenth worldwide in overall cases of COVID-19 and third in the Western Hemisphere behind the United States and Brazil. See "COVID-19 Coronavirus Pandemic," Worldometer, 2021, accessed April 20, 2021, https://www.worldometers.info/coronavirus.
21. While numbers tying social class to voting practices in Mexico are difficult to find, it appears that López Obrador won strong majorities among people who termed the economy or poverty as their primary issues. See Roderic Ai Camp and Shannan L. Mattiace, *Politics in Mexico: The Path of a New Democracy*, 7th ed. (Oxford: Oxford University Press, 2020), 265.
22. See Marissa K. López, *Racial Immanence: Chicanx Bodies beyond Representation* (New York: New York University Press, 2019), 7.
23. Amy Sara Carroll, *REMEX: Toward an Art History of the NAFTA Era* (Austin: University of Texas Press, 2017), 7–8.
24. For a discussion of early- to mid-twentieth-century tensions between Mexican and Mexican American / Chicano populations, see Octavio Paz, *El laberinto de la soledad. Postdata. Vuelta a El laberinto de la soledad* (Mexico City: FCE, 2004), "El pachuco y otros extremos"; Rodolfo F. Acuña *Anything but Mexican: Chicanos in Contemporary Los Angeles*, 2nd ed. (New York: Verso, 2020), x.

    For discussions of more recent frictions between these communities see Mariángela Rodríguez, *Tradición, identidad, mito y metáfora: Mexicanos y chicanos en California* (Mexico City: Centro de Investigaciones y Estudios Superiores en Antropología Social, 2005), 16–17; Carlos G. Vélez-Ibáñez, prologue to *Tradición, identidad, mito y metáfora: Mexicanos y chicanos en California*, by Mariángela Rodríguez (Mexico City: Centro de Investigaciones y Estudios Superiores en Antropología Social), 6–7.
25. Patricia H. Hamm, "How México Built Support for the Negotiation of the North American Free Trade Agreement: Targeting Mexican Diaspora in the United States" (PhD diss., University of California, Irvine, 2001), 109–233.
26. M. López, *Racial Immanence*, 7. For a discussion of the term *ethnoracial*, see Linda Martin Alcoff, "Is Latina/o Identity a Racial Identity?," in *Hispanics/Latinos in the United States*, ed. Jorge J. E. Gracia and Pablo De Grieff (New

York: Routledge, 2000), 42; Jorge Duany, "Puerto Rican, Hispanic, or Latino? Recent Debates on National and Pan-Ethnic Identities," *Centro Journal* 15, no. 2 (2003): 266; Patricia Silver, *Sunbelt Diaspora: Race, Class, and Latino Politics in Puerto Rican Orlando*, (Austin: University of Texas Press, 2020), 12; Silvio Torres-Saillant, "Inventing the Race: Latinos and the Ethnoracial Pentagon," *Latino Studies* 1, no. 1 (2003): 147.

27. Some critics go as far as referring to Chicanx populations as an "internal colony" of the United States. Tomás Almaguer, "Historical Notes on Chicano Oppression: The Dialectics of Racial and Class Domination in North América," in *The Aztlán Mexican Studies Reader, 1974–2016*, ed. Héctor Calderón (Los Angeles: UCLA Chicano Studies Research Center Press, 2018), 52–55.

28. While distinct from one another, the terms *Chicano*, *Chicana*, and *Chicanx* generally refer to people born in the United States to parents of Mexican descent. Of course, like any generalized definition for a term, this one has its shortcomings. Many people who arrive in the United States at a young age after being born in Mexico, for example, may identify with the label. The Chicano science-fiction author Ernest Hogan—whom I discuss in greater depth in Chapter 2—has only one parent of Mexican descent.

29. For a history of internal divisions among Mexican American and Chicanx populations in the United States, see Ramón A. Gutiérrez, "Unraveling America's Hispanic Past: Internal Stratification and Class Boundaries," in *The Chicano Studies Reader*, ed. Chon A. Noriega et al. (Los Angeles: UCLA Chicano Studies Research Center Press, 2016), 345–54.

30. Cristóbal Salinas Jr. and Adele Lozano, "Mapping and Recontextualizing the Evolution of the Term *Latinx*: An Environmental Scanning in Higher Education," *Journal of Latinos and Education* 18, no. 4 (2019): 302.

31. Nicole Trujillo-Pagán, "Crossed Out by LatinX: Gender Neutrality and Genderblind Sexism." *Latino Studies* 16, no. 3 (2018): 399. See also Gilbert Guerra and Gilbert Orbea, "The Argument against the Use of the Term 'Latinx,'" *Phoenix* (Swarthmore, PA), Nov. 19, 2015. https://swarthmorephoenix.com/author/gilberts1.

32. Claudia Milian, *LatinX*, (Minneapolis: University of Minnesota Press, 2019), 2; María Scharrón-del Río and Alan A. Aja, "*Latinx*: Inclusive Language as Liberation Praxis," *Journal of Latinx Psychology* 8, no. 1 (2020): 8–10; Juan Velasco, "The X in Race and Gender: Rethinking Chicano/a Cultural Production through the Paradigms of Xicanisma and Me(x)icanness," in *The Chicana/o Cultural Studies Reader*, ed. Angie Chabram-Dernersesian (New York: Routledge, 2006), 204–8.

33. Walter Benn Michaels, *The Beauty of a Social Problem: Photography, Autonomy, Economy* (Chicago: University of Chicago Press, 2015), 63; see also Jodi Melamed, *Represent and Destroy: Rationalizing Violence in the New Racial Capitalism*, (Minneapolis: University of Minnesota Press, 2011), xvii.

34. M. López, *Racial Immanence*, 4.

35. For discussions of race as a socioeconomic process that uses phenotype to assign a person their role in the economy, see Michael Omi and Howard Winant, *Racial Formation in the United States: From the 1960s to the 1990s*, 2nd ed. (New York: Routledge, 1994), 1–5; Vijay Prashad, *Everybody Was Kung Fu Fighting: Afro-Asian Connections and the Myth of Cultural Purity* (Boston, MA: Beacon Press, 2001), chapter 1.
36. M. López, *Racial Immanence*, 7; Lysa Rivera, "Future Histories and Cyborg Labor: Reading Borderlands Science Fiction after NAFTA," *Science Fiction Studies* 39, no. 3 (2012).
37. Lysa Rivera, "Chicana/o Cyberpunk after el Movimiento," *Aztlán: A Journal of Chicano Studies* 40, no. 2 (2015): 190.
38. Gloria Anzáldúa, *Borderlands / La frontera: The New Mestiza*, 3rd ed. (San Francisco: Aunt Lute, 2007), chapter 4. See also Norma Alarcón, "Chicana Femenism: In the Tracks of 'the' Native Woman," in Chabram-Dernersesian, *The Chicana/o Studies Reader*, 185–87; Catherine Ramírez, "Cyborg Femenism: The Science Fiction of Octavia E. Butler and Gloria Anzaldúa," in *Reload: Rethinking Women + Cyberculture*, edited by Mary Flanagan and Austin Booth (Cambridge: Massachusetts Institute of Technology Press, 2002), 391.

    Notions of robo-sacer resistance invoke Estelle Tarica's (2014) notion of "countervictimization," or the act of contesting dehumanizing biopolitical discourses that blame victims for their plights. See Estelle Tarica, "La biopolítica en contra de sí: Víctimas y contravíctimas en el México contemporáneo," in *Heridas abiertas: Biopolítica y representación en América Latina*, eds. Mabel Moraña and Ignacio M. Sánchez Prado (Madrid: Iberoamericana, 2014), 204–5.
39. Rebecca Janzen, *The National Body in Mexican Literature: Collective Challenges to Biopolitical Control* (New York: Palgrave MacMillan, 2015), 7–8; Mabel Moraña, "Introducción: *Heridas abiertas*," in Moraña and Sánchez Prado, *Heridas abiertas*, 8.
40. José Manuel Valenzuela Arce, "El *cruising* de la muerte. Biocultura: Biopíticas, biorresistencias y bioproxemias," in Moraña and Sánchez Prado, *Heridas abiertas*, 170.
41. Ignacio M. Sánchez Prado, "Máquinas de precarización: Afectos y violencias de la cultura neoliberal," in *Precariedades, exclusiones y emergencias*, eds. Mabel Moraña and José Manuel Valenzuela Arce (Mexico City: Universidad Autónoma Metropolitana), 104–5. See also Antar Martínez-Guzmán, "Masculine Subjectivities and Necropolitics: Precarization and Violence at the Mexican Margins," *Subjectivity* 12, no. 4 (Dec. 2019): 288–308; Mabel Moraña, "Escasez y modernidad," in Moraña and Valenzuela Arce, *Precariedades, exclusiones y emergencias*, 25.
42. Wendy Brown, *Undoing the Demos: Neoliberalism's Stealth Revolution* (New York: Zone, 2015), 33–34; see also Rosana Reguillo, "La turbulencia en el paisaje: De jóvenes, necropolítica y 43 esperanzas," in *Juvenicidio: Aytotzinapa y las vidas precarias en América Latina y España*, ed. José Manuel Valenzuela

Arce (Barcelona: Ned Ediciones, 2015), 65; Rosana Reguillo, "Precariedad(es): Necropolítica y máquinas de guerra," in Moraña and Valenzuela Arce, *Precariedades, exclusiones y emergencias*, 53–55.
43. Judith Butler, *Precarious Life: The Powers of Mourning and Violence* (New York: Verso, 2006), 37–38.
44. M. López, *Racial Immanence*, 2.
45. Sergio González Rodríguez, *The Femicide Machine*, trans. Michael Parker-Stainback (Los Angeles: Semiotext(e), 2012), 26–39.
46. Manuel Castells, *The Information Age: Economy, Society and Culture*, vol. 1, *The Rise of the Network Society*, 2nd ed. (Malden, MA: Blackwell Press, 2000), 375–406.
47. Joseba Gabilondo, "Postcolonial Cyborgs: Subjectivity in the Age of Cybernetic Reproduction," in *The Cyborg Handbook*, eds. Chris Hables Gray, Heidi J. Figueroa-Sarriera, and Steven Mentor (New York: Routledge, 1995), 424.
48. For a discussion of how marginalized people of Latin American descent throughout the world have used technology to advocate for themselves and build community, see David S. Dalton and David Ramírez Plascencia, "Introduction: Imagining Latinidad in Digital Diasporas," in Dalton and Ramírez Plascencia, *Imagining Latinidad: Digital Diasporas and Public Engagement among Latin American Migrants* (Leiden, Netherlands: Brill, 2023), 9–11. Certainly, a digital divide remains in effect that disproportionately excludes both Mexican and Chicanx individuals from global online discourse. See Jen Schradie, *The Revolution that Wasn't: How Digital Activism Favors Conservatives* (Cambridge, MA: Harvard University Press, 2019), 15–16, 271–72.
49. My definition of what constitutes a cyborg builds on the argument of Chris Hables Gray, who states that "a cyborg is a self-regulating organism that combines the natural and artificial together in one system. [. . .] If you have been technologically modified in any significant way, from an implanted pacemaker to a vaccination that reprogrammed your immune system, then you are definitely a cyborg." See Chris Hables Gray, *Cyborg Citizen: Politics in the Posthuman Age* (New York: Routledge, 2001), 1–6.
50. David S. Dalton, *Mestizo Modernity: Race, Technology, and the Body in Postrevolutionary Mexico* (Gainesville: University of Florida Press, 2018), 16.
51. Donna Haraway, *Simians, Cyborgs and Women: The Reinvention of Nature* (London: Free Association of Books, 1991), 153. Certainly, Haraway's (1991) writings are frequently problematic as they relate to nonwhite and third-world actors. See J. Andrew Brown, "El oficio del *cyborg*: Nuevas direcciones para una identidad poshumana en América Latina," in Moraña and Sánchez Prado, *Heridas abiertas*, 247–50. *Robo Sacer* aims to build on Haraway's thought while at the same time focusing on how the conceptualization of cyborg being (and resistance) changes in the Mexican and Chicanx contexts.
52. Dalton, *Mestizo Modernity*, 21–27; Haraway, *Simians, Cyborgs and Women*, 169.
53. Jennifer González, "Envisioning Cyborg Bodies: Notes from the Research," in

Gray, Figueroa-Sarriera, and Mentor, *The Cyborg Handbook*; Haraway, *Simians, Cyborgs and Women*, chapters 8 and 9; N. Katherine Hayles, *How We Became Posthuman: Virtual Bodies in Cybernetics, Literature, and Informatics*, (Chicago: University of Chicago Press, 1999); Teresa López-Pellisa, *Patologías de la realidad virtual: Cibercultura y ciencia ficción*, (Madrid: FCE, 2015), 192–242; Chela Sandoval, *Methodology of the Oppressed* (Minneapolis: University of Minnesota Press, 2000).

54. Haraway, *Simians, Cyborgs and Women*, 186.
55. For a discussion of *bios* as the Aristotelean good life, see Agamben, *Homo Sacer*, 1–3. The exact nature of the subaltern's access to discourse remains a point of contention within subaltern studies.
56. David S. Dalton, "Exploiting Liminal Legality: Inclusive Citizenship Models in the Online Discourse of United We Dream," in Dalton and Ramírez Plascencia, *Imagining Latinidad*; Cecilia Menjívar, "Liminal Legality: Salvadoran and Guatemalan Immigrants' Lives in the United States," *American Journal of Sociology* 111, no. 4 (2006); Lindsay Pérez Huber, "Constructing 'Deservingness': DREAMers and Central American Unaccompanied Children in the National Immigration Debate," *Association of Mexican American Educators Journal* 9, no. 3 (2015): 26–27.
57. R. Andrés Guzmán, *Universal Citizenship: Latina/o Studies at the Limits of Identity* (Austin: University of Texas Press, 2019), 7.
58. Amaya, *Citizenship Excess*, 16–18.
59. Sandoval, *Methodology of the Oppressed*, 168.
60. Catherine Ramírez, "Cyborg Femenism: The Science Fiction of Octavia E. Butler and Gloria Anzaldúa," in *Reload: Rethinking Women + Cyberculture*, eds. Mary Flanagan and Austin Booth (Cambridge: Massachusetts Institute of Technology Press, 2002), 375.
61. Sandoval, *Methodology of the Oppressed*, 167–70; C. Ramírez, "Cyborg Femenism," 383–88.
62. Gayatri Chakravorty Spivak, "Can the Subaltern Speak?," in *Marxism and the Interpretation of Culture*, eds. Lawrence Grossberg and Cary Nelson (Urbana: University of Illinois Press, 1988), 308. Certainly, we should note that many thinkers point out that Spivak's assertion of the subaltern's inability to speak only applies to political speaking; the subaltern can and do speak among themselves in ways that remain largely illegible to the state on a daily basis. See José Rabasa, *Without History: Subaltern Studies, the Zapatista Insurgency, and the Specter of History* (Pittsburgh, PA: University of Pittsburgh Press, 2010), 4.
63. Haraway, *Simians, Cyborgs and Women*, 163.
64. Rosi Braidotti, *The Posthuman*, (Malden, MA: Polity Press, 2013), 115.
65. Braidotti, *The Posthuman*, 116–20.
66. See Román de la Campa, "Teoría, literatura y tutela del error," in Moraña and Sánchez Prado, *Heridas abiertas*, 65–66.

67. Michael Hardt and Antonio Negri, *Empire* (Cambridge, MA: Harvard University Press, 2000), 218.
68. Eden Medina, Ivan da Costa Marques, and Christina Holmes. "Introduction: Beyond Imported Magic," in *Beyond Imported Magic: Essays on Science, Technology, and Society in Latin America*, eds. Eden Medina, Ivan da Costa Marques, and Christina Holmes (Cambridge: Massachusetts Institute of Technology Press, 2014), 1–3; Ivan da Costa Marques, "Cloning Computers: From Rights of Possession to Rights of Creation," *Science as Culture* 14, no. 2 (2003).
69. At its core, the term Global South refers to those people living in poor nations to the south of North America and Western Europe. Certainly, the idea of the South as a single monolithic whole is emblematic of the fact that it has been largely defined by the North. See Roxanne Lynn Doty, *Imperial Encounters: The Politics of Representation in North-South Relations* (Minneapolis: University of Minnesota Press, 1996), 1–14.
70. Néstor García Canclini, *Latinoamericanos buscando lugar en este siglo* (Buenos Aires: Paidós, 2002), 80. For discussions on how Latin American actors can domesticize foreign technologies, see Hilda Chacón, introduction to *Online Activism in Latin America*, ed. Hilda Chacón (New York: Routledge, 2019), 6; Dalton and Ramírez Plascencia, eds., *Imagining Latinidad*; Medina, Marques, and Holmes, *Beyond Imported Magic*, 2; Sandoval, *Methodology of the Oppressed*, 176; Claire Taylor and Thea Pitman, *Latin American Identity in Online Cultural Production* (New York: Routledge, 2013), 11.
71. Giorgio Agamben, *The Open: Man and Animal*, trans. Kevin Attell (Redwood City, CA: Stanford University Press, 2004), 8; see also Ariadna Estévez, "Biopolítica y necropolítica: ¿Constitutivos u opuestos?" *Espiral: Estudios sobre Estado y Sociedad* 25, no. 73 (2018): 16.
72. Juan Manuel Valenzuela Arce and Mabel Moraña, "Vidas carenciadas, y resistencias sociales," in Moraña and Valenzuela Arce, *Precariedades, exclusiones y emergencias*, 16.
73. Ricardo Domínguez, "Digital Zapatismo," in *Info Wars: [Ars Electronica 98]*, eds. Gerfried Stocker and Christine Schöpf (Wien: Springer, 1998); see also Jill Lane, "Electronic Disturbance Theater: Timeline 1994-2004." *TDR: The Drama Review* 47, no. 2 (2003): 136–42.
74. Dorothy E. Denning, "Activism, Hacktivism, and Cyberterrorism: The Internet as a Tool for Influencing Foreign Policy," in *Networks and Netwars: The Future of Terror, Crime, and Militancy*, eds. John Arquilla and David Ronfeldt (Santa Monica: RAND Corporation, 2001), 265–66.
75. Jorge Alberto Lizama, "El poder de las redes sociales: Hacktivismo vs. páginas web del gobierno mexicano," in *La cultura del espectáculo y el escándalo: Los media en la sociedad actual*, ed. Nery Córdova (Mazatlán: Universidad Autónoma de Sinaloa, 2007), 9–13; Alexandra Whitney Samuel, "Hacktivism and the Future of Political Participation" (PhD diss., Harvard University, 2004).

76. Graham Meikle, "Electronic Civil Disobedience and Symbolic Power," in *Cyber Conflict and Global Politics*, eds. Athina Karatzogianni (New York: Routledge, 2010), 179–81; Joe Ashbrook Nickell, "Takin' It to the . . . Screen," *Wired*, June 6, 1998, https://www.wired.com/1998/06/takin-it-to-the-screen.
77. Gray, *Cyborg Citizen*, 44.
78. Gray, *Cyborg Citizen*, 44.
79. Pierre Bourdieu, *Acts of Resistance: Against the Tyranny of the Market*, trans. Richard Nice (New York: The New Press, 1998), 85, emphasis in original.
80. For a discussion on how the state of exception codes Latin American lives as bare and expendable, see Irmgard Emmelhainz, *La tiranía del sentido común: La reconversión neoliberal en México* (Mexico City: Paradiso Editores, 2016), 17; Walter Mignolo, *The Darker Side of Western Modernity: Global Futures, Decolonial Options* (Durham, NC: Duke University Press, 2011), 199.
81. For discussions of "gore capitalism," see Sayak Valencia, *Gore Capitalism*, trans. John Pluecker (South Pasadena, CA: Semiotext(e), 2018); for discussions on necropolitics, see Achille Mbembe, *Necropolitics*, trans. Steven Corcoran (Durham, NC: Duke University Press, 2019); for discussions on necropolitical capitalism see Franco "Bifo" Berardi, "Prólogo. Necro-capitalismo y sensibilidad," in *La tiranía del sentido común*, by Irmgard Emmelhainz, 9–13 (Mexico City: Paradiso Editores, 2016); for discussions of "necrocapitalism" see Subhabrata Bobby Banerjee, "Necrocapitalism," *Organization Studies* 29, no. 12 (2008); for discussions of "necropolitical neoliberal projects" see Valenzuela Arce and Moraña, "Vidas carenciadas," 15; see also Clara Valverde Gefaell, *De la necropolítica neoliberal, a la empatía radical: Violencia discreta, cuerpos excluidos y repolitización* (Madrid: Icaria, 2016).
82. See Estévez, "Biopolítica," 19–20; Horacio Legrás, "Biopolítica: Vicisitudes de una idea," in Moraña and Sánchez Prado, *Heridas abiertas*, 41–44.
83. Emmelhainz, *La tiranía del sentido común*, 16.
84. Mbembe, *Necropolitics*, 70.
85. Indeed, Agamben has faced some criticism among Latin Americanists who assert that he does not focus as much on coloniality as he should. See Sánchez Prado, "Prologo," in Moraña and Sánchez Prado, *Heridas abieras*, 25.
86. Estévez, "Biopolítica," 18; Marina Gržinić and Šefik Tatlić, *Necropolitics, Racialization, and Global Capitalism: Historicization of Biopolitics and Forensics of Politics, Art, and Life* (Lanham, MD: Lexington Books, 2014); Valverde Gefaell, *De la necropolítica*.
87. Mbembe, *Necropolitics*, 55; see also Estévez, "Biopolítica," 19–20.
88. Estévez, "Biopolítica"; Valencia, *Gore Capitalism*, 205–50. For a further discussion of necropolitics and migration in the Mexican context, see Amarela Varela Huerta, ed., *Necropolítica y migración en la frontera vertical mexicana: Un ejercicio de conocimiento situado* (Mexico City: UNAM, 2020).
89. Estévez, "Biopolítica," 19.
90. Valencia, *Gore Capitalism*, 211, emphasis mine.

91. Foucault, *The History of Sexuality*, 140; Mbembe, *Necropolitics*, 80; Bruno Bosteels, "De la violencia a la columa: Viejos y nuevos sujetos emergentes en México," in Moraña and Valenzuela Arce, *Precariedades, exclusiones y emergencias*, 80–81.
92. Agamben, *State of Exception*, 1–31; Mbembe, *Necropolitics*, 98–100.
93. For other excellent titles that interrogate the intersections of race and biopolitics see Gržinić and Tatlić, *Necropolitics, Racialization*; Ariadna Estévez, *Necropolitical Production and Management of Forced Migration* (Lanham, MD: Lexington Books, 2021).
94. Mbembe, *Necropolitics*, 38–39; see also Jean Franco, "Una historia que carece enteramente de historia," in Moraña and Sánchez Prado, *Heridas abiertas*.
95. Mbembe, *Necropolitics*, 177.
96. Haraway, *Simians, Cyborgs and Women*, 149–51.
97. See also Braidotti, *The Posthuman*, 115–42.
98. Valencia, *Gore Capitalism*, 206, emphasis in original.
99. Reguillo, "Precariedad(es)," 59–65.
100. Ángel Rama, *The Lettered City*, trans. John Charles Chasteen (Durham, NC: Duke University Press, 1996), 98–100.
101. Ariadna Estévez, *Human Rights and Free Trade in Mexico: A Discursive and Sociopolitical Perspective* (New York: Palgrave MacMillan, 2008), 34–50; Brian L. Price, *Cult of Defeat in Mexico's Historical Fiction: Failure, Trauma, and Loss* (New York: Palgrave MacMillan, 2012), 103; Peter Watt and Roberto Zepeda, *Drug War Mexico: Politics, Neoliberalism and Violence in the New Narcoeconomy* (London: Zed Books, 2012), 141–78.
102. Gareth Williams, *The Mexican Exception: Sovereignty, Police, and Democracy* (New York: Palgrave MacMillan, 2011), 11.
103. Williams, *The Mexican Exception*, 12.
104. Andreas Waldkirch, "The Effects of Foreign Direct Investment in Mexico since NAFTA," *World Economy* 33, no. 5 (2010).
105. Roberto Esposito, *Bíos: Biopolitics and Philosophy*, trans. Timothy Campbell (Minneapolis: University of Minnesota Press, 2008), 45–77. See Dalton, *Mestizo Modernity*, 100–107.
106. Peter H. Smith, *Talons of the Eagle: Latin America, the United States, and the World* (Oxford: Oxford University Press, 2008), 226.
107. Kevin R. Johnson, "Free Trade and Closed Borders: NAFTA and Mexican Immigration to the United States," *Immigration and Nationality Law Review*, no. 16 (1994): 940.
108. Josiah McC Heyman, "'Illegality' and the US-Mexico Border: How It Is Produced and Resisted," in *Constructing Immigrant "Illegality": Critiques, Experiences, and Responses*, ed. Cecilia Menjívar and Daniel Kanstroom (Cambridge: Cambridge University Press, 2013), 112–14.
109. Abraham Acosta, *Thresholds of Illiteracy: Theory, Latin America, and the Crisis of Resistance* (New York: Fordham University Press, 2014), 224–25.

110. Anjali Browning, "Corn, Tomatoes, and a Dead Dog: Mexican Agricultural Restructuring and Rural Responses to Declining Maize Production in Oaxaca, Mexico," *Mexican Studies/Estudios Mexicanos* 29, no. 1 (2013); Raúl E. Fernández and Gilbert G. González, *A Century of Chicano History: Empire, Nations and Migration* (New York: Routledge, 2012), xiv; Alyshia Gálvez, *Eating NAFTA: Trade, Food Policies, and the Destruction of Mexico* (Oakland: University of California Press, 2018), 159–72; Steven Zahniser and William Coyle, *US-Mexico Corn Trade During the NAFTA Era: New Twists on an Old Story*, US Department of Agriculture, Economic Research Service FDS-04D-01, May 2004), https://www.ers.usda.gov/webdocs/outlooks/36451/49338_fds04d01.pdf?v=374.2.
111. Justin Paulson, "Peasant Struggles and International Solidarity: The Case of Chiapas," *Socialist Register* 37 (2001): 278.
112. Valencia, *Gore Capitalism*, 70–75.
113. Miguel López-Lozano, *Utopian Dreams, Apocalyptic Nightmares: Globalization in Recent Mexican and Chicano Narrative*, (West Lafayette, IN: Purdue University Press, 2008), 5–15.
114. More's *Utopia* received a posthumous publication in English in 1551.
115. Silvana Serafin, "Eu-topos/ou-topos: Utopías y futuro," *Oltreoceano-Rivista Sulle Migrazioni* 18 (2021): 14–17.
116. Vivien Greene, "Utopia/Dystopia," *American Art* 25, no. 2 (2011): 2.
117. For a discussion about different strategies for economic integration in early 1990s Latin America, see Jorge G. Castañeda, *Utopia Unarmed: The Latin American Left after the Cold War* (New York: Knopf, 1993), 312–16. For a discussion of strategies for economic integration during the first decade of the twenty-first century, see Smith, *The Talons of the Eagle*, 284–89.
118. Néstor García Canclini, *Hybrid Cultures: Strategies for Entering and Leaving Modernity*, trans. Christopher L. Chiappari and Silvia L. López (Minneapolis: University of Minnesota Press, 1995).
119. Carlos Monsiváis, "De la cultura mexicana en vísperas del Tratado de Libre Comercio," in *La educación y la cultura ante el Tratado de Libre Comercio*, eds. Gilberto Guevara Niebla and Néstor García Canclini (Mexico City: Nueva Imagen, 1992), 209.
120. Castañeda, *Utopia Unarmed*, 316, 322–24.
121. Fernández and González, *A Century of Chicano History*, 110–12.
122. Emmelhainz, *La tiranía del sentido común*, 19; Stuart Hall, "Signification, Representation, Ideology: Althusser and the Post-Structuralist Debates," *Critical Studies in Media Communication* 2, no. 2 (1985): 105.
123. Louis Althusser, "Ideology and Ideological State Apparatuses: Notes towards an Investigation," in *Cultural Theory: An Anthology*, ed. Imre Szesman and Timothy Kaposy (Malden, MA: Wiley-Blackwell, 2011), 241.
124. Emmelhainz, *La tiranía del sentido común*, 100–117.
125. Armando Bartra, "Mexico: Yearnings and Utopias: The Left in the Third Millenium," in *The New Latin American Left: Utopia Reborn*, eds. Patrick

Barrett, Daniel Chavez, and César Rodríguez Garavito (London: Pluto Press, 2008), 213.
126. Emmelhainz, *La tiranía del sentido común*, 16.
127. In this case, I build on Tzvetan Todorov's definition of the fantastic as a genre that sits at the threshold between the real world and a fictitious one. See Tzvetan Todorov, *The Fantastic: A Structural Approach to a Literary Genre*, trans. Richard Howard (Ithaca, NY: Cornell University Press, 1975), 24–40. That said, I am less inclined to accept his argument that we leave the fantastic mode when we determine the cause of an apparently supernatural event. See Todorov, *The Fantastic*, 25. Rather, I find the umbrella of fantastic literature to be a valuable means of viewing an array of genres *and modes* like SF, magical realism, horror, and the gothic alongside one another.
128. John Rieder, *Colonialism and the Emergence of Science Fiction* (Middletown, CT: Wesleyan University Press, 2008), 6.
129. Rieder, *Colonialism and the Emergence of Science Fiction*, 6–10.
130. Mbembe, *Necropolitics*, 163.
131. Catherine Ramírez, "Deus ex Machina: Tradition, Technology and the Chicanafuturist Art of Marion C. Martinez," *Aztlán: A Journal of Chicano Studies* 29, no. 2 (2004).
132. Catherine Ramírez, "Afrofuturism/Chicanafuturism: Fictive Kin," *Aztlán: A Journal of Chicano Studies* 33, no. 1 (2008): 187.
133. L. Rivera, "Chicana/o Cyberpunk after el Movimiento," 187–88.
134. David S. Dalton, "Science Fiction vs. Magical Realism: Oppositional Aesthetics and Contradictory Political Discourses in Sergio Arau's *A Day without a Mexican*," in *Peter Lang Companion to Latin American Science Fiction*, eds. Silvia Kurlat Ares and Ezequiel De Rosso (New York: Peter Lang, 2021).
135. M. Elizabeth Ginway, *Cyborgs, Sexuality, and the Undead: The Body in Mexican and Brazilian Speculative Fiction* (Nashville, TN: Vanderbilt University Press, 2020), 1. Cathryn Josefina Merla-Watson and B. V. Olguín also employ the phrase *Latin@ Speculative Arts* when speaking of these fictions from a US-Latinx and Chicanx perspective. The term offers certain advantages over *Chicanafuturism*, particularly its ability to apply to a wider array of texts than the latter. That said, the terms overlap significantly, and many of the scholars in Merla-Watson and Olguín's edited volume prefer the more politically charged term of *Chicanafuturism*. See Cathryn Josefina Merla-Watson and B. V. Olguín, "Introduction: Altermundos: Reassessing the Past, Present, and Future of the Chican@ and Latin@ Speculative Arts," in *Altermundos: Latin@ Speculative Litearture, Film, and Popular Culture*, ed. Cathryn Josefina Merla-Watson and B. V. Olguín (Los Angeles: UCLA Chicano Studies Research Center Press, 2017).
136. See Stephen C. Tobin and Libia Brenda, "Genre in Mexico and the Crazy, Joyful Adventure of the Anthology for the Mexicanx Initiative," *Latin American Literature Today* 8, no. 12 (2018). At the same time, Tobin and Brenda make the

curious observation that the term *speculative fiction* in English is frequently dropped when titles and terms are translated into Spanish.

137. This approach proves useful in navigating a literary terrain that has historically favored modes like magical realism over SF. See J. Andrew Brown and M. Elizabeth Ginway, introduction to *Latin American Science Fiction: Theory and Practice* (New York: Palgrave MacMillan, 2012), 1.

138. Carlos Gerardo Zermeño Vargas, "Fantasticidad, encuentros con lo monstruoso e identidades inestables en dos novelas mexicanas: Patricia Laurent Kullick y Guadalupe Nettel" (PhD diss., Instituto Tecnologico y Estudios Superiores de Monterrey, 2017), 13.

139. Silvia Kurlat Ares, "Prólogo," in *Historia de la ciencia ficción latinoamericana I: Desde los orígenes hasta la modernidad*, eds. Teresa López-Pellisa and Silvia G. Kurlat Ares (Madrid: Iberoamericana, 2020), 12; see also Luis C. Cano, *Los espíritus de la ciencia ficción: Espiritismo, periodismo y cultura popular en las novelas de Eduardo Holmberg, Francisco Miralles y Pedro Castera* (Chapel Hill: University of North Carolina Press, 2017), 54.

140. The deep ties between SF and dystopia in Mexican letters that has existed since at least Eduardo Urzaiz's publication of *Eugenia* in 1919. See Rachel Haywood Ferreira, *The Emergence of Latin American Science Fiction* (Middletown, CT: Wesleyan University Press, 2010), 66–67.

141. López-Lozano, *Utopian Dreams, Apocalyptic Nightmares*, 1–4, 15–26; David Seed, *Science Fiction: A Very Short Introduction* (Oxford: Oxford University Press, 2011), 81–96.

142. López-Lozano, *Utopian Dreams, Apocalyptic Nightmares*, 3.

143. Dalton, *Mestizo Modernity*, 52–58; Jerry Hoeg, *Science, Technology, and Latin American Narrative in the Twentieth Century and Beyond* (Bethlehem, PA: Lehigh University Press, 2000), 73–82; Silvia Spitta, "Of Brown Buffaloes, Cockroaches, and Others: *Mestizaje* North and South of the Río Bravo," *Revista de Estudios Hispánicos* 35, no. 3 (2001): 334. For a discussion about the "retro-labeling" of certain strands of Latin American literature as SF, see Haywood Ferreira, *The Emergence of Latin American Science Fiction*, 1–11.

144. Dalton, *Mestizo Modernity*. Joshua Lund, *The Mestizo State: Reading Race in Modern Mexico* (Minneapolis: University of Minnesota Press, 2012); Pedro Palou, *El fracaso del mestizo* (Mexico City: Paidós, 2014).

145. See Ignacio M. Sánchez Prado, "El mestizaje en el corazón de la utopía: *La raza cósmica* entre Aztlán y América Latina," *Revista Canadiense de Estudios Hispánicos* 33, no. 2 (2009).

146. "El plan espiritual de Aztlán," 1969, http://www.cwu.edu/~mecha/documents/plan_de_aztlan.pdf. For a discussion of Aztlán from the Mexican tradition, see Lori Boornazian Diel, *The Codex Mexicanus: A Guide to Life in Late Sixteenth-Century New Spain* (Austin: University of Texas Press, 2018), 116–20.

147. Denise A. Segura and Beatriz M. Pesquera, "Beyond Indifference and Antipathy: The Chicana Movement and Chicana Feminist Discourse," in Noriega et al.,

*The Chicano Studies Reader*, 360–62; Adaljiza Sosa Riddell, "Chicanas and El Movimiento," in Noriega et al., *The Chicano Studies Reader*.

148. Alarcón, "Chicana Femenism," 185. For a discussion about the struggles to apply the term Chicana to people from previous time periods, see Deena J. González, "Chicana Identity Matters," in Noriega et al., *The Chicano Studies Reader*.

149. Rafael Pérez-Torres, "Refiguring Aztlán," in Noriega et al., *The Chicano Studies Reader*, 173.

150. Chabram-Dernersesian, "I Throw Punches for My Race, But I Don't Want to Be a Man: Writing US—Chica-nos (Gil, Us)/Chicanas—into the Movement Script," in Chabram-Dernersesian, *The Chicana/o Studies Reader*.

151. Cherríe Moraga, "Queer Aztlán: The Re-Formation of Chicano Tribe," in *Aztlán: Essays on the Chicano Homeland*, rev. ed., eds. Rodolfo Anaya, Francisco A. Lomelí and Enrique R. Lamadrid (Albuquerque: University of New Mexico Press, 2017), 255.

152. Dylan A. T. Miner, *Creating Aztlán: Chicano Art, Indigenous Sovereignty, and Lowriding across Turtle Island* (Tucson: University of Arizona Press, 2014), 37.

153. Segura and Pesquera, "Beyond Indifference and Antipathy," 358; David S. Dalton, "Eugenics and Doubly Marginalized Mexican and Chicana Women: Documenting the Left-Right Consensus on Reproductive Health in Renee Tajima-Peña's *No más bebés*," in Dalton and Weatherford, *Healthcare in Latin America*, 134–38.

154. Anzaldúa, *Borderlands/La frontera*, 108–13.

155. C. Ramírez, "Cyborg Femenism," 390.

156. Jennifer Browdy de Hernández, "On Home Ground: Politics, Location, and the Construction of Identity in Four American Women's Autobiographies," *MELUS* 22, no. 4 (1997): 33–34; Ivy Schweitzer, "For Gloria Anzaldúa: Collecting America, Performing Friendship," *PMLA* 12, no. 1 (2006).

157. Taylor and Pitman, *Latin American Identity*, 145.

158. Taylor and Pitman, *Latin American Identity*, 146. Certainly, Jerry Hoeg recognized the similarities between mestizaje and cyborg identity when he wrote on cybermestizaje and, especially cybermestizas. See Hoeg, *Science, Technology*, chapter 7.

159. For a discussion of mestizaje and cyborg theory, see Dalton, *Mestizo Modernity*, introduction.

160. Chela Sandoval, "Forward: Unfinished Words: The Crossing of Gloria Anzaldúa," in *EntreMundos/AmongWorlds: New Perspectives on Gloria Anzaldúa*, ed. AnaLouise Keating (New York: Palgrave MacMillan, 2005), xiii; see also Susana Ramírez, "Recovering Gloria Anzaldúa's Sci-fi Roots: Nepantler@ Visions in the Unpublished and Published Speculative Precursors to *Borderlands*," in Merla-Watson and Olguín, *Altermundos*.

161. Catherine Ramírez, "Foreword: The Time Machine: From Afrofuturism to Chicanafuturism and Beyond," in Merla-Watson and Olguín, *Altermundos*, ix–xi. Curtis Marez details Octavia Butler's continued relevance in Chicanx

studies and the Chicanx Movement. See Curtis Marez, "Octavia E. Butler after the Chicanx Movement," *Women's Studies: An Interdisciplinary Journal* 47, no. 7 (2018): 756–59.
162. S. Ramírez, "Recovering Gloria Anzaldúa's Sci-fi Roots," 58.
163. Hardt and Negri, *Empire*, 216.
164. Emmelhainz, *La tiranía del sentido común*, 107.
165. See Agamben, *Homo Sacer*, 12.
166. See Haraway, *Simians, Cyborgs and Women*, 154; Sandoval, *Methodology of the Oppressed*, 166–77.
167. Sophie Esch, *Modernity at Gunpoint: Firearms, Politics, and Culture in Mexico and Central America* (Pittsburgh, PA: University of Pittsburgh Press, 2018), 21.
168. Radhika Gajjala, "Internet Constructs of Identity and Ignorance: 'Third-World' Contexts and Cyberfeminism," *Works and Days* 17/18, no. 33/34/35/36 (1999); Joy James, "'Concerning Violence': Frantz Fanon's Rebel Intellectual in Search of a Black Cyborg," *South Atlantic Quarterly* 11, no. 1 (2013); Sarah Juliet Lauro, Tiffany Gilmore, and Jenni G. Halpin, "Glass Wombs, Cyborg Women, and Kangaroo Mothers: How a Third-World Practice May Resolve the Techno/Feminist Debate," *TEXT Technology*, no. 1 (2007).

## CHAPTER 1

1. While *Cronos* was released in 1993, del Toro filmed it in 1992.
2. Agamben, *Homo Sacer*, 8.
3. María Herrera-Sobek, "Writing the Toxic Environment: Ecocriticism and Chicana Literary Imagination," in *A Contested West: New Readings of Place in Western American Literature*, eds. Martin Simonson, David Río, and Amaia Ibarraran (London: Portal Editions, 2013), 182.
4. Numerous critics have highlighted the discursive significance of Cerezita's name, which means "cherry" in English. Some argue that it associates her with virginity and the author's name. See Linda Margarita Greenberg, "Learning for the Dead: Wounds, Women, and Activism in Cherríe Moraga's *Heroes and Saints*," *MELUS: Multi-Ethnic Literature of the US* 34, no. 1 (2009): 176. Others claim that it also associates her with Ceres, "the ancient goddess of fertility." See Marilyn Chandler McEntyre, "Sickness in the System: The Health Costs of the Harvest," *Journal of Medical Humanities* 28, no. 2 (2007): 100.
5. For a list of scholars who discuss the significance of Jesús Gris's name, see Ann Davies, "Guillermo del Toro's *Cronos*: The Vampire as Embodied Heterotopia," *Quarterly Review of Film and Video* 25, no. 5 (2008): 400; Héctor Fernández L'Hoeste, "De insectos y otros demonios: Breves apuntes sobre las obsesiones de Guillermo del Toro," *Cifra Nueva* 12, no. 2 (2000): 44; Richard Harrington, "*Cronos*," *Washington Post*, May 22, 1994, https://www.washingtonpost.com/wp-srv/style/longterm/movies/videos/cronosnrharrington_a0abc7.htm; S. T. Joshi, "The Magical Spirituality of a Lapsed Catholic: Atheism and Anti-Clericalism," in *The Supernatural Cinema of Guillermo del Toro*, ed. John H. Morehead

(Jefferson, NC: McFarland, 2015), 14; Israel Muñoz Gallarte, "El bestiario clásico de Guillermo del Toro," *Ámbitos: Revista de Estudios de Ciencias Sociales y Humanidades*, no. 27 (2012): 49–50; Robin Murray and Joseph Heumann, *Monstrous Nature: Environment and Horror on the Big Screen* (Lincoln: University of Nebraska Press, 2016), 36.

6. Passariello, Phyllis, "Desperately Seeking *Something*: Che Guevara as Secular Saint," in *The Making of Saints: Contesting Sacred Ground*, ed. James F. Hopgood (Tuscaloosa: University of Alabama Press, 2005); Desirée A. Martín, *Borderlands Saints: Secular Sanctity in Chicano/a and Mexican Culture* (New Brunswick, NJ: Rutgers University Press, 2013).
7. Martín, *Borderlands Saints*, 4.
8. Agamben, *Homo Sacer*, 12.
9. See Anzaldúa, *Borderlands/La frontera*, 103; see also Theresa Delgadillo, *Spiritual Mestizaje: Religion, Gender, Race, and Nation in Contemporary Chicana Narrative*, (Durham, NC: Duke University Press, 2011), chapter 1.
10. Anzaldúa, *Borderlands/La frontera*, 103.
11. For a discussion on how cyborg subjectivity makes certain bodies illegibile to society at large, see Dalton, *Mestizo Modernity*, 22–23; Haraway, *Simians, Cyborgs and Women*, 151–55.
12. For a discussion of contemporary cases of the environmental challenges that migrant workers continue to face, see Carolina L. Balazs, Rachel Morello-Frosch, Alan E. Hubbard, and Isha Ray, "Environmental Justice Implications of Arsenic Contamination in California's San Joaquin Valley: A Cross-Sectional, Cluster-Design Examining Exposure and Compliance in Community Drinking Water Systems," *Environmental Health* 11 no, 1 (2012).
13. The limited list of works that have discussed the juxtaposition of SF and magical realism include the following critics: José Arnulfo Durán de Alba "Ciencia ficción + Realismo mágico = Utopía," *Escritos: Revista del Centro de Ciencias del Lenguaje* 21 (2000); and my own chapter Dalton, "Science Fiction vs. Magical Realism."
14. Vivian Carol Sobchack, *Screening Space: The American Science Fiction Film* (New Brunswick, NJ: Rutgers University Press, 1997), 29–55.
15. Christopher P. Tourney, "The Moral Character of Mad Scientists: A Cultural Critique of Science," *Science, Technology, and Human Values* 17, no. 4 (1992): 414.
16. Gabriel Eljaiek-Rodríguez, *Selva de fantasmas: El gótico en la literatura y el cine latinoamericanos* (Bogotá: Editorial Pontificia Universidad Javeriana, 2017), 181.
17. Sobchack, *Screening Space*, 29–30.
18. Eljaiek-Rodríguez, *Selva de fantasmas*, 187–88.
19. Alejo Carpentier, "On the Marvelous Real in America," in *Magical Realism: Theory, History, Community*, eds. Lois Parkinson Zamora and Wendy B. Faris (Durham, NC: Duke University Press, 1995), 86–88; Luis Leal, "Magical Realism in Spanish American Literature," trans. Wendy B. Faris, in *Magical Realism:*

*Theory, History, Community*, edited by Lois Parkinson Zamora and Wendy B. Faris (Durham, NC: Duke University Press, 1995), 121.

20. See Alberto Fuguet and Sergio Gómez, "Prólogo," *McOndo*, (Barcelona: Grijalbo-Mondadori, 1997), 17; Diana Palaversich, *De Macondo a McOndo: Senderos de la postmodernidad latinoamericana* (Barcelona: Plaza y Valdés, 2005), 33–36; Pedro Ángel Palou, Eloy Urroz, Ignacio Padilla, and Ricardo Chávez Castañeda, "Manifiesto del Crack," Confabulario, April 9, 1996, https://confabulario.eluniversal.com.mx/manifiesto-del-crack-1996.

21. Stephen Slemon, "Magic Realism as Postcolonial Discourse," in Zamora and Faris, *Magical Realism*, 407–26.

22. Gavin O'Toole, "A New Nationalism for a New Era: The Political Ideology of Mexican Neoliberalism," *Bulletin of Latin American Research* 22, no. 3 (2003).

23. Alfredo Saad-Filho and Deborah Johnston, introduction to *Neoliberalism: A Critical Reader*, eds. Alfredo Saad-Filho and Deborah Johnston (London: Pluto Press, 2005), 2.

24. Gérard Duménil and Dominique Lévy argue that the neoliberal transition was already underway in Reagan's California. See Gérard Duménil and Dominique Lévy, "The Neoliberal (Counter-)Revolution," in Saad-Filho and Deborah Johnston, *Neoliberalism*, 10–11. For a discussion of the policy moves that brought California into a neoliberal economic order, see David E. Keefe, "Governor Regan, Welfare Reform, and AFDC Fertility," *Social Service Review* 57, no. 2 (1983): 234–39.

25. Julie Guthman, "Neoliberalism and the Making of Food Politics in California," *Geoforum* 39, no. 3 (2008): 1178.

26. Jill Harrison, "Abandoned Bodies and Spaces of Sacrifice: Pesticide Drift Activism and the Contestation of Neoliberal Environmental Politics in California," *Geoforum* 39, no. 3 (2008).

27. Kathy Perkins and Roberta Uno, "Cherríe Moraga," in *Contemporary Plays by Women of Color*, comp. Kathy Perkins and Roberta Uno (New York: Routledge, 2006), 230. For a discussion of how this play fits within Moraga's larger body of work, see Irma Mayorga, "Cherríe Moraga," in *Twentieth-Century American Dramatists*, 3rd series, ed. Christopher J. Wheatley (Detroit, MI: Thomson Gale, 2002).

28. M. Coye and L. Goldman, *Summary of Environmental Data: McFarland Childhood Cancer Cluster Investigation, Phase III Report* (Sacramento: California Department of Health Services, Environmental Epidemiology and Toxicology Program, 1991); Herrera-Sobek, "Writing the Toxic Environment," 183.

29. For a discussion of the environmental activism of César Chávez and Dolores Huerta, see Richard Griswold del Castillo and Richard A. Garcia, *César Chávez: A Triumph of Spirit* (Norman: University of Oklahoma Press, 1995), 136.

30. Cherríe Moraga, "Author's Notes," in *Heroes and Saints and Other Plays*, by Cherríe Moraga (Albuquerque, NM: West End Press, 2007), 89. Babett Rubóczki, "Environment and the Somatic Body in Cherríe Moraga's *Heroes*

*and Saints* and Edwidge Danticat's *The Farming of Bones*," *Revista de Estudios Norteamericanos* 25 (2021): 78–79.

31. Cherríe Moraga, *Heroes and Saints*, in *Contemporary Plays by Women of Color*, comps. Kathy A. Perkins and Roberta Uno (New York: Routledge, 2006), 233.
32. For studies that view the play through the lens of magical realism, see Maria Alicia C. Garza, "High Crimes against the Flesh: The Embodiment of Violent Otherization in Cherríe Moraga's *Heroes and Saints*," *Letras Femeninas* 30, no. 1 (2004): 22; Angelika Köhler, "The Body as Borderland: Reconceptualization of the Body in Recent Chicana Literature," in *Body Signs: The Latino/a Body in Cultural Production*, ed. Astrid M. Fellner (Berlin: Lit, 2012), 193. At the same time, other critics have asserted a surreal aesthetic. See Suzanne Bost, *Encarnación: Illness and Body Politics in Chicana Feminist Literature* (New York: Fordham University Press, 2010), 117; Kerstin Knopf, "Cherríe Moraga, *Heroes and Saints* (1992)," in *Drama, Part II*, ed. Susanne Peters and Klaus Stierstorfer (Trier: Wissenschaftlicher, 2006), 375. Others have ascribed a fantastic element to the play. See İnci Bilgin Tekin, *Myths of Oppression Revisited in Cherríe Moraga's and Liz Lochhead's Drama* (Stuggart: Ibidem-Verl, 2012), 83. In general, these critics use competing lenses to view and interpret the same elements.
33. Haraway, *Simians, Cyborgs and Women*, 175.
34. For a fascinating discussion of the interface between the written text of the playscript and the performance of a bodiless head, see Telory W. Davies, "Race, Gender, and Disability: Cherríe Moraga's Bodiless Head," *Journal of Dramatic Theory and Criticism* 21, no. 1 (2006): 34–38; Ikue Kina, "Cherríe Moraga's Ecofeminist Aesthetics toward Reclaiming Chicana Body in *Heroes and Saints* and *Watsonville*: Some Place Not Here," *Tamkang Review* 40, no. 1 (2009): 80; Joanna L. Mitchell, "Haunting the Chicana: The Queer Child and the Abject Mother in the Writing of Cherríe Moraga," in *Unveiling the Body in Hispanic Women's Literature: From Nineteenth-Century Spain to Twenty-First-Century United States*, ed. Renée Scott and Arleen Chiclana y González (Lewiston, NY: Edwin Mellen Press, 2006), 216; Priscilla Solis Ybarra, *Writing the Goodlife: Mexican American Literature and the Environment* (Tucson: University of Arizona Press, 2016), 155.
35. Solis Ybarra, *Writing the Goodlife*, 155–56.
36. W. B. Worthen, "Staging América: The Subject of History in Chicano/a Theatre," *Theatre Journal* 49, no. 2 (1997): 111. See Elizabeth Jacobs, "The Ecologies of Protest in the Theatre of Aztlán," *Comparative American Studies* 10, no. 1 (2012): 97.
37. María J. Durán, "Bodies That Should Matter: Chicana/o Farmworkers, Slow Violence, and the Politics of (In)visibility in Cherríe Moraga's *Heroes and Saints*," *Aztlan: A Journal of Chicano Studies* 42, no. 1 (2017): 54–55.
38. Cerezita's cyborg nature helps to explain the deconstructive nature that many critics have noted in her performance of—and interaction with—constructs

of race, gender, sexuality, and even disability. See T. Davies, "Race, Gender, and Disability," 31; Köhler, "The Body as Borderland," 194.

39. Durán, "Bodies That Should Matter," 46–52; T. Davies, "Race, Gender, and Disability," 30; Garza, "High Crimes against the Flesh," 32–33; Elizabeth Arden Thomas, "Poisoning the Mother/Land: An Ecofeminist Dramaturgy in José Rivera's *Marisol* and Cherríe Moraga's *Heroes and Saints*," *Theatre History Studies* 35 (2016): 156.

40. Julia de Foor Jay, "(Re)Claiming the Race of the Mother: Cherríe Moraga's *Shadow of a Man*, *Giving Up the Ghost*, and *Heroes and Saints*," in *Women of Color: Mother-Daughter Relationships in Twentieth-Century Literature*, ed. Elizabeth Brown-Guillory (Austin: University of Texas Press, 1996), 108; Irma Mayorga, "Invisibility's Contusions: Violence in Cherríe Moraga's *Heroes and Saints* and *The Hungry Woman* and Luis Valdez's *Zoot Suit*," in *Violence in American Drama: Essays on Its Staging, Meanings, and Effects*, ed. Alfonso Ceballos Muñoz, Ramón Espejo Romero, and Bernardo Muñoz Martínez (Jefferson, NC: McFarland, 2011), 162.

41. Dalton, *Mestizo Modernity*, 108.

42. Haraway, *Simians, Cyborgs and Women*, 181.

43. Nina Lykke, "Between Monsters, Goddesses, and Cyborgs: Feminist Confrontations with Science," in *The Gendered Cyborg: A Reader*, ed. Gill Kirkup, Linda Janes, Kath Woodward, and Fiona Hovenden (New York: Routledge, 2000), 82.

44. Lykke, "Between Monsters, Goddesses, and Cyborgs," 85.

45. Kina, "Cherríe Moraga's Ecofeminist Aesthetics," 84–85.

46. Julie Avril Minich, *Accessible Citizenships: Disability, Nation, and the Cultural Politics of Greater Mexico* (Philadelphia, PA: Temple University Press, 2014), 58; Esther Sánchez-Pardo González, "The Desire Called Utopia: Re-Imagining Collectivity in Moraga and Castillo," *Estudios Ingleses de la Universidad Complutense* 17 (2009): 95–104. For discussions of *Heroes and Saints* as a nationalist play, see Catriona Rueda-Esquibel, *With Her Machete in Her Hand: Reading Chicana Lesbians* (Austin: University of Texas Press, 2006), 153–62.

47. Moraga, *Heroes and Saints*, 237.

48. Thomas, "Poisoning the Mother/Land," 154. See also T. Davies, "Race, Gender, and Disability," 32; McEntyre, "Sickness in the System," 99.

49. Durán, "Bodies That Should Matter," 46; see also Rob Nixon, *Slow Violence and Environmentalism of the Poor* (Cambridge, MA: Harvard University Press, 2011), 2.

50. Peggy Reynolds et al., "The Four County Study of Childhood Cancer: Clusters in the Context," *Statistics in Medicine* 15 (1996): 696.

51. Reynolds et al., "The Four County Study," 696.

52. Peggy Reynolds et al., "Childhood Cancer and Agricultural Pesticide Use: An Ecologic Study in California," *Environmental Health Perspectives* 1, no. 3 (2002): 320–21.

53. Balazs et al., "Environmental Justice Implications," 8–10.
54. Knopf, "Cherríe Moraga, *Heroes and Saints*," 376.
55. Arianne Burford, "Cartographies of a Violent Landscape: Viramontes' and Moraga's Remapping of Feminisms in *Under the Feet of Jesus* and *Heroes and Saints*," *Genders* 47 (2008), https://www.colorado.edu/gendersarchive1998-2013/2008/02/01/cartographies-violent-landscape-viramontes-and-moragas-remapping-feminisms-under-feet; Cynthia Degnan, "[Ex]posing Sightlines: The Staging of Power in Cherríe Moraga's *Heroes and Saints*," *Atenea* 23, no. 2 (2003): 141.
56. Knopf, "Cherríe Moraga, *Heroes and Saints*," 376.
57. According to Elizabeth Jacobs, this scene asserts an ancient comradery between people of Chicanx and Indigenous descent in America. See Jacobs, "Ecologies of Protest," 93.
58. Moraga, *Heroes and Saints*, 234–35.
59. Durán, "Bodies That Should Matter," 58.
60. Greenberg, "Learning from the Dead," 165, emphasis mine.
61. Moraga, *Heroes and Saints*, 235.
62. Anne Shea, "'Don't Let Them Make You Feel You Did a Crime': Immigration Law, Labor Rights, and Farmworker Testimony," *MELUS* 28, no. 1 (2003): 127.
63. William Acree, "The Trial of Theatre: *Fiat iustitia, et pereat mundus*," *Latin American Theatre Review* 40, no. 1 (2006): 42.
64. Frank Obenland, "'To Meet a Broader and Wiser Revolution': Notions of Collectivity in Contemporary Mexican American Drama," *Amerikastudien/ American Studies* 57, no. 2 (2012): 272.
65. Moraga, *Heroes and Saints*, 238.
66. Moraga, *Heroes and Saints*, 238. Carla Jonsson argues that bilingual scenes like this serve two purposes: they help non-bilingual audiences understand the dialogue, and they "enrich the linguistic experience for the bilingual audience," See Carla Jonsson, "Functions of Code-Switching in Bilingual Theater: An Analysis of Three Chicano Plays," *Journal of Pragmatics* 42, no. 5 (2010): 1303; see also Carla Jonsson, "Representing Voice in Chicano Theatre through the Use of Orthography: An Analysis of Three Plays by Cherríe Moraga," in *The Representation of the Spoken Mode in Fiction: How Authors Write How People Talk*, ed. Carolina P. Amador Moreno and Ana Nunes (Lewiston, NY: Edwin Mellen Press, 2009), 104–8.
67. Moraga, *Heroes and Saints*, 239.
68. Moraga, *Heroes and Saints*, 247.
69. Héctor Calderón, *Narratives of Greater Mexico: Essays on Chicano Literary History, Genre, and Borders* (Austin: University of Texas Press, 2004), 131.
70. Rueda-Esquibel, *With Her Machete*, 158–59.
71. Armando Lampe, "Religión y política en América Latina: La confrontación entre Juan Pablo II y Ernesto Cardenal en 1983," *Anuario Latinoamericano Ciencias Políticas y Relaciones Internacionales* 3 (2016): 21–22.

72. "Nicaraguan Poet-Priest Cardenal Leaves Hospital, Thanks Pope," AP News, February 20, 2019, https://apnews.com/article/e54eab9738284e7494dd33e7965d9e38.
73. Moraga, *Heroes and Saints*, 257.
74. Moraga, *Heroes and Saints*, 257. Indeed, Cerezita's bodilessness paradoxically accentuates her sexuality. See Mitchell, "Haunting the Chicana," 215.
75. Greenberg, "Learning from the Dead," 177.
76. Several scholars have identified a queering nature to this scene. See Rueda-Esquibel, *With Her Machete*, 156–57; Kina, "Cherríe Moraga's Ecofeminist Aesthetics, 86–87. Indeed, Leah Garland discusses how Moraga uses queer sexualities to redefine certain aspects of the Catholic Church. See Leah Garland, *Contemporary Latina/o Performing Arts of Moraga, Tropicana, Fusco, and Bustamante* (New York: Peter Lang, 2009), 31–39.
77. Garland, *Contemporary Latina/o*, 35; Knopf, "Cherríe Moraga, Heroes and Saints (1992)," 379; Yvonne Yarbro-Bejarano, *The Wounded Heart: Writing on Cherríe Moraga* (Austin: University of Texas Press, 2001), 72.
78. Obenland, "'To Meet a Broader,'" 188.
79. Many Chicana feminists evoke the pre-Columbian deities associated with the image of the Virgin of Guadalupe because they provide avenues for agency that the Catholic saint does not. See Alicia Arrizón, "Mythical Performativity: Relocating Aztlán in Chicana Feminist Cultural Productions," *Theatre Journal* 42, no. 1 (2000): 37–42.
80. Dalton, *Mestizo Modernity*, 138.
81. Yvonne Yarbro-Bejarano, "Chicana Literature from a Chicana Feminist Perspective," *Americas Review* 15 (1987): 141. See also Araceli Esparza, "Cherríe Moraga's Changing Consciousness of Solidarity," in *The Un/Making of Latina/o Citizenship: Culture, Politics, and Aesthetics*, ed. Ellie D. Hernández, and Eliza Rodríguez y Gibson (New York: Palgrave MacMillan, 2014), 147.
82. "Cherríe Moraga: Chicana Writer, Activist, Pioneer," *Yale Daily News* (New Haven, CT), Sept. 27, 2013, https://yaledailynews.com/blog/2013/09/27/chicana-writer-activist-pioneer.
83. Knopf views this act as sacrificial because Cerezita has long viewed her hair as her only beautiful feature. Knopf, "Cherríe Moraga, Heroes and Saints," 385.
84. Yvonne Yarbro-Bejarano, *The Wounded Heart*, 74–75.
85. Martin, *Borderlands Saints*, 4.
86. Yarbro-Bejarano, *The Wounded Heart*, 75.
87. Garza, "High Crimes against the Flesh," 30.
88. McEntyre, "Sickness in the System," 100–101.
89. Mitchell, "Haunting the Chicana," 216.
90. Jocelyn Sherman, "UFW Remembers Rene Lopez who sacrificed his life for La Causa (1962–1983)," United Farm Workers, Sept. 21, 2017, https://ufw.org/ufw-remembers-rene-lopez-who-sacrificed-his-life-for-la-causa-1962-1983.
91. Moraga, *Heroes and Saints*, 261.

92. Degnan, "[Ex]posing Sightlines," 143.
93. Mayorga, "Invisibility's Conclusions," 163
94. Solis Ybarra, *Writing the Goodlife*, 157; see also Yarbro-Bejarano, *The Wounded Heart*, 66.
95. Mayorga, "Invisibility's Conclusions," 163; Julie Avril Minich, "'You Gotta Make Aztlán Any Way You Can': Disability in Cherríe Moraga's *Heroes and Saints*," in *Disability and Mothering: Liminal Spaces of Embodied Knowledge*, ed. Cynthia Lewiecki-Wilson and Jen Celio (Syracuse, NY: Syracuse University Press, 2011), 270–74.
96. John Waldron, "Introduction: Culture Monopolies and Criticism: A Way Out?" *Discourse* 26, no. 1–2 (2004): 6.
97. Deborah Shaw, *The Three Amigos: The Transnational Filmmaking of Guillermo del Toro, Alejando González Iñárritu, and Alfonso Cuarón* (Manchester: Manchester University Press, 2013), 36.
98. Prior to filming *Cronos*, del Toro had built a successful career in Mexican national television. Ignacio M. Sánchez Prado, *Screening Neoliberalism: Transforming Mexican Cinema, 1988–2012* (Nashville, TN: Vanderbilt University Press, 2014), 162.
99. Erica Segre, "'La desnacionalización de la pantalla': Mexican Cinema in the 1990s," in *Changing Reels: Latin American Cinema against the Odds*, ed. Rob Rix and Roberto Rodríguez-Saona (Leeds: Trinity and All Saints University College, 1997), 35–37.
100. Indeed, the movie itself was a product of transnational funding. See Álvaro Fernández, "*Cronos*: El origen del alquimista—Estudio de caso," *El ojo que piensa: Revista de cine iberoamericano* 3 (2011), http://www.elojoquepiensa.cucsh.udg.mx/index.php/elojoquepiensa/article/view/35/35; Laurence Davies, "Guillermo del Toro's *Cronos*, or the Pleasures of Impurity," in *Gothic Science Fiction 1980–2010*, ed. Sara Wesson and Emily Alder (Liverpool: Liverpool University Press, 2011), 88–89; Shaw, *The Three Amigos*, 24–26. Dolores Tierney, "Transnational Political Horror in *Cronos* (1993), *El espinazo del diablo* (2001), and *El laberinto del fauno* (2006)," in *The Transnational Fantasies of Guillermo del Toro*, edited by Ann Davies, Deborah Shaw, and Dolores Tierney (New York: Palgrave MacMillan, 2014), 164.
101. Sánchez Prado, *Screening Neoliberalism*, 166; Anne Marie Stock, "Authentically Mexican? *Mi querido Tom Mix* and *Cronos* Reframe Critical Questions," in *Mexico's Cinema: A Century of Film and Filmakers*, ed. Joanne Hershfield and David R. Maciel (Wilmington, DE: Scholarly Resources Books, 2005), 276.
102. Waldron, "Introduction," 18.
103. Beatriz Trigo, "*Cronos* by Guillermo del Toro," *Chasqui: Revista de Literatura Latinoamericana* 30, no. 1 (2001): 177.
104. Shaw, *The Three Amigos*, 21.
105. Tierney, "Transnational Political Horror," 161–62; Christina L. Sisk, "Entre el Cha Cha Chá y el Estado: El cine nacional mexicano y sus arquetipos," *A Contra Corriente* 8, no. 3 (2011): 168.

106. Ignacio M. Sánchez Prado, "Monstruos neoliberales: Capitalismo y terror en *Cronos* y *Somos lo que hay*," in *Aproximaciones al cine de terror en Latinoamérica y el Caribe*, ed. Rosana Díaz-Zambrana and Patricia Tomé (San Juan: Editorial Isla Negra, 2012), 47–49.
107. Micah K. Donohue, "Translatio Vampyri: Transamerican Vampires and Transnational Capital in Guillermo del Toro's *Cronos*," *Comparative American Studies* 14, no. 2 (2016): 130.
108. Stacy Rusnak, "Mexican Cinema in a Global Age: The Films of Guillermo Del Toro, Alfonso Cuarón, and Alejandro González Iñarritu" (PhD diss., Georgia State University, 2010), 63–67.
109. Gabriel Eljaiek-Rodríguez, "Bloodsucking Bugs: Horacio Quiroga and the Latin American Transformation of Vampires," in Morehead, *Supernatural Cinema*, 151–52.
110. Mabel Moraña, *The Monster as War Machine*, trans. Andrew Ascherl (Amherst, MA: Cambria Press, 2018), 372.
111. A. Davies, "Guillermo del Toro's *Cronos*," 399.
112. Edward King and Joanna Page, *Posthumanism and the Graphic Novel in Latin America* (London: University College London Press, 2017), 86.
113. Karl Marx, *Capital: A Critique of Political Economy*, vol. 1, book 1: *The Process of Production of Capital*, translated by Samuel Moore and Edward Aveling, edited by Frederick Engels, first English ed. 1887. Marx Engels Archive, 1999, https://www.marxists.org/archive/marx/works/download/pdf/Capital-Volume-I.pdf, 163; see also Donohue, "Translatio Vampyri," 131–35; Rusnak, "Mexican Cinema in a Global Age," 64.
114. John Kraniauskas, "*Cronos* and the Political Economy of Vampirism: Notes on a Historical Constellation," in *Cultural Margins: Cannibalism and the Colonial World*, ed. Francis Barker, Peter Hulme, and Margaret Iversen (Cambridge: Cambridge University Press, 1998), 144–47.
115. Eljaiek-Rodríguez, *Selva de fantasmas*, 182.
116. Adriana Gordillo, "*Aura*, 'Constancia,' and 'Sleeping Beauty': Carlos Fuentes's Little History on Photography," in *Latin American Gothic in Literature and Culture*, ed. Sandra Casanova-Vizcaíno and Inés Ordiz (New York: Routledge, 2018), 173; see also David S. Dalton, "Liberation and the Gothic in Carlos Solórzano's *Las manos de Dios*," in Casanova-Vizcaíno and Ordiz, *Latin American Gothic*, 87.
117. Eljaiek-Rodríguez, "Bloodsucking Bugs," 146–49.
118. Justo Planas Cabrejo, "Cronos en el laberinto de lo *unheimlich*," *Imagofagia: Revista de la Asociación Argentina de Estudios de Cine y Audiovisual*, no. 16 (2017): 250. Fernández L'Hoeste, "De insectors y otros demonios," 44; Raúl Rodríguez-Hernández and Claudia Schaefer, "Sublime Horror: Transparency, Melodrama, and the Mise-en-scene of Two Mexican Vampire Films," in *The Universal Vampire: Origins and Evolution of a Legend*, ed. Barbara Brodman and James E. Doan (Madison, WI: Fairleigh Dickinson University Press, 2013), 231–32.

119. Geoffery Kantaris, "Cyborgs, Cities, and Celluloid: Memory Machines in Two Latin American Cyborg Films," in *Latin American Cyberculture and Cyberliterature*, ed. Claire Taylor and Thea Pitman (Liverpool: University of Liverpool Press, 2007), 56–57.
120. Lauren Berg, "Globalization and the Modern Vampire," *Film Matters* 2, no. 3 (2011): 10.
121. Waldron, "Introduction," 19–20; Eric White, "Insects and Automata in Hoffmann, Balzac, Carter, and del Toro," *Journal of the Fantastic in the Arts* 19, no. 3 (2008): 376.
122. Haraway, *Simians, Cyborgs and Women*, 152.
123. Murray and Heumann, *Monstrous Nature*, 33. Óscar Pérez approaches Gris's desire for penetration from the device through a queer lens. See Óscar Pérez, "A Queer Reading of *Nuevo Cine Mexicano*," *Film International*, no. 70 (2014): 79–81.
124. Murray and Heumann, *Monstrous Nature*, 34.
125. Francisco de León, "El horror se queda en casa," *Pasavento: Revista de Estudios Hispánicos* 1, no. 1 (2013): 38; Tierney, "Transnational Political Horror," 165.
126. Dale Hudson, *Vampires, Race, and Transnational Hollywood* (Edinburgh: Edinburgh University Press, 2017), 217.
127. Alessandro Yuri Alegrette, "Entre o horror e a beleza: A sublime estética gótica dos filmes de Guillermo del Toro," *Revista abusões* 1, no. l (2016): 15–19; Stock, "Authentically Mexican?" 15–19.
128. Sánchez Prado, *Screening Neoliberalism*, 163.
129. Shaw, *The Three Amigos*, 36–38.
130. Elaine L. Graham, *Representations of the Post/Human: Monsters, Aliens, and Others in Popular Culture* (New Brunswick, NJ: Rutgers University Press, 2002), 63–83.
131. Eljaiek-Rodríguez, *Selva de fantasmas*, 186.
132. A. Davies, "Guillermo del Toro's *Cronos*," 401; see also Moraña, *Monster as War Machine*, 374.
133. Geoffery Kantaris, "Cyborgs, Cities, and Celluloid," 56–58; see also Persephone Braham, *From Amazons to Zombies: Monsters in Latin America* (Lewisburg, PA: Bucknell University Press, 2015), 174; Chaudhuri Shohini, "Visit of the Body Snatchers: Alien Invasion Themes in Vampire Narratives," *Camera Obscura* 14, no. 1–2 (1997): 191. For a discussion of medicalized cyborgs, see J. Andrew Brown *Cyborgs in Latin America* (New York: Palgrave MacMillan, 2010), 26, 140.
134. L. Davies, "Guillermo del Toro's *Cronos*," 92.
135. Shaw, *The Three Amigos*, 23.
136. Sánchez Prado, *Screening Neoliberalism*, 166–67. For a discussion that highlights the pre-NAFTA conflicts between the United States and Mexico in this film, see Ann Davies, "Slime and Subtlety: Monsters in del Toro's Spanish-Language Films," in Morehead, *Supernatural Cinema*, 53. For a study showing

the macroeconomic growth that occurred during the Mexican Miracle, see Fernando Carmona et al., *El milagro mexicano* (Mexico City: Editorial Nuestro Tiempo, 1970).
137. Sánchez Prado, *Screening Neoliberalism*, 166–67.
138. Shaw, *The Three Amigos*, 24.
139. Ann Davies, "Guillermo del Toro's Monsters: Matter Out of Place," in Davies, Shaw, and Tierney, *Transnational Fantasies*, 29.
140. Sánchez Prado, "Monstruos neoliberales," 51.
141. Alegrette, "Entre o horror," 18; A. Davies, "Slime and Subtlety," 54; Kraniauskas, "*Cronos* and the Political Economy," 146; Tierney, "Transnational Political Horror," 164–65.
142. Tierney, "Transnational Political Horror," 164–65.
143. Moraña, *The Monster as War Machine*, 371; see also Óscar Martínez Agíss, "Reinventando al vampiro: *Cronos* de Guillermo del Toro," in *Nuevas narrativas mexicanas*, ed. Marco Kunz, Cristina Mondragón, and Dolores Phillipps-López (Barcelona: Red ediciones S.L, 2012), 318; Sidney Sondergard, "The Ambivalence of Creative Desire: Theogonic Myth and Monstrous Offspring," in Morehead, *Supernatural Cinema*, 93–96.
144. Brad O'Brien, "Fulcanelli as a Vampiric Frankenstein and Jesus as His Vampiric Monster: The Frankenstein and Dracula Myths in Guillermo del Toro's *Cronos*," in *Monstrous Adaptations: Generic and Thematic Mutations in Horror and Film*, ed. Richard J. Hand and Jay McRoy (Manchester: Manchester University Press, 2007), 176.
145. Melissa Olson, "Dracula the Anti-Christ: New Resurrection of an Immortal Prejudice," in *Images of the Modern Vampire: The Hip and the Atavistic*, ed. Barbara Brodman and James E. Doan, 29–40 (Madison, WI: Fairleigh Dickinson University Press, 2013), 35–37; Bruno D. Starrs, "Keeping the Faith: Catholicism in *Dracula* and its Adaptations," *Journal of Dracula Studies* 6 (2004): 6.
146. Javier Martín Párraga, "La reinvención del mito vampírico en *Cronos*, de Guillermo del Toro," *Frame* 6 (2010): 60.
147. Doug Jones, foreword to Morehead, *The Supernatural Cinema of Guillermo del Toro*, 4.
148. Shaw, *The Three Amigos*, 25.
149. Pérez, "Queer Reading," 80; Raúl Rodríguez-Hernández and Claudia Schaefer, "*Cronos* and the Man of Science: Madness, Monstrosity, Mexico," *Revista de Estudios Hispánicos* 33, no. 1 (1999): 94.
150. A. Davies, "Guillermo del Toro's *Cronos*," 401.
151. L. Davies, "Guillermo del Toro's *Cronos*," 92n3; Rusnak, "Mexican Cinema in a Global Age," 78–79; Shaw, *The Three Amigos*, 24; Tierney, "Transnational Political Horror," 164.
152. For a discussion of Mexico's reticence in fully protecting the rights of immigrants living within its borders, see Jürgen Buchenau, "The Limits of the Cosmic Race: Immigrant and Nation in Mexico, 1850–1950," in *Immigration*

*and National Identities in Latin America*, ed. Nicola Foote and Michael Goebel (Gainesville: University Press of Florida, 2014); Pablo Yankelevich, *Los otros: Raza, normas y corrupción en la gestión de la extranjería en México, 1900–1950* (Mexico City: Colegio de México, 2019).

153. Joshi, "Magical Spirituality," 14; see also Eljaiek-Rodríguez, "Bloodsucking Bugs," 156.
154. Jones, Foreward.
155. Rodríguez-Hernández and Schaefer, "*Cronos* and the Man of Science," 90.
156. Tierney, "Transnational Political Horror," 167.
157. Agamben, *Homo Sacer*, 41.
158. Agamben, *Homo Sacer*, 48–51.
159. The child protagonists of del Toro's cinema often receive parental guidance from a monstrous figure after losing a parental figure. See Alexandra West, "Where the Wild Things Are: Monsters and Children," in Morehead, *Supernatural Cinema*, 132.
160. Waldron, "Introduction," 22.
161. Braham, *From Amazons to Zombies*, 174.
162. Jessica Balanzategui, "The Child Transformed by Monsters: The Monstrous Beauty of Childhood Trauma," in Morehead, *Supernatural Cinema*, 78.
163. Dalton, *Mestizo Modernity*, 146–61.
164. Simone Weil, *Gravity and Grace*, trans. Arthur Wills (New York: Routledge, 2004), 69.
165. Braham, *From Amazons to Zombies*, 175, emphasis mine.
166. Sánchez Prado, *Screening Neoliberalism*, 169.
167. Shaw, *The Three Amigos*, 30.
168. Estévez, "Biopolítica."

## CHAPTER 2

1. Ignacio M. Sánchez Prado, "Ending the World with Words: Bernardo Fernández (BEF) and the Institutionalization of Science Fiction in Mexico," in Ginway and Brown, *Latin American Science Fiction*, 114.
2. Javier Cabrera Hormazábal, "Panorámica de la ciencia ficción mexicana: Mundos posibles y utopía en *Ruido gris* de Juan José Rojo," (master's thesis, Universidad de Chile, 2013), 33. Pepe Rojo recently removed "Ruido gris" from his website following a re-edition of the story alongside "Yonke."
3. Armando Rendon, Jenny Irizary, and Scott Duncan-Fernandez, "Ernesto [*sic*] Hogan: Father of Chicano Scifi Interview May 2020," *Somos en Escrito Interviews/Entrevistas*, May 26, 2020. https://somosenescrito.weebly.com/interviews-entrevistas/ernesto-hogan-father-of-chicano-scifi-interview-may-2020.
4. Rendon, Irizary, and Duncan-Fernandez, "Ernesto [*sic*] Hogan."
5. See Brown and Ginway, Introduction, 1–2.
6. Ernest Hogan, *Smoking Mirror Blues*, (La Grande: Wordcraft of Oregon, 2001), 195. According to Elsa del Campo Ramírez, the simulation of Marilyn

testifies to a process that "downgrad[es] religion to iconography, or, perhaps, transform[s] iconolatry into a creed." See Elsa del Campo Ramírez, "Postethnicity and Antiglobalization in Chicana/o Science Fiction: Ernest Hogan's *Smoking Mirror Blues* and Beatrice Pita's *Lunar Braceros 2125-2148*," *Journal of Transnational American Studies* 9, no. 1 (2018): 392–93.

7. Several fans and critics view Hogan as a postcyberpunk author. For a fan perspective, see James Palmer, review of *Smoking Mirror Blues* (Wordcraft Speculative Writers Series), *New York Journal of Books*, Oct. 1, 2010, https://www.nyjournalofbooks.com/book-review/smoking-mirror-blues-wordcraft-speculative-writers-series; for an academic perspective, see Lysa Rivera, "*Mestizaje* and Heterotopia in Ernest Hogan's *High Aztech*," in *Black and Brown Planets: The Politics of Race in Science Fiction*, ed. Isiah Lavender (Jackson: University Press of Mississippi, 2014), 146–47. For a discussion of the novel as a cyberpunk text, see Daoine S. Bachran, "From Code to Codex: Tricksterizing the Digital Divide in Ernest Hogan's *Smoking Mirror Blues*," in *Altermundos: Latin@ Speculative Literature, Film, and Popular Culture*, eds. Cathryn Josefina Merla-Watson and B V. Olguín (Los Angeles: UCLA Chicano Studies Research Center Press, 2017), 112.

8. See Mike Featherstone and Roger Burrows, "Cultures of Technological Embodiment: An Introduction," in *Cyberspace/Cyberbodies/Cyberpunk: Cultures of Technological Embodiment*, ed. Mike Featherstone and Roger Burrows (London: Sage Publications, 1995), 7–8; Katie Hafner and John Markoff, *Cyberpunk: Outlaws and Hackers on the Computer Frontier* (New York: Touchstone, 1991), 10–11.

9. Brown and Ginway, Introduction, 8–9.

10. Josh Rios, "A Possible Future Return to the Past," *Somatechnics* 7, no. 1 (2017): 66.

11. Pre-Columbian religious traditions prove particularly important in Hogan's oeuvre. See Frederick Luis Aldama, "Introduction: On Matters of Form in Contemporary Latino Poetry," in *Formal Matters in Contemporary Latino Poetry*, ed. Frederick Luis Aldama (New York: Palgrave MacMillan, 2016), 9; Frederick Luis Aldama, "Confessions of a Latin@ Sojourner in *SciFilandia*," In *Latin@ Rising: An Anthology of Latin@ Science Fiction and Fantasy*, ed. Matthew David Goodwin (San Antonio, TX: Wings Press, 2017), xvi.

12. Mbembe, *Necropolitics*, 175.

13. Mbembe, *Necropolitics*, 176.

14. Naief Yehya, "Revolt, Confusion, and Cult of the Trivial in Mexican Cyberculture," in *Technology and Culture in Twentieth-Century Mexico*, ed. Araceli Tinajero and Brian J. Freeman (Tuscaloosa: University of Alabama Press), 132. Castells, *The Information Age*, 357.

15. Bachran, "From Code to Codex," 111–16.

16. For a discussion on how the rise of the information economy has developed hand-in-hand with neoliberal reforms regarding such disparate elements as the de-unionization of labor and the deregulation of finance, see Robert Neubauer,

"Neoliberalism in the Information Age, or Vice Versa?: Global Citizenship, Technology, and Hegemonic Ideology," *TripleC* 9, no. 2 (2011): 200–3.

17. García Canclini's *Hybrid Cultures: Strategies for Entering and Leaving Modernity* (1995) now reads like a hopeful though ultimately naïve treatise on the potential of the neoliberal order to reconcile the problems facing Latin America. The author has recognized as much in his own work. For a more tempered take with both critical and hopeful essays, see Gilberto Guevara Niebla and Néstor García Canclini, eds., *La educación y la cultura ante el tratado de libre comercio* (Mexico City: Nueva Imagen, 1994).

18. See Bachran, "From Code to Codex," 125.

19. See Darío González, Nelson, "El *neuropunk* y la ciencia ficcón hispanoamericana," *Revista Iberoamericana* 83, no. 259–260 (2017): 355–56; Grace A. Martin, "For the Love of Robots: Posthumanism in Latin American Science Fiction between 1960–1999" (PhD diss., University of Kentucky, 2015), 199.

20. Alexander P. Shafer, "Queering Bodies: Aliens, Cyborgs, and Spacemen in Mexican and Argentine Science Fiction" (PhD diss., University of California, Riverside, 2017), 92.

21. Hernán Manuel García, "Tecnociencia y cibercultura en México: *Hackers* en el cuento *cyberpunk* mexicano," *Revista Iberoamericana* 78, no. 238–239 (2012): 336.

22. Hernán Manuel García, "La globalización desfigurada o la post-globalización imaginada: La estética cyberpunk (post)mexicana" (PhD dissertation, University of Kansas, 2011), 109–11; Martin, "For the Love of Robots," 199; Shafer, "Queering Bodies," 85.

23. Rodrigo Gómez, "TV Azteca y la industria televisiva mexicana en tiempos de integración regional (TLCAN) y desregulación económica," *Comunicación y Sociedad*, no. 1 (2004). Certainly, Televisa and TV Azteca functioned as a duopoly by the first decade of the twenty-first century. Felipe Gaytán Alcalá and Juliana Fregoso Bonilla, "La ley Televisa de México," *Chasqui: Revista Latinoamericana de Comunicación*, no. 94 (2006): 42.

24. Andrew Paxman and Alex M. Saragoza, "Globalization and Latin Media Powers: The Case of Mexico's Televisa," *Continental Order?: Integrating North America for Cybercapitalism*, ed. Vincent Mosco and Dan Schiller (Lanham, MD: Rowman & Littlefield, 2001), 65.

25. Gómez, "TV Azteca," 75.

26. Omar Hernández and Emile McAnany, "Cultural Industries in the Free Trade Age: A Look at Mexican Television," in *Fragments of a Golden Age*, ed. Gilbert M. Joseph, Anne Rubenstein, and Eric Zolov (Durham, NC: Duke University Press, 2001), 393–94; Gómez, "TV Azteca," 77.

27. Nery Córdova, "El espectáculo y la massmediación sociocultural," in Córdova, *La cultura del espectáculo*, 122.

28. Córdova, "espectáculo y la massmediación," 122.

29. Adriana Garay, "'Escurrirá sangre' por la TV," *Reforma* (Mexico City), Dec. 30, 1996.

30. Agamben, *Homo Sacer*, 9.
31. Agamben, *Homo Sacer*, 83.
32. See Gálvez, *Eating NAFTA*, 10–18; Asa Cristina Laurell, "Three Decades of Neoliberalism in Mexico: The Destruction of Society," *International Journal of Health Services* 45, no. 2 (2015): 250–52.
33. Stephen C. Tobin, "Televisual Subjectivities in Pepe Rojo's Speculative Fiction from Mexico: 1996–2003," *Alambique: Revista Académica de Ciencia Ficción y Fantasía* 4 (2016): 5–6.
34. Andrea L. Bell, and Yolanda Molina-Gavilán. "Introduction: Science Fiction in Latin America and Spain," in *Cosmos Latinos: An Anthology of Science Fiction from Latin America and Spain*, ed. Andrea L. Bell and Yolanda Molina-Gavilán (Middletown, CT: Wesleyan University Press, 2003), 15.
35. Tobin, "Televisual Subjectivities," 1–3.
36. Martin, "For the Love of Robots," 203.
37. Tobin, "Televisual Subjectivities," 4.
38. Héctor Fernández L'Hoeste, "El futuro en cuentos: De OVNIs e implantes oculares en la ciencia ficción mexicana," *Revista Iberoamericana* 83, no. 259–260 (2017): 496; Shafer, "Queering Bodies," 90.
39. M. Elizabeth Ginway, "Do implantado ao ciborge: O corpo social na ficção científica brasileira," *Revista Iberoamericana* 73, no. 221 (2007): 789; Shafer, "Queering Bodies," 35.
40. García, "globalización desfigurada," 97.
41. Shafer, "Queering Bodies," 87.
42. Pepe Rojo, "Gray Noise," trans. Andrea Bell, in Bell and Molina-Gavilán, *Cosmos Latinos*, 245.
43. Rojo, "Gray Noise," 247.
44. M. Elizabeth Ginway, "The Politics of Cyborgs in Mexico and Latin America," *Semina: Ciência Sociais e Humana* 34, no. 2 (2013): 167.
45. Rojo, "Gray Noise," 247.
46. Martin, "For the Love of Robots," 214. See also Tobin, "Televisual Subjectivities," 3.
47. Fernández L'Hoeste, "Futuro en cuentos," 495.
48. Fernández L'Hoeste, "Futuro en cuentos," 496.
49. Fernández L'Hoeste, "Futuro en cuentos," 496.
50. For a discussion of the pleasurably tight couplings between flesh and metal, see Haraway, *Simians, Cyborgs and Women*, 152. Ginway, "Politics of Cyborgs," 167.
51. Rojo, "Gray Noise," 245.
52. Rojo, "Gray Noise," 253.
53. The use of the verb "chingar" in the Spanish version of this text is one of the few elements that explicitly place the story in Mexico. See Pepe Rojo, "Ruido gris" (Mexico City: Universidad Autónoma Metropolitana, 1996), 33.
54. Rojo, "Gray Noise," 257–58.
55. Rojo, "Gray Noise," 258.

56. Rojo, "Gray Noise," 258.
57. Frederic Jameson, "Future City," *New Left Review* 21 (2003): 76; Slavoj Zizek, "Slavoj Zizek on Occupy Wall Street: A Moving Speech," P2P Foundation Blog, Oct. 15, 2011, https://blog.p2pfoundation.net/slavoj-zizek-on-occupy-wall-street-a-moving-speech/2011/10/15.
58. Rojo, "Gray Noise," 245.
59. Althusser, "Ideology and Ideological," 204–6.
60. Rojo, "Gray Noise," 264.
61. Rojo, "Ruido gris," 45.
62. Jameson, "Future City," 76.
63. Bachran, "From Code to Codex," 118.
64. Bachran, "From Code to Codex," 125. Indeed, another critic argues that Hogan's mediasphere celebrates diversity only as a means of monetizing—and fetishizing—human difference. See del Campo Ramírez, "Postethnicity and Antiglobalization," 395.
65. Hogan, *Smoking Mirror Blues*, 6.
66. Hogan, *Smoking Mirror Blues*, 35.
67. Bachran, "From Code to Codex," 116.
68. Hogan, *Smoking Mirror Blues*, 44.
69. Del Campo Ramírez, "Postethnicity and Antiglobalization," 392.
70. Ernest Hogan, "Chicanonautica Manifesto," *Aztlan: A Journal of Chicano Studies* 40, no. 2 (2015): 131–34. Some critics argue that Hogan's aesthetic has influenced the work of other US authors of color. Paul Allatson, "From 'Latinidad' to 'Latinid@des': Imaging the Twenty-First Century," in *The Cambridge Companion to Latina/o American Literature*, ed. John Morán González (Cambridge: Cambridge University Press, 2016), 142n6.
71. See also del Campo Ramírez, "Postethnicity and Antiglobalization," 386; L. Rivera, "*Mestizaje* and Heterotopia," 141–57.
72. Del Campo Ramírez, "Postethnicity and Antiglobalization," 387.
73. L. Rivera, "Chicana/o Cyberpunk," 196.
74. See Susana Rostas "'Mexicanidad': The Resurgence of the Indian in Popular Mexican Nationalism," *Cambridge Journal of Anthropology* 23, no. 1 (2002): 21; see also Bachran, "From Code to Codex," 120–25.
75. See Anzaldúa, *Borderlands/La frontera*, chapter 7; Pérez-Torres, "Refiguring Aztlán," 173–74; Sandoval, *Methodology of the Oppressed*, 166–77.
76. For a detailed reading of the different groups that compose Chicano populations in the United States, see Gutiérrez, "Unraveling America's," 345–54.
77. Guillermo Bonfil Batalla, *México profundo: Una civilización negada* (Mexico City: SEP/CIESAS, 1987), 41–42.
78. Carl G. Jung et al., *Man and His Symbols* (New York: Dell, 1968), 103.
79. Del Campo Ramírez recognizes an implicit dialogue with Jung in the novel, but she does not connect it to Tezcatlipoca, the trickster god. See del Campo Ramírez, "Postethnicity and Antiglobalization," 383.

80. For a discussion of the Orientalization of nonhegemonic societies, see Edward Said *Orientalism* (New York: Penguin, 2003), 50–72.
81. Hogan, *Smoking Mirror Blues*, 13–14.
82. Anzaldúa, *Borderlands/La frontera*, 64.
83. Hogan, *Smoking Mirror Blues*, 22.
84. Anzaldúa, *Borderlands/La frontera*, 105–6.
85. For a discussion about the misogyny that prevailed during the Chicano Movement, see Segura and Pesquera, "Beyond Indifference," 360–62.
86. See Haraway, *Simians, Cyborgs and Women*, 151.
87. Hogan, *Smoking Mirror Blues*, 15–16.
88. Hogan, *Smoking Mirror Blues*, 193.
89. Diel, *The Codex Mexicanus*, 116–20.
90. Pérez-Torres, "Refiguring Aztlán," 172.
91. Arrizón, "Mythical Performativity," 26; Maria Hsia Chang, "Multiculturalism, Immigration, and Aztlan," *Social Contract* 10, no. 3 (2000): 208–10; Hernán Manuel García, "Hacia una poética de la tecnología periférica: *Post-cyberpunk y picaresca en Sleep Dealer* de Alex Rivera," *Revista Iberoamericana* 83, no. 259–260 (2017).
92. Chabram-Dernersesian, "I Throw Punches," 172–75; Moraga, "Queer Aztlán," 256–59.
93. See L. Rivera, "*Mestizaje* and Heterotopia."
94. See Anzaldúa, *Borderlands/La frontera* for an example par excellence of this sort of work.
95. See Claudio Lomnitz, *Exits from the Labyrinth: Culture and Ideology in the Mexican National Space* (Berkeley: University of California Press, 1992), 1–22; Bachran, "From Code to Codex," 113.
96. Haraway, *Simians, Cyborgs and Women*, 152.
97. Hogan, *Smoking Mirror Blues*, 113.
98. N. Katherine Hayles, *How We Think: Digital Media and Contemporary Technogenesis* (Chicago: University of Chicago Press, 2012), 3.
99. Hogan, *Smoking Mirror Blues*, 111.
100. Hayles, *How We Think*, 96, 95–103.
101. Hayles, *How We Became Posthuman*, 5.
102. Hogan, *Smoking Mirror Blues*, 112.
103. Rampant sexuality is a frequent element of Hogan's narrative. See Cynthia Ward, "*Cortez on Jupiter*, by Ernest Hogan," *Cascadia Subduction Zone* 5, no. 2 (2015): 12.
104. Hogan, *Smoking Mirror Blues*, 202.
105. Hogan, *Smoking Mirror Blues*, 209.
106. Hogan, *Smoking Mirror Blues*, 160.
107. Enrique Florescano, *Quetzalcóatl y los mitos fundadores de Mesoamérica* (Mexico City: Debolsillo, 2017), 86–88.

## CHAPTER 3

1. Luis Martín-Cabrera, "The Potentiality of the Commons: A Materialist Critique of Cognitive Capitalism from the Cyberbracer@s to the Ley Sinde," *Hispanic Review* 80, no. 4 (2012): 590–91.
2. Ande Davis, "Consumed by El Otro Lado: Alterations of the Neoliberal Self in *Sleep Dealer*," *Chiricú Journal: Latina/o Literatures, Arts, and Cultures* 4, no. 1 (2019): 45.
3. Martín-Cabrera, "Potentiality of the Commons," 590.
4. Alfredo Suppia, "Quando a realidade parece ficção, é hora de fazer *mockumentary*," *Ciência e Cultura* 65, no. 1 (2013).
5. Kitty Calavita, *Inside the State: The Bracero Program, Immigration, and the I.N.S* (New York: Routledge, 1992), 4–10. For a discussion of Operation Gatekeeper, see Melissa Ann Castillo-Garsow, "A Mexican State of Mind: New York City and the New Borderlands of Culture" (PhD diss., Yale University, 2017), 8. Many would argue that the exploitation of migrant workers extends into the present. See Ronald L. Mize and Alicia C. S. Swords, *Consuming Mexican Labor: From the Bracero Program to NAFTA* (Toronto: University of Toronto Press, 2011), xxxii–xxxvi.
6. See Joshua Clover, "The Future in Labor," *Film Quarterly* 63, no. 1 (2009): 8; Ginway, "Politics of Cyborgs," 166.
7. B. V. Olguín, "'Contrapuntal Cyborgs?': The Ideological Limits and Revolutionary Potential of Latin@ Science Fiction," *Aztlán: A Journal of Chicano Studies* 41, no. 1 (2016): 230; Rebecca M. Schreiber, "The Undocumented Everyday: Migrant Rights and Visual Strategies in the Work of Alex Rivera," *Journal of American Studies* 50, no. 2 (2016).
8. Marissa K. López, "The Xicano Future is Now: Poetry, Performance, and Prolepsis," *ASAP/Journal* 4, no. 2 (2019): 409; China Medel, "The Ghost in the Machine: The Biopolitics of Memory in Alex Rivera's *Sleep Dealer*," *Camera Obscura* 33, no. 1 (2018): 115–16.
9. Camilla Fojas, *Migrant Labor and Border Securities in Pop Culture* (New York: Routledge, 2017), 35.
10. The company's spelling—it does not place an accent on the word "Rio"—linguistically illustrates the marginalization of Spanish and non-Anglo ways of knowing in this dystopian world. See Amy Sara Carroll, "From *Papapapá* to *Sleep Dealer*: Alex Rivera's Undocumentary Poetics," *Social Identities: Journal for the Study of Race, Nation and Culture* 19, no. 3–4 (2013): 493.
11. Sarah D. Wald, "Farmworker Activism," in *The Cambridge Companion to Literature and Food*, ed. J. Michelle Coghlan (Cambridge: Cambridge University Press, 2020), 205.
12. Curtis Marez, *Farm Worker Futurism: Speculative Technologies of Resistance* (Minneapolis: University of Minneapolis Press, 2016), 35.
13. Ana María Manzanas Calvo and Paula Barba Guerrero, "Redrawing the Boundary: From Carlos Fuentes's *La frontera de cristal* (1995) to Rosaura

Sánchez and Beatrice Pita's *Lunar Braceros 2125–2148* (2009)," *Excentric Narratives: Journal of Anglophone Literature, Culture and Media*, no. 3 (2019).
14. Christopher González, "Latino Sci-Fi: Cognition and Narrative Design in Alex Rivera's *Sleep Dealer*," in *Latinos and Narrative Media*, ed. Frederick Luis Aldama (New York: Palgrave MacMillan, 2013), 222.
15. del Campo Ramírez, "Postethnicity and Antiglobalization," 389; Ana María Manzanas Calvo and Jesús Benito, *Occupying Space in American Literature and Culture: Static Heroes, Social Movements and Empowerment* (New York: Routledge, 2014) 94–97; Kristy L. Ulibarri, "Speculating Latina Radicalism: Labour and Motherhood in *Lunar Braceros 2125–2148*," *Feminist Review* 116 (2017): 91. For a discussion of the historically loaded nature of the term *reservation*, see Brittany Henry, "Unsettling Utopia: The Politics of Hope in North American Dystopian Fiction" (PhD diss., Rice University, 2018), 169.
16. Geoffrey Kantaris, "Terminal City: Immaterial Migrations, Virtual Detachments and the North-South Divide (Alex Rivera's *Sleep Dealer*, 2008)," in *South and North: Contemporary Urban Orientations*, ed. Kerry Bystrom, Ashleigh Harris, and Andrew J. Webber (New York: Routledge, 2018), 144.
17. Mbembe, *Necropolitics*, 83.
18. Mbembe, *Necropolitics*, 85.
19. Mark Manion and Abby Goodrum, "Terrorism or Civil Disobedience: Toward a Hacktivist Ethic," *Computers and Society* 30, no. 2 (2000): 14.
20. Ricardo Domínguez, "Electronic Civil Disobedience: Inventing the Future of Online Agitprop Theater," *PMLA* 124, no 5 (2009): 1807; Stefan Wray, "On Electronic Civil Disobedience," *Peace Review: A Journal of Social Justice* 11, no. 1 (1999): 109.
21. García, "Hacia una poética," 336; Marez, *Farm Worker Futurism*, 163.
22. Sandoval, *Methodology of the Oppressed*, 173; see also García, "Hacia una poética," 327.
23. Haraway, *Simians, Cyborgs and Women*, 191.
24. Haraway, *Simians, Cyborgs and Women*, 170–73.
25. García, "Hacia una poética," 331.
26. Marez, *Farm Worker Futurism*, 161.
27. Jennifer M. Lozano, "Alex Rivera's Multimedia Storytelling, Humor, and Transborder Latinx Futurity," in *Latinx Ciné in the Twenty-First Century*, ed. Frederick Luis Aldama (Tucson: University of Arizona Press, 2019), 267.
28. Miranda, "Techno/Memo," 255; Gabriela Nuñez, "The Future of Food?: Indigenous Knowledges and Sustainable Food Systems in Latin@ Speculative Fiction," in Merla-Watson and Olguín, *Altermundos*, 237.
29. Taylor and Pitman, *Latin American Identity*, 162.
30. Anzaldúa, *Borderlands/La frontera*, 109.
31. For a list of studies that view the film as a US or US-Latinx production, see Frederick Luis Aldama, "Toward a Transfrontera-LatinX Aesthetic: An Interview with Filmmaker Alex Rivera," *Latino Studies* 15, no. 3 (2017): 373–80; Andrés Amerikaner, "Xerox Men: Technological Tropes in U.S. Latino/a

Displacement Literature," *Symploke* 25, no. 1–2 (2017); Ande Davis, "Consumed by El Otro Lado."

32. For a list of studies that view the film as Mexican, see Pablo Brescia, "*Sleep Dealer* y el México futuro: ¿Borrón y cuenta nueva?," in *Nationbuilding en el cine mexicano desde la Época de Oro hasta el presente*, ed. Friedhelm Schmidt-Welle and Christian Wehr (Madrid: Iberoamericana, 2015); Betina Keizman, "Relecturas (cinematográficas) de la migración mexicana," *Amérique Latine Histoire et Mémoire: Les Cahiers ALHIM* 23 (2012); Martínez-Guzmán, "Masculine Subjectivities." I have previously noted ties between this film and Mexican Golden Age cinema. David S. Dalton, "*Robo Sacer*: 'Bare Life' and Cyborg Labor beyond the Border in Alex Rivera's *Sleep Dealer*," *Hispanic Studies Review* 1, no. 2 (2016): 20.

33. For a list of studies that view the film as a transnational production, see Evert Hamner, "Virtual Immigrants: Transfigured Bodies and Transnational Spaces in Science Fiction Cinema," in *Simultaneous Worlds: Global Science Fiction Cinema*, ed. Jennifer L. Feeley and Sarah Ann Wells (Minneapolis: University of Minnesota Press, 2015); Kantaris, "Terminal City"; Pepe Rojo, "Border Technologies," *Review: Literature and Arts of the Americas* 48, no. 1 (2015): 10n4; Carolina Rueda, "The Everlasting *Sleep Dealer*: Alex Rivera's Visionary Mind and Fantasy Nightmares in Present Times," *Studies in Spanish and Latin American Cinemas* 14, no. 3 (2017).

34. Sophia A. McClennen, *Globalization and Latin American Cinema: Toward a New Critical Paradigm* (New York: Palgrave MacMillan, 2018), 473.

35. Tracey Daniels-Lerberg, "Watershed Ethics and Dam Politics: Mapping Biopolitics, Race, and Resistance in *Sleep Dealer* and *Watershed*," in *Make Waves: Water in Contemporary Literature and Film*, ed. Paula Anca Farca (Reno: University of Nevada Press, 2019), 119.

36. Javier Duran, "Virtual Borders, Data Aliens, and Bare Bodies: Culture, Securitization, and the Biometric State," *Journal of Borderlands Studies* 25, no. 3–4 (2010): 224; L. Rivera, "Future Histories," 425–27.

37. Medel, "The Ghost in the Machine," 114. We should note that nothing in the film explicitly associates Luz with South America, but the actress is Chilean, and her accent sets her apart from the Mexican characters throughout.

38. Altha Cravey, Joseph Palis, and Gabriela Valdivia, "Imagining the Future from the Margins: Cyborg Labor in Alex Rivera's *Sleep Dealer*," *GeoJournal* 80, no. 6 (2015): 869.

39. For a Marxist approach, see Matthew David Goodwin, "The Technology of Labor, Migration, and Protest," in *The Routledge Companion to Latina/o Popular Culture*, ed. Frederick Luis Aldama (New York: Routledge, 2016); Alfredo Suppia and and Igor Oliveira. "Cibertíteres: Discurso marxista e a colisão entre o público e privado no cinema de Alex Rivera," *Ciberlegenda* 1, no. 26 (2012); Alfredo Suppia, "Remote Exploitations: Alex Rivera's Materialist SF Cinema in the Age of Cognitive Capitalism," in *Red Alert: Marxist Approaches to Science*

Fiction Cinema, ed. Ewa Mazierska and Alfredo Suppia (Detroit, MI: Wayne State University Press, 2014); Jelena Šesnić, "Dreams Deferred: The Concept of the US-Mexican Borderlands between the Global North and the Global South," Americana: E-Journal of American Studies in Hungary 7, no. 1 (2011); L. Rivera, "Future Histories." For a post-Marxist take, see Jodi Melamed, "Post-Marxism, American Studies, and Post-Capitalist Futures," in Approaches to American Cultural Studies, ed. Antje Dallmann, Eva Bosenberg, and Martin Klepper (New York: Routledge, 2016), 139–43.

40. Arturo Vargas, "Movilidades posapocalípticas: Un nuevo acercamiento a la película de la migración irregular," Nomenclatura: Aproximaciones a los estudios hispánicos 2 (2012): 10.

41. Fabio Chee, "Science Fiction and Latino Studies Today... and in the Future," in Aldama, Routledge Companion, 114.

42. See Cordelia E. Barrera, "Cyborg Bodies, Strategies of Consciousness and Ecological Revolution in the Mexico-US Borderlands," Chicana/Latina Studies 14, no. 1 (2014); Katarzyna Olga Beilin and Sainath Suryanarayanan, "Step Out to Shadowtime, Hurry Like a Plant: Corporeal and Corporate Time for the Anthropocene Generation," Transmodernity 6, no. 2 (2016); Sharada Balachandran Orihuela and Andrew Carl Hageman, "The Virtual Realities of US/Mexico Border Ecologies in Maquilapolis and Sleep Dealer," Environmental Communication 5, no. 2 (2011); Jungwon Park, "La frontera en ruinas: El cuerpo enfermo y la biopolítica global en Maquilapolis y Sleep Dealer," Revista Iberoamericana 84, no. 265 (2018): 1128–30.

43. Micah K. Donohue, "Borderlands Gothic Science Fiction: Alienation as Intersection in Rivera's Sleep Dealer and Lavín's 'Llegar a la orilla,'" Science Fiction Studies 45, no. 1 (2018).

44. Marez, Farm Worker Futurism, 137; A. Vargas, "Movilidades posapocalípticas," 11. For other comparisons to popular and Hollywood cinema, see Suppia, "Remote Exploitations," 205–6; Kantaris, "Terminal City," 145–47; Keizman, "Relecturas (cinematográficas)," 3–5; Raúl Rodríguez-Hernández and Claudia Schaefer, "Do Cybraceros Dream of a Good Night's Sleep?" in Apocalyptic Chic: Visions of the Apocalypse and Post-Apocalypse in Literature and Visual Arts, ed. Barbara Brodman and James E. Doan (Lanham, MD: Rowman and Littlefield, 2017); Suppia and Oliveira, "Cibertíteres," 195; Libia Villazana, "Transnational Virtual Mobility as a Reification of Deployment of Power: Exploring Transnational Processes in the Film Sleep Dealer," Transnational Cinemas 4, no. 2 (2013): 220.

45. Sara Ann Wells, "The Scar and the Node: Border Science Fiction and the Mise-en-scène of Globalized Labor," Global South 8, no. 1 (2014): 74.

46. Duran, "Virtual Borders," 224.

47. Duran, "Virtual Borders," 226.

48. García, "Hacia una poética," 335–37; see also Hamner, "Virtual Immigrants," 156.

49. Olguín, "Contrapuntal Cyborgs?," 223.

50. Davis, "Consumed by El Otro Lado," 52.
51. Thomas Prasch, "Aquaterrorists and Cybraceros: The Dystopian Borderlands of Alex Rivera's *Sleep Dealer* (2008)," in *Border Visions: Identity and Diaspora in Film*, ed. Jakub Kazecki, Karen A. Ritzenhoff, and Cynthia J. Miller (Lanham, MD: Scarecrow Press, 2013).
52. Ramírez, J. Jesse, "*Sleep Dealer*, or, Tijuana, Ciudad del Futuro," unpublished paper. Ramírez implicitly cites José Martí's famous "Nuestra América."
53. For a discussion on water rights in the film, see Prasch, "Aquaterrorists and Cybraceros," 49–53; Daniels-Lerberg, "Watershed Ethics"; Villazana, "Transnational Virtual Mobility," 220–21.
54. Samantha Kountz, "The Other Side of the Wall: Technology and Borders in *Sleep Dealer*," *International Journal of Humanities and Cultural Studies* 1, no. 4 (2016): 290–91.
55. For a discussion on pre-emption in the film, see Amy Sara Carroll, "From *Papapapá* to *Sleep Dealer*," 494; Prasch, "Aquaterrorists and Cybraceros," 49–52. For a discussion of the privatization of military functions, see Louise Amoore, "Biometric Borders: Governing Mobilities in the War on Terror," *Political Geography* 25 (2006): 340–49; Donohue, "Borderlands Gothic," 57.
56. Michael Martínez Raguso, "All of the Work, with None of the Workers: The Technology of Consumption in *Sleep Dealer*," in *Future Humans in Fiction and Film*, ed. Louisa Mackay Demerjian and Karen F. Stein (Cambridge: Cambridge Scholars Publishing, 2018), 119.
57. Medel, "The Ghost in the Machine," 118.
58. Martínez-Raguso, "All of the Work," 119.
59. Benedict Anderson, *Imagined Communities: Reflections on the Origin and Spread of Nationalism*, 2nd ed. (New York: Verso, 1991), 7.
60. Ana María Manzanas Calvo and Jesús Benito Sánchez, *Hospitality in American Literature and Culture: Spaces, Bodies, Borders* (New York: Routledge, 2016), 101; Prasch, "Aquaterrorists and Cybraceros," 49–50; Šesnić, "Dreams Deferred."
61. McKenzie Wark, *Gamer Theory* (Cambridge, MA: Harvard University Press, 2007), 1–8.
62. Martínez-Raguso, "All of the Work," 127.
63. Hayles, *How We Became Posthuman*, 1–2.
64. Iskandar Zulkarnain, "Polyspatial Resistance for the Sake of the 'Real' Subalterns: Electronic Civil Disobedience as a Form of Hacktivism," in *On and Off the Page: Mapping Place in Text and Culture*, ed. M. B. Hackler and Ari J. Adipurwawidjana (Cambridge: Cambridge Scholars Press, 2009), 221–24.
65. Agamben, *Homo Sacer*, 89.
66. For a discussion of Rudy's alienation, see Suppia, "Remote Exploitations," 208. For a discussion of the humanization of Miguel, see Daniels-Lerberg, "Watershed Ethics," 132.
67. Manzanas Calvo and Sánchez, *Hospitality*, 101.
68. Barrera, "Cyborg Bodies," 36.

69. Shelley Streeby, "Speculative Archives: Histories of the Future of Education," *Pacific Coast Philology* 49, no. 1 (2014): 38.
70. J. González, "Envisioning Cyborg Bodies," 268–78; Haraway, *Simians, Cyborgs and Women*, 173–81; Sandoval, *Methodology of the Oppressed*, 167–70.
71. Barrera, "Cyborg Bodies," 46.
72. Barrera, "Cyborg Bodies," 30.
73. See Michel Foucault, "The Technologies of the Self," in Rabinow and Rose, *The Essential Foucault*, 145–69.
74. T. Jake Dionne, "Tropics of Reality Television: Introducing Metaphor and Coloniality through *Drones!*," *Teaching Media Quarterly* 7, no. 3 (2019): 3.
75. J. V. Miranda, "Techno/Memo: The Politics of Cultural Memory in Alex Rivera's *Sleep Dealer*," in *Latinx Ciné in the Twenty-First Century*, ed. Frederick Luis Aldama (Tucson: University of Arizona Press, 2019), 255–56; Rodríguez-Hernández and Schaefer, "Do *Cybraceros* Dream," 152.
76. Rueda, "The Everlasting *Sleep Dealer*," 338.
77. Daoine S. Bachran, "From Recovery to Discovery: Ethnic American Science Fiction and (Re)Creating the Future" (PhD diss., University of New Mexico, 2016), 155.
78. Sandoval, *Methodology of the Oppressed*, 174.
79. Rebecca Lemov, "On Not Being There: The Data-Driven Body at Work and at Play," *Hedgehog Review* 17, no. 2 (2015): 46.
80. Tom Barry, *Mexico: A Country Guide* (Albuquerque: Resource Center Press, 1992), 143; Sergio Guadalupe Sánchez Díaz, *Diálogos desde la subalternidad, la resistencia y la resiliencia: Cultura obrera en las maquiladoras de Ciudad Juárez* (Mexico City: Universidad Autónoma Metropolitana, 2011), 199–200.
81. Sánchez Díaz, *Diálogos*, 129–40. For a discussion on the dehumanizing potential of the maquiladora economy, see Chapter 4 of this book.
82. Marina Pereira Penteado, "Do cotágio ao isolamento: O futuro distópico insistente em *The Rag Doll Plagues* e *Sleep Dealer*," *Revista Línguas & Letras* 16, no. 33 (2015): 155.
83. Duran, "Virtual Borders," 224.
84. Park, "La frontera en ruinas," 1122.
85. Guillermo Alonso Meneses, "Migra, coyotes, paisanos y muertitos: Sobre la analiticidad y el sentido de ciertos factores de la migración clandestina en la frontera norte," *El bordo: Retos de frontera* 7 (2001).
86. R. Scott Frey, "The Transfer of Core-Based Hazardous Production Processes to the Export Processing Zones of the Periphery: The Maquiladora Centers of Northern Mexico," *Journal of World-Systems Research* 9, no. 2 (2003); Christopher Woodruff and Rene Zenteno, "Migration Networks and Microenterprises in Mexico," *Journal of Development Economics* 82 (2007).
87. Aziz N. Berdiev, Yoonbai Kim, and Chun-Ping Chang, "Remittances and Corruption," *Economic Letters* 188 (2013), http://econ.ccu.edu.tw/manage/1382434267_a.pdf.

88. Acosta, *Thresholds of Illiteracy*, 231–35.
89. Suppia, "Remote Exploitations," 206.
90. Lysa Rivera, "Neoliberalism and Dystopia in U.S.-Mexico Borderlands Fiction," in *Blast, Corrupt, Dismantle, Erase: Contemporary North American Dystopian Literature*, ed. Brett Josef Brubisic, Gisele M. Baxter, and Tara Lee (Waterloo, Ont.: Wilfrid Laurier University Press, 2014), 304.
91. McClennen, *Globalization and Latin American Cinema*, 470; Christina L. Sisk, "Disembodied and Deportable Labor at the US Mexico-Border: Representations of the Mexican Body in Film," *Transmodernity* 3, no. 2 (2014): 42, 50–51.
92. For a discussion of how Marx's vampire interfaces with this film, see Donohue, "Borderlands Gothic," 50; Markus Heide, "Cosmopolitics in Border Film: *Amores perros* (2000) and *Sleep Dealer* (2008)," *Comparative American Studies* 11, no. 1 (2013): 89–108. For a discussion of the breakdown of nodeworker bodies, see Kantaris, "Terminal City," 155; Sisk, "Disembodied and Deportable," 54.
93. Kerry Mackereth, "Maids and Family Androids: Racialised Post-Care Imaginaries in *Humans* (2015–), *Sleep Dealer* (2008) and *Her* (2013)," *Feminist Review* 123 (2019): 35; see also Kountz, "Other Side of the Wall," 295.
94. Amerikaner, "Xerox Men," 120; Debra A. Castillo, "Rasquache Aesthetics in Alex Rivera's 'Why Cybraceros'" *Nordlit* 31 (2014): 11–13; Orihuela and Hagerman, "Virtual Realities of US/Mexico," 177; L. Rivera, "Future Histories," 426
95. Manzanas Calvo and Sánchez, *Hospitality*, 98.
96. See Emmelhainz, *La tiranía del sentido común*, 115.
97. Davis, "Consumed by El Otro Lado," 47.
98. Steven Rawle, *Transnational Cinema: An Introduction* (New York: Palgrave MacMillan, 2018), 105–6.
99. For an interview where Rivera discusses the "power" in the construction of Luz's character, see Javier Ramírez, "Sci-Fi-ing Immigration and the US-Mexico Border: An Interview with Filmmaker Alex Rivera," *Chiricú Journal: Latina/o Literature, Art, and Culture* 1, no. 1 (2016): 100. For critical studies that cast Luz in a positive light, see William A. Nericcio, "Latina/o Dystopias on the Verge of an Electric, Pathological Tomorrow: Alex Rivera's *Sleep Dealer*," *Review: Literature and Arts of the Americas* 48, no. 1 (2015): 50; L. Rivera, "Future Histories," 425; others go as far as arguing that Memo narrates the events of the film through True Node. Sisk, "Disembodied and Deportable," 51.
100. Medel, "The Ghost in the Machine," 115–17, 122–31.
101. Fiona Jeffries, "Cyborg Resistance on the Digital Assembly Line: Global Connectivity as a Terrain of Struggle for the Commons in Alex Rivera's *Sleep Dealer*," *Journal of Communication Inquiry* 39, no. 1 (2015): 25; Miranda, "Techno/Memo," 259.
102. Mackereth, "Aids and Family Androids," 32; Rueda, "The Everlasting *Sleep Dealer*," 338–39; Wells, "The Scar and the Node," 80.
103. María Gil Poisa, "Ciudad, frontera y espacio en *Sleep Dealer*," in *Geographies of Identity: Mapping, Crossing, and Transgressing Urban and Human Boundaries*,

ed. Esther Álvarez Lopez (Madrid: Instituto Franklin, Universidad Alacalá de Hernández, 2016), 118; Naief Yehya, *Drone Visions: A Brief Cyberpunk History of Killing Machines* (San Diego, CA: Hyperbole Books, 2020), 118.
104. Rodríguez-Hernández and Schaefer, "Do *Cybraceros* Dream," 155.
105. Carroll, "From *Papapá* to *Sleep Dealer*, 495. For a discussion of the gender-based overtones surrounding TruNode labor, particularly notions of "women's work," see Medel, "The Ghost in the Machine," 126–27.
106. Ramez Naam, *More Than Human: Embracing the Promise of Biological Enhancement* (New York: Broadway Books, 2005), 202–5.
107. Suppia and Oliveira, "Cibertíteres," 192.
108. For a discussion on how these nodes have facilitated Luz's ability to peer into Memo's mind and profit by selling his stories, see Heide, "Cosmopolitics in Border Film," 104.
109. Medel, "The Ghost in the Machine," 115.
110. Jeffries, "Cyborg Resistance," 27.
111. Camilla Fojas, "Border Securities, Drone Cultures, and Alex Rivera's *Sleep Dealer*," in Aldama, *Latinx Ciné in the Twenty-First Century*, 240; Barrera, "Cyborg Bodies," 30.
112. Medel, "The Ghost in the Machine," 127–31.
113. Amerikaner, "Xerox Men," 121.
114. Sandoval, *Methodology of the Oppressed*, 20.
115. García, "Hacia una poética," 340–41.
116. Orihuela and Hageman, "Virtual Realities of US/Mexico," 173.
117. Manuel F. Medina, "Las fronteras globales imaginadas en *Sleep Dealer*, de Alex Rivera," *Olho d'água* 4, no. 2 (2012): 55.
118. Sisk, "Disembodied and Deportable," 55.
119. Olguín, "Contrapuntal Cyborgs?," 225.
120. Marissa K. López, *Chicano Nations: The Hemispheric Origins of Mexican American Literature* (New York: New York University Press, 2011), 202.
121. Beilin and Suryanarayanan, "Step Out to *Shadowtime*," 27; Mark Bould, *Science Fiction: Routledge Film Guidebooks* (New York: Routledge, 2012), 195. The scholars dialogue with Walter Mignolo who defines "re-existing" as an attempt to awaken pre-Columbian ways of knowing. See Walter Mignolo, "Coloniality Is Far from Over, and So Must Be Decoloniality," *Afterall: Journal of Art, Context and Enquiry* 43, no. 1 (2017): 41.
122. Fojas, "Border Securities," 84; see also Bachran, "From Recovery to Discovery," 154.
123. Miranda, "Techno/Memo," 261.
124. Throughout the novella, the authors refer to those who live on the reservations as reslifers.
125. L. Rivera, "Future Histories," 428. Others argue that the novella is, ultimately, "a critical vision of past and present global capitalism." See Ulibarri, "Speculating Latina Radicalism," 89.

126. M. González, "Labor Movements," 2; Fojas, "Border Securities," 242; see also Derek Lee, "Postquantum: *A Tale for the Time Being, Atomik Aztex*, and Hacking Modern Space Time," *MELUS: The Society for the Study of the Multi-Ethnic Literature of the United States* 43, no. 1 (2020): 2.
127. Angie Chabram-Dernersesian, "Bucking Tradition: Sci Fi with a Chicana/o Latina/o Twist," *Confluencia* 26, no. 1 (2010): 192; Marez, *Farm Worker Futurism*, 158; Henry, "Unsettling Utopia," 170.
128. Streeby, "Speculative Archives," 35.
129. Manzanas Calvo and Barba Guerrero, "Redrawing the Boundary," 130.
130. Joy Ann Sánchez-Taylor, "Science Fiction/Fantasy and the Representation of Ethnic Futurity" (PhD diss., University of South Florida, 2014), 117–18.
131. Henry, "Unsettling Utopia," 159–66.
132. Bachran, "From Recovery to Discovery," 121. According to Pacharee Sudhinaraset, Lydia's use of nanotexts draws to mind the communications strategies of Subcomandante Marcos during the Zapatista Uprising of 1994. See Olguín, "Contrapuntal Cyborgs?," 228; Pacharee Sudhinaraset, "The End of Innocence: Women of Color Literature, Utopia, and the Cultural Politics of U.S. Cold War Racial Liberalism" (PhD diss., University of Washington, 2013), 277–301.
133. José Roberto Flores, "Raza especulativa: Reimaginando el discurso racial en la narrativa mexicoamericana (1970–2010)" (PhD diss., Arizona State University, 2017), 261.
134. M. López, *Racial Immanence*, 129–30; Christopher Perreira, "Speculative Futurity and the Eco-cultural Politics of *Lunar Braceros: 2125–2148*," in *Latinx Environmentalisms: Place, Justice, and the Decolonial*, ed. Sarah D. Wald et al. (Philadelphia, PA: Temple University Press, 2019), 94–95.
135. M. López, *Racial Immanence*, 136
136. M. López, *Racial Immanence*, 137.
137. Alicia Gaspar de Alba, *Chicano Art: Inside/Outside the Master's House: Cultural Politics and the Cara Exhibition* (Austin: University of Texas Press, 1998), 14.
138. Sandoval, *Methodology of the Oppressed*, 167.
139. Manfred E. Clynes and Nathan S. Kline, "Cyborgs and Space," in Gray, Figueroa-Sarriera, and Mentor, *The Cyborg Handbook*, 29–31.
140. Olguín, "Contrapuntal Cyborgs?," 227.
141. Rosaura Sánchez and Beatrice Pita, *Lunar Braceros 2125-2148* (Moorpark, CA: Floricanto Press, 2019), 29.
142. Manzanas Calvo and Barba Guerrero, "Redrawing the Boundary," 132.
143. Agamben, *State of Exception*, 2.
144. Chris Hables Gray, "An Interview with Manfred E. Clynes," in Gray, Figueroa-Sarriera, and Mentor, *The Cyborg Handbook*, 49.
145. Ulibarri, "Speculating Latina Radicalism," 90.
146. Michel Foucault, "About the Concept of the 'Dangerous Individual' in

Nineteenth-Century Legal Psychiatry," in Rabinow and Rose, *The Essential Foucault*, 210.
147. L. Rivera, "Future Histories," 430.
148. Sánchez and Pita, *Lunar Braceros*, 40.
149. Sánchez and Pita, *Lunar Braceros*, 41.
150. Sánchez and Pita, *Lunar Braceros*, 42.
151. Perreira, "Speculative Futurity," 98; See also Manzanas Calvo and Benito, *Occupying Space*, 93.
152. L. Rivera, "*Mestizaje* and Heterotopia," 158; Peter H. Eichstaedt, *If You Poison Us: Uranium and Native Americans* (Santa Fe, NM: Red Crane Books, 1994).
153. Herrera-Sobek, "Writing the Toxic Environment," 174–75.
154. Sánchez and Pita, *Lunar Braceros*, 118.
155. Sánchez and Pita, *Lunar Braceros*, 114.
156. Sánchez-Taylor, "Science Fiction/Fantasy," 139.
157. Sánchez and Pita, *Lunar Braceros*, 59.
158. Ulibarri, "Speculating Latina Radicalism," 90.
159. Sánchez and Pita, *Lunar Braceros*, 54.
160. Sánchez and Pita, *Lunar Braceros*, 67–68.
161. Hanna Burdette, *Revealing Rebellion in Abiayala: The Insurgent Poetics of Contemporary Indigenous Literature* (Tucson: University of Arizona Press, 2019), 209.
162. del Campo Ramírez, "Postethnicity and Antiglobalization," 388–89; Renee Hudson, "Former Futures and Absent Histories in María Cristina Mena, Rosaura Sánchez, and Beatrice Pita," *New Centennial Review* 19, no. 2 (2019): 80–83.
163. R. Hudson, "Former Futures," 72.
164. Many of the acts of Cali-Texas reverberate with a type of "border fascism." See Curtis Marez, "The Future in the Present, or, When Cages Crumble," *American Quarterly* 71, no. 2 (2020).
165. Ylce Irizarry, *Chicana/o and Latina/o Fiction: The New Memory of Latinidad* (Urbana: University of Illinois Press, 2016), 12.
166. del Campo Ramírez, "Postethnicity and Antiglobalization," 388.
167. Sánchez and Pita, *Lunar Braceros*, 30.
168. Sánchez and Pita have criticized El Movimiento directly in academic writing. See Rosaura Sánchez and Beatrice Pita, "Marxism, Materialism, and Latino/a Literature: What Is at Stake?," in *Dialectical Imaginaries: Materialist Approaches to U.S. Latino/a Literature in the Age of Neoliberalism*, ed. Marcial González and Carlos Gallego (Ann Arbor: University of Michigan Press, 2018), 23.
169. R. Hudson, "Former Futures," 83.
170. R. Hudson, "Former Futures," 84; Ulibarri, "Speculating Latina Radicalism," 91.
171. Sánchez and Pita, *Lunar Braceros*, 89.
172. Sánchez and Pita, *Lunar Braceros*, 65.

173. Sánchez and Pita, *Lunar Braceros*, 67.
174. Sánchez and Pita, *Lunar Braceros*, 72.
175. Sánchez and Pita, *Lunar Braceros*, 89.
176. Sánchez and Pita, *Lunar Braceros*, 89.
177. Olguín, "Contrapuntal Cyborgs?," 230.
178. Agamben, *Homo Sacer*, 89.
179. Sánchez and Pita, *Lunar Braceros*, 106.
180. Sánchez and Pita, *Lunar Braceros*, 112.
181. Sánchez and Pita, *Lunar Braceros*, 112.
182. Nuñez, "The Future of Food?," 239–42; Henry, "Unsettling Utopia," 172–74.
183. Olguín, "Contrapuntal Cyborgs?," 230.
184. Manzanas Calvo and Benito, *Occupying Space*, 97.
185. Manzanas Calvo and Benito, *Occupying Space*, 97.
186. Henry, "Unsettling Utopia," 174.
187. Sánchez and Pita, *Lunar Braceros*, 81.
188. For a discussion of revolutionary mothering in the novella, see Henry, "Unsettling Utopia," 193–98; for a discussion of the reimagination of the family unit see R. Hudson, "Former Futures," 85–87; for a discussion of Pedro as quasi-cyborg, see Olguín, "Contrapuntal Cyborgs?," 229. For a discussion of the novel's deconstruction of the family unit, see Ulibarri, "Speculating Latina Radicalism," 86–88; see also Henry, "Unsettling Utopia," 80; López, *Racial Immanence*, 134.
189. His biological mother is Lydia, and his biological father is Gabriel, his mother's first lover; he and Lydia froze a fertilized egg long before they ever went to jail, and Gabriel was murdered by Cali-Texas operatives in Brazil. Lydia raises him with Frank as his biological mother in Chinganaza; however, because she can no longer carry a child after her stint on the moon, she asks her comrade, Leticia— who is in a relationship with Maggie—to be a surrogate mother. Furthermore, Pedro is raised by Tom and Betty when Lydia returns to Cali-Texas in what is almost certainly a failed attempt to tear down the reservations. For a discussion of communal parenting in the novella, see del Campo Ramírez, "Postethnicity and Antiglobalization," 394–95.
190. Ulibarri, "Speculating Latina Radicalism," 87.
191. Sánchez and Pita, *Lunar Braceros*, 116. Indeed, the authors explore this armed uprising in their sequel, *Keep Me Posted: Logins from Tomorrow*, where armed resistance and robo-sacer hacktivism work together hand-in-hand in a strategy of radical resistance. See Rosaura Sánchez and Beatrice Pita, *Keep Me Posted: Logins from Tomorrow* (Moorpark, CA: Floricanto Press, 2020).

**CHAPTER 4**

1. In a private conversation, Gabriela Damián Miravete confirmed to me that the character Marisela is named after Marisela Escobedo Ortiz, the social activist from Juárez who was assassinated in 2010 for protesting her daughter's murder in 2008.

2. Kathleen Staudt and Irasema Coronado, "Binational Civic Action for Accountability: Antiviolence Organizing in Ciudad Juárez / El Paso," in Gaspar de Alba and Guzmán, *Making a Killing: Femicide, Free Trade, and La Frontera* (Austin: University of Texas Press, 2010), 166–75.
3. See Alicia Gaspar de Alba and Georgina Guzmán, eds. *Making a Killing: Femicide, Free Trade, and La Frontera* (Austin: University of Texas Press, 2010). Several recent Chicanx studies readers have dedicated chapters to the Juárez feminicides. See Noriega et al., *The Chicano Studies Reader*; Calderón, *The Aztlán Mexican Studies Reader*.
4. "Mexico Selects *Backyard* for Oscar Consideration," *Reuters* (London), Sept. 24, 2009, https://www.reuters.com/article/us-oscars-mexico/mexico-selects-backyard-for-oscar-consideration-idUSTRE58N0V820090924.
5. While *Bordertown* and *Backyard/El traspatio* share a great deal in common, *Backyard/El traspatio* more explicitly engages the role of technology and modernization not only in casting women workers as expendable, but also in imagining avenues for resistance.
6. Cristina Rivera Garza, *Grieving: Dispatches from a Wounded country*, trans. Sarah Booker (New York: The Feminist Press, 2020), 85–93; Cristina Rivera Garza, *The Restless Dead: Necrowriting and Disappropriation*, trans. Robin Myers (Nashville, TN: Vanderbilt University Press, 2020), 152–54.
7. Amanda Petersen, "Breaking Silences and Revealing Hosts: Spectral Moments of Gendered Violence in Mexico," *iMex Revista: México Interdisciplinario/ Interdisciplinary Mexico* 16, no. 2 (2019): 26.
8. See Yolanda Mercader, "El cine ante los feminicidios de Ciudad Juárez," in *Cine y frontera: Territorios ilimitados de la mirada*, ed. Graciela Martínez Zalce and Juan Carlos Vargas (Mexico City: Bonilla Artigas Editores, 2014), 217.
9. Berman titled her screenplay *Backyard*. Carrera revised it to *Backyard/El traspatio*. To avoid confusion, I will refer to the film as *Backyard/El traspatio* throughout. In those cases where I need to distinguish between the screenplay and the movie, I will use the terms *Berman's screenplay* and *Carrera's film*.
10. Julia Monárrez Fragoso, *Trama de una injusticia: Feminicidio sexual sistémico en Ciudad Juárez* (Tijuana: El Colegio de la Frontera Norte, 2009), 90–97.
11. My usage of the term immunization differs from those scholars who use the term to refer to a numbness against feminicide that could happen as it receives greater coverage. See Rosa-Linda Fregoso and Cynthia Bejarano, "Introduction: A Cartography of Feminicide in the Américas," in *Terrorizing Women: Feminicide in the Americas*, ed. Rosa-Linda Fregoso and Cynthia Bejarano (Durham, NC: Duke University Press, 2010), 1.
12. Contemporary Mexican authors frequently use phantasmagoric discourse to emphasize the continued dystopian nature of the country's politics. See Carolyn Wolfenzon, *Nuevos fantasmas recorren México: Lo espectral en la literatura mexicana del siglo XXI* (Madrid: Iberoamericana, 2020), 26.
13. Jean Franco, *Cruel Modernity* (Durham, NC: Duke University Press, 2013),

230, 217–25; see also Micah K. Donohue, "Borderlands Hyperbole, Critical Dystopias, and Transfeminist Utopian Hope: Gaspar de Alba's *Desert Blood* and Valencia's *Capitalismo gore*," *Utopian Studies* 31, no. 3 (2021): 559.

14. Melissa Wright, "The Dialectics of Still Life: Murder, Women, and the Maquiladoras," *Public Culture* 11, no. 3 (1999).

15. Monárrez Fragoso, *Trama de una injusticia*, 102–3; Círila Quintero Ramírez, "Trabajo femenino en las maquiladoras: ¿Explotación o liberación?," in *Bordeando la violencia contra las mujeres en la frontera norte de México*, ed. Julia Estela Monárrez Fragoso and María Socorro Tabuenca Córdoba (Tijuana: El Colegio de la Frontera Norte, 2007).

16. Jorge Carrillo, "La importancia del impacto del TLC en la industria maquiladora en América Latina," in *Reestructuración productiva, mercado de trabajo y sindicatos en América Latina*, ed. Enrique de la Garza Toledo (Buenos Aires: Consejo Latinoamericano de Ciencias Sociales, 2000), 162–66; González Rodríguez, *The Femicide Machine*, 9; Melissa Wright, "El lucro, la democracia y la mujer pública: Estableciendo las conexiones," in Monárrez Fragoso and Tabuenca Córdoba, *Bordeando la violencia*. That said, William C. Gruben challenges the popular narrative that NAFTA accelerated maquiladora growth through statistical analyses. Whether or not he is correct, maquiladoras clearly are transnational, neoliberal institutions. William C. Gruben, "Was NAFTA behind Mexico's High Maquiladora Growth?," *Economic and Financial Review of Dallas*, no. Q3 (2001).

17. Alarcón, "Chicana Femenism," 187; Sánchez Díaz, *Diálogos*, 256–64.

18. Héctor Domínguez-Ruvalcaba and Patricia Ravelo Blancas, *Desmantelamiento de la ciudadanía: Políticas de terror en la frontera norte* (Mexico City: Eón, 2011), 27–28.

19. González Rodríguez, *The Femicide Machine*, 32.

20. González Rodríguez, *The Femicide Machine*, 9.

21. Amnesty International has directed significant attention to the Juárez femicides in recent years, denouncing them and calling for concrete actions to oppose them. See "Intolerable Killings: Ten Years of Abductions and Murders in Ciudad Juárez and Chihuahua," Amnesty International, Aug 10, 2003, https://www.amnesty.org/en/documents/AMR41/027/2003/en.

22. This attitude appears to reflect those of maquiladoras in real-world Juárez. See Monárrez Fragoso, *Trama de una injusticia*, 86.

23. For a definition of *femicide*, see Diana E. H. Russell and Roberta H. Harmes, *Femicide in Global Perspective* (London: Teacher's College Press, 2001), 4.

24. While the term *feminicidio* was coined to discuss violence against women in Juárez, the practice occurs throughout the nation, the Hispanic world, and beyond.

25. Fregoso and Bejarano, "Introduction," 3–4; For a list of studies that have come to employ the term *feminicide* rather than *femicide*, see Adriana Carmona López, Alma Gómez Caballero, and Lucha Castro Rodríguez, "Feminicide in Latin America in the Movement for Women's Human Rights," in Fregoso and Bejarano,

*Terrorizing Women*, 158–59; see also Nuala Finnegan, *Cultural Representations of* Feminicidio *at the US-Mexico Border* (New York: Routledge, 2018), 2–5; Franco, *Cruel Modernity*, 92; Rita Laura Segato, "Territory, Sovereignty, and Crimes of the Second State: The Writing on the Body of Murdered Women," trans. Sara Koopman, in Fregoso and Bejarano, *Terrorizing Women*; Stuadt and Coronado, "Binational Civic Action," 158–66. Some scholars have even begun to leave the term *feminicidio* untranslated. See Finnegan, *Cultural Representations of* Feminicido.

26. See James C. Harrington, "¡Alto a la impunidad!: Legal Relief for Femicide in Juárez?," in *Gender Violence at the U.S.-Mexico Border: Media Representation and Public Response*, ed. Ignacio Corona and Héctor Domínguez-Ruvalcaba (Tucson: University of Arizona Press, 2010), 158–63; María Socorro Tabuenca Córdoba, "Ghost Dance in Ciudad Juárez at the End/Beginning of the Millennium," in Gaspar de Alba and Guzmán, *Making a Killing*, 100–113

27. Mabel Moraña, *Pensar el cuerpo: Historia, materialidad y símbolo* (Barcelona: Herder, 2021), 316.

28. Finnegan, *Cultural Representations*, 36–41.

29. For examples of documentary films that discuss the desaparecidas, see Cristina Michaus's *Juárez: Desierto de esperanza* (2001); Lourdes Portillo's *Señorita extraviada* (2002); Rafael Bonilla's *La batalla de las cruces: Una década de impunidad y violencia contra las mujeres* (2005); José Antonio Cordero and Alejandra Sánchez's *Bajo Juárez: La ciudad devorando a sus hijas* (2006); Alex Flores and Lorena Vassolo's *Juarez: The City where Women Are Disposable* (2007). See Miguel López-Lozano, "Women in the Global Machine: Patrick Bard's *La frontera*, Carmen Galán Benítez's *Tierra marchita*, and Alicia Gaspar de Alba's *Desert Blood: The Juárez Murders*," in Corona and Domínguez-Ruvalcaba, *Gender Violence*, 130.

30. Alfonso Varona, "Entrevista a Sabina Berman," *Latin American Theatre Review* 47, no. 1 (2013): 143–44.

31. Alicia Vargas Amésquita, "El cuerpo femenino como metáfora del territorio-nación en *Backyard: El traspatio* de Carlos Carrera," in *Mexican Transnational Cinema and Literature*, ed. Maricruz Castro Ricalde, Mauricio Calderón Díaz, and James Ramsey (New York: Peter Lang, 2017), 272.

32. Ignacio M. Sánchez Prado, "*Amores perros*: Exotic Violence and Neoliberal Fear," trans. Kara N. Moranski, *Journal of Latin American Cultural Studies* 15, no. 1 (2006): 40.

33. We should note that *Backyard/El traspatio* is not the only borderlands film to engage feminicide through a thriller or slasher aesthetic. For a discussion of other films to build on this aesthetic, see María Socorro Tabuenca Córdoba "Representations of Femicide in Border Cinema," in Corona and Domínguez-Ruvalcaba, *Gender Violence*, 89.

34. Emily Hind, "Estado de excepción y feminicidio: *El traspatio/Backyard* (2009) de Carlos Carrera y Sabina Berman," *Colorado Review of Hispanic Studies* 8 (2010): 30; Celina Manzoni, "Discursos del cuerpo y construcción de memoria,"

*Taller de letras* 49 (2011): 165; Dana A. Meredith and Luis Alberto Rodríguez Cortés, "Expanding Outrage: Representations of Gendered Violence and Feminicide in Mexico," in *Modern Mexican Culture: Critical Foundations*, ed. Stuart A. Day (Tucson: University of Arizona Press, 2017), 246–47; Angélica Tornero, "La vida dañada: Documentos de cultura sobre Ciudad Juárez," *Elementos* 92 (2013).
35. Carol J. Clover, *Men, Women, and Chain Saws: Gender in the Modern Horror Film*, (Princeton, NJ: Princeton University Press, 1992), 28.
36. Jessica Robinso, *Life Lessons from Slasher Films* (Lanham, MD: Scarecrow Press, 2012), 3–7.
37. Clover, *Men, Women, and Chain Saws*, 21.
38. See Tabuenca Córdoba, "Ghost Dance," 96–97.
39. See Rupsayar Das, "Representation of Violence against Women in Indian Print Media: A Comparative Analysis," *Global Media Journal* 3, no. 1 (2012): 3–5.
40. Ashley Wellman, Michele Bisaccia Meitl, and Patrick Kinkade, "Lady and the Vamp: Roles, Sexualization, and Brutalization of Women in Slasher Films," *Sexuality and Culture* 25 (2021): 674.
41. Elizabeth Villalobos, "Asesinos fronterizos: *Performance* de transgresión de los derechos humanos en el imaginario social del norte y sur de México" (PhD diss., University of Kansas, 2014), 158.
42. See Lydia Cristina Huerta Moreno, "Affecting Violence: Narratives of Los Feminicidios and their Ethical and Political Reception" (PhD diss., University of Texas at Austin, 2012), 113; Angélica Tornero, "Discursos híbridos y perspectiva en *2666* de Roberto Bolaño y en *Backyard/El traspatio* de Carlos Carrera," *Cuaderno Internacional de Estudios Humanísticos y Literatura* 20 (2013): 25; Hugo Valdez, "Los cinefotógrafos creadores de la imagen fílmica en México," *Varia* 20 (2012).
43. John Kenneth Muir, *Horror Films FAQ: All That's Left to Know about Slashers, Vampires, Zombies, Aliens, and More* (Milwaukee, WI: Applause Theatre and Cinema Books, 2013), 244.
44. Héctor Domínguez-Ruvalcaba, "Death on the Screen: Imagining Violence in Border Media," in Corona and Domínguez-Ruvalcaba, *Gender Violence*, 66.
45. Villalobos, "Asesinos fronterizos," 197.
46. Kara M. Kvaran, "'You're All Doomed!': A Socioeconomic Analysis of Slasher Films," *Journal of American Studies* 50, no. 4 (2016).
47. Nina Namaste, "Not Just a Ciudad Juárez Problem: Extreme Capitalsim, Masculinity, and Impunity in Sabina Berman's *Backyard*," *Contemporary Theatre Review* 22, no. 2 (2012): 492; Huerta Moreno, "Affecting Violence," 121.
48. Sayak Valencia and Sonia Herrera Sánchez, "From Cinema to the *Live* Regime: Pedagogies of Cruelty and Social Anesthesia in Two Latin American Movies," in *Gender-Based Violence in Latin American and Iberian Cinemas*, ed. Rebeca Maseda García, María José Gámez Fuentes, and Barbara Zecchi (New York: Routledge, 2020), 183; see also Vargas Amésquita, "El cuerpo femenino, 279–80.
49. Vargas Amésquita, "El cuerpo femenino, 280–81; see also González Rodríguez, *The Femicide Machine*, 32.

50. Anna Kingsley, "Framing the Body: The Juárez Feminicides in Contemporary Mexican Visual Culture (1993–2013)" (PhD diss., University of London, 2017), 147.
51. Sabina Berman, *Backyard*, *Gestos* 20, no. 39 (2005): 124. When dialogues between Berman's screenplay and Carrera's film are similar, I will quote the language from the screenplay.
52. Berman, *Backyard*, 125.
53. Carla de Pozzio, "El TLCAN: Y su representación en el femincidio de Ciudad Juárez" (master's thesis, Bowling Green State University, 2010), 105.
54. Joshua Briones, "Paying the Price for NAFTA: NAFTA's Effect on Women and Children Laborers in Mexico," *UCLA Women's Law Journal* 9 (1998): 303–12.
55. Stuart A. Day, *Outside Theater: Alliances that Shape Mexico* (Tucson: University of Arizona Press, 2017), 142.
56. Hind, "Estado de excepción," 31. For a further discussion of extralegal activities in Juárez and throughout the border region, see Kathleen Stuadt and Howard Campbell, "The Other Side of the Ciudad Juárez Femicide Story," *ReVista: Harvard Review of Latin America* 7, no. 2 (2008); José Manuel Valenzuela Arce and Mabel Moraña, "Entrada: Precariedad y exclusión social: Dispositivos estructurantes del proyecto neoliberal," in Moraña and Valenzuela Arce, *Precariedades, exclusiones y emergencias*, 12–13.
57. Carrera makes clear his critique of Chihuahua governor Francisco Barrio Terrazas (1992–1998) through his casting of Enoc Leaño, who captures the look and mannerisms of the actual governor. Yolanda Reyes, "Personajes femeninos contestatarios del cine mexicano del siglo XXI: Subvirtiendo la Época de Oro" (PhD diss., National University of Ireland, Galway, 2012), 188.
58. Harrington, "¡Alto a la impunidad!," 156–57.
59. Berman, *Backyard*, 151. A similar scene occurs in Carrera's filmic adaptation.
60. See Sayak Valencia and Sonia Herrera Sánchez, "Pornomiseria, violencia machista y mirada colonial en los filmes *Backyard: El traspatio* y *La mujer del animal*," *Anclajes* 34, no. 3 (2020): 18.
61. Such discourses lead to a type of silencing and even appropriation of women's activism in Juárez. See Clara E. Rojas, "The V-Day March in Mexico: Appropriation and Misuse of Local Women's Activism," in Gaspar de Alba and Guzmán, *Making a Killing*, 201.
62. Grace C. Spencer, "Her Body Is a Battlefield: The Applicability of the Alien Tort Statute to Corporate Human Rights Abuses in Juarez, Mexico," *Gonzaga Law Review* 40 (2004): 512–13.
63. José Manuel Valenzuela Arce, "Ciudad Juárez: La frontera más bonita," *Alternativas*, no. 3 (2014): 12.
64. Anna Costanza Baldry and Maria José Magalhães. "Prevention of Femicide," in *Femicide across Europe: Theory, Research and Prevention*, ed. Shalva Weil, Consuelo Corradi, and Marceline Naudi (Bristol, UK: Policy Press, 2018), 82–83.
65. Vargas Amésquita, "El cuerpo femenino," 282.

66. Olimpia Arellano-neri, "Cinematographic and Literary Representations of the Femicides in Ciudad Juárez" (PhD diss., University of Cincinnati, 2013), 133.
67. Arellano-neri, "Cinematographic and Literary," 116.
68. Huerta Moreno, "Affecting Violence," 124.
69. Verónica Oxman, "At the Border of the Gender Abyss: Discussing Masculinity and Feminicide in Ciudad Juárez," in *Engaging Men in Building Gender Equality*, ed. Michael Flood and Richard Howson (Newcastle: Cambridge Scholars Publishing, 2015), 131.
70. Rita Cancino and Pablo Rolando Cristoffanini claim that the juxtaposition of different profiles of killer provides a more nuanced understanding of the Juárez feminicides, where the causes and articulations are multifaceted and only tangentially related. Rita Cancino and Pablo Roland Cristoffanini, "La violencia en América Latina," *Sociedad y Discurso* 23 (2013): 7.
71. Clover, *Men, Women, and Chain Saws*, 33.
72. Clover, *Men, Women, and Chain Saws*, 41–42.
73. Day, *Outside Theater*, 145.
74. Kingsley, "Framing the Body," 154.
75. Kingsley's argument implicitly recognizes Cutberto's relatively positive representation.
76. Kingsley, "Framing the Body," 156.
77. Domínguez-Ruvalcaba, "Death on the Screen," 64.
78. See Sánchez Prado, "*Amores perros*."
79. Sonia Herrera Sánchez, "Cine de ficción y feminicidio: El caso de Ciudad Juárez," *Mientras Tanto*, no. 121 (2014): 72.
80. Hind, "Estado de excepción," 34.
81. Namaste, "Not Just a Ciudad Juárez Problem," 486–87; see also Priscila Meléndez, "The Body and the Law in the Mexico/US Borderlands: Violence and Violations in *El viaje de los cantores* by Hugo Salcedo and *Backyard* by Sabina Berman," *Modern Drama* 54, no. 1 (2011): 28; Ana Elena Puga, "Female Alliances and Women's Histories in Contemporary Mexican and Argentine Drama," in *Contemporary Women Playwrights: Into the Twenty-First Century*, eds. Penny Farfan and Lesley Ferris (New York: Palgrave MacMillan, 2013), 40–41; Reyes, "Personajes femeninos contestatarios," 183.
82. Sánchez Prado, *Screening Neoliberalism*, 174.
83. Agamben, *Homo Sacer*, 136–43.
84. Justin Castro, *Radio in Revolution: Wireless Technology and State Power in Mexico, 1897–1938* (Lincoln: University of Nebraska Press, 2016); Sonia Robles, *Mexican Waves: Radio Broadcasting along Mexico's Northern Border, 1930–1950*, (Tucson: University of Arizona Press, 2019), 71–93.
85. Antoni Castells-Talens and José Manuel Ramos Rodríguez, "Technology for Cultural Survival: Indigenous-Language Radio at the End of the Twentieth Century," in Tinajero and Freeman, *Technology and Culture*, 183–85.
86. Day, *Outside Theater*, 137; Estela Valverde, "New Latin American Film:

Addressing the Negative Culturescapes and Glocalising Transnational Problems," *Crítica Contemporánea: Revista de Teoría Política* 2 (2012): 139.
87. Berman, *Backyard*, 110.
88. Berman, *Backyard*, 162.
89. Reyes, "Personajes femeninos contestatarios," 186; Villalobos, "Asesinos fronterizos," 197.
90. Marshall McLuhan, *Understanding Media: The Extensions of Man* (Scarborough, Ont.: Mentor Books, 1964), 264.
91. Hayles, *How We Became Posthuman*, 34; see also Brown, *Cyborgs in Latin America*, 147–48.
92. Pablo M. Zavala, "La producción antifeminicidista mexicana: Autoría, representación y feminismo en la frontera juarense," *Chasqui* 45, no. 2 (2016): 57–58.
93. Berman, *Backyard*, 168. It is worth noting that Peralta gives a similar monologue when the governor visits Juárez in Carrera's version as well. However, the governor arrives prior to Juana's murder, and the official castigates Blanca for fabricating evidence to arrest a man who is clearly guilty of feminicide.
94. Sayak Valencia and Herrera Sánchez, "From Cinema," 183.
95. Berman, *Backyard*, 172. The governor makes a similar statement in Carrera's film. However, unlike what we see in Berman's screenplay, the people of Juárez fail to save Blanca from losing her badge, and she ultimately leaves for the United States. That said, the film alludes to the potential to subvert officialist channels through radio when Blanca blackmails the Comandante, telling him that Peralta will reveal every case of police corruption on his show if they decide to charge her with any crimes.
96. See McLuhan, *Understanding Media*, 261.
97. Berman, *Backyard*, 172.
98. See Day, *Outside Theater*, 144–46.
99. Clover, *Men, Women, and Chain Saws*, ix–xiii, 35–41.
100. Hind, "Estado de excepción," 36–37; Sánchez Prado, *Screening Neoliberalism*, 219.
101. For a discussion of the androgeneity of Final Girl characters, see Angel D. Weaver et al., "Embodying the Moral Code?: Thirty Years of Final Girls in Slasher Films," *Psychology of Popular Media Culture* 4, no. 1 (2015): 39; for a discussion of the "boyishness" of these characters, see Clover, *Men, Women, and Chain Saws*, 40.
102. Hind, "Estado de excepción," 39.
103. De la Reguera's performance fits within a body of maquiladora cinema that has cast actors with significant star power in principal roles in order to ensure commercial successes both with Mexican and international audiences. See Niamh Thornton, *Tastemakers and Tastemaking: Mexico and Curated Screen Violence* (Albany: State University of New York Press, 2020), 129–30.
104. Wellman, Meitl, and Kinkade, "Lady and the Vamp," 663.
105. Hind, "Estado de excepción," 36.

106. Hind, "Estado de excepción," 37.
107. See Clover, *Men, Women, and Chain Saws*, 35; Vargas Amésquita, "El cuerpo femenino, 373–78.
108. For a discussion of the tropes of the slasher—which include going through dark alleys—see Mathias Clasen and Todd K. Platts, "Evolution and Slasher Films," in *Evolution and Popular Narrative*, ed. Dirk Vanderbeke and Brett Cooke (Leiden, Netherlands: Brill, 2019), 31.
109. Clover, *Men, Women, and Chain Saws*, 41; see also Valencia and Herrera Sánchez, "From Cinema to the *Live* Regime," 184.
110. Arellano-neri, "Cinematographic and Literary," 116.
111. Meredith and Rodríguez Cortés, "Expanding Outrage," 246.
112. Clover, *Men, Women, and Chain Saws*, 46. Indeed, slasher cinema's cathartic tendencies play a key role in the viewing experience of these films. See Vera Dika, *Games of Terror:* Halloween, Friday the 13th, *and the Films of the Stalker Cycle* (London: Associated University Presses, 1990), 10.
113. For a discussion on the shortcomings of armed insurrection as robo-sacer resistance, see Chapter 5 in this book.
114. Clover, *Men, Women, and Chain Saws*, 37.
115. Zermeño Vargas, "Fantasticidad, encuentros," 21.
116. For a discussion of feminicide throughout Mexico, see Mercedes Olivera, "Violencia feminicida: Violence against Women and Mexico's Structural Crisis," trans. Victoria J. Furio, in Fregoso and Bejarano, *Terrorizing Women*, 49.
117. Finnegan, *Cultural Representations of* Feminicido, 8.
118. The award went to an English translation called "They Will Dream in the Garden" that was published in *Latin American Literature Today*, https://latinamericanliteraturetoday.org/2018/05/they-will-dream-garden-gabriela-damian-miravete. "2018 Otherwise Award," Otherwise Award, 2019, https://otherwiseaward.org/award/2018-otherwise-award. In 2019, the Tiptree Award's name was changed to the Otherwise Award.
119. Alexis Lothian, "Gabriela Damián Miravete Wins 2018 Tiptree Award!: Honor and Long List Announced," *Otherwise Award* (Madison, WI), Mar. 22, 2018. https://otherwiseaward.org/2019/03/gabriela-damian-miravete-wins-2018-tiptree-award-honor-and-long-list-announced. The translator, Adrian Demopulos, was also recognized "with a special honor for a wonderful translation."
120. Hans Moravec, *Mind Children: The Future of Robot and Human Intelligence* (Cambridge, MA: Harvard University Press, 1988), 121.
121. Hayles, *How We Became Posthuman*, 36.
122. López-Pellisa, *Patologías de la realidad*, 155.
123. Moravec, *Mind Children*, 121.
124. Cecilia Eudave, "El cuerpo como espacio de lo insólito en la narrativa mexicana reciente escrita por mujeres," in *Realidades fracturadas: Estéticas de lo insólito en la narrativa en lengua española (1980–2018)*, ed. Natalia Álvarez Méndez and Ana Abello Verano (Madrid: Visor Libros, 2019), 54.
125. Williams, *The Mexican Exception*, 25.

126. Eudave, "El cuerpo como espacio," 54.
127. For a discussion on how continued capitalist expansion necessitates the loss of female lives, see Alicia Gaspar de Alba "Poor Brown Female: The Miller's Compensation for 'Free' Trade," in Gaspar de Alba and Guzmán, *Making a Killing*; Gaspar de Alba and Guzmán, "Introduction: *Feminicidio*: The 'Black Legend' of the Border," in Gaspar de Alba and Guzmán, *Making a Killing*; González Rodríguez, *The Femicide Machine*, 7–14; Steven S. Volk and Marian E. Schlotterbeck "Gender, Order, and Femicide: Reading the Popular Culture of Murder in Ciudad Juárez," in Noriega et al., *The Chicano Studies Reader*, 613–15. For a discussion of how feminicide itself becomes the threat to state sovereignty, see Sergio Villalobos-Ruminot, "Biopolítica y soberanía: Notas sobre la ambigüedad del corpus literario," in Moraña and Sánchez Prado, *Heridas abiertas*, 54.
128. Williams, *The Mexican Exception*, 66.
129. Esposito, *Bíos*, 45–77; Timothy Campbell, "Translator's Introduction: *Bíos*, Immunity, Life: The Thought of Roberto Esposito," in *Bíos: Biopolitics and Philosophy*, trans. Timothy Campbell (Minneapolis: University of Minnesota Press, 2008), vii–xlii.
130. Williams, *The Mexican Exception*, 11.
131. Esposito, *Bíos*, 92.
132. López-Pellisa, *Patologías de la realidad*, 124–26.
133. Jacques Derrida, *Specters of Marx: The State of the Debt, the Work of Mourning, and the New International* (New York: Routledge, 1994), 4–8.
134. Derrida, *Specters of Marx*, 51.
135. Avery Gordon, *Ghostly Matters: Haunting and the Sociological Imagination* (Minneapolis: University of Minnesota Press, 1997), 97–98.
136. David S. Dalton, "Una espectralidad cibernética: Cuestionando un presente *hauntológico* en *Historias del séptimo sello*, de Norma Yamille Cuéllar," *iMex Revista: México Interdisciplinario/Interdisciplinary Mexico* 8, no. 16 (2019): 84. The silhouettes fit within a broader theorization of a ghostly posthuman that has appeared in the writings of Mexican women writers during the neoliberal period.
137. Throughout this chapter, I cite the English translation of the story by Adrian Demopulos. However, I use the original Spanish for names and terms.
138. Franco 2013, *Cruel Modernity*, 208–13; Alberto Ribas-Casasayas and Amada L. Petersen, eds., *Espectros: Ghostly Hauntings in Contemporary Transhispanic Narratives* (Lewisburg, PA: Bucknell University Press, 2016), 133–35; Marta Sierra, "*Memento Mori*: Photography and Narrative in Cristina Rivera Garza's *Nadie me verá llorar*," in Ribas-Casasayas and Petersen, *Espectros*.
139. Oswaldo Estrada, "Vivir a muerte: Escrituras dolientes y denuncias de género en *El silencio de los cuerpos*," *Letras Femeninas* 43, no. 2 (2018): 73.
140. Sergio González Rodríguez, "Prólogo," in *El silencio de los cuerpos: Relatos sobre feminicidos*, ed. Olga Alarcón et al. (Mexico City: Ediciones B, 2015), 8. See also Olivera, "Violencia feminicida," 50–51.

141. Valencia, *Gore Capitalism*, 206, emphasis in original.
142. David E. Johnson, *Violence and Naming: On Mexico and the Promise of Literature* (Austin: University of Texas Press, 2019), 51.
143. Carol Clark D'Lugo, *The Fragmented Novel in Mexico: The Politics of Form* (Austin: University of Texas Press, 1997), xii.
144. For a discussion of how real-world structural barriers to female education facilitate violence against women, see Olivera, "Violencia feminicida," 58, nt. 4.
145. Elvia R. Arriola, "Accountability for Murder in the *Maquiladoras*: Linking Corporate Indifference to Gender Violence at the U.S.-Mexico Border," in Gaspar de Alba and Guzmán, *Making a Killing*, 36–50.
146. Rivera Garza, *Grieving*, 89.
147. Lane, "Electronic Disturbance Theater," 136–39; Zulkarnain, "Polyspatial Resistance," 226.
148. Haraway, *Simians, Cyborgs and Women*, 154; Sandoval, *Methodology of the Oppressed*, 20.
149. For a discussion of literature that eschews the possibility of achieving a type of immortality through technology, see Moraña, *Pensar el cuerpo*, 317–18.
150. Haraway, *Simians, Cyborgs and Women*, 151.
151. While I am aware of no credible charges tying TelMex directly to feminicide in Mexico, we should note that the company epitomizes the neoliberal order that has played an integral role in the systemic murder of women in places like Ciudad Juárez. See Gaspar de Alba and Guzmán, *Making a Killing*; Valencia, *Gore Capitalism*; González Rodríguez, *The Femicide Machine*.
152. Braidotti, *The Posthuman*, 112.
153. Rivera Garza, *The Restless Dead*, 10.
154. Rivera Garza, *The Restless Dead*, 10–20.
155. González Rodríguez, "Prólogo," 8–9; Monárrez Fragoso, *Trama de una injusticia*, 42–63.
156. See Alberto Ribas-Casasayas and Amanda L. Petersen, "Introduction: Theories of the Ghost in a Transhispanic Context," in Ribas-Casasayas and Petersen, *Espectros*, 2.
157. Ginway, *Cyborgs, Sexuality, and the Undead*, 107.
158. Wolfenzon, *Nuevos fantasmas*, 26.
159. Umberto Eco, *Travels in Hyperreality: Essays* (San Diego, CA: Harcourt, 1983), 7.
160. Eco, *Travels*, 18–21.
161. Ribas-Casasayas and Petersen, "Introduction," 2.
162. Rivera Garza, *The Restless Dead*, 11.
163. For a discussion of the need to grant greater agency to posthuman actors, see J. Andrew Brown, "El oficio del *cyborg*," 248–49.
164. See Ribas-Casasayas and Petersen, "Introduction," 3.
165. Tabaré Azcona Muñoz, "The Poetics of Invocation: Haunted Writing and Political Subjectification in Twenty-First-Century Mexico" (MA thesis, University of Colorado, 2017), 48.

166. See Williams, *The Mexican Exception*.
167. Oswaldo Estrada, "Vivir a muerte," 74.

## CHAPTER 5

1. For a discussion of narco and necropolitics, see R. Guy Emerson, *Necropolitics: Living Death in Mexico* (New York: Palgrave MacMillan, 2019), 9–11.
2. Rafael Acosta, "Taming Heroes: Deep Time, Affect, and Economies of Honor and Glory in Contemporary Mexico," *Revista de Estudios Hispánicos* 52, no. 3 (2018); Rafael Acosta, *Drug Lords, Cowboys, and Desperados: Violent Myths of the U.S.-Mexico Frontier* (Notre Dame, IN: University of Notre Dame Press, 2021), 31–38. The narco has rocketed to fame across Latin America. For a discussion of the presence of the narco in Mexican, Colombian, and Latin American music, see Kristine Vanden Berg, *Narcos y sicaros en la ciudad letrada* (Valencia: Albatros, 2019), 35–40.
3. Acosta, *Drug Lords, Cowboys*, 2.
4. Oswaldo Zavala, *Los cárteles no existen: Narcotráfico y cultura en México* (Mexico City: Malpaso, 2018), 14–16; see also Jorge Volpi, *El insomnio de Bolívar: Cuatro consideraciones intempestivas sobre América Latina en el siglo XXI* (Mexico City: Random House Mondadori, 2009), 127.
5. David S. Dalton, "Immunizing the *Zetas*: Drug Violence and Zombie Biopolitics in Pedro M. Valencia's *Con Z de zombie*," *Revista de Literatura Mexicana Contemporánea* 24, no. 73 (2018): 139–48; David S. Dalton, "From Sensationalist Media to the Narcocorrido: Drones, Sovereignty, and Exception along the US-Mexican Border," in Plaw, Gurgel, and Ramírez Plascencia, *Politics of Technology*, 85–90; Valencia, *Gore Capitalism*, 55–58.
6. John Helmer, *Drugs and Minority Oppression* (New York: Seabury Press, 1975), 165n3; Kenneth B. Nunn, "Race, Crime and the Pool of Surplus Criminality: Or Why the 'War on Drugs' was a War on Blacks," *Journal of Gender, Race, and Justice* 6, no. 2 (2002): 416–17.
7. Nixon, Richard, "Remarks about an Intensified Program for Drug Abuse Prevention and Control," Office of the Under Secretary of Defense for Personnel & Readiness, June 17, 1971, https://prhome.defense.gov/Portals/52/Documents/RFM/Readiness/DDRP/docs/41%20Nixon%20Remarks%20Intensified%20Program%20for%20Drug%20Abuse.pdf.
8. Dan Baum, "Legalize It All: How to Win the War on Drugs," *Harper's Magazine*, April 2016. https://harpers.org/archive/2016/04/legalize-it-all.
9. Avelardo Valdez and Charles D. Kaplan, "Deconstructing US Marijuana Prohibition Policies in the Early Twentieth Century: An Intersectional Theoretical Approach," *Aztlán: A Journal of Chicano Studies* 44, no. 1 (2019).
10. Lina Britto, *Marijuana Boom: The Rise and Fall of Colombia's First Drug Paradise* (Oakland: University of California Press, 2020); Smith, *The Talons of the Eagle*, 245–51.

11. George W. Grayson, *Mexico: Narco-Violence and a Failed State?* (New Brunswick, NJ: Transaction Publishers, 2011), 27–29.
12. Raúl Diego Rivera Hernández, *Narratives of Vulnerability in Mexico's War on Drugs* (New York: Palgrave MacMillan, 2020), 3.
13. It is hard to gauge the extent of fraud in the election of 2006. Many of the specific allegations centered on partisan canvasing and the decision of outgoing president Vicente Fox to endorse Calderón, both of which, while frowned upon in Mexico due to its single-party history, are common practices in democracies throughout the world. See R. Michael Alvarez, Thad E. Hall, and Susan D. Hyde, "Introduction: Studying Election Fraud," in *Election Fraud: Detecting and Deterring Electoral Manipulation*, ed. R. Michael Alvarez, Thad E. Hall, and Susan D. Hyde (Washington, DC: Brookings Institution Press, 2009), 5. Cristina Rivera Garza refers to the election as "potentially fraudulent"—rather than certainly fraudulent—for precisely this reason. See Rivera Garza, *The Restless Dead*, 1. For a discussion of the distinction between "legality" and "legitimacy" in the election, see Todd A. Eisenstadt, "The Origins and Rationality of the 'Legal versus Legitimate' Dichotomy Invoked in Mexico's 2006 Post-Electoral Conflict," *PS: Political Science and Politics* 40, no. 1 (2007).
14. For a list of studies discussing how Calderón executed the War on Drugs to gain international favor, see César Morales Oyarvide, "La guerra contra el narcotráfico en México. Debilidad del Estado, orden local y fracaso de una estrategia," *Aposta: Revista de Ciencias Sociales* 50 (2011): 12–14; Alonso Vázquez Moyers and Germán Espino Sánchez. "La producción discursiva en la guerra contra el narcotráfico en el sexenio de Calderón: En busca de la legitimidad perdida," *Discurso y Sociedad* 9, no. 4 (2015): 497–500; Sonja Wolf and Gonzalo Celorio Morayta, "La guerra de México contra el narcotráfico y la iniciativa Mérida: Piedras angulares en la búsqueda de legitimidad," *Foro Internacional* 51, no. 4 (2011): 672. At the same time we should note that much of the political class within Mexico favored the military action as well. The Operativo Conjunto Michoacán, for example, enjoyed broad support from the Conferencia Nacional de Gobernadores (CONANGO; National Conference of Governors). See Luis Astorga, *"¿Qué querían que hiciera?": Inseguridad y delincuencia organizada en el gobierno de Felipe Calderón* (Mexico City: Grijalbo, 2015), 23–24. Clearly, political leaders throughout the country recognized the fact that they benefitted as well from a militarized response to drug trafficking. See also John Saxe-Fernández, "Diseños imperiales sobre México y América Latina," *Temas de Nuestra América* 25, no. 47 (2009): 104–5.
15. Rivera Garza, *The Restless Dead*, 2.
16. Williams, *The Mexican Exception*, 3–4.
17. Emerson, *Necropolitics*, 179–86.
18. One film critic notes the ambiguously dystopian nature of the film when he refers to it as "post-apocalyptic, pre-apocalyptic or merely apocalypse adjacent." See Guy Lodge, "Film Review: *Buy Me a Gun*," *Variety*, May 31, 2018, https://variety.com/2018/film/reviews/buy-me-a-gun-review-1202826446.

19. Anaya's decision to have Rosa as his protagonist is especially noteworthy given the charge of a "flat characterization of women" in his earlier works. See Cordelia Candelaria, "Rudolfo A. Anaya (30 October 1937– )," in *Chicano Writers: First Series*, ed. Francisco A. Lomelí and Carl R. Shirley, (Detroit, MI: Thomson Gale, 1989), 29.
20. I use the spelling *ChupaCabra* throughout this section of the book because that is the spelling that Anaya employs throughout his trilogy.
21. Rudolfo Anaya, *Curse of the ChupaCabra* (Albuquerque: University of New Mexico Press, 2006), 89.
22. Perhaps because he published this novel in 2018, ten years after *Roswell UFO*, Anaya turns the CD from *Roswell UFO* into a flash drive in *Billy the Kid*.
23. Esch, *Modernity at Gunpoint*, 21.
24. Esch, *Modernity at Gunpoint*, 22.
25. See David J. Hess, "On Low-Tech Cyborgs," in Gray, Figueroa-Sarriera, and Mentor, *The Cyborg Handbook*.
26. Haraway, *Simians, Cyborgs and Women*, 178.
27. For a discussion of friendly selves, see Haraway, *Simians, Cyborgs and Women*, 151. For a discussion of the role of firearms in conquering the Americas, see Esch, *Modernity at Gunpoint*, 4.
28. Agamben, *The Open*, 7–8.
29. For a discussion of how individuals view remarkable and illogical events as quotidian in the magical-real mode, see Carpentier, "On the Marvelous Real"; Leal, "Magical Realism." For critiques about how this literary mode casts Latin Americans—particularly those of Black and Indigenous descent—as essentialistically primitive, see Román de la Campa, "Magical Realism and World Literature: A Genre for the Times?" *Revista Canadiense de Estudios Hispánicos* 23, no. 2 (1999).
30. Brown and Ginway, "Introduction," 1.
31. Volpi, *El insomnio de Bolívar*, 185, 185–91.
32. Amanda Rueda, "Nuevas condiciones de la internacionalización de los cines de América Latina y plataformas profesionales de festivales. El caso de Cine en Construcción." *Archivos de la Filmoteca* 77 (2019): 77–78.
33. Christopher Warnes, *Magical Realism and the Postcolonial Novel: Between Faith and Irreverence* (New York: Palgrave MacMillan, 2009), 12.
34. Warnes, *Magical Realism*, 14.
35. Ricardo Bedoya Wilson, *El cine latinoamericano del siglo XXI: Tendencias y tratamientos* (Lima: Fondo Editorial Universidad de Lima, 2020. Kindle, Feb. 18, 2021), 400.
36. Laura Reyes, "Contribuciones cinematográficas al diálogo necesario para la reconstrucción de Guatemala: Gasolina, Las marimbas del infierno y *Polvo de Julio Hernández Cordón*," *La BloGoteca de Babel* 7 (2018): 3.
37. Olivia Cosentino, "Slower Cinema: Violence, Affect, and Spectatorship in *Las elegidas*," *Journal of Latin American Cultural Studies* 60, no. 3 (2021): 70.

38. The movie first appeared for rent and purchase on only two platforms: iStore and Google Play. More recently, it also appears on Amazon Prime. Indeed, despite numerous international awards, Hernández Cordón has historically struggled to make his films available on DVD or streaming platforms. See María Lourdes Cortés, "Filmmaking in Central America: An Overview," *Studies in Spanish and Latin American Cinemas* 15, no. 2 (2018): 157.
39. Carlos Belmonte Grey, "Territory and Central American and Mexican Youth in the Cinematic Work of Julio Hernández Cordón," *Comunicación y Medios* 38 (2018): 102.
40. Hispano Durón, "New Central American Cinema (2001–2010)" (PhD diss., University of Kansas, 2014), 50–51.
41. See Sebastião Guilherme Albano, "Elipse, história, política, memoria: *Las marimbas del infierno* e *O soma o redor*," *Fotocinema: Revista Científica de Cine y Fotografías* 9 (2014): 72.
42. Rueda, "Nuevas condiciones," 77–78. The director depended on film festivals for funding in *Cómprame un revólver* as well. See Minerva Campos, "Un impulso transnacional al cine latinoamericano de festivales: El programa Cine en Construcción," *Foro Hispánico* 51 (2016): 77n7; M. Cortés, "Filmmaking in Central America," 149–50. The film earned a respectable $1,903,503 MXN in the national box office along with showings at several major film festivals including Cannes. See *Anuario Estadístico de Cine Mexicano / Statistical Yearbook of Mexican Cinema* (Mexico City: Ministry of Culture, IMCINE, 2019), http://www.imcine.gob.mx/wp-content/uploads/2020/05/Anuario-Estad%C3%ADstico-de-Cine-Mexicano.pdf.
43. Valeria Grinberg Pla, "Against Anomie: Julio Hernández Cordón's Post-War Trilogy—*Gasolina/Gasoline* (2008), *Las marimbas del infierno/The Marimbas of Hell* (2010) and *Polvo/Dust* (2012)," *Studies in Spanish and Latin American Cinemas* 15, no. 2 (2018): 203–7.
44. María Lourdes Cortés, "Gasolina: Ocio, vacío y violencia en un viaje sin destino," in *Pereza: Historia de los afectos*, ed. Armando Casas (Mexico City: UNAM, Ebook, 2018).
45. Andrea Cabezas Vargas and Júlia González de Canales Carcereny, "Central American Cinematographic Aesthetics and Their Role in International Film Festivals," *Studies in Spanish and Latin American Cinemas* 15, no. 2 (2018): 180.
46. Cabezas Vargas and González de Canales Carcereny, "Central American Cinematographic Aesthetics," 180. The director's focus on sexual diversity has contributed to his popularity in France, even making it possible to rescue earlier films, like *Las marimbas del infierno* (2012), whose original distributor succumbed to bankruptcy. See Cédric Lépine, "Distribución de películas latinoamericanas en Francia en 2018," *Cinémas d'amérique latine* 27 (2019).
47. Grinberg Pla, "Against Anomie," 204.
48. M. Cortés, "Gasolina"; see also Reyes, "Contribuciones cinematográficas," 1–2.

49. Cortés, "Gasolina."
50. All English translations of the dialogue in this film reflect those in the subtitles.
51. Hayles, *How We Became Posthuman*, 3.
52. Herbert Sussman and Gerhard Joseph, "Prefiguring the Posthuman: Dickens and Prosthesis," *Victorian Literature and Culture* 32, no. 2 (2004): 618.
53. Hayles, *How We Became Posthuman*, 196–97.
54. Linda F. Hogle, "Tales from the Cryptic: Technology Meets Organism in the Living Cadaver," in Gray, Figueroa-Sarriera, and Mentor, *The Cyborg Handbook*, 204–8.
55. Haraway, *Simians, Cyborgs and Women*, 150, 163.
56. Esch, *Modernity at Gunpoint*, 21–22.
57. Bertold Brecht, "A Short Organum for the Theatre," Tensta Konsthall, 1945, 6. http://www.tenstakonsthall.se/uploads/139-Brecht_A_Short_Organum_for_the_Theatre.pdf.
58. Cabezas Vargas and González de Canales Carcereny, "Central American Cinematographic Aesthetics," 175–76.
59. Valencia, *Gore Capitalism*, 213, emphasis in original.
60. For a discussion of the absent state in Hernández Cordón's work, see Lorena Antezana Barrios and Marcela Rosales, "Editorial monográfico 'comunicación y espacialidad,'" *Comunicación y medios* 27, no. 38 (2018): 10. For a discussion of the absent state in historiographies of drug economies, see Britto, *Marijuana Boom*, 9–12.
61. Valencia, *Gore Capitalism*, 51–58; O. Zavala, *Los cárteles no existen*, 16.
62. Luis Astorga, *Seguridad, traficantes y militares* (Mexico City: Tusquets, 2007), 183–272, 54.
63. Esch, *Modernity at Gunpoint*, 189.
64. Esch, *Modernity at Gunpoint*, 181–82.
65. Agamben, *State of Exception*, 4.
66. For a discussion of how drug traffickers have contributed to feminicide in the country, see Domínguez-Ruvalcaba and Ravelo Blancas, *Desmantelamiento de la ciudadanía*, 93–106; González Rodríguez, *The Femicide Machine*, 40–70.

    I say this claim is problematic because, while drug traffickers and organized crime have undoubtedly contributed to feminicide in Mexico, the majority of cases of violence against women are cases of domestic abuse. See Julia E. Monárrez Fragoso, "Violencia de género, violencia de pareja, feminicidio y pobreza," in *Violencia contra las mujeres: Inseguridad ciudadana en Ciudad Juárez*, ed. Julia Estela Monárrez Fragoso et al. (Tijuana: El Colegio de la Frontera Norte, 2010), 240–46; Rodolfo Rubio Salas, "Características de la violencia de pareja en Chihuahua y algunas entidades fronterizas del norte de México," in Monárrez Fragoso et al., *Violencia contra las mujeres*; César M. Fuentes Flores, "La violencia de pareja en el entorno urbano del estado de Chihuahua: hacia el diseño de políticas públicas," in Monárrez Fragoso et al., *Violencia contra las mujeres*.

67. Johnson, *Violence and Naming*, 44.
68. Michaela M. Rogers, "Exploring the Domestic Abuse Narratives of Trans and Nonbinary People and the Role of Cisgenderism in Identity Abuse, Misgendering, and Pathologizing," *Violence against Women* 27, no. 12–13 (2020).
69. Esch, *Modernity at Gunpoint*, 22.
70. Warnes, *Magical Realism*, 2–3.
71. See Warnes, *Magical Realism*, 8.
72. Warnes, *Magical Realism*, 13.
73. Kim Anderson Sasser, *Magical Realism and Cosmopolitanism: Strategizing Belonging* (New York: Palgrave MacMillan, 2014), 21.
74. Héctor Domínguez-Ruvalcaba, *De la sensualidad a la violencia de género: La modernidad y la nación en las representaciones de la masculinidad en el México contemporáneo* (Mexico City: CIESAS, 2013), 58.
75. Helene Price, "Unsavoury Representations in Laura Esquivel's *Como agua para chocolate*," in *A Companion to Magical Realism*, ed. Stephen M. Hart and Wen-chin Ouyang (Suffolk: Tamesis, 2005); Sasser, *Magical Realism*, 5.
76. González Rodríguez, *The Femicide Machine*, 44. For further reading on the dangers faced by women and girls in northern Mexico, see Julia E. Monárrez Fragoso "Las diversas representaciones del feminicidio y los asesinatos de mujeres en Ciudad Juárez, 1993–2005," in Monárrez Fragoso et al., *Violencia contra las mujeres*, 364–68.
77. It is worth noting that *Cómprame un revólver* is technically a Mexican/Colombian production. Indeed, the film was one of the most critically acclaimed Colombian pictures of 2018, and it was one of twenty-three transnational coproductions that Colombia's Fondo para el Desarrollo Cinematográfico considered for funding. See Isabella Soto Salazar, "Ruta para la coproducción en Colombia" (senior thesis, Universidad Autónoma de Occidente, 2017), 64–65; see also Ana Milena Fúquene Daza and Daniel Mauricio Rodríguez Sevilla, "Apartes del cine colombiano" (senior thesis, Universidad Cooperativa de Colombia, 2020), 48.
78. Sasser, *Magical Realism*, 6.
79. Haraway, *Simians, Cyborgs and Women*, 151. This scene also communicates a problematic politics of transness due to the fact that the boss loses their influence over Huck as Huck comes to understand the criminal's nonbinary gender identity. See Sarah Wyble, "The Undermining of Queer and Feminist Agendas in Julio Hernández Cordón's *Cómprame un revólver*," paper presented at the Southeast Conference of Latin American Studies, Charlotte, NC, March 2022.
80. Esch, *Modernity at Gunpoint*, 21.
81. Haraway, *Simians, Cyborgs and Women*, 151.
82. Bruce Dick and Silvio Sirias, introduction to *Conversations with Rudolfo Anaya*, ed. Bruce Dick and Silvio Sirias (Jackson: University of Mississippi Press, 1998), xiii; Francisco Lomelí, "Chican@ Literary Imagination: Trajectory and Evolution of Canon Building from the Margins," in *The Forked Juniper:*

Critical Perspectives on Rudolfo Anaya, ed. Roberto Cantú (Norman: University of Oklahoma Press, 2016).

83. Manuel Broncano, "'We Are All Serafina's Children': Racial Landscapes in Rudolfo Anaya," in *Landscapes of Writing in Chicano Literature*, ed. Imelda Martín-Junquera (New York: Palgrave MacMillan, 2013), 122. See also Angelika Köhler, "The New World Man: Magical Realism in Rudolfo Anaya's *Bless Me, Ultima*," in *U.S. Latino Literatures and Cultures: Transnational Perspectives*, ed. Francisco Lomelí and Karin Ikas (Heidelberg: Universitätsverlag Winter, 2000); Enrique Lamadrid, "Myth as the Cognitive Process of Popular Culture in Rudolfo Anaya's *Bless Me, Ultima*: The Dialectics of Knowledge," *Hispania* 68, no. 3 (1985).

   Others refer to Anaya's brand of magical realism as "Southwest mysticism." See Robert F. Gish, "Rudolfo A. Anaya," in *Updating the Literary West*, ed. Max Westbrook and Dan Flores (Fort Worth: Texas Christian University Press, 1999), 534. Still others call it "native metaphysics." See Enrique Lamadrid, "The Dynamics of Myth in the Creative Vision of Rudolfo Anaya," in *Pasó por aquí: Critical Essays on the New Mexican Literary Tradition, 1542–1988* (Albuquerque: University of New Mexico Press, 1989), 243.

84. For a discussion of the tension and communion that occurs in the New Mexican landscape throughout Anaya's oeuvre, see Alfred Jung, "Regionalist Motifs in Rudolfo A. Anaya's Fiction (1972–82)," in *Missions in Conflict: Essays on U.S.-Mexican Relations and Chicano Culture*, ed. Renate von Bardeleben, Dietrich Briesemeister, and Juan Bruce-Novoa (Tübingen: Stauffenburg Verlag Brigitte Narr GmbH, 1986). For a discussion of the importance of the Chicanx Indigenous ancestry of Chicanx peoples and cultures in Anaya's thought, see David King Dunaway and Sara Spurgeon, *Writing the Southwest* (Albuquerque: University of New Mexico Press, 1995), 20.

85. While I have avoided the term Hispanic throughout this book, the terms *Hispano* and *Hispana* prove valuable in the New Mexican context because they were historically used to denote people of Spanish (read: *mestizo*) descent. Given that this is an older term, I will not employ the nonbinary *Hispanx*.

86. Andrea J. Pitts, *Nos/Otras: Gloria E. Anzaldúa, Multiplicitous Agency, and Resistance* (Albany: State University of New York Press, 2021), 61.

87. Sandoval, *Methodology of the Oppressed*, 168.

88. Joanna Zylinska, "'The Future . . . Is Monstrous': Prosthetics as Ethics," in *The Cyborg Experiments: The Extensions of the Body in the Media Age*, ed. Joanna Zylinska (London: Continuum, 2002), 216.

89. Anzaldúa, *Borderlands/La frontera*, 105.

90. Anzaldúa, *Borderlands/La frontera*, 105–7.

91. For a discussion of the interconnectedness among the New Mexican landscape, the individuals who live there, and the community at large in Anaya's narrative, see Carmen Lydia Flys Junquera, "*La Tierra*: Sense of Place in Contemporary Chicano Literature," in *Spanish Perspectives on Chicano Literature: Literary and*

*Cultural Essays*, ed. Jesús Rosales, Vanessa Fonseca, and Francisco A. (Columbus: Ohio State University Press, 2017), 140; Manuel Broncano, "Landscapes of the Magical: Cather's and Anaya's Explorations of the Southwest," in *Willa Cather and the American Southwest*, ed. John N. Swift and Joseph R. Urgo (Lincoln: University of Nebraska Press, 2002), 126; Dunaway and Spurgeon, *Writing the Southwest*, 16.

92. Enrique Lamadrid, "De vatos y profetas: Cultural Authority and Literary Presence in the Writing of Rudolfo Anaya," in Cantú, *The Forked Juniper*, 201.

93. Robert Con Davis-Undiano, *Mestizos Come Home!: Making and Claiming Mexican American Identity* (Norman: University of Oklahoma Press, 2017), 104.

94. White settlers exploited those residents of New Mexico and California that had lived there previous to annexation. Nevertheless, larger numbers of people immigrated to California, and the government engaged in programs of Native American genocide in that territory. See Benjamin Madley, *An American Genocide: The United States and the California Indian Catastrophe, 1846–1873* (New Haven, CT: Yale University Press, 2016). Settlers and the government engaged in similar acts in New Mexico as well. Nevertheless, overall migration to the state was much lower, and the original inhabitants have maintained a much stronger presence there.

95. William A. Calvo-Quirós, "Sucking Vulnerability: Neoliberalism, the Chupacabras, and the Post-Cold War Years," in Hernández and Rodríguez y Gibson, *The Un/Making of Latina/o Citizenship*, 224.

96. For Anaya, Aztlán functions as a figurative, mythic space that facilitates "communal and cultural cohesion" among Chicanx communities throughout the nation. See Rudolfo Anaya, "Aztlán: A Homeland without Boundaries," in *Aztlán: Essays on the Chicano Homeland*, ed. Rudolfo A. Anaya and Francisco Lomelí (Albuquerque: University of New Mexico Press, 1991). Robert Con Davis-Undiano, "The Emergence of New World Studies: Anaya, Aztlán, and the New Chicana," *Genre: Forms of Discourse and Culture* 32, no. 1–2 (1999): 121; Horst Tonn, "Imagining the Local and the Global in the Work of Rudolfo A. Anaya," in Cantú, *The Forked Juniper*, 242.

97. Lamadrid, "De vatos y profetas," 199; Benjamin Radford, *Tracking the Chupacabra: The Vampire Beast in Fact, Fiction, and Folklore* (Albuquerque: University of New Mexico Press, 2011), 47. These assertions aside, the novels seem, more precisely, to be aimed at a young adult readership.

98. Calvo-Quirós, "Sucking Vulnerability," 223. The illicit drug trade has long interested Anaya due to its disastrous effects in Mexican and Chicanx communities. See Abelardo Baeza, "Rudolfo A. Anaya," in *Twentieth-Century American Western Writers*, ed. Richard H. Cracroft (Detroit, MI: Thomson Gale,), 16; Héctor Calderón, *Narratives of Greater Mexico*, 36.

99. Bruce Dick and Silvio Sirias, introduction to Dick and Sirias, *Conversations with Rudolfo Anaya*, xii. Early in his career, Anaya expressed frustration with the pressure to politicize his literature. See Juan Bruce-Novoa, "Rudolfo Anaya,"

in Dick and Sirias, *Conversations with Rudolfo Anaya*, 18–21; David Johnson and David Apodaca, "Myth and the Writer: A Conversation with Rudolfo Anaya" in Bruce and Sirias, *Conversations with Rudolfo Anaya*, 37–38.

100. Lamadrid, "The Dynamics of Myth," 246. Numerous authors have written extensively on how the author uses the myth of the La Llorona to engage the intersectionalities of race, class, and gender in New Mexican and Chicanx society. See Sophia Emmanouilidou, "Mythography and the Reconstitution of Chicano Identity in Rudolfo Alfonso Anaya's *The Legend of La Llorona*," in *Transcultural Localisms: Responding to Ethnicity in a Globalized World*, ed. Yiorgos Kalogeras and Eleftheria Arapoglou (Heidelberg: Universitätsverlag Winter GmbH, 2006); Ewelina Krok, "The Figure of La Llorona as a Central Cultural Paradigm in Contemporary Chicano/a Literature," in *Kulturelles Wissen und Intertextualität: Theoriekonzeptionen und Fallstudien zur Kontextualisierung von Literatur*, ed. Marion Gymnich, Birgit Neumann, Ansgar Nünning (Trier: Wissenschaftlicher Verlag Trier, 2006), 200–202; An Van Hecke, "Hybrid Voices in the Borderlands: Translation and Reconstruction of Mexican Images in Rudolfo Anaya," *Confluencia: Revista Hispánica de Cultura y Literatura* 29, no. 2 (2014).

101. Radford, *Tracking the Chuapacabra*, 3.
102. Radford, *Tracking the Chupacabra*, 3–19.
103. Ginway, *Cyborgs, Sexuality, and the Undead*, 150; Moraña, *The Monster as War Machine*, 400–402.
104. William A. Calvo-Quirós, "Chupacabras, the Strange Case of Carlos Salinas de Gortari and His Transformation into the *Chupatodo*," in *Crossing the Borders of the Imagination*, ed. María del Mar Ramón Torrijos (Madrid: Instituto Franklin de Estudios Norteamericanos, Universidad de Alcalá, 2014), 90–93.
105. Julio Cañero Serrano, "Rudolfo Anaya's Narrative as an Example of Chicano Proletarianization within an Internal Colonial Framework," in Lomelí and Ikas, *U.S. Latino Literatures*, 191–97.
106. Marx, *Capital*, 163.
107. Anaya, *Curse of the ChupaCabra*, 43.
108. Moraña, *The Monster as War Machine*, 400.
109. Volpi, *El insomnio de Bolívar*, 126–30.
110. Anaya, *Curse of the ChupaCabra*, 16.
111. Agamben, *Homo Sacer*, 160–65; Agamben, *The Open*, 15.
112. Anaya, *Curse of the ChupaCabra*, 47.
113. Anaya, *Curse of the ChupaCabra*, 47.
114. Rudolfo Anaya, *ChupaCabra Meets Billy the Kid* (Norman: University of Oklahoma Press, 2008), 120.
115. Calvo-Quirós, "Sucking Vulnerability," 224.
116. Calvo-Quirós, "Sucking Vulnerability," 227.
117. Aishih Wehbe Herrera, "Performing Masculinity, Performing the Self: Rudolfo Anaya's *Bless Me, Ultima* and *Heart of Aztlan*," *Revista Canaria de Estudios Ingleses* 66 (2013): 112. For a discussion of Anaya's interest in Carl Jung, see

Margarite Fernández Olmos, *Rudolfo A. Anaya: A Critical Companion* (Westport, CT: Greenwood Publishing Group, 1999), 41–44; Antonio Márquez, "The Achievement of Rudolfo A. Anaya," in *The Magic of Words: Rudolfo A. Anaya and His Writings*, ed. Paul Vassallo (Albuquerque: University of New Mexico Press, 1982), 45–48.

118. Davis-Undiano, *Mestizos Come Home!*, 11; Scott P. Sanders, "Southwestern Gothic: Alienation, Integration, and Rebirth in the Works of Richard Shelton, Rudolfo Anaya, and Leslie Silko," *Weber Studies: An Interdisciplinary Humanities Journal* 4, no. 2 (1987).
119. Carmen Lydia Flys Junquera, "Rudolfo Anaya's Shifting Sense of Place," in Martín Junquera, *Landscapes of Writing*, 162.
120. Ralph E. Rodríguez, *Brown Gumshoes: Detective Fiction and the Search for Chicana/o Identity* (Austin: University of Texas Press, 2005), 119.
121. Rudolfo Anaya, "Mythical Dimensions/Political Reality," in *The Multicultural Southwest*, ed. Gabriel A. Meléndez et al. (Tucson: University of Arizona Press, 2001), 267.
122. Anaya, *Curse of the ChupaCabra*, 129.
123. Anaya, *Curse of the ChupaCabra*, 130, emphasis mine.
124. Susan Baker Sotelo, *Chicano Detective Fiction: A Critical Study of Five Novelists*. Jefferson, NC: McFarland, 2005), 42.
125. Christina Garcia Lopez, *Calling the Soul Back: Embodied Spirituality in Chicanx Narrative* (Tucson: University of Arizona Press, 2019), 5. See also Anzaldúa, *Borderlands/La frontera*, 70.
126. Rosaura Sánchez, "Rudolfo Anaya's Historical Memory," in Cantú, *The Forked Juniper*, 222.
127. Anaya, *Curse of the ChupaCabra*, 140.
128. Anaya, *Curse of the ChupaCabra*, 160–61.
129. Anaya, *Curse of the ChupaCabra*, 161.
130. Calvo-Quirós, "Sucking Vulnerability," 226.
131. Valencia, *Gore Capitalism*, 63–68; O. Zavala, *Los cárteles no existen*.
132. Anaya, *ChupaCabra Meets Billy the Kid*, 27.
133. Rudolfo Anaya, *ChupaCabra and the Roswell UFO* (Albuquerque: University of New Mexico Press, 2008), 137.
134. Anaya, *ChupacCabra and the Roswell UFO*, 137.
135. Roberto Cantú, introduction to *The Forked Juniper*, 12.
136. José Vasconcelos, *El monismo estético* (Mexico City: Tip Murguía, 1918). See also Cantú, "Introduction," 12.
137. Dalton, *Mestizo Modernity*, 35; Patrick Romanell, "Bergson in Mexico: A Tribute to Vasconcelos," *Philosophy and Phenomenological Research* 21, no. 4 (1961): 503–8.
138. Lund, *The Mestizo State*, x-xiv.
139. Robert Con Davis-Undiano, "Mestizos Critique the New World: Vasconcelos, Anzaldúa, and Anaya," *Lit: Literature Interpretation Theory* 11, no. 2 (2000).

140. See Andrea J. Pitts, "Toward an Aesthetics of Race: Bridging the Writings of Gloria Anzaldúa and José Vasconcelos," *Inter-American Journal of Philosophy* 5, no. 1 (2014).
141. John-Michael Rivera, "Billy the Kid's Corpse and the Specter of Mexican Manhood," in *Decolonizing Latinx Masculinities*, ed. Arturo J. Aldama and Frederick Luis Aldama (Tucson: University of Arizona Press, 2020), 27.
142. David Correia, *Properties of Violence: Law and Land Grant Struggle in Northern New Mexico* (Athens: University of Georgia Press, 2013), 1–12.
143. J. Rivera, "Billy the Kid's Corpse," 27.
144. Cecilia J. Aragón, "*Los corridos de Billy the Kid—El Bilito*: Contemporary Ballads and Songs about Billy the Kid from Native New Mexicans, Rudolfo Anaya and Simón Álvarez," *Camino Real: Estudios de las Hispanidades Norteamericanas* 3, no. 5 (2011): 42.
145. J. Rivera, "Billy the Kid's Corpse," 27–28.
146. Joel Jacobsen, *Such Men as Billy the Kid: The Lincoln County War Reconsidered* (Lincoln: University of Nebraska Press, 1994), 211–12.
147. For a discussion of how "autobiographical elements" drove Anaya's literature, see Bridget Kevane, *Latino Literature in America* (Westport, CT: Greenwood Publishing, 2003), 34. For a discussion of the ties among Billy the Kid and the Native American and Hispanic populations of New Mexico, see Aragón, "*Los corridos de Billy the Kid*," 39.
148. J. Rivera, "Billy the Kid's Corpse," 30.
149. Quoted in Manuel Otero, *The Real Billy the Kid* (New York: R. R. Wilson, 1936), 160.
150. For a discussion of different oral histories about Billy the Kid's interactions with the Mexican inhabitants of New Mexico, see Aragón, "*Los corridos de Billy the Kid*," 39–41.
151. Robert M. Utley, *Wanted: The Outlaw Lives of Billy the Kid and Ned Kelly* (New Haven, CT: Yale University Press, 2015), 51.
152. Anaya, *ChupaCabra Meets Billy the Kid*, 72.
153. Chabram-Dernersesian, "I Throw Punches for My Race," 168.
154. Chabram-Dernersesian, "I Throw Punches for My Race."
155. Anaya, *ChupaCabra Meets Billy the Kid*, 74.
156. John-Michael Rivera, *The Emergence of Mexican America: Recovering Stories of Mexican Peoplehood in U.S. Culture* (New York: New York University Press, 2006), 121.
157. Anaya, *ChupaCabra Meets Billy the Kid*, 79–80.
158. Anaya, *ChupaCabra Meets Billy the Kid*, 27.
159. Yehya, *Drone Visions*, 64.
160. Anaya, *ChupaCabra Meets Billy the Kid*, 120–21.
161. J. Rivera, "Billy the Kid's Corpse," 29; see also Aragón "*Los corridos de Billy the Kid—El Bilito*," 39; J. Rivera, *Emergence of Mexican America*, 110–34.
162. Anaya, *ChupaCabra Meets Billy the Kid*, 145.

163. Anaya, *ChupaCabra Meets Billy the Kid*, 150.
164. Anaya, *ChupaCabra Meets Billy the Kid*, 155.
165. See Esch, *Modernity at Gunpoint*, 21.

## CONCLUSION

1. Avery Plaw, Barbara Carvalho Gurgel, and David Ramírez Plascencia, introduction to Plaw, Gurgel, and Ramírez Plascencia, *Politics of Technology*, 1.
2. Ruth Levitas, *Utopia as Method: The Imaginary Reconstitution of Society* (New York: Palgrave MacMillan, 2013), 110.
3. López-Lozano, *Utopian Dreams, Apocalyptic Nightmares*, 23–26.
4. Taylor and Pitman, *Latin American Identity*; Claire Taylor, *Place and Politics in Latin American Digital Culture* (New York: Routledge, 2014).
5. Hilda Chacón, introduction to Chacón, *Online Activism in Latin America*, 19–20.
6. Sergio Delgado Moya, "A Theater of Displacement: Staging Activism, Poetry, and Migration through a Transborder Immigrant Tool," in Chacón, *Online Activism in Latin America*.
7. Emily Hind, "On Pirates and Tourists: Ambivalent Approaches to *El Blog del Narco*," in Chacón, *Online Activism in Latin America*; Amber Workman, The Uses and Limits of Ethnic Humor and New Media in *¡Ask a Mexican!*" In Chacón, *Online Activism in Latin America*.
8. Dalton, "Exploiting Liminal Legality."
9. United States Citizenship and Immigration Services has documented the country of origin of all registered recipients of DACA. See Approximate Active DACA Recipients: Country of Birth as of September 4, 2017 (United States Citizenship and Immigration Services), https://www.uscis.gov/sites/default/files/document/data/daca_population_data.pdf. For a discussion of how 1.5-generation activists coordinated virtual and physical demonstrations, see Laura Corrunker, "'Coming out of the Shadows': DREAM Act Activism in the Context of Global Anti-Deportation Activism," *Indiana Journal of Global Legal Studies* 19, no. 1 (2012): 158–63; Walter Nicholls, "Voice and Power in the Immigrant Rights Movement," in Menjívar and Kanstroom, *Constructing Immigrant "Illegality,"* 236; William A. Schwab, *Right to DREAM: Immigration Reform and America's Future* (Fayetteville: University of Arkansas Press, 2013), 124.
10. Sarah C. Bishop, "Undocumented Immigrant Media Makers and the Search for Connection Online," *Critical Studies in Media Communication* 34 no. 5 (2017): 423; Thomas Piñeros Shields, "DREAMers Rising: Constituting the Undocumented Student Immigrant Movement" (PhD diss., Brandeis University, 2014), 145–50.
11. See Barack H. Obama, "Remarks by the President in Address to the Nation on Immigration," The White House: President Barack Obama, November 20, 2014, https://obamawhitehouse.archives.gov/the-press-office/2014/11/20/remarks-President-address-nation-immigration.
12. Dalton, "Exploiting Liminal Legality."
13. See, for example, the case of Mexican migrants in Japan who have created communities through YouTube and other social media. Yunuen Ylce Mandujano-Salazar,

"YouTube Channels of Mexicans Living in Japan: Virtual Communities and Bi-Cultural Imagery Construction," in Dalton and Ramírez Plascencia, *Imagining Latinidad*, 153–66.

14. See, for example, the case of diasporic communities of Latin American descent who have used technology to advocate for their communities against gentrification in cities like London. See Jessica Retis and Patria Román-Velázquez. "Latin Americans in London: Digital Diasporas and Social Activism," in Dalton and Ramírez Plascencia, *Imagining Latinidad*, 110–13.
15. The initiative began on the campus of the University of California, Berkely before expanding to other parts of San José and later to the University of California, Los Angeles. The company now has operations in Miami, Detroit, Pittsburgh, New Mexico, and Washington. See KiwiBot for Business, https://www.kiwibot.com.
16. Miguel Figliozzi and Dylan Jennings, "Autonomous Delivery Robots and Their Potential Impacts on Urban Freight Energy Consumption and Emissions," *Transportation Research Procedia* 46 (2020).
17. Sabrina Touami, "Vehicules de Livraison Autonomes: Une Solution pour L'avenir?," (master's thesis, Université Gustave Eiffel, 2020).
18. Lasse Hulgaard and Frederik Moesgaard. "Digital Interfaces for Urban Spaces" (master's thesis, Copenhagen Business School, 2020), 22; Mason Marks, "Robots in Space: Sharing Our World with Autonomous Delivery Vehicles," paper presented at the We Robot Conference, Miami, FL, March 2019, https://robots.law.miami.edu/2019/wp-content/uploads/2019/03/Mason-Marks-Robots-in-Space-WeRobot-2019-3-14.pdf.
19. Annalee Newitz, "The Robots Won't Steal Your Jobs, It Will Be Worse than That." *New Scientist* 242, no. 3236 (2019).
20. Emma Rooholfada, "Kiwi Hires Colombian Students to Supervise KiwiBots," *Daily Californian* (Berkeley, CA), Oct. 15, 2019, https://www.dailycal.org/2019/10/15/kiwi-hires-colombian-students-to-supervise-kiwibots.
21. Rieder, *Colonialism and the Emergence*.
22. Schradie, *The Revolution that* Wasn't, 7.
23. See Lilia Fernández, "Race Baiting, Identity Politics, and the Impact of the Conservative Economic Agenda on Latinos/as," *Latino Studies* 16, no. 4 (2018); Bernadette Nadya Jaworsky, *The Boundaries of Belonging: Online Work of Immigration-Related Social Movement Organizations* (New York: Palgrave Macmillan, 2016), 11–20.
24. See David S. Dalton, "Unos anticonceptivos apocalípticos: Inconmensurabilidades semánticas entre la ciencia médica y la religion, en *La píldora maravillosa* de Jesús Pavlo Tenorio," *Revista de Medicina y Humanidades* 8, no. 1 (2016): 84–85.
25. I use the term Chicano here because the film explicitly codes her enemies as male.
26. Agamben, *Homo Sacer*, 136–43.
27. The film shows several moments where Riley interacts with Black characters—particularly women—who have also suffered at the hands of the Mexican cartel.

In so doing, it imagines a shared solidarity among white and Black Americans against a supposedly foreign threat represented by people of Latin American descent.
28. For a discussion of Santa Muerte in Mexican culture, see José Gil Olmos, *La Santa Muerte: La virgen de los olvidados* (Mexico City: Debolsillo, 2012).
29. For a discussion about *Peppermint* as a film of feminist empowerment that South Korean cinema has used as a blueprint in its own productions, see Hyekyong Sim, "Acting 'Like a Woman': South Korean Female Action Heroines," *Journal of Japanese and Korean Cinema* 12, no. 2 (2020): 116.
30. Box Office Mojo. *Peppermint*, 2018. https://www.boxofficemojo.com/release/rl738493953.
31. Mexican migration to the United States has dropped so drastically in recent years that Mexicans now represent less than 50 percent of undocumented immigrants in the country. Certainly, the drop in Mexican migration has coincided with increased migration from Central America, and most of these migrants enter the country by crossing through Mexico first. See Jeffrey S. Passel and D'vera Cohn, "Mexicans Decline to Less than Half the U.S. Unauthorized Immigrant Population for the First Time," Pew Research Center, 2019, https://www.pewresearch.org/fact-tank/2019/06/12/us-unauthorized-immigrant-population-2017.
32. Sánchez Prado, *Screening Neoliberalism*, 5–7.
33. Several historians have shown that central Church leadership in the Vatican had no interest in helping Mexican clerics. Instead, they simply wanted peace and order. See Jürgen Buchenau, *Blood in the Sand: The "Sonoran Dynasty" in the Mexican Revolution* (Lincoln: University of Nebraska Press, forthcoming); Steven J. C. Andes, *The Vatican and Catholic Activism in Mexico and Chile: The Politics of Transnational Catholicism, 1920–1940* (Oxford: Oxford University Press, 2014,) 70–87.
34. Renée de la Torre, Cristina Gutiérrez, and Alberto Hernández. "Religious Reconfiguration in Mexico: Beliefs and Practices National Survey, 2016," *Social Compass* 67, no. 3 (2020).
35. Mbembe, *Necropolitics*, 175–76.

# References

Acosta, Abraham. *Thresholds of Illiteracy: Theory, Latin America, and the Crisis of Resistance.* New York: Fordham University Press, 2014.
Acosta, Rafael. *Drug Lords, Cowboys, and Desperados: Violent Myths of the U.S.-Mexico Frontier.* Notre Dame, IN: University of Notre Dame Press, 2021.
———. "Taming Heroes: Deep Time, Affect, and Economies of Honor and Glory in Contemporary Mexico." *Revista de Estudios Hispánicos* 52, no. 3 (2018): 815–36.
Acree, William. "The Trial of Theatre: *Fiat iustitia, et pereat mundus.*" *Latin American Theatre Review* 40, no. 1 (2006): 39–60.
Acuña, Rodolfo F. *Anything but Mexican: Chicanos in Contemporary Los Angeles*, 2nd ed. New York: Verso, 2020.
Agamben, Giorgio. *Homo sacer: Sovereign Power and Bare Life.* Translated by Daniel Heller-Roazen. Redwood City, CA: Stanford University Press, 1998.
———. *State of Exception.* Translated by Daniel Heller Roazen. Redwood City, CA: Stanford University Press, 2005.
———. *The Open: Man and Animal.* Translated by Kevin Attell. Redwood City, CA: Stanford University Press, 2004.
Alarcón, Norma. "Chicana Femenism: In the Tracks of 'the' Native Woman." In Chabram-Dernersesian, *The Chicana/o Studies Reader* 183–90.
Albano, Sebastião Guilherme. "Elipse, história, política, memoria: *Las marimbas del infierno* e *O soma o redor.*" *Fotocinema: Revista Científica de Cine y Fotografías*, no. 9 (2014): 65–83.
Aldama, Frederick Luis. "Confessions of a Latin@ Sojourner in *SciFilandia.*" In *Latin@ Rising: An Anthology of Latin@ Science Fiction and Fantasy*, edited by Matthew David Goodwin, xv–xx. San Antonio, TX: Wings Press, 2017.
———. "Introduction: On Matters of Form in Contemporary Latino Poetry." In *Formal Matters in Contemporary Latino Poetry*, edited by Frederick Luis Aldama, 1–32. New York: Palgrave MacMillan, 2016.

———, ed. *Latinx Ciné in the Twenty-First Century*. Tucson: University of Arizona Press, 2019.

———, ed. *The Routledge Companion to Latina/o Popular Culture*. New York: Routledge, 2016.

———. "Toward a Transfrontera-LatinX Aesthetic: An Interview with Filmmaker Alex Rivera." *Latino Studies* 15, no. 3 (2017): 373–80.

Alegrette, Alessandro Yuri. "Entre o horror e a beleza: A sublime estética gótica dos filmes de Guillermo del Toro." *Revista abusões* 1, no. 1 (2016): 13–30.

Allatson, Paul. "From 'Latinidad' to 'Latinid@des': Imaging the Twenty-First Century." In *The Cambridge Companion to Latina/o American Literature*, edited by John Morán González, 128–44. Cambridge: Cambridge University Press, 2016.

Alcoff, Linda Martín. "Is Latina/o Identity a Racial Identity?" In *Hispanics/Latinos in the United States*, edited by Jorge J. E. Gracia and Pablo De Grieff, 23–44. New York: Routledge, 2000.

Almaguer, Tomás. "Historical Notes on Chicano Oppression: The Dialectics of Racial and Class Domination in North América." In Calderón, *The Aztlán Mexican Studies Reader*, 38–70.

Alonso Meneses, Guillermo. "Migra, coyotes, paisanos y muertitos: Sobre la analiticidad y el sentido de ciertos factores de la migración clandestina en la frontera norte." *El bordo: Retos de frontera*, no. 7 (2001).

Althusser, Louis. "Ideology and Ideological State Apparatuses: Notes Towards an Investigation." In *Cultural Theory: An Anthology*, edited by Imre Szesman and Timothy Kaposy, 204–22. Malden, MA: Wiley-Blackwell, 2011.

Alvarez, R. Michael, Thad E. Hall, and Susan D. Hyde. "Introduction: Studying Election Fraud." In *Election Fraud: Detecting and Deterring Electoral Manipulation*, edited by R. Michael Alvarez, Thad E. Hall, and Susan D. Hyde, 1–20. Washington, DC: Brookings Institution Press, 2009.

Amaya, Héctor. *Citizenship Excess: Latinas/os, Media, and the Nation*. New York: New York University Press, 2013.

Amerikaner, Andres. "Xerox Men: Technological Tropes in U.S. Latino/a Displacement Literature." *Symploke* 25, no. 1–2 (2017): 113–23.

Amoore, Louise. "Biometric Borders: Governing Mobilities in the War on Terror." *Political Geography* 25, no. 3 (2006): 336–51.

Anaya, Rudolfo. "Aztlán: A Homeland without Boundaries." In *Aztlán: Essays on the Chicano Homeland*, edited by Rudolfo A. Anaya and Francisco Lomelí, 230–41. Albuquerque: University of New Mexico Press, 1991.

———. *ChupaCabra and the Roswell UFO*. Albuquerque: University of New Mexico Press, 2008.

———. *ChupaCabra Meets Billy the Kid*. Norman: University of Oklahoma Press, 2018.

———. *Curse of the ChupaCabra*. Albuquerque: University of New Mexico Press, 2006.

———. "Mythical Dimensions/Political Reality." In *The Multicultural Southwest*, edited by Gabriel A. Meléndez, Jane M. Young, Patricia Moore, and Patrick Pynes, 267–72. Tucson: University of Arizona Press, 2001.

Anderson, Benedict. *Imagined Communities: Reflections on the Origin and Spread of Nationalism*, 2nd ed. New York: Verso, 1991.

Andes, Steven J. C. *The Vatican and Catholic Activism in Mexico and Chile: The Politics of Transnational Catholicism, 1920–1940*. Oxford: Oxford University Press, 2014.

Antezana Barrios, Lorena, and Marcela Rosales. "Editorial monográfico 'comunicación y espacialidad.'" *Comunicación y medios* 27, no. 38 (2018): 9–10.

*Anuario Estadístico de Cine Mexicano 2019 / Statistical Yearbook of Mexican Cinema*. Mexico City: Ministry of Culture, IMCINE, 2019. http://www.imcine.gob.mx/wp-content/uploads/2020/05/Anuario-Estad%C3%ADstico-de-Cine-Mexicano.pdf.

Anzaldúa, Gloria. *Borderlands / La frontera: The New Mestiza*, 3rd ed. San Francisco: Aunt Lute, 2007.

Aragón, Cecilia J. "*Los corridos de Billy the Kid—El Bilito*: Contemporary Ballads and Songs about Billy the Kid from Native New Mexicans, Rudolfo Anaya and Simón Álvarez." *Camino Real: Estudios de las Hispanidades Norteamericanas* 3, no. 5 (2011): 37–57.

Arellano-neri, Olimpia. "Cinematographic and Literary Representations of the Femicides in Ciudad Juárez." PhD diss., University of Cincinnati, 2013.

Arriola, Elvia R. "Accountability for Murder in the *Maquiladoras*: Linking Corporate Indifference to Gender Violence at the U.S.-Mexico Border." In Gaspar de Alba and Guzmán, *Making a Killing*, 25–62.

Arrizón, Alicia. "Mythical Performativity: Relocating Aztlán in Chicana Feminist Cultural Productions." *Theatre Journal* 42, no. 1 (2000): 23–49.

Artz, Georgeanne M. "Immigration and Meatpacking in the Midwest." *Choices: The Magazine of Food, Farm, and Resource Issues* 27, no. 2 (2012). https://www.choicesmagazine.org/choices-magazine/theme-articles/immigration-and-agriculture/immigration-and-meatpacking-in-the-midwest-.

Astorga, Luis. *"¿Qué querían que hiciera?": Inseguridad y delincuencia organizada en el gobierno de Felipe Calderón*. Mexico City: Grijalbo, 2015.

———. *Seguridad, traficantes y militares*. Mexico City: Tusquets, 2007.

Azcona Muñoz, Tabaré. "The Poetics of Invocation: Haunted Writing and Political Subjectification in Twenty-First-Century Mexico." MA thesis, University of Colorado, 2017.

Bachran, Daoine S. "From Recovery to Discovery: Ethnic American Science Fiction and (Re)Creating the Future." PhD diss., University of New Mexico, 2016.

———. "From Code to Codex: Tricksterizing the Digital Divide in Ernest Hogan's *Smoking Mirror Blues*." In Merla-Watson and B. V. Olguín, *Alternmundos*, 111–27.

Baeza, Abelardo. "Rudolfo A. Anaya." In *Twentieth-Century American Western Writers*, edited by Richard H. Cracroft, 11–19. Detroit, MI: Thomson Gale, 1999.

Bajo Juárez: La ciudad devorando a sus hijas, directed by José Antonio Cordero and Alejandra Sánchez. Morelia, MX: FOPROCINE, IMCINE, Pepa Films, 2008. DVD.

Balanzategui, Jessica. "The Child Transformed by Monsters: The Monstrous Beauty of Childhood Trauma." In Morehead, *Supernatural Cinema*, 76–92.

Balazs, Carolina L., Rachel Morello-Frosch, Alan E. Hubbard, and Isha Ray. "Environmental Justice Implications of Arsenic Contamination in California's San Joaquin Valley: A Cross-Sectional, Cluster-Design Examining Exposure and Compliance in Community Drinking Water Systems." *Environmental Health* 11 no, 1 (2012): 2–12.

Baldry, Anna Costanza, and Maria José Magalhães. "Prevention of Femicide." In *Femicide across Europe: Theory, Research and Prevention*, edited by Shalva Weil, Consuelo Corradi, and Marceline Naudi, 71–92. Bristol, UK: Policy Press, 2018.

Banerjee, Subhabrata Bobby. "Necrocapitalism." *Organization Studies* 29, no. 12 (2008): 1542–63.

Barrera, Cordelia E. "Cyborg Bodies, Strategies of Consciousness and Ecological Revolution in the Mexico-US Borderlands." *Chicana/Latina Studies* 14, no. 1 (2014): 28–55.

Barry, Tom. *Mexico: A Country Guide*. Albuquerque, NM: Resource Center Press, 1992.

Bartra, Armando. "Mexico: Yearnings and Utopias: The Left in the Third Millenium." In *The New Latin American Left: Utopia Reborn*, edited by Patrick Barrett, Daniel Chavez, and César Rodríguez Garavito, 186–214. London: Pluto Press, 2008.

Baum, Dan. "Legalize It All: How to Win the War on Drugs." *Harper's Magazine*, April 2016. https://harpers.org/archive/2016/04/legalize-it-all.

Bedoya Wilson, Ricardo. *El cine latinoamericano del siglo XXI: Tendencias y tratamientos*. Lima: Fondo Editorial Universidad de Lima, 2020. Kindle, Feb. 18, 2021.

Beilin, Katarzyna Olga, and Sainath Suryanarayanan. "Step Out to *Shadowtime*, Hurry Like a Plant: Corporeal and Corporate Time for the Anthropocene Generation." *Transmodernity* 6, no. 2 (2016): 20–43.

Bell, Andrea L., and Yolanda Molina-Gavilán, eds. *Cosmos Latinos: An Anthology of Science Fiction from Latin America and Spain*. Middletown, CT: Wesleyan University Press, 2003.

Bell, Andrea L., and Yolanda Molina-Gavilán. "Introduction: Science Fiction in Latin America and Spain." In Bell and Molina-Gavilán, *Cosmos Latinos*, 1–19.

Belmonte Grey, Carlos. "Territory and Central American and Mexican Youth in the Cinematic Work of Julio Hernández Cordón." *Comunicación y Medios*, no. 38 (2018): 100–111.

Benjamin, Walter. "On the Concept of History." Trans. Dennis Redmond, 2005. Marxists Internet Archive. Accessed April 20, 2021. https://www.marxists.org/reference/archive/benjamin/1940/history.htm.

Berardi, Franco "Bifo." "Prólogo. Necro-capitalismo y sensibilidad." In *La tiranía del sentido común*, by Irmgard Emmelhainz, 9–13. Mexico City: Paradiso Editores, 2016.

Berdiev, Aziz N., Yoonbai Kim, and Chun-Ping Chang. "Remittances and Corruption." *Economic Letters* 188, no. 1 (2013): 182–85. http://econ.ccu.edu.tw/manage/1382434267_a.pdf.

Berg, Lauren. "Globalization and the Modern Vampire." *Film Matters* 2, no. 3 (2011): 8–12.

Berman, Sabina. *Backyard*. *Gestos* 20, no. 39 (2005): 109–81.

Bishop, Sarah C. "Undocumented Immigrant Media Makers and the Search for Connection Online." *Critical Studies in Media Communication* 34 no. 5 (2017): 415–31.

Bonilla, Rafael, dir. *La batalla de las cruces: Una década de impunidad y violencia contra las mujeres*. 2005; Tlalpan, MX: Centro de Investigaciones y Estudios Superiores en Antropología Social; Campo Imaginario, 2005. DVD.

Bonfil Batalla, Guillermo. *México profundo: Una civilización negada*. Mexico City: Secretaría de Educación Pública; Centro de Investigaciones Económicas, Administrativas y Sociales, 1987.

Bost, Suzanne. *Encarnación: Illness and Body Politics in Chicana Feminist Literature*. New York: Fordham University Press, 2010.

Bosteels, Bruno. "De la violencia a la columa: Viejos y nuevos sujetos emergentes en México." In Moraña and Valenzuela Arce, *Precariedades, exclusiones y emergencias*, 75–98.

Bould, Mark. *Science Fiction: Routledge Film Guidebooks*. New York: Routledge, 2012.

Bourdieu, Pierre. *Acts of Resistance: Against the Tyranny of the Market*. Translated by Richard Nice. New York: The New Press, 1998.

Braham, Persephone. *From Amazons to Zombies: Monsters in Latin America*. Lewisburg, PA: Bucknell University Press, 2015.

Braidotti, Rosi. *The Posthuman*. Malden, MA: Polity Press, 2013.

Brecht, Bertolt. "A Short Organum for the Theatre," 1945. Tensta Konsthall, accessed Feb 17, 2021. http://www.tenstakonsthall.se/uploads/139-Brecht_A_Short_Organum_for_the_Theatre.pdf.

Brescia, Pablo. "*Sleep Dealer* y el México futuro: ¿Borrón y cuenta nueva?" In *Nationbuilding en el cine mexicano desde la Época de Oro hasta el presente*, edited by Friedhelm Schmidt-Welle and Christian Wehr, 275–82. Madrid: Iberoamericana, 2015.

Briones, Joshua. "Paying the Price for NAFTA: NAFTA's Effect on Women and Children Laborers in Mexico." *UCLA Women's Law Journal* 9, no. 2 (1998): 301–27.

Britto, Lina. *Marijuana Boom: The Rise and Fall of Colombia's First Drug Paradise*. Oakland: University of California Press, 2020.

Broncano, Manuel. "Landscapes of the Magical: Cather's and Anaya's Explorations of the Southwest." In *Willa Cather and the American Southwest*, edited by John

N. Swift and Joseph R. Urgo, 124–35. Lincoln: University of Nebraska Press, 2002.

———. "'We Are All Serafina's Children': Racial Landscapes in Rudolfo Anaya." In Martín Junquera, *Landscapes of Writing*, 120–30.

Browdy de Hernández, Jennifer. "On Home Ground: Politics, Location, and the Construction of Identity in Four American Women's Autobiographies." *MELUS* 22, no. 4 (1997): 21–38.

Brown, J. Andrew. *Cyborgs in Latin America*. New York: Palgrave MacMillan, 2010.

———. "El oficio del *cyborg*: Nuevas direcciones para una identidad poshumana en América Latina." In Moraña and Sánchez Prado, *Heridas abiertas*, 247–58.

Brown, J. Andrew, and M. Elizabeth Ginway. Introduction to Ginway and Brown, *Latin American Science Fiction*, 1–15.

Brown, Wendy. *Undoing the Demos: Neoliberalism's Stealth Revolution*. New York: Zone, 2015.

Browning, Anjali. "Corn, Tomatoes, and a Dead Dog: Mexican Agricultural Restructuring and Rural Responses to Declining Maize Production in Oaxaca, Mexico." *Mexican Studies / Estudios Mexicanos* 29, no. 1 (2013): 85–199.

Bruce-Novoa, Juan. "Rudolfo Anaya." In Bruce and Sirias, *Conversations with Rudolfo Anaya*, 11–28.

Buchenau, Jürgen. "The Limits of the Cosmic Race: Immigrant and Nation in Mexico, 1850–1950." In *Immigration and National Identities in Latin America*, edited by Nicola Foote and Michael Goebel, 66–90. Gainesville: University Press of Florida, 2014.

———. *Blood in the Sand: The "Sonoran Dynasty" in the Mexican Revolution*. Lincoln: University of Nebraska Press, forthcoming.

Burdette, Hannah. *Revealing Rebellion in Abiayala: The Insurgent Poetics of Contemporary Indigenous Literature*. Tucson: University of Arizona Press, 2019.

Burford, Arianne. "Cartographies of a Violent Landscape: Viramontes' and Moraga's Remapping of Feminisms in *Under the Feet of Jesus* and *Heroes and Saints*." *Genders*, no. 47 (2008). https://www.colorado.edu/gendersarchive1998-2013/2008/02/01/cartographies-violent-landscape-viramontes-and-moragas-remapping-feminisms-under-feet.

Butler, Judith. *Precarious Life: The Powers of Mourning and Violence*. New York: Verso, 2006.

Cabezas Vargas, Andrea, and Júlia González de Canales Carcereny. "Central American Cinematographic Aesthetics and Their Role in International Film Festivals." *Studies in Spanish and Latin American Cinemas* 15, no. 2 (2018): 163–86.

Cabrera Hormazábal, Javier. "Panorámica de la ciencia ficción mexicana: Mundos posibles y utopía en *Ruido gris* de Juan José Rojo." Master's thesis, Universidad de Chile, 2013. http://repositorio.uchile.cl/bitstream/handle/2250/113087/FI-Cabrera%20Javier.pdf.

Calavita, Kitty. *Inside the State: The Bracero Program, Immigration, and the I.N.S.* New York: Routledge, 1992.

Calderón, Héctor. *Narratives of Greater Mexico: Essays on Chicano Literary History, Genre, and Borders.* Austin: University of Texas Press, 2004.

———, ed. *The Aztlán Mexican Studies Reader, 1974-2016.* Los Angeles: UCLA Chicano Studies Research Center Press, 2018.

Calvo-Quirós, William A. "Chupacabras, the Strange Case of Carlos Salinas de Gortari and his Transformation into the *Chupatodo*." In *Crossing the Borders of the Imagination*, edited by María del Mar Ramón Torrijos, 89–102. Madrid: Instituto Franklin de Estudios Norteamericanos, Universidad de Alcalá, 2014.

———. "Sucking Vulnerability: Neoliberalism, the Chupacabras, and the Post–Cold War Years." In Hernández and Rodríguez y Gibson, *The Un/Making of Latina/o Citizenship*, 211–30.

Camp, Roderic Ai, and Shannan L. Mattiace. *Politics in Mexico: The Path of a New Democracy*, 7th ed. Oxford: Oxford University Press, 2020.

Campbell, Timothy. "Translator's Introduction: *Bíos*, Immunity, Life: The Thought of Roberto Esposito." In *Bíos: Biopolitics and Philosophy*. Translated by Timothy Campbell, vii–xlii. Minneapolis: University of Minnesota Press, 2008.

Campos, Minerva. "Un impulso transnacional al cine latinoamericano de festivales: El programa Cine en Construcción." *Foro Hispánico: Revista Hispánica de Flandes y Holanda*, no. 51 (2016): 72–81.

Cancino, Rita, and Pablo Rolando Cristoffanini. "La violencia en América Latina." *Sociedad y Discurso*, no. 23 (2013): 1–12.

Candelaria, Cordelia. "Rudolfo A. Anaya (30 October 1987– )." In *Chicano Writers: First Series*, edited by Francisco A. Lomelí and Carl R. Shirley, 24–35. Detroit, MI: Thomson Gale, 1989.

Cano, Luis C. *Los espíritus de la ciencia ficción: Espiritismo, periodismo y cultura popular en las novelas de Eduardo Holmberg, Francisco Miralles y Pedro Castera.* Chapel Hill: University of North Carolina Press, 2017.

Cantú, Roberto. Introduction to Cantú, *The Forked Juniper*, 3–26.

———, ed. *The Forked Juniper: Critical Perspectives on Rudolfo Anaya.* Norman: University of Oklahoma Press, 2016.

Cañero Serrano, Julio. "Rudolfo Anaya's Narrative as an Example of Chicano Proletarianization within an Internal Colonial Framework." In Lomelí and Ikas, *U.S. Latino Literatures*, 191–99.

Carmona, Fernando, Guillermo Montano, Jorge Carrión, and Alonso Aguilar. *El milagro mexicano*. Mexico City: Editorial Nuestro Tiempo, 1970.

Carmona López, Adriana, Alma Gómez Caballero, and Lucha Castro Rodríguez. "Feminicide in Latin America in the Movement for Women's Human Rights." In Fregoso and Bejarano, *Terrorizing Women*, 157–76.

Carpentier, Alejo. "On the Marvelous Real in America." In Zamora and Faris, *Magical Realism*, 75–88.

Carrera, Carlos, dir. *Backyard/El traspatio*. 2009; Los Angles: Paramount Pictures, 2009. DVD.

Carrillo, Jorge. "La importancia del impacto del TLC en la industria maquiladora en América Latina." In *Reestructuración productiva, mercado de trabajo y sindicatos en América Latina*, edited by Enrique de la Garza Toledo, 157–79. Buenos Aires: Consejo Latinoamericano de Ciencias Sociales, 2000.

Carroll, Amy Sara. "From *Papapapá* to *Sleep Dealer*: Alex Rivera's Undocumentary Poetics." *Social Identities* 19, no. 3–4 (2013): 485–500.

———. *REMEX: Toward an Art History of the NAFTA Era*. Austin: University of Texas Press, 2017.

Casanova-Vizcaíno, Sandra, and Inés Ordiz, eds. *Latin American Gothic in Literature and Culture*. New York: Routledge, 2018.

Castañeda, Jorge G. *Utopia Unarmed: The Latin American Left after the Cold War*. New York: Knopf, 1993.

Castells, Manuel. *The Information Age: Economy, Society and Culture*, vol. 1, *The Rise of the Network Society*, 2nd ed. Malden, MA: Blackwell Press, 2000.

Castells-Talens, Antoni and José Manuel Ramos Rodríguez. "Technology for Cultural Survival: Indigenous-Language Radio at the End of the Twentieth Century." In Tinajero and Freeman, *Technology and Culture*, 178–93.

Castillo, Debra A. "Rasquache Aesthetics in Alex Rivera's 'Why Cybraceros.'" *Nordlit*, no. 31 (2014): 7–23.

Castillo-Garsow, Melissa Ann. "A Mexican State of Mind: New York City and the New Borderlands of Culture." PhD diss., Yale University, 2017.

Castro, Justin. *Radio in Revolution: Wireless Technology and State Power in Mexico, 1897–1938*. Lincoln: University of Nebraska Press, 2016.

Chabram-Dernersesian, Angie. "Bucking Tradition: Sci Fi with a Chicana/o Latina/o Twist." *Confluencia* 26, no. 1 (2010): 192–94.

———. "I Throw Punches for My Race, But I Don't Want to Be a Man: Writing US—Chica-nos (Gil, Us)/Chicanas—into the Movement Script." In Chabram-Dernersesian, *The Chicana/o Studies Reader*, 165–82. New York: Routledge, 2006.

———, ed. *The Chicana/o Cultural Studies Reader*. New York: Routledge, 2006.

Chacón, Hilda. Introduction to *Online Activism in Latin America*, edited by Hilda Chacón, 1–30. New York: Routledge, 2019.

———, ed. *Online Activism in Latin America*. New York: Routledge, 2019.

Chacón, Mario A. *Untitled Image*. Cover Illustration. In Sánchez and Pita, *Lunar Braceros 2125–2148*, book cover.

———. *Untitled Image*. Internal Illustration. In Sánchez and Pita, *Lunar Braceros 2125–2148*, 17.

Chang, Maria Hsia. "Multiculturalism, Immigration, and Aztlan." *Social Contract* 10, no. 3 (2000): 207–11.

Chaudhuri, Shohini. "Visit of the Body Snatchers: Alien Invasion Themes in Vampire Narratives." *Camera Obscura* 14, no. 1–2 (1997): 180–98. https://doi.org/10.1215/02705346-14-1-2_40-41-180.

Chee, Fabio. "Science Fiction and Latino Studies Today and in the Future." In Aldama, *Routledge Companion*, 126–35.

Clasen, Mathias, and Todd K. Platts. "Evolution and Slasher Films." In *Evolution and Popular Narrative*, edited by Dirk Vanderbeke and Brett Cooke, 23–42. Leiden, Netherlands: Brill, 2019.

Clover, Carol J. *Men, Women, and Chain Saws: Gender in the Modern Horror Film.* Princeton, NJ: Princeton University Press, 1992.

Clover, Joshua. "The Future in Labor." *Film Quarterly* 63, no. 1 (2009): 6–8.

Clynes, Manfred E., and Nathan S. Kline. "Cyborgs and Space." In Gray, Figueroa-Sarriera, and Mentor, *The Cyborg Handbook*, 29–34.

Córdova, Nery. "El espectáculo y la massmediación sociocultural." In Córdova, *La cultura del espectáculo*, 106–44.

———, ed. *La cultura del espectáculo y el escándalo: Los media en la sociedad actual*. Mazatlán: Universidad Autónoma de Sinaloa, 2007.

Corona, Ignacio, and Héctor Domínguez-Ruvalcaba, eds. *Gender Violence at the U.S.-Mexico Border: Media Representation and Public Response.* Tucson: University of Arizona Press, 2010.

Correia, David. *Properties of Violence: Law and Land Grand Struggle in Northern New Mexico*. Athens: University of Georgia Press, 2013.

Corrunker, Laura. "'Coming Out of the Shadows': DREAM Act Activism in the Context of Global Anti-Deportation Activism." *Indiana Journal of Global Legal Studies* 19, no. 1 (2012): 143–68.

Cortés, María Lourdes. "Filmmaking in Central America: An Overview." *Studies in Spanish and Latin American Cinemas* 15, no. 2 (2018): 143–61.

———. "*Gasolina*: Ocio, vacío y violencia en un viaje sin destino." In *Pereza: Historia de los afectos*, edited by Armando Casas, no pagination. Mexico City: UNAM. Ebook, 2018.

Cosentino, Olivia. "Slower Cinema: Violence, Affect, and Spectatorship in *Las elegidas*." *Journal of Latin American Cultural Studies* 60, no. 3 (2021): 62–82.

Coye, M., and L. R. Goldman. *Summary of Environmental Data: McFarland Childhood Cancer Cluster Investigation, Phase III Report*. Sacramento: California Department of Health Services, Environmental Epidemiology and Toxicology Program, 1991.

Cravey, Altha, Joseph Palis, and Gabriela Valdivia. "Imagining the Future from the Margins: Cyborg Labor in Alex Rivera's *Sleep Dealer*." *GeoJournal* 80, no. 6 (2015): 867–80.

Dalton, David S. "Eugenics and Doubly Marginalized Mexican and Chicana Women: Documenting the Left-Right Consensus on Reproductive Health in Renee Tajima-Peña's *No más bebés*." In Dalton and Weatherford, *Healthcare in Latin America*, 130–39.

———. "Exploiting Liminal Legality: Inclusive Citizenship Models in the Online Discourse of United We Dream." In Dalton and Ramírez Plascencia, *Imagining Latinidad*, 59–79.

———. "Immunizing the *Zetas*: Drug Violence and Zombie Biopolitics in Pedro M. Valencia's *Con Z de zombie*." *Revista de Literatura Mexicana Contemporánea* 24, no. 73 (2018): 137–50.

———. "From Sensationalist Media to the Narcocorrido: Drones, Sovereignty, and Exception along the US-Mexican Border." In Plaw, Gurgel, and Ramírez Plascencia, *Politics of Technology*, 80–94.

———. "Liberation and the Gothic in Carlos Solórzaon's *Las manos de Dios*." In Casanova-Vizcaíno and Ordiz, *Latin American Gothic*, 84–95.

———. *Mestizo Modernity: Race, Technology, and the Body in Postrevolutionary Mexico*. Gainesville: University of Florida Press, 2018.

———. "*Robo Sacer*: 'Bare Life' and Cyborg Labor beyond the Border in Alex Rivera's *Sleep Dealer*." *Hispanic Studies Review* 1, no. 2 (2016): 15–29.

———. "Una espectralidad cibernética: Cuestionando un presente *hauntológico* en *Historias del séptimo sello*, de Norma Yamille Cuéllar." *iMex Revista: México Interdisciplinario / Interdisciplinary Mexico* 8, no. 16 (2019): 84–97.

———. "Unos anticonceptivos apocalípticos: Inconmensurabilidades semánticas entre la ciencia médica y la religion, en *La píldora maravillosa* de Jesús Pavlo Tenorio." *Revista de Medicina y Humanidades* 8, no. 1 (2016): 83–94.

———. "Science Fiction vs. Magical Realism: Oppositional Aesthetics and Contradictory Political Discourses in Sergio Arau's *A Day without a Mexican*." In *Peter Lang Companion to Latin American Science Fiction*, edited by Silvia Kurlat Ares and Ezequiel De Rosso, 43–53. New York: Peter Lang, 2021.

Dalton, David S., and David Ramírez Plascencia. 2022. "Introduction: Imagining Latinidad in Digital Diasporas." In Dalton and Ramírez Plascencia, *Imagining Latinidad*, 1–21.

———, eds. *Imagining Latinidad: Digital Diasporas and Public Engagement among Latin American Migrants*. Leiden, Netherlands: Brill, 2023.

Dalton, David S., and Douglas J. Weatherford, eds. *Healthcare in Latin America: History, Society, Culture*. Gainesville: University of Florida Press, 2022.

———. Introduction to Dalton and Weatherford, *Healthcare in Latin America*, 1–15.

Damián Miravete, Gabriela. "Soñarán en el jardín." *Latin American Literature Today* 1, no. 6 (2018). https://latinamericanliteraturetoday.org/es/2018/04/they-will-dream-garden-gabriela-damian-miravete.

———. "They Will Dream in the Garden." Translated by Adrian Demopulos. *Latin American Literature Today* 1, no. 6 (2018). https://latinamericanliteraturetoday.org/2018/05/they-will-dream-garden-gabriela-damian-miravete.

Daniels-Lerberg, Tracey. "Watershed Ethics and Dam Politics: Mapping Biopolitics, Race, and Resistance in *Sleep Dealer* and *Watershed*." In *Make Waves: Water in Contemporary Literature and Film*, edited by Paula Anca Farca, 117–36. Reno: University of Nevada Press, 2019.

Darío González, Nelson. "El *neuropunk* y la ciencia ficcón hispanoamericana." *Revista Iberoamericana* 83, no. 259–260 (2017): 345–64.

Das, Rupsayar. "Representation of Violence against Women in Indian Print Media: A Comparative Analysis." *Global Media Journal* 3, no. 1 (2012): 1–24.

Davies, Anne. "Guillermo del Toro's *Cronos*: The Vampire as Embodied Heterotopia." *Quarterly Review of Film and Video* 25, no. 5 (2008): 395–403.
———. "Guillermo del Toro's Monsters: Matter Out of Place." In Davies, Shaw, and Tierney, *Transnational Fantasies*, 29–44.
———. "Slime and Subtlety: Monsters in del Toro's Spanish-Language Films." In Morehead, *Supernatural Cinema*, 41–57.
Davies, Anne, Deborah Shaw, and Dolores Tierney, eds. *The Transnational Fantasies of Guillermo del Toro*. New York: Palgrave MacMillan, 2014.
Davies, Laurence. "Guillermo del Toro's *Cronos*, or the Pleasures of Impurity." In *Gothic Science Fiction 1980-2010*, edited by Sara Wesson and Emily Alder, 87–101. Liverpool: Liverpool University Press, 2011.
Davies, Telory W. "Race, Gender, and Disability: Cherríe Moraga's Bodiless Head." *Journal of Dramatic Theory and Criticism* 21, no. 1 (2006): 29–44.
Davis, Ande. "Consumed by El Otro Lado: Alterations of the Neoliberal Self in *Sleep Dealer*." *Chiricú Journal: Latina/o Literatures, Arts, and Cultures* 4, no. 1 (2019): 38–55.
Davis-Undiano, Robert Con. *Mestizos Come Home!: Making and Claiming Mexican American Identity*. Norman: University of Oklahoma Press, 2017.
———. "Mestizos Critique the New World: Vasconcelos, Anzaldúa, and Anaya." *Lit: Literature Interpretation Theory* 11, no. 2 (2000): 117–42.
———. "The Emergence of New World Studies: Anaya, Aztlán, and the New Chicana." *Genre: Forms of Discourse and Culture* 32, no. 1–2 (1999): 115–40.
Day, Stuart A. *Outside Theater: Alliances that Shape Mexico*. Tucson: University of Arizona Press, 2017.
Degnan, Cynthia. "[Ex]posing Sightlines: The Staging of Power in Cherrie Moraga's *Heroes and Saints*." *Atenea* 23, no. 2 (2003): 139–51.
de la Campa, Román. "Magical Realism and World Literature: A Genre for the Times?" *Revista Canadiense de Estudios Hispánicos* 23, no. 2 (1999): 205–19.
———. "Teoría, literatura y tutela del error." In Moraña and Sánchez Prado, *Heridas abiertas*, 65–77.
de la Torre, Renée, Cristina Gutiérrez, and Alberto Hernández. "Religious Reconfiguration in Mexico: Beliefs and Practices National Survey, 2016." *Social Compass* 67, no. 3 (2020): 349–71.
del Campo Ramírez, Elsa. "Postethnicity and Antiglobalization in Chicana/o Science Fiction: Ernest Hogan's *Smoking Mirror Blues* and Beatrice Pita's *Lunar Braceros 2125-2148*." *Journal of Transnational American Studies* 9, no. 1 (2018): 383–401.
Delgadillo, Theresa. *Spiritual Mestizaje: Religion, Gender, Race, and Nation in Contemporary Chicana Narrative*. Durham, NC: Duke University Press, 2011.
Delgado Moya, Sergio. "A Theater of Displacement: Staging Activism, Poetry, and Migration through a Transborder Immigrant Tool." In Chacón, *Online Activism in Latin America*, 33–57.
del Toro, Guillermo. *Cronos*. 1993; Mexico City: October Films, 1994. DVD.

de León, Francisco. "El horror se queda en casa." *Pasavento: Revista de Estudios Hispánicos* 1, no. 1 (2013): 35–46.

Denning, Dorothy E. "Activism, Hacktivism, and Cyberterrorism: The Internet as a Tool for Influencing Foreign Policy." In *Networks and Netwars: The Future of Terror, Crime, and Militancy*, edited by John Arquilla and David Ronfeldt, 239–88. Santa Monica: RAND Corporation, 2001. https://www.rand.org/pubs/monograph_reports/MR1382.html.

de Pozzio, Carla. "El TLCAN: Y su representación en el femincidio de Ciudad Juárez." Master's thesis, Bowling Green State University, 2010.

Derrida, Jacques. *Specters of Marx: The State of the Debt, the Work of Mourning, and the New International*. New York: Routledge, 1994.

Dick, Bruce, and Silvio Sirias eds. *Conversations with Rudolfo Anaya*. Jackson: University of Mississippi Press, 1998.

———. Introduction to Bruce and Sirias, *Conversations with Rudolfo Anaya*, ix–xvii.

Diel, Lori Boornazian. *The Codex Mexicanus: A Guide to Life in Late Sixteenth-Century New Spain*. Austin: University of Texas Press, 2018.

Dika, Vera. *Games of Terror: Halloween, Friday the 13th, and the Films of the Stalker Cycle*. London: Associated University Presses, 1990.

Dionne, T. Jake. "Tropics of Reality Television: Introducing Metaphor and Coloniality through *Drones!*" *Teaching Media Quarterly* 7, no. 3 (2019): 2–20.

D'Lugo, Carol Clark. *The Fragmented Novel in Mexico: The Politics of Form*. Austin: University of Texas Press, 1997.

Domínguez, Ricardo. "Digital Zapatismo." In *Info Wars: [Ars Electronica 98]*, edited by Gerfried Stocker and Christine Schöpf, 53–58. Wien: Springer, 1998.

———. "Electronic Civil Disobedience: Inventing the Future of Online Agitprop Theater." *PMLA* 124, no 5 (2009): 1806–12.

Domínguez-Ruvalcaba, Héctor. "Death on the Screen: Imagining Violence in Border Media." In Corona and Domínguez-Rubalcaba, *Gender Violence*, 60–80.

———. *De la sensualidad a la violencia de género: La modernidad y la nación en las representaciones de la masculinidad en el México contemporáneo*. Mexico City: CIESAS, 2013.

Domínguez-Ruvalcaba, Héctor, and Patricia Ravelo Blancas. *Desmantelamiento de la ciudadanía: Políticas de terror en la frontera norte*. Mexico City: Eón, 2011.

Donohue, Micah K. "Translatio Vampyri: Transamerican Vampires and Transnational Capital in Guillermo del Toro's *Cronos*." *Comparative American Studies* 14, no. 2 (2016): 126–38.

———. "Borderlands Gothic Science Fiction: Alienation as Intersection in Rivera's *Sleep Dealer* and Lavín's 'Llegar a la orilla.'" *Science Fiction Studies* 45, no. 1 (2018): 48–68.

———. "Borderlands Hyperbole, Critical Dystopias, and Transfeminist Utopian Hope: Gaspar de Alba's *Desert Blood* and Valencia's *Capitalismo gore*." *Utopian Studies* 31, no. 3 (2021): 553–72.

Doty, Roxanne Lynn. *Imperial Encounters: The Politics of Representation in North-South Relations*. Minneapolis: University of Minnesota Press, 1996.
Duany, Jorge. "Puerto Rican, Hispanic, or Latino? Recent Debates on National and Pan-Ethnic Identities." *Centro Journal* 15, no. 2 (2003): 256–67.
Dunaway, David King, and Sara Spurgeon. *Writing the Southwest*. Albuquerque: University of New Mexico Press, 2003.
Duménil, Gérard, and Dominique Lévy. "The Neoliberal (Counter-)Revolution." In Saad-Filho and Johnston, *Neoliberalism*, 9–19.
Duran, Javier. "Virtual Borders, Data Aliens, and Bare Bodies: Culture, Securitization, and the Biometric State." *Journal of Borderlands Studies* 25, no. 3–4 (2010): 219–30.
Durán, María J. "Bodies that Should Matter: Chicana/o Farmworkers, Slow Violence, and the Politics of (In)visibility in Cherríe Moraga's *Heroes and Saints*." *Aztlan: A Journal of Chicano Studies* 42, no. 1 (2017): 45–71.
Durán de Alba, José Arnulfo. "Ciencia ficción + Realismo mágico = Utopía." *Escritos: Revista del Centro de Ciencias del Lenguaje*, no. 21 (2000): 37–48.
Durón, Hispano. *New Central American Cinema (2001–2010)*. PhD diss., University of Kansas, 2014.
Eco, Umberto. *Travels in Hyperreality: Essays*. San Diego, CA: Harcourt, 1983.
Eichstaedt, Peter H. *If You Poison Us: Uranium and Native Americans*. Santa Fe, NM: Red Crane Books, 1994.
Eisenstadt, Todd A. "The Origins and Rationality of the 'Legal versus Legitimate' Dichotomy Invoked in Mexico's 2006 Post-Electoral Conflict." *PS: Political Science and Politics* 40, no. 1 (2007): 39–43.
Eljaiek-Rodríguez, Gabriel. "Bloodsucking Bugs: Horacio Quiroga and the Latin American Transformation of Vampires." In Morehead, *Supernatural Cinema*, 146–62.
———. *Selva de fantasmas: El gótico en la literatura y el cine latinoamericanos*. Bogotá: Editorial Pontificia Universidad Javeriana, 2017.
"El plan espiritual de Aztlán." 1969. America in the Sixties and Seventies, Jan. 2018. https://60sand70samerica.voices.wooster.edu/wp-content/uploads/sites/101/2018/01/el-plan-de-aztlan.pdf.
Emerson, R. Guy. *Necropolitics: Living Death in Mexico*. New York: Palgrave MacMillan, 2019.
Emmelhainz, Irmgard. *La tiranía del sentido común: La reconversión neoliberal en México*. Mexico City: Paradiso Editores, 2016.
Emmanouilidou, Sophia. "Mythography and the Reconstitution of Chicano Identity in Rudolfo Alfonso Anaya's *The Legend of La Llorona*." In *Transcultural Localisms: Responding to Ethnicity in a Globalized World*, edited by Yiorgos Kalogeras and Eleftheria Arapoglou, 129–41. Heidelberg: Universitätsverlag Winter GmbH, 2006.
Esch, Sophie. *Modernity at Gunpoint: Firearms, Politics, and Culture in Mexico and Central America*. Pittsburgh, PA: University of Pittsburgh Press, 2018.

Esparza, Araceli. "Cherríe Moraga's Changing Consciousness of Solidarity." In Hernández and Rodrígues y Gibson, *The Un/Making of Latina/o Citizenship*, 145–66.

Esposito, Roberto. *Bíos: Biopolitics and Philosophy.* Translated by Timothy Campbell. Minneapolis: University of Minnesota Press, 2008.

Estévez, Ariadna. "Biopolítica y necropolítica: ¿Constitutivos u opuestos?" *Espiral: Estudios sobre Estado y Sociedad* 25, no. 73 (2018): 9–43.

———. *Human Rights and Free Trade in Mexico: A Discursive and Sociopolitical Perspective*. New York: Palgrave MacMillan, 2008.

———. *Necropolitical Production and Management of Forced Migration*. Lanham, MD: Lexington Books, 2021.

Estrada, Oswaldo. "Vivir a muerte: Escrituras dolientes y denuncias de género en *El silencio de los cuerpos.*" *Letras Femeninas* 43, no. 2 (2018): 68–83.

Eudave, Cecilia. "El cuerpo como espacio de lo insólito en la narrativa mexicana reciente escrita por mujeres." In *Realidades fracturadas: Estéticas de lo insólito en la narrativa en lengua española (1980–2018)*, edited by Natalia Álvarez Méndez and Ana Abello Verano, 43–58. Madrid: Visor Libros, 2019.

Featherstone, Mike, and Roger Burrows. "Cultures of Technological Embodiment: An Introduction." In *Cyberspace/Cyberbodies/Cyberpunk: Cultures of Technological Embodiment*, edited by Mike Featherstone and Roger Burrows, 1–20. London: Sage Publications, 1995.

Fernández, Álvaro. "*Cronos*: El origen del alquimista—Estudio de caso." *El ojo que piensa: Revista de cine iberoamericano*, no. 3 (2011). http://www.elojoquepiensa.cucsh.udg.mx/index.php/elojoquepiensa/article/view/35/35.

Fernández, Lilia. "Race Baiting, Identity Politics, and the Impact of the Conservative Economic Agenda on Latinos/as." *Latino Studies* 16, no. 4 (2018): 524–30.

Fernández, Raúl E., and Gilbert G. González. *A Century of Chicano History: Empire, Nations and Migration*. New York: Routledge, 2012.

Fernández L'Hoeste, Héctor. "El futuro en cuentos: De OVNIs e implantes oculares en la ciencia ficción mexicana." *Revista Iberoamericana* 83, no. 259–260 (2017): 483–99.

———. "De insectos y otros demonios: Breves apuntes sobre las obsesiones de Guillermo del Toro." *Cifra Nueva* 12, no. 2 (2000): 41–50.

Fernández Olmos, Margarite. *Rudolfo A. Anaya: A Critical Companion*. Westport, CT: Greenwood Publishing Group, 1999.

Figliozzi, Miguel, and Dylan Jennings. "Autonomous Delivery Robots and Their Potential Impacts on Urban Freight Energy Consumption and Emissions." *Transportation Research Procedia*, no. 46 (2020): 21–28.

Finnegan, Nuala. *Cultural Representations of* Feminicidio *at the US-Mexico Border*. New York: Routledge, 2018.

Flores Alex, and Lorena Vassolo, dirs. *Juarez: The City where Women Are Disposable*. Toronto: Las Perlas del Mar Films, 2007. DVD.

Flores, José Roberto. "Raza especulativa: Reimaginando el discurso racial en la narrativa mexicoamericana (1970–2010)." PhD diss., Arizona State University, 2017.

Florescano, Enrique. *Quetzalcóatl y los mitos fundadores de Mesoamérica*. Mexico City: Debolsillo, 2017.

Flys Junquera, Carmen Lydia. "*La Tierra*: Sense of Place in Contemporary Chicano Literature." In *Spanish Perspectives on Chicano Literature: Literary and Cultural Essays*, edited by Jesús Rosales, Vanessa Fonseca, and Francisco A. Lomelí, 139–54. Columbus: Ohio State University Press, 2017.

———. "Rudolfo Anaya's Shifting Sense of Place." In Martín Junquera *Landscapes of Writing*, 161–71.

Fojas, Camilla. "Border Securities, Drone Cultures, and Alex Rivera's *Sleep Dealer*." In Aldama, *Latinx Ciné in the Twenty-First Century*, 237–66.

———. *Migrant Labor and Border Securities in Pop Culture*. New York: Routledge, 2017.

Foucault, Michel. "About the Concept of the 'Dangerous Individual' in Nineteenth-Century Legal Psychiatry." In Rabinow and Rose, *The Essential Foucault*, 208–28.

———. "Technologies of the Self." In Rabinow and Rose, *The Essential Foucault*, 145–69.

———. "The Birth of Biopolitics." In Rabinow and Rose, *The Essential Foucault*, 202–7.

———. *The History of Sexuality: Volume I: An Introduction*. Translated by Robert Hurley. New York: Pantheon Books, 1990.

Franco, Jean. *Cruel Modernity*. Durham, NC: Duke University Press, 2013.

———. "Una historia que carece enteramente de historia." In Moraña and Sánchez Prado, *Heridas abiertas*, 155–64.

Fregoso, Rosa-Linda, and Cynthia Bejarano, eds. *Terrorizing Women: Feminicide in the Americas*. Durham, NC: Duke University Press, 2010.

———. "Introduction: A Cartography of Feminicide in the Américas." In Fregoso and Bejarano, *Terrorizing Women*, 1–42.

Frey, R. Scott. "The Transfer of Core-Based Hazardous Production Processes to the Export Processing Zones of the Periphery: The Maquiladora Centers of Northern Mexico." *Journal of World-Systems Research* 9, no. 2 (2003): 317–54.

Frey, William H. *Diversity Explosion: How New Racial Demographics are Remaking America*. Washington, DC: Brookings Institution Press, 2018.

Fuentes Flores, César M. "La violencia de pareja en el entorno urbano del estado de Chihuahua: Hacia el diseño de políticas públias." In Monárrez Fragoso et al., *Violencia contra las mujeres*, 335–60.

Fuguet, Alberto, and Sergio Gómez. "Prólogo." *McOndo*. Barcelona: Grijalbo-Mondadori, 1997.

Fúquene Daza, Ana Milena, and Daniel Mauricio Rodríguez Sevilla. "Apartes del cine colombiano." Senior tesis, Universidad Cooperativa de Colombia, 2020.

https://repository.ucc.edu.co/bitstream/20.500.12494/17668/5/2020_cine_colombiano.pdf.

Gabilondo, Joseba. "Postcolonial Cyborgs: Subjectivity in the Age of Cybernetic Reproduction." In Gray, Figueroa-Sarriera, and Mentor, *The Cyborg Handbook*, 423–32.

Gajjala, Radhika. "Internet Constructs of Identity and Ignorance: 'Third-World' Contexts and Cyberfeminism." *Works and Days* 17/18, no. 33/34/35/36 (1999): 117–37.

Galeano, Eduardo. *Las venas abiertas de América Latina*. Mexico City: Siglo Veintiuno Editores, 2004.

Gálvez, Alyshia. *Eating NAFTA: Trade, Food Policies, and the Destruction of Mexico*. Oakland: University of California Press, 2018.

García, Hernán Manuel. "Hacia una poética de la tecnología periférica: Post-cyberpunk y picaresca en *Sleep Dealer* de Alex Rivera." *Revista Iberoamericana* 83, no. 259–260 (2017): 327–44.

———. "La globalización desfigurada o la post-globalización imaginada: La estética cyberpunk (post)mexicana." PhD diss., University of Kansas, 2011.

———. "Tecnociencia y cibercultura en México: *Hackers* en el cuento *cyberpunk* mexicano." *Revista Iberoamericana* 78, no. 238–239 (2012): 329–48.

García Canclini, Néstor. *Hybrid Cultures: Strategies for Entering and Leaving Modernity*. Translated by Christopher L. Chiappari and Silvia L. López. Minneapolis: University of Minnesota Press, 1995.

———. *Latinoamericanos buscando lugar en este siglo*. Buenos Aires: Paidós, 2002.

Garcia Lopez, Christina. *Calling the Soul Back: Embodied Spirituality in Chicanx Narrative*. Tucson: University of Arizona Press, 2019.

Garland, Leah. *Contemporary Latina/o Performing Arts of Moraga, Tropicana, Fusco, and Bustamante*. New York: Peter Lang, 2009.

Garza, Maria Alicia C. "High Crimes against the Flesh: The Embodiment of Violent Otherization in Cherríe Moraga's *Heroes and Saints*." *Letras Femeninas* 30, no. 1 (2004): 26–39.

Gaspar de Alba, Alicia. *Chicano Art: Inside/Outside the Master's House: Cultural Politics and the Cara Exhibition*. Austin: University of Texas Press, 1998.

———. "Poor Brown Female: The Miller's Compensation for 'Free' Trade." In Gaspar de Alba and Guzmán, *Making a Killing*, 63–93.

Gaspar de Alba, Alicia, and Georgina Guzmán, eds. *Making a Killing: Femicide, Free Trade, and La Frontera*. Austin: University of Texas Press, 2010.

———. "Introduction: *Feminicidio*: The 'Black Legend' of the Border." In Gaspar de Alba and Guzmán, *Making a Killing*, 1–22.

Gaytán Alcalá, Felipe, and Juliana Fregoso Bonilla. "La ley Televisa de México." *Chasqui: Revista Latinoamericana de Comunicación*, no. 94 (2006): 40–45.

Gil Olmos, José. *La Santa Muerte: La virgen de los olvidados*. Mexico City: Debolsillo, 2012.

Ginway, M. Elizabeth. *Cyborgs, Sexuality, and the Undead: The Body in Mexican and Brazilian Speculative Fiction*. Nashville, TN: Vanderbilt University Press, 2020.

———. "Do implantado ao ciborge: O corpo social na ficção científica brasileira." *Revista Iberoamericana* 73, no. 221 (2007): 787–99.

———. "The Politics of Cyborgs in Mexico and Latin America." *Semina: Ciência Sociais e Humana* 34, no. 2 (2013): 161–72.

Ginway, M. Elizabeth, and J. Andrew Brown, eds. *Latin American Science Fiction: Theory and Practice*. New York: Palgrave MacMillan, 2012.

Gish, Robert F. "Rudolfo A. Anaya." In *Updating the Literary West*, edited by Max Westbrook and Dan Flores, 532–36. Fort Worth: Texas Christian University Press, 1999.

Gómez, Rodrigo. "TV Azteca y la industria televisiva mexicana en tiempos de integración regional (TLCAN) y desregulación económica." *Comunicación y Sociedad*, no. 1 (2004): 51–90.

González, Christopher. "Latino Sci-Fi: Cognition and Narrative Design in Alex Rivera's *Sleep Dealer*." In *Latinos and Narrative Media*, edited by Frederick Luis Aldama, 211–23. New York: Palgrave MacMillan, 2013.

González, Deena J. "Chicana Identity Matters." In Noriega et al., *The Chicano Studies Reader*, 375–87.

González, Jennifer. "Envisioning Cyborg Bodies: Notes from Current Research." In Gray, Figueroa-Sarriera, and Mentor, *The Cyborg Handbook*, 267–79.

González Rodríguez, Sergio. *The Femicide Machine*. Translated by Michael Parker-Stainback. Los Angeles: Semiotext(e), 2012.

———. "Prólogo." In *El silencio de los cuerpos: Relatos sobre feminicidios*, compiled by Olga Alarcón, Raquel Castro, Gabriela Damián Miravete, Iris García Cuevas, Susana Iglesias, Abril Posas, Ivonne Reyes Chiquete, Cristina Rivera Garza, Tania Tagle, and Sergio González Rodríguez. Mexico City: Ediciones B, 2015.

Goodwin, Matthew David. "The Technology of Labor, Migration, and Protest." In Aldama, *Routledge Companion*, 120–28.

Gordon, Avery. *Ghostly Matters: Haunting and the Sociological Imagination*. Minneapolis: University of Minnesota Press, 1997.

Gordillo, Adriana. "*Aura*, 'Constancia,' and 'Sleeping Beauty': Carlos Fuentes's Little History on Photography." In Casanova-Vizcaíno and Ordiz, *Latin American Gothic*, 172–88.

Graham, Elaine L. *Representations of the Post/Human: Monsters, Aliens, and Others in Popular Culture*. New Brunswick, NJ: Rutgers University Press, 2002.

Gray, Chris Hables. "An Interview with Manfred E. Clynes." In Gray, Figueroa-Sarriera, and Mentor, *The Cyborg Handbook*, 43–53.

———. *Cyborg Citizen: Politics in the Posthuman Age*. New York: Routledge, 2001.

Gray, Chris Hables, Heidi J. Figueroa-Sarriera, and Steven Mentor, eds. *The Cyborg Handbook*. New York: Routledge, 1995.

Grayson, George W. *Mexico: Narco-Violence and a Failed State?* New Brunswick, NJ: Transaction Publishers, 2011.

Greenberg, Linda Margarita. "Learning for the Dead: Wounds, Women, and Activism in Cherríe Moraga's *Heroes and Saints*." *MELUS: Multi-Ethnic Literature of the U.S.* 34, no. 1 (2009): 163–84.

Greene, Vivien. "Utopia/Dystopia." *American Art* 25, no. 2 (2011): 2–7.

Grinberg Pla, Valeria. "Against Anomie: Julio Hernández Cordón's Post-War Trilogy—*Gasolina/Gasoline* (2008), *Las marimbas del infierno/The Marimbas of Hell* (2010) and *Polvo/Dust* (2012)." *Studies in Spanish and Latin American Cinemas* 15, no. 2 (2018): 203–16.

Griswold del Castillo, Richard, and Richard A. Garcia. *César Chávez: A Triumph of Spirit*. Norman: University of Oklahoma Press, 1995.

Gruben, William C. "Was NAFTA behind Mexico's High Maquiladora Growth?" *Economic and Financial Review of Dallas*, no. Q3 (2001): 11–21. https://ideas.repec.org/a/fip/fedder/y2001iqiiip11-21.html.

Gržinić, Marina, and Šefik Tatlić. *Necropolitics, Racialization, and Global Capitalism: Historicization of Bioplitics and Forensics of Politics, Art, and Life*. Lanham, MD: Lexington Books, 2014.

Guthman, Julie. "Neoliberalism and the Making of Food Politics in California." *Geoforum* 39, no. 3 (2008): 1171–83.

Gutiérrez, Ramón A. "Unraveling America's Hispanic Past: Internal Stratification and Class Boundaries." In Noriega et al., *The Chicano Studies Reader*, 345–57.

Guevara Niebla, Gilberto, and Néstor García Canclini, eds. *La educación y la cultura ante el tratado de libre comercio*. Mexico City: Nueva Imagen, 1994.

Guzmán, R. Andrés. *Universal Citizenship: Latina/o Studies at the Limits of Identity*. Austin: University of Texas Press, 2019.

Hafner, Katie, and John Markoff. *Cyberpunk: Outlaws and Hackers on the Computer Frontier*. New York: Touchstone, 1991.

Hall, Stuart. "Signification, Representation, Ideology: Althusser and the Post-Structuralist Debates." *Critical Studies in Media Communication* 2, no. 2 (1985): 91–114.

Hamm, Patricia H. "How México Built Support for the Negotiation of the North American Free Trade Agreement: Targeting Mexican Diaspora in the United States." PhD diss., University of California, Irvine, 2001.

Hamner, Evert. "Virtual Immigrants: Transfigured Bodies and Transnational Spaces in Science Fiction Cinema." In *Simultaneous Worlds: Global Science Fiction Cinema*, edited by Jennifer L. Feeley and Sarah Ann Wells. Minneapolis: University of Minnesota Press, 2015.

Hanrahan, Brian and Paulina Aroch Fugellie. "Reflections on the Transformation in Mexico." *Journal of Latin American Cultural Studies* 28, no. 1 (2019): 113–37.

Haraway, Donna. *Simians, Cyborgs and Women: The Reinvention of Nature*. London: Free Association of Books, 1991.

Hardt, Michael, and Antonio Negri. *Empire*. Cambridge, MA: Harvard University Press, 2000.

Harrington, James C. "¡Alto a la impunidad!: Legal Relief for Femicide in Juárez?" In Corona and Domínguez-Ruvalcaba, *Gender Violence*, 155–76.

Harrison, Jill. "Abandoned Bodies and Spaces of Sacrifice: Pesticide Drift Activism and the Contestation of Neoliberal Environmental Politics in California." *Geoforum* 39, no. 3 (2008): 1197–214.

Hayles, N. Katherine. *How We Became Posthuman: Virtual Bodies in Cybernetics, Literature, and Informatics.* Chicago: University of Chicago Press, 1999.
———. *How We Think: Digital Media and Contemporary Technogenesis.* Chicago: University of Chicago Press, 2012.
Haywood Ferreira, Rachel. *The Emergence of Latin American Science Fiction.* Middletown, CT: Wesleyan University Press, 2010.
Heide, Markus. "Cosmopolitics in Border Film: *Amores perros* (2000) and *Sleep Dealer* (2008)." *Comparative American Studies* 11, no. 1 (2013): 89–108.
Helmer, John. *Drugs and Minority Oppression.* New York: Seabury Press, 1975.
Henry, Brittany. "Unsettling Utopia: The Politics of Hope in North American Dystopian Fiction." PhD diss., Rice University, 2018.
Hernández, Ellie D., and Eliza Rodríguez y Gibson, eds. *The Un/Making of Latina/o Citizenship: Culture, Politics, and Aesthetics.* New York: Palgrave MacMillan, 2014.
Hernández, Omar, and Emile McAnany. "Cultural Industries in the Free Trade Age: A Look at Mexican Television." In *Fragments of a Golden Age*, edited by Gilbert M. Joseph, Anne Rubenstein, and Eric Zolov, 389–414. Durham, NC: Duke University Press, 2001.
Hernández Cordón, Julio, dir. *Cómprame un revólver.* Chapultepec: Zima Entertainment, Woo Films, 2019.
Herrera Sánchez, Sonia. "Cine de ficción y feminicidio: El caso de Ciudad Juárez." *Mientras Tanto*, no. 121 (2014): 63–84.
———. "Writing the Toxic Environment: Ecocriticism and Chicana Literary Imagination." In *A Contested West: New Readings of Place in Western American Literature*, edited by Martin Simonson, David Río, and Amaia Ibarraran, 173–87. London: Portal Editions, 2013.
Hess, David J. "On Low-Tech Cyborgs." In Gray, Figueroa-Sarriera, and Mentor, *The Cyborg Handbook*, 371–78.
Heyman, Josiah McC. "'Illegality' and the US-Mexico Border: How It Is Produced and Resisted." In Menjívar and Kanstroom, *Constructing Immigrant "Illegality,"* 111–35.
Hind, Emily. "Estado de excepción y feminicidio: *El traspatio/Backyard* (2009) de Carlos Carrera y Sabina Berman." *Colorado Review of Hispanic Studies*, no. 8 (2010): 27–42.
———. "On Pirates and Tourists: Ambivalent Approaches to *El Blog del Narco.*" In Chacón, *Online Activism in Latin America*, 113–27.
Hoeg, Jerry. *Science, Technology, and Latin American Narrative in the Twentieth Century and Beyond.* Bethlehem, PA: Lehigh University Press, 2000.
Hogan, Ernest. "Chicanonautica Manifesto." *Aztlan: A Journal of Chicano Studies* 40, no. 2 (2015): 131–34.
———. *Cortez On Jupiter.* San Francisco: Strange Particle Press, 2014.
———. *High Aztech.* New York: Tor, 1992.
———. *Smoking Mirror Blues.* La Grande: Wordcraft of Oregon, 2001.
Hogle, Linda F. "Tales from the Cryptic: Technology Meets Organism in the Living Cadaver." In Gray, Figueroa-Sarriera, and Mentor, *The Cyborg Handbook*, 203–18.

Hudson, Dale. *Vampires, Race, and Transnational Hollywood*. Edinburgh: Edinburgh University Press, 2017.

Hudson, Renee. "Former Futures and Absent Histories in María Cristina Mena, Rosaura Sánchez, and Beatrice Pita." *New Centennial Review* 19, no. 2 (2019): 69–92.

Huerta Moreno, Lydia Cristina. "Affecting Violence: Narratives of Los Feminicidios and their Ethical and Political Reception." PhD diss., University of Texas at Austin, 2012.

Hulgaard, Lasse, and Frederik Moesgaard. "Digital Interfaces for Urban Spaces." Master's thesis, Copenhagen Business School, 2020. https://research-api.cbs.dk/ws/portalfiles/portal/66776948/988781_Digital_Interfaces_for_Urban_Spaces.pdf.

Irizarry, Ylce. *Chicana/o and Latina/o Fiction: The New Memory of Latinidad*. Urbana: University of Illinois Press, 2016.

Jacobs, Elizabeth. "The Ecologies of Protest in the Theatre of Aztlán." *Comparative American Studies* 10, no. 1 (2012): 95–107.

Jacobsen, Joel. *Such Men as Billy the Kid: The Lincoln County War Reconsidered*. Lincoln: University of Nebraska Press, 1994.

James, Joy. "'Concerning Violence': Frantz Fanon's Rebel Intellectual in Search of a Black Cyborg." *South Atlantic Quarterly* 11, no. 1 (2013): 57–70.

Jameson, Frederic. "Future City." *New Left Review*, no. 21 (2003): 65–79.

Janzen, Rebecca. *The National Body in Mexican Literature: Collective Challenges to Biopolitical Control*. New York: Palgrave MacMillan, 2015.

Jaworsky, Bernadette Nadya. *The Boundaries of Belonging: Online Work of Immigration-Related Social Movement Organizations*. New York: Palgrave Macmillan, 2016.

Jay, Julia de Foor. "(Re)claiming the Race of the Mother: Cherríe Moraga's *Shadow of a Man*, *Giving Up the Ghost*, and *Heroes and Saints*." In *Women of Color: Mother-Daughter Relationships in Twentieth-Century Literature*, edited by Elizabeth Brown-Guillory, 95–116. Austin: University of Texas Press, 1996.

Jeffries, Fiona. "Cyborg Resistance on the Digital Assembly Line: Global Connectivity as a Terrain of Struggle for the Commons in Alex Rivera's *Sleep Dealer*." *Journal of Communication Inquiry* 39, no. 1 (2015): 21–37.

Johnson, David, and David Apodaca. "Myth and the Writer: A Conversation with Rudolfo Anaya." In Bruce and Sirias, *Conversations with Rudolfo Anaya*, 29–48.

Johnson, David E. *Violence and Naming: On Mexico and the Promise of Literature*. Austin: University of Texas Press, 2019.

Johnson, Kevin R. "Free Trade and Closed Borders: NAFTA and Mexican Immigration to the United States." *Immigration and Nationality Law Review*, no. 16 (1994): 937–78.

Jones, Doug. Foreword to Morehead, *Supernatural Cinema*, 7–10.

Jonsson, Carla. "Functions of Code-Switching in Bilingual Theater: An Analysis of Three Chicano Plays." *Journal of Pragmatics: An Interdisciplinary Journal of Language Studies* 42, no. 5 (2010): 1296–310.

---. "Representing Voice in Chicano Theatre through the Use of Orthography: An Analysis of Three Plays by Cherríe Moraga." In *The Representation of the Spoken Mode in Fiction: How Authors Write How People Talk*, edited by Carolina P. Amador Moreno and Ana Nunes, 101–23. Lewiston, NY: Edwin Mellen Press, 2009.

Joshi, S. T. "The Magical Spirituality of a Lapsed Catholic: Atheism and Anti-Clericalism." In Morehead, *Supernatural Cinema*, 11–20.

Jung, Alfred. "Regionalist Motifs in Rudolfo A. Anaya's Fiction (1972–82)." In *Missions in Conflict: Essays on U.S.-Mexican Relations and Chicano Culture*, edited by Renate von Bardeleben, Dietrich Briesemeister, and Juan Bruce-Novoa, 159–67. Tübingen: Stauffenburg Verlag Brigitte Narr GmbH, 1986.

Jung, Carl G., M. L. von Franz, Joseph L. Henderson, Jolande Jacobi, and Aniela Jaffé. *Man and His Symbols*. New York: Dell, 1968.

Kantaris, Geoffrey. "Cyborgs, Cities, and Celluloid: Memory Machines in Two Latin American Cyborg Films." In *Latin American Cyberculture and Cyberliterature*, edited by Claire Taylor and Thea Pitman, 50–69. Liverpool: University of Liverpool Press, 2007.

---. "Terminal City: Immaterial Migrations, Virtual Detachments and the North-South Divide (Alex Rivera's *Sleep Dealer*, 2008)." In *South and North: Contemporary Urban Orientations*, edited by Kerry Bystrom, Ashleigh Harris, Andrew J. Webber, 141–59. New York: Routledge, 2018.

Keefe, David E. "Governor Regan, Welfare Reform, and AFDC Fertility." *Social Service Review* 57, no. 2 (1983): 234–53.

Keizman, Betina. "Relecturas (cinematográficas) de la migración mexicana." *Amérique Latine Histoire et Mémoire: Les Cahiers ALHIM*, no. 23 (2012): 1–8. https://journals.openedition.org/alhim/4232.

Kevane, Bridget. *Latino Literature in America*. Westport, CT: Greenwood Publishing, 2003.

Kina, Ikue. "Cherríe Moraga's Ecofeminist Aesthetics toward Reclaiming Chicana Body in *Heroes and Saints* and *Watsonville*: Some Place Not Here." *Tamkang Review* 40, no. 1 (2009): 77–96.

King, Edward and Joanna Page. *Posthumanism and the Graphic Novel in Latin America*. London: University College London Press, 2017.

Kingsley, Anna. "Framing the Body: The Juárez Feminicides in Contemporary Mexican Visual Culture (1993–2013)." PhD diss., University of London, 2017.

Knopf, Kerstin. "Cherríe Moraga, *Heroes and Saints* (1992)." In *Drama, Part II*, edited by Susanne Peters and Klaus Stierstorfer, 369–88. Trier: Wissenschaftlicher, 2006.

Köhler, Angelika. "The Body as Borderland: Reconceptualization of the Body in Recent Chicana Literature." In *Body Signs: The Latino/a Body in Cultural Production*, edited by Astrid M. Fellner, 189–200. Berlin: Lit, 2012.

---. "The New World Man: Magical Realism in Rudolfo Anaya's *Bless Me, Ultima*." In Lomelí and Ikas, *U.S. Latino Literatures*, 201–13.

Kountz, Samantha. "The Other Side of the Wall: Technology and Borders in *Sleep Dealer*." *International Journal of Humanities and Cultural Studies* 1, no. 4 (2016): 287–99.

Kraniauskas, John. "*Cronos* and the Political Economy of Vampirism: Notes on a Historical Constellation." In *Cultural Margins: Cannibalism and the Colonial World*, edited by Francis Barker, Peter Hulme, and Margaret Iversen, 142–57. Cambridge: Cambridge University Press, 1998.

Krok, Ewelina. "The Figure of La Llorona as a Central Cultural Paradigm in Contemporary Chicano/a Literature." In *Kulturelles Wissen und Intertextualität: Theoriekonzeptionen und Fallstudien zur Kontextualisierung von Literatur*, edited by Marion Gymnich, Birgit Neumann, Ansgar Nünning, 195–207. Trier: Wissenschaftlicher Verlag Trier, 2006.

Kurlat Ares, Silvia G. "Prólogo." In *Historia de la ciencia ficción latinoamericana I: Desde los orígenes hasta la modernidad*, edited by Teresa López-Pellisa and Silvia G. Kurlat Ares, 9–17. Madrid: Iberoamericana, 2020.

Kvaran, Kara M. "'You're All Doomed!': A Socioeconomic Analysis of Slasher Films." *Journal of American Studies* 50, no. 4 (2016): 953–70.

Lamadrid, Enrique. "De vatos y profetas: Cultural Authority and Literary Presence in the Writing of Rudolfo Anaya." In Cantú, *The Forked Juniper*, 197–209.

———. "Myth as the Cognitive Process of Popular Culture in Rudolfo Anaya's *Bless Me, Ultima*: The Dialectics of Knowledge." *Hispania* 68, no. 3 (1985): 496–501.

———. "The Dynamics of Myth in the Creative Vision of Rudolfo Anaya." In *Pasó por aquí: Critical Essays on the New Mexican Literary Tradition, 1542–1988*. Albuquerque: University of New Mexico Press, 1989.

Lampe, Armando. "Religión y política en América Latina: La confrontación entre Juan Pablo II y Ernesto Cardenal en 1983." *Anuario Latinoamericano Ciencias Políticas y Relaciones Internacionales*, no. 3 (2016): 19–34.

Lane, Jill. "Electronic Disturbance Theater: Timeline 1994–2004. *TDR: The Drama Review* 47, no. 2 (2003): 129–44.

Laresgoiti, Francisco, dir. *2033*. 2008; Mexico City: Casa de Cine, 2010. DVD.

Laurell, Asa Cristina. "Three Decades of Neoliberalism in Mexico: The Destruction of Society." *International Journal of Health Services* 45, no. 2 (2015): 246–64.

Lauro, Sarah Juliet, Tiffany Gilmore, and Jenni G. Halpin. "Glass Wombs, Cyborg Women, and Kangaroo Mothers: How a Third-World Practice May Resolve the Techno/Feminist Debate." *TEXT Technology*, no. 1 (2007): 73–94.

Leal, Luis. "Magical Realism in Spanish American Literature." Translated by Wendy B. Faris. In *Magical Realism: Theory, History, Community*, edited by Lois Parkinson Zamora and Wendy B. Faris, 119–24. Durham, NC: Duke University Press, 1967.

Lee, Derek. "Postquantum: *A Tale for the Time Being, Atomik Aztex*, and Hacking Modern Space Time." *MELUS: The Society for the Study of the Multi-Ethnic Literature of the United States* 43, no. 1 (2020): 1–26.

Legrás, Horacio. "Biopolítica: Vicisitudes de una idea." In Moraña and Sánchez Prado, *Heridas abiertas*, 31–46.

Leibler, Jessica, Jeanne A. Jordan, Kristen Brownstein, Lina Lander, Lance B. Price, Melissa J. Perry. "*Staphylococcus aureus*: Nasal Carriage among Beefpacking Workers in a Midwestern United States Slaughterhouse." *PLOS One* 11, no. 2 (2016): 1–11.

Lemov, Rebecca. "On Not Being There: The Data-Driven Body at Work and at Play." *Hedgehog Review* 17, no. 2 (2015): 44–55.

Lépine, Cédric. "Distribución de películas latinoamericanas en Francia en 2018." *Cinémas d'amérique latine*, no. 27 (2019): 144–53. https://doi.org/10.4000/cinelatino.6257.

Levitas, Ruth. *Utopia as Method: The Imaginary Reconstitution of Society*. New York: Palgrave MacMillan, 2013.

Lizama, Jorge Alberto. "El poder de las redes sociales: Hacktivismo vs. páginas web del gobierno mexicano." In Córdova, *La cultura del espectáculo*, 3–20.

Lomelí, Francisco. "Chican@ Literary Imagination: Trajectory and Evolution of Canon Building from the Margins." In Cantú, *The Forked Juniper*, 179-98.

Lomelí, Francisco, and Karin Ikas, eds. *U.S. Latino Literatures and Cultures: Transnational Perspectives*. Heidelberg: Universitätsverlag Winter, 2000.

Lomnitz, Claudio. *Exits from the Labyrinth: Culture and Ideology in the Mexican National Space*. Berkeley: University of California Press, 1992.

López, Marissa K. *Chicano Nations: The Hemispheric Origins of Mexican American Literature*. New York: New York University Press, 2011.

———. *Racial Immanence: Chicanx Bodies beyond Representation*. New York: New York University Press, 2019.

———. "The Xicano Future is Now: Poetry, Performance, and Prolepsis." *ASAP/Journal* 4, no. 2 (2019): 403–28.

López-Lozano, Miguel. *Utopian Dreams, Apocalyptic Nightmares: Globalization in Recent Mexican and Chicano Narrative*. West Lafayette, IN: Purdue University Press, 2008.

———. "Women in the Global Machine: Patrick Bard's *La frontera*, Carmen Galán Benítz's *Tierra marchita*, and Alicia Gaspar de Alba's *Desert Blood: The Juárez Murders*." In Corona and Domínguez-Ruvalcaba, *Gender Violence*, 129–51.

López-Pellisa, Teresa. *Patologías de la realidad virtual: Cibercultura y ciencia ficción*. Madrid: FCE, 2015.

Lozano, Jennifer M. "Alex Rivera's Multimedia Storytelling, Humor, and Transborder Latinx Futurity." In Aldama, *Latinx Ciné in the Twenty-First Century*, 267–85.

Lund, Joshua. *The Mestizo State: Reading Race in Modern Mexico*. Minneapolis: University of Minnesota Press, 2012.

Lykke, Nina. "Between Monsters, Goddesses, and Cyborgs: Feminist Confrontations with Science." In *The Gendered Cyborg: A Reader*, edited by Gill Kirkup, Linda Janes, Kath Woodward, and Fiona Hovenden, 74–87. New York: Routledge, 2000.

Madley, Benjamin. *An American Genocide: The United States and the California Indian Catastrophe, 1846–1873*. New Haven: Yale University Press, 2016.

Mackereth, Kerry. "Maids and Family Androids: Racialised Post-Care Imaginaries in *Humans* (2015– ), *Sleep Dealer* (2008) and *Her* (2013)." *Feminist Review* 123, no. 1 (2019): 24–39.

Mandujano-Salazar, Yunuen Ylce. "YouTube Channels of Mexicans Living in Japan: Virtual Communities and Bi-Cultural Imagery Construction." In Dalton and Ramírez Plascencia, *Imagining Latinidad*, 154–70.

Manion, Mark, and Abby Goodrum. "Terrorism or Civil Disobedience: Toward a Hacktivist Ethic." *Computers and Society* 30, no. 2 (2000): 14–19.

Manzanas Calvo, Ana María, and Jesús Benito Sánchez. *Hospitality in American Literature and Culture: Spaces, Bodies, Borders*. New York: Routledge, 2016.

Manzanas Calvo, Ana María, and Jesús Benito. *Occupying Space in American Literature and Culture: Static Heroes, Social Movements and Empowerment*. New York: Routledge, 2014.

Manzanas Calvo, Ana María, and Paula Barba Guerrero. "Redrawing the Boundary: From Carlos Fuentes's *La frontera de cristal* (1995) to Rosaura Sánchez and Beatrice Pita's *Lunar Braceros 2125–2148* (2009)." *Excentric Narratives: Journal of Anglophone Literature, Culture and Media*, no. 3 (2019): 122–35.

Manzoni, Celina. "Discursos del cuerpo y construcción de memoria." *Taller de letras*, no. 49 (2011): 159–69.

Marez, Curtis. "Octavia E. Butler, After the Chicanx Movement." *Women's Studies: An Interdisciplinary Journal* 47, no. 7 (2018): 755–60.

———. "The Future in the Present, or, When Cages Crumble." *American Quarterly* 71, no. 2 (2020): 337–42.

———. *Farm Worker Futurism: Speculative Technologies of Resistance*. Minneapolis: University of Minneapolis Press, 2016.

Marks, Mason. "Robots in Space: Sharing Our World with Autonomous Delivery Vehicles." Paper Presented at the We Robot Conference, Miami, FL, March 2019. https://robots.law.miami.edu/2019/wp-content/uploads/2019/03/Mason-Marks-Robots-in-Space-WeRobot-2019-3-14.pdf.

Marques, Ivan da Costa. "Cloning Computers: From Rights of Possession to Rights of Creation." *Science as Culture* 14, no. 2 (2003): 139–60.

Márquez, Antonio. "The Achievement of Rudolfo A. Anaya." In *The Magic of Words: Rudolfo A. Anaya and His Writings*, edited by Paul Vassallo, 33–52. Albuquerque: University of New Mexico Press, 1982.

Martín, Desirée. *Borderlands Saints: Secular Sanctity in Chicano/a and Mexican Culture*. New Brunswick, NJ: Rutgers University Press, 2013.

Martin, Grace A. "For the Love of Robots: Posthumanism in Latin American Science Fiction between 1960–1999." PhD diss., University of Kentucky, 2015.

Martín-Cabrera, Luis. "The Potentiality of the Commons: A Materialist Critique of Cognitive Capitalism from the Cyberbracer@s to the Ley Sinde." *Hispanic Review* 80, no. 4 (2012): 583–605.

Martín-Junquera, Imelda, ed. *Landscapes of Writing in Chicano Literature*. New York: Palgrave MacMillan, 2013.

Martín Párraga, Javier. "La reinvención del mito vampírico en *Cronos*, de Guillermo del Toro." *Frame*, no. 6 (2010): 57–67.

Martínez Agíss, Oscar. "Reinventando al vampiro: *Cronos* de Guillermo del Toro." In *Nuevas narrativas mexicanas*, edited by Marco Kunz, Cristina Mondragón, and Dolores Phillipps-López. Barcelona: Red ediciones S.L, 2012.

Martínez-Guzmán, Antar. "Masculine Subjectivities and Necropolitics: Precarization and Violence at the Mexican Margins." *Subjectivity* 12 (2019): 288–308.

Martínez-Raguso, Michael. "All of the Work, with None of the Workers: The Technology of Consumption in *Sleep Dealer*." In *Future Humans in Fiction and Film*, edited Louisa Mackay Demerjian and Karen F. Stein, 116–30. Cambridge: Cambridge Scholars Publishing, 2018.

Marx, Karl. *Capital: A Critique of Political Economy*, vol. 1, book 1: *The Process of Production of Capital*. Translated by Samuel Moore and Edward Aveling, edited by Frederick Engels, first English ed. 1887. Marx Engels Archive, 1999. https://www.marxists.org/archive/marx/works/download/pdf/Capital-Volume-I.pdf.

Mayorga, Irma. "Cherríe Moraga." In *Twentieth-Century American Dramatists*, 3rd series, edited by Christopher J. Wheatley, 245–67. Detroit, MI: Thomson Gale, 2002.

———. "Invisibility's Contusions: Violence in Cherríe Moraga's *Heroes and Saints* and *The Hungry Woman* and Luis Valdez's *Zoot Suit*." In *Violence in American Drama: Essays on Its Staging, Meanings, and Effects,* edited by Alfonso Ceballos Muñoz, Ramón Espejo Romero, and Bernardo Muñoz Martínez, 151–71. Jefferson, NC: McFarland, 2011.

Mbembe, Achille. *Necropolitics*. Translated by Steven Corcoran. Durham, NC: Duke University Press, 2019.

McClennen, Sophia A. *Globalization and Latin American Cinema: Toward a New Critical Paradigm*. New York: Palgrave MacMillan, 2018.

McEntyre, Marilyn Chandler. "Sickness in the System: The Health Costs of the Harvest." *Journal of Medical Humanities* 28, no. 2 (2007): 97–104.

McLuhan, Marshall. *Understanding Media: The Extensions of Man*. Scarborough. Ont.: Mentor Books, 1964.

Medel, China. "The Ghost in the Machine: The Biopolitics of Memory in Alex Rivera's *Sleep Dealer.*" *Camera Obscura* 33, no. 1 (2018): 113–37.

Medina, Eden, Ivan da Costa Marques, and Christina Holmes. "Introduction: Beyond Imported Magic." In *Beyond Imported Magic: Essays on Science, Technology, and Society in Latin America*, edited by Eden Medina, Ivan da Costa, and Christina Holmes, 1–23. Cambridge, MA: MIT Press, 2014.

Medina, Manuel F. "Las fronteras globales imaginadas en *Sleep Dealer*, de Alex Rivera." *Olho d'água* 4, no. 2 (2012): 52–61.

Meikle, Graham. "Electronic Civil Disobedience and Symbolic Power." In *Cyber Conflict and Global Politics*, edited by Athina Karatzogianni, 177–87. New York: Routledge, 2010.

Melamed, Jodi. "Post-Marxism, American Studies, and Post-Capitalist Futures." In *Approaches to American Cultural Studies*, edited by Antje Dallmann, Eva Bosenberg, and Martin Klepper, 135–44. New York: Routledge, 2016.

———. *Represent and Destroy: Rationalizing Violence in the New Racial Capitalism.* Minneapolis: University of Minnesota Press, 2011.

Meléndez, Priscila. "The Body and the Law in the Mexico/U.S. Borderlands: Violence and Violations in *El viaje de los cantores* by Hugo Salcedo and *Backyard* by Sabina Berman." *Modern Drama* 54, no. 1 (2011): 24–44.

Menjívar, Cecilia. "Liminal Legality: Salvadoran and Guatemalan Immigrants' Lives in the United States." *American Journal of Sociology* 111, no. 4 (2006): 999–1037.

Menjívar, Cecilia, and Daniel Kanstroom, eds. *Constructing Immigrant 'Illegality': Critiques, Experiences, and Responses.* Cambridge: Cambridge University Press, 2013.

Mercader, Yolanda. "El cine ante los feminicidios de Ciudad Juárez." In *Cine y frontera: Territorios ilimitados de la mirada*, edited by Graciela Martínez Zalce and Juan Carlos Vargas, 207–30. Mexico City: Bonilla Artigas Editores, 2014.

———. "Introduction: Altermundos: Reassessing the Past, Present, and Future of the Chican@ and Latin@ Speculative Arts." In Merla-Watson and Olguín, *Altermundos*, 1–36.

Meredith, Dana A., and Luis Alberto Rodríguez Cortés. "Expanding Outrage: Representations of Gendered Violence and Feminicide in Mexico." In *Modern Mexican Culture: Critical Foundations*, edited by Stuart A. Day, 237–58. Tucson: University of Arizona Press, 2017.

Merla-Watson, Cathryn Josefina, and B. V. Olguín, eds. *Altermundos: Latin@ Speculative Literature, Film, and Popular Culture.* Los Angeles: UCLA Chicano Studies Research Center Press, 2017.

Michaels, Walter Benn. *The Beauty of a Social Problem: Photography, Autonomy, Economy.* Chicago: University of Chicago Press, 2015.

Michaus, Cristina, dir. *Juárez: Desierto de esperanza.* 2001. Mexico City: Tenzin Producciones, 2002. VHS.

Mignolo, Walter. "Coloniality Is Far from Over, and So Must Be Decoloniality." *Afterall: A Journal of Art, Context and Enquiry* 43, no. 1 (2017): 38–45.

———. *The Darker Side of Western Modernity: Global Futures, Decolonial Options.* Durham, NC: Duke University Press, 2011.
Milian, Claudi. *LatinX.* Minneapolis: University of Minnesota Press, 2019.
Miner, Dylan A. T. *Creating Aztlán: Chicano Art, Indigenous Sovereignty, and Lowriding across Turtle Island.* Tucson: University of Arizona Press, 2014.
Minich, Julie Avril. *Accessible Citizenships: Disability, Nation, and the Cultural Politics of Greater Mexico.* Philadelphia, PA: Temple University Press, 2014.
———. "'You Gotta Make Aztlán Any Way You Can': Disability in Cherríe Moraga's *Heroes and Saints.*" In *Disability and Mothering: Liminal Spaces of Embodied Knowledge,* edited by Cynthia Lewiecki-Wilson and Jen Celio, 260–74. Syracuse, NY: Syracuse University Press, 2011.
Miranda, J. V. "Techno/Memo: The Politics of Cultural Memory in Alex Rivera's *Sleep Dealer.*" In Aldama, *Latinx Ciné in the Twenty-First Century,* 249–66.
Mitchell, Joanna L. "Haunting the Chicana: The Queer Child and the Abject Mother in the Writing of Cherríe Moraga." In *Unveiling the Body in Hispanic Women's Literature: From Nineteenth-Century Spain to Twenty-First-Century United States,* edited by Renée Scott and Arleen Chiclana y González, 203–22. Lewiston, NY: Edwin Mellen Press, 2006.
Mize, Ronald L., and Alicia C. S. Swords. *Consuming Mexican Labor: From the Bracero Program to NAFTA.* Toronto: University of Toronto Press, 2011.
Monárrez Fragoso, Julia. "Las diversas representaciones del feminicidio y los asesinatos de mujeres en Ciudad Juárez, 1993–2005." In Monárrez Fragoso et al., *Violencia contra las mujeres,* 361–89.
———. *Trama de una injusticia: Feminicidio sexual sistémico en Ciudad Juárez.* Tijuana: El Colegio de la Frontera Norte, 2009.
———. "Violencia de género, violencia de pareja, feminicidio y pobreza." In Monárrez Fragoso et al., *Violencia contra las mujeres,* 361–89.
Monárrez Fragoso, Julia Estela, and María Socorro Tabuenca Córdoba, eds. *Bordeando la violencia contra las mujeres en la frontera norte de México.* Tijuana: El Colegio de la Frontera Norte, 2007.
Monárrez Fragoso, Julia Estela, Luis E. Cervera Gómez, César M. Fuentes Flores, and Rodolfo Rubio Salas, eds. *Violencia contra las mujeres: Inseguridad ciudadana en Ciudad Juárez.* Tijuana: El Colegio de la Frontera Norte, 2010.
Monsiváis, Carlos. "De la cultura mexicana en vísperas del Tratado de Libre Comercio." In *La educación y la cultura ante el Tratado de Libre Comercio,* edited by Gilberto Guevara Niebla and Néstor García Canclini, 179–209. Mexico City: Nueva Imagen, 1992.
Moore, Jazmyn T., Jessica N. Ricaldi, Charles E. Rose, Jennifer Fuld, Monica Parise, Gloria J. Kang, Anne K. Driscoll et al. "Disparities in Incidence of COVID-19 among Underrepresented Racial/Ethnic Groups in Counties Identified as Hotspots during June 5–18, 2020—22 States, February–June 2020." *Morbidity and Mortality Weekly Report* 69, no. 33 (2020): 1122–26.
Moraga, Cherríe. "Author's Notes." In *Heroes and Saints and Other Plays,* by Cherríe Moraga, 89. Albuquerque, NM: West End Press, 2007.

———. *Heroes and Saints*. In Perkins and Uno, *Contemporary Plays by Women of Color*, 233–61.

———. "Queer Aztlán: The Re-Formation of Chicano Tribe." In *Aztlán: Essays on the Chicano Homeland*, rev. ed., edited by Rodolfo Anaya, Francisco A. Lomelí y Enrique R. Lamadrid, 253–72. Albuquerque: University of New Mexico Press, 2017.

———. *Watsonville: Some Place Not Here*. In *Watsonville: Some Place Not Here; Circle in the Dirt: El Pueblo de East Palo Alto*, by Cherríe Moraga. Albuquerque, NM: West End Press, 2005.

Morales Oyarvide, César. "La guerra contra el narcotráfico en México. Debilidad del Estado, orden local y fracaso de una estrategia." *Aposta: Revista de Ciencias Sociales*, no. 50 (2011): 1–35.

Moraña, Mabel. "Escasez y modernidad." In Moraña and Valenzuela Arce, *Precariedades, exclusiones y emergencias*, 25–36.

———. "Introducción: *Heridas abiertas*." In Moraña and Sánchez Prado, *Heridas abiertas*, 7–22.

———. *Pensar el cuerpo: Historia, materialidad y símbolo*. Barcelona: Herder, 2021.

———. *The Monster as War Machine*. Translated by Andrew Ascherl. Amherst, NY: Cambria Press, 2018.

Moraña, Mabel, and Ignacio M. Sánchez Prado, eds. *Heridas abiertas: Biopolítica y representación en América Latina*. Madrid: Iberoamericana, 2014.

Moraña, Mabel, and José Manuel Valenzuela Arce, eds. *Precariedades, exclusiones y emergencias: Necropolítica y sociedad civil en América Latina*. Mexico City: Universidad Autónoma Metropolitana, 2014.

Moravec, Hans. *Mind Children: The Future of Robot and Human Intelligence*. Cambridge, MA: Harvard University Press, 1988.

More, Thomas. *Utopia*. 1516. Scotts Valley, CA: CreateSpace, 2015.

Morehead, John H., ed. *The Supernatural Cinema of Guillermo del Toro*. Jefferson, NC: McFarland, 2015.

Morel, Pierre, dir. *Peppermint*. Los Angeles: STX Entertainment, 2018. Streaming.

Muir, John Kenneth. *Horror Films FAQ: All that's Left to Know about Slashers, Vampires, Zombies, Aliens, and More*. Milwaukee, WI: Applause Theatre and Cinema Books, 2013.

Muñoz Gallarte, Israel. "El bestiario clásico de Guillermo del Toro." *Ámbitos: Revista de Estudios de Ciencias Sociales y Humanidades*, no. 27 (2012): 47–52.

Murray, Robin, and Joseph Heumann. *Monstrous Nature: Environment and Horror on the Big Screen*. Lincoln: University of Nebraska Press, 2016.

Naam, Ramez. *More Than Human: Embracing the Promise of Biological Enhancement*. New York: Broadway Books, 2005.

Namaste, Nina. "Not Just a Ciudad Juárez Problem: Extreme Capitalism, Masculinity, and Impunity in Sabina Berman's *Backyard*." *Contemporary Theatre Review* 22, no. 2 (2012): 485–98.

Nava, Gregory, dir. *Bordertown*. 2007; Berlin: Möbious Entertainment, 2008. DVD.

Nericcio, William A. "Latina/o Dystopias on the Verge of an Electric, Pathological Tomorrow: Alex Rivera's *Sleep Dealer*." *Review: Literature and Arts of the Americas* 48, no. 1 (2015): 48–54.

Neubauer, Robert. "Neoliberalism in the Information Age, or Vice Versa?: Global Citizenship, Technology, and Hegemonic Ideology." *TripleC* 9, no. 2 (2011): 195–230.

Newitz, Annalee. "The Robots Won't Steal Your Jobs, It Will Be Worse than That." *New Scientist* 242, no. 3236 (2019): 24.

Nicholls, Walter. "Voice and Power in the Immigrant Rights Movement." In Menjívar and Kanstroom, *Constructing Immigrant "Illegality,"* 225–45.

Nixon, Rob. *Slow Violence and Environmentalism of the Poor*. Cambridge, MA: Harvard University Press, 2011.

Noriega, Chon A., Eric Ávila, Karen Mary Davalos, Chela Sandoval, Rafael Pérez-Torres, eds. *The Chicano Studies Reader: An Anthology of Aztlán, 1970–2015*. Los Angeles: UCLA Chicano Studies Research Center Press, 2016.

Nunn, Kenneth B. "Race, Crime and the Pool of Surplus Criminality: Or Why the 'War on Drugs' was a War on Blacks." *Journal of Gender, Race, and Justice* 6, no. 2 (2002): 381–446.

Nuñez, Gabriela. "The Future of Food?: Indigenous Knowledges and Sustainable Food Systems in Latin@ Speculative Fiction." In Merla-Watson and Olguín, *Altermundos*, 235–48.

Obenland, Frank. "'To Meet a Broader and Wiser Revolution': Notions of Collectivity in Contemporary Mexican American Drama." *Amerikastudien/American Studies* 57, no. 2 (2012): 271–90.

O'Brien, Brad. "Fulcanelli as a Vampiric Frankenstein and Jesus as His Vampiric Monster: The Frankenstein and Dracula Myths in Guillermo del Toro's *Cronos*." In *Monstrous Adaptations: Generic and Thematic Mutations in Horror and Film*, edited by Richard J. Hand and Jay McRoy, 172–80. Manchester: Manchester University Press, 2007.

Olguín, B. V. "'Contrapuntal Cyborgs?': The Ideological Limits and Revolutionary Potential of Latin@ Science Fiction." *Aztlán: A Journal of Chicano Studies* 41, no. 1 (2016): 217–33.

Olivera, Mercedes. "Violencia feminicida: Violence against Women and Mexico's Structural Crisis." Translated by Victoria J. Furio. In Fregoso and Bejarano, *Terrorizing Women*, 49–58.

Olson, Melissa. "Dracula the Anti-Christ: New Resurrection of an Immortal Prejudice." In *Images of the Modern Vampire: The Hip and the Atavistic*, edited by Barbara Brodman and James E. Doan, 29–40. Madison, WI: Fairleigh Dickinson University Press, 2013.

Omi, Michael, and Howard Winant. *Racial Formation in the United States: From the 1960s to the 1990s*, 2nd ed. New York: Routledge, 1994.

Orihuela, Sharada Balachandran, and Andrew Carl Hageman. "The Virtual Realities of US/Mexico Border Ecologies in *Maquilapolis* and *Sleep Dealer*." *Environmental Communication* 5, no. 2 (2011): 166–86.

Otero, Manuel. *The Real Billy the Kid*. New York: R. R. Wilson, 1936.

O'Toole, Gavin. "A New Nationalism for a New Era: The Political Ideology of Mexican Neoliberalism." *Bulletin of Latin American Research* 22, no. 3 (2003): 269–90.

Oxman, Verónica. "At the Border of the Gender Abyss: Discussing Masculinity and Feminicide in Ciudad Juárez." In *Engaging Men in Building Gender Equality*, edited by Michael Flood and Richard Howson, 126–34. Newcastle: Cambridge Scholars Publishing, 2015.

Palaversich, Diana. *De Macondo a McOndo: Senderos de la postmodernidad latinoamericana*. Barcelona: Plaza y Valdés, 2005.

Palou, Pedro. *El fracaso del mestizo*. Mexico City: Paidós, 2014.

Park, Jungwon. "La frontera en ruinas: El cuerpo enfermo y la biopolítica global en *Maquilapolis* y *Sleep Dealer*." *Revista Iberoamericana* 84, no. 265 (2018): 1117–33.

Parlee, Lorena, Lenny Bourin, Mike Farrell, César Chavez, and Dolores Huerta. *The Wrath of Grapes*. United Farm Workers, 1986. YouTube, posted by Paul Langan, Nov. 22, 2016. https://www.youtube.com/watch?v=Wq4804ftL4A.

Passariello, Phyllis. "Desperately Seeking *Something*: Che Guevara as Secular Saint." In *The Making of Saints: Contesting Sacred Ground*, edited by James F. Hopgood, 75–89. Tuscaloosa: University of Alabama Press, 2005.

Paulson, Justin. "Peasant Struggles and International Solidarity: The Case of Chiapas." *Socialist Register*, no. 37 (2001): 275–88.

Paxman, Andrew, and Alex M. Saragoza. "Globalization and Latin Media Powers: The Case of Mexico's Televisa." *Continental Order?: Integrating North America for Cybercapitalism*, edited by Vincent Mosco and Dan Schiller, 64–85. Lanham, MD: Rowman and Littlefield, 2001.

Paz, Octavio. *El laberinto de la soledad. Postdata. Vuelta a El laberinto de la soledad*. Mexico City: FCE, 2004.

Pereira Penteado, Marina. "Do cotágio ao isolamento: O futuro distópico insistente em *The Rag Doll Plagues* e *Sleep Dealer*." *Revista Línguas & Letras* 16, no. 33 (2015): 149–64.

Pérez, Óscar. "A Queer Reading of *Nuevo Cine Mexicano*." *Film International*, no. 70 (2014): 69–83.

Pérez Huber, Lindsay. "Constructing 'Deservingness': DREAMers and Central American Unaccompanied Children in the National Immigration Debate." *Association of Mexican American Educators Journal* 9, no. 3 (2015): 22–34.

Pérez-Torres, Rafael. "Refiguring Aztlán." In Noriega et al., *The Chicano Studies Reader*, 171–89.

Perkins, Kathy A., and Roberta Uno. "Cherríe Moraga." In Perkins and Uno, *Contemporary Plays by Women of Color*, 230–32.

———, eds. *Contemporary Plays by Women of Color*. New York: Routledge, 2006.
Perreira, Christopher. "Speculative Futurity and the Eco-Cultural Politics of *Lunar Braceros: 2125–2148*." In *Latinx Environmentalisms: Place, Justice, and the Decolonial*, edited by Sarah D. Wald, David J. Vázquez, Priscilla Solis Ybarra, and Sarah Jaquette Ray, 87–103. Philadelphia, PA: Temple University Press, 2019.
Petersen, Amanda. "Breaking Silences and Revealing Hosts: Spectral Moments of Gendered Violence in Mexico." *iMex Revista: México Interdisciplinario/ Interdisciplinary Mexico* 16, no. 2 (2019): 22–40.
Piñeros Shields, Thomas. "DREAMers Rising: Constituting the Undocumented Student Immigrant Movement." PhD diss., Brandeis University, 2014.
Pitts, Andrea J. *Nos/Otras: Gloria E. Anzaldúa, Multiplicitous Agency, and Resistance*. Albany: State University of New York Press, 2021.
———. "Toward an Aesthetics of Race: Bridging the Writings of Gloria Anzaldúa and José Vasconcelos." *Inter-American Journal of Philosophy* 5, no. 1 (2014): 80–100.
Planas Cabrejo, Justo. "*Cronos* en el laberinto de lo *unheimlich*." *Imagofagia: Revista de la Asociación Argentina de Estudios de Cine y Audiovisual*, no. 16 (2017): 244–66.
Plaw, Avery, Barbara Carvalho Gurgel, and David Ramírez Plascencia. Introduction to Plaw, Gurgel, and Ramírez Plascencia, *Politics of Technology*, 1–12.
———, eds. *The Politics of Technology in Latin America*, vol. 1, *Data Protection, Homeland Security and the Labor Market*. New York: Routledge, 2020.
Poisa, María Gil. "Ciudad, frontera y espacio en *Sleep Dealer*." In *Geographies of Identity: Mapping, Crossing, and Transgressing Urban and Human Boundaries*, edited by Esther Álvarez Lopez, 115–23. Madrid: Instituto Franklin, Universidad Alacalá de Hernández, 2016.
Portillo, Lourdes, dir. *Señorita extraviada/Missing Young Woman*. 2001; New York City: Women Make Movies, 2002. DVD.
Prasch, Thomas. "Aquaterrorists and Cybraceros: The Dystopian Borderlands of Alex Rivera's *Sleep Dealer* (2008)." In *Border Visions: Identity and Diaspora in Film*, edited by Jakub Kazecki, Karen A. Ritzenhoff, and Cynthia J. Miller, 43–58. Lanham, MD: Scarecrow Press, 2013.
Prashad, Vijay. *Everybody Was Kung Fu Fighting: Afro-Asian Connections and the Myth of Cultural Purity*. Boston, MA: Beacon Press, 2001.
Price, Brian L. *Cult of Defeat in Mexico's Historical Fiction: Failure, Trauma, and Loss*. New York: Palgrave MacMillan, 2012.
Price, Helene. "Unsavoury Representations in Laura Esquivel's *Como agua para chocolate*." In *A Companion to Magical Realism*, edited by Stephen M. Hart and Wen-chin Ouyang, 181–90. Suffolk: Tamesis, 2005.
Puga, Ana Elena. "Female Alliances and Women's Histories in Contemporary Mexican and Argentine Drama." In *Contemporary Women Playwrights: Into*

*the 21st Century*, edited by Penny Farfan and Lesley Ferris, 35–49. New York: Palgrave MacMillan, 2013.

Quintero Ramírez, Círila. "Trabajo femenino en las maquiladoras: ¿Explotación o liberación?" In Monárrez Fragoso and Tabuenca Córdoba, *Bordeando la violencia*, 191–218.

Rabasa, José. *Without History: Subaltern Studies, the Zapatista Insurgency, and the Specter of History*. Pittsburgh, PA: University of Pittsburgh Press, 2010.

Rabinow, Paul, and Nikolas Rose, eds. *The Essential Foucault*. New York: The New Press, 2003.

Radford, Benjamin. *Tracking the Chupacabra: The Vampire Beast in Fact, Fiction, and Folklore*. Albuquerque: University of New Mexico Press, 2011.

Rama, Angel. *The Lettered City*. Translated by John Charles Chasteen. Durham, NC: Duke University Press, 1996.

Ramírez, Catherine. "Afrofuturism/Chicanafuturism: Fictive Kin." *Aztlán: A Journal of Chicano Studies* 33, no. 1 (2008): 185–94.

———. "Cyborg Femenism: The Science Fiction of Octavia E. Butler and Gloria Anzaldúa." In *Reload: Rethinking Women + Cyberculture*, edited by Mary Flanagan and Austin Booth, 374–402. Cambridge: Massachusetts Institute of Technology Press, 2002.

———. "Deus ex Machina: Tradition, Technology and the Chicanafuturist Art of Marion C. Martinez." *Aztlán: A Journal of Chicano Studies* 29, no. 2 (2004): 55–92.

———. "Foreward: The Time Machine: From Afrofuturism to Chicanafuturism and Beyond." In Merla-Watson and Olguín, *Altermundos*, ix–xii.

Ramírez, Javier. "Sci-Fi-ing Immigration and the US-Mexico Border: An Interview with Filmmaker Alex Rivera." *Chiricú Journal: Latina/o Literature, Art, and Culture* 1, no. 1 (2016): 95–105.

Ramírez, J. Jesse. "*Sleep Dealer*, or, Tijuana, Ciudad del Futuro." Unpublished paper.

Ramírez, Susana. "Recovering Gloria Anzaldúa's Sci-fi Roots: Nepantler@ Visions in the Unpublished and Published Speculative Precursors to *Borderlands*." In Merla-Watson and Olguín, *Altermundos*, 55–71.

Rawle, Steven. *Transnational Cinema: An Introduction*. New York: Palgrave MacMillan, 2018.

Reguillo, Rossana. "La turbulencia en el paisaje: De jóvenes, necropolítica y esperanzas." In *Juvenicidio: Aytotzinapa y las vidas precarias en América Latina y España*, edited by José Manuel Valenzuela Arce, 59–78. Barcelona: Ned Ediciones, 2015.

———. "Precariedad (es): necropolítica y máquinas de guerra." In Moraña and Valenzuela Arce, *Precariedades, exclusiones y emergencias*, 53–74.

Retis, Jessica, and Patria Román-Velázquez. "Latin Americans in London: Digital Diasporas and Social Activism." In Dalton and Ramírez Plascencia, *Imagining Latinidad*, 100–18.

Reyes, Laura. "Contribuciones cinematográficas al diálogo necesario para la reconstrucción de Guatemala: Gasolina, Las marimbas del infierno y *Polvo* de Julio Hernández Cordón." *La BloGoteca de Babel*, no. 7 (2018): 1–24.

Reyes, Yolanda. "Personajes femeninos contestatarios del cine mexicano del siglo XXI: Subvirtiendo la Época de Oro." PhD diss., National University of Ireland, Galway, 2012.

Reynolds, Peggy, Daniel F. Smith, Enid Satariano, David O. Nelson, Lynn R. Goldman, and Raymond R. Neutra. "The Four County Study of Childhood Cancer: Clusters in the Context." *Statistics in Medicine* 15, no. 7–9 (1996): 683–97.

Reynolds, Peggy, Julie Von Behren, Robert B. Gunier, Debbie E. Golberg, Andrew Hertz, and Martha E. Harnly. "Childhood Cancer and Agricultural Pesticide Use: An Ecologic Study in California." *Environmental Health Perspectives* 1, no. 3 (2002): 319–24.

Ribas-Casasayas, Alberto, and Amanda L. Petersen, eds. *Espectros: Ghostly Hauntings in Contemporary Transhispanic Narratives*. Lewisburg, PA: Bucknell University Press, 2016.

———. "Introduction: Theories of the Ghost in a Transhispanic Context." In Ribas-Casasayas and Petersen, *Espectros*, 1–12.

Rieder, John. *Colonialism and the Emergence of Science Fiction*. Middletown, CT: Wesleyan University Press, 2008.

Rios, Josh. "A Possible Future Return to the Past." *Somatechnics* 7, no. 1 (2017): 59–73.

Rivera, Alex. "Cybracero Systems." http://www.cybracero.com/. Accessed Jun. 18, 2016.

———, dir. *Sleep Dealer*. 2008; Sundance, CO: Maya Entertainment, 2008. DVD.

———, dir. *Why Cybraceros?* 1997. Los Angeles: LA Freewaves, Dec. 3, 2012, https://www.youtube.com/watch?v=Xr1eqKcDZq4.

Rivera, Lysa. "Chicana/o Cyberpunk after el Movimiento." *Aztlán: A Journal of Chicano Studies* 40, no. 2 (2015): 187–202.

———. "Future Histories and Cyborg Labor: Reading Borderlands Science Fiction after NAFTA." *Science Fiction Studies* 39, no. 3 (2012): 415–36.

———. "*Mestizaje* and Heterotopia in Ernest Hogan's *High Aztech*." In *Black and Brown Planets: The Politics of Race in Science Fiction*, edited by Isiah Lavender, 146–62. Jackson: University Press of Mississippi, 2014.

———. "Neoliberalism and Dystopia in U.S.-Mexico Borderlands Fiction." In *Blast, Corrupt, Dismantle, Erase: Contemporary North American Dystopian Literature*, edited by Brett Josef Brubisic, Gisele M. Baxter, and Tara Lee, 291–310. Waterloo, Canada: Wilfrid Laurier University Press, 2014.

Rivera Garza, Cristina. *Grieving: Dispatches from a Wounded country*. Translated by Sarah Booker. New York: The Feminist Press, 2020.

———. *The Restless Dead: Necrowriting and Disappropriation*. Translated by Robin Myers. Nashville, TN: Vanderbilt University Press, 2020.

Rivera Hernández, Raúl Diego. *Narratives of Vulnerability in Mexico's War on Drugs*. New York: Palgrave MacMillan, 2020.

Rivera, John-Michael. "Billy the Kid's Corpse and the Specter of Mexican Manhood." In *Decolonizing Latinx Masculinities*, edited by Arturo J. Aldama and Frederick Luis Aldama, 23–37. Tucson: University of Arizona Press, 2020.

———. *The Emergence of Mexican America: Recovering Stories of Mexican Peoplehood in U.S. Culture*. New York: New York University Press, 2006.

Robles, Sonia. *Mexican Waves: Radio Broadcasting along Mexico's Northern Border, 1930–1950*. Tucson: University of Arizona Press, 2019.

Robinso, Jessica. *Life Lessons from Slasher Films*. Lanham, MD: Scarecrow Press, 2012.

Rodríguez, Mariángela. *Tradición, identidad, mito y metáfora: Mexicanos y chicanos en California*. Mexico City: Centro de Investigaciones y Estudios Superiores en Antropología Social, 2005.

Rodríguez, Ralph E. *Brown Gumshoes: Detective Fiction and the Search for Chicana/o Identity*. Austin: University of Texas Press, 2005.

Rodríguez-Hernández, Raúl, and Claudia Schaefer. "*Cronos* and the Man of Science: Madness, Monstrosity, Mexico." *Revista de Estudios Hispánicos* 33, no. 1 (1999): 85–108.

———. "Do *Cybraceros* Dream of a Good Night's Sleep?" In *Apocalyptic Chic: Visions of the Apocalypse and Post-Apocalypse in Literature and Visual Arts*, edited by Barbara Brodman and James E. Doan, 149–64. Lanham, MD: Rowman and Littlefield, 2017.

———. "Sublime Horror: Transparency, Melodrama, and the Mise-en-scene of Two Mexican Vampire Films." In *The Universal Vampire: Origins and Evolution of a Legend*, edited by Barbara Brodman and James E. Doan, 225–38. Madison, WI: Fairleigh Dickinson University Press, 2013.

Rogers, Michaela M. "Exploring the Domestic Abuse Narratives of Trans and Nonbinary People and the Role of Cisgenderism in Identity Abuse, Misgendering, and Pathologizing." *Violence against Women* 27, no. 12–13 (2020): 2187–207.

Rojas, Clara E. "The V-Day March in Mexico: Appropriation and Misuse of Local Women's Activism." In Gaspar de Alba and Guzmán, *Making a Killing*, 201–10.

Rojo, Pepe. "Border Technologies." *Review: Literature and Arts of the Americas* 48, no. 1 (2015): 6–14.

———. "Gray Noise." Translated by Andrea Bell. In Bell and Molina-Gavilán, *Cosmos Latinos*, 244–65.

———. "Ruido gris." Mexico City: Universidad Autónoma Metropolitana, 1996.

Romanell, Patrick. "Bergson in Mexico: A Tribute to José Vasconcelos." *Philosophy and Phenomenological Research* 21, no. 4 (1961): 501–13.

Rostas, Susana. "'Mexicanidad': The Resurgence of the Indian in Popular Mexican Nationalism." *Cambridge Journal of Anthropology* 23, no. 1 (2002): 20–38.

Rubio Salas, Rodolfo. "Características de la violencia de pareja en Chihuahua y algunas entidades fronterizas del norte de México." In Monárrez Fragoso et al., *Violencia contra las mujeres*, 275–334.

Rubóczki, Babett. "Environment and the Somatic Body in Cherríe Moraga's *Heroes and Saints* and Edwidge Danticat's *The Farming of Bones*." *Revista de Estudios Norteamericanos*, no. 25 (2021): 75–89.

Rueda, Amanda. "Nuevas condiciones de la internacionalización de los cines de América Latina y plataformas profesionales de festivales: El caso de Cine en Construcción." *Archivos de la Filmoteca*, no. 77 (2019): 59–78.

Rueda, Carolina. "The Everlasting *Sleep Dealer*: Alex Rivera's Visionary Mind and Fantasy Nightmares in Present Times." *Studies in Spanish & Latin American Cinemas* 14, no. 3 (2017): 333–48.

Rueda-Esquibel, Catriona. *With Her Machete in Her Hand: Reading Chicana Lesbians*. Austin: University of Texas Press, 2006.

Rusnak, Stacy. "Mexican Cinema in a Global Age: The Films of Guillermo Del Toro, Alfonso Cuarón, and Alejandro González Iñarritu." PhD diss., Georgia State University, 2010.

Russell, Diana E. H., and Roberta H. Harmes. *Femicide in Global Perspective*. London: Teacher's College Press, 2001.

Saad-Filho, Alfredo and Deborah Johnston. Introduction to Saad-Filho and Johnston, *Neoliberalism: A Critical Reader*, 1–6.

Saad-Filho, Alfredo, and Deborah Johnston, eds. *Neoliberalism: A Critical Reader*. London: Pluto Press, 2005.

Said, Edward. *Orientalism*. New York: Penguin, 2003.

Salinas, Cristóbal, Jr., and Adele Lozano. "Mapping and Recontextualizing the Evolution of the Term *Latinx*: An Environmental Scanning in Higher Education." *Journal of Latinos and Education* 18, no. 4 (2019): 302–15.

Samuel, Alexandra Whitney. "Hacktivism and the Future of Political Participation." PhD diss., Harvard University, 2004.

Sánchez, Rosaura. "Rudolfo Anaya's Historical Memory." In Cantú, *The Forked Juniper*, 221–40.

Sánchez, Rosaura, and Beatrice Pita. *Keep Me Posted: Logins from Tomorrow*. Moorpark, CA: Floricanto Press, 2020.

———. *Lunar Braceros 2125-2148*. 2009. Moorpark, CA: Floricanto Press, 2019.

———. "Marxism, Materialism, and Latino/a Literature: What Is at Stake?" In *Dialectical Imaginaries: Materialist Approaches to U.S. Latino/a Literature in the Age of Neoliberalism*, edited by Marcial González and Carlos Gallego, 21–46. Ann Arbor: University of Michigan Press, 2018.

Sánchez Díaz, Sergio Guadalupe. *Diálogos desde la subalternidad, la resistencia y la resiliencia. Cultura obrera en las maquiladoras de Ciudad Juárez*. Mexico City: Universidad Autónoma Metropolitana, 2011.

Sánchez-Pardo González, Esther. "The Desire Called Utopia: Re-Imagining Collectivity in Moraga and Castillo." *Estudios Ingleses de la Universidad Complutense*, no. 17 (2009): 95–114.

Sánchez Prado, Ignacio M. "*Amores perros*: Exotic Violence and Neoliberal Fear." Translated by Kara N. Moranski. *Journal of Latin American Cultural Studies* 15, no. 1 (2006): 39–57.

———. "El mestizaje en el corazón de la utopía: *La raza cósmica* entre Aztlán y América Latina." *Revista Canadiense de Estudios Hispánicos* 33, no. 2 (2009): 381–404.

———. "Ending the World with Words: Bernardo Fernández (BEF) and the Institutionalization of Science Fiction in Mexico." In Ginway and Brown, *Latin American Science Fiction*, 111–32.

———. "Máquinas de precarización: Afectos y violencias de la cultura neoliberal." In Moraña and Valenzuela Arce, *Precariedades, exclusiones y emergencias*, 99–126.

———. "Monstruos neoliberales: Capitalismo y terror en *Cronos* y *Somos lo que hay*." In *Aproximaciones al cine de terror en Latinoamérica y el Caribe*, edited by Rosana Díaz-Zambrana and Patricia Tomé, 47–63. San Juan: Editorial Isla Negra, 2012.

———. "Prólogo." In Moraña and Sánchez Prado, *Heridas abiertas*, 23–29.

———. *Screening Neoliberalism: Transforming Mexican Cinema, 1988–2012*. Nashville, TN: Vanderbilt University Press, 2014.

Sánchez-Taylor, Joy Ann. "Science Fiction/Fantasy and the Representation of Ethnic Futurity." PhD diss., University of South Florida, 2014.

Sanders, Scott P. "Southwestern Gothic: Alienation, Integration, and Rebirth in the Works of Richard Shelton, Rudolfo Anaya, and Leslie Silko." *Weber Studies: An Interdisciplinary Humanities Journal* 4, no. 2 (1987). https://weberstudies.weber.edu/archive/archive%20A%20%20Vol.%201-10.3/Vol.%204.2/4.2sanders.htm.

Sandoval, Chela. "Forward: Unfinished Words: The Crossing of Gloria Anzaldúa." In *EntreMundos/AmongWorlds: New Perspectives on Gloria Anzaldúa*, edited by AnaLouise Keating, xiii–xvi. New York: Palgrave MacMillan, 2005.

———. *Methodology of the Oppressed*. Minneapolis: University of Minnesota Press, 2000.

Sasser, Kim Anderson. *Magical Realism and Cosmopolitanism: Strategizing Belonging*. New York: Palgrave MacMillan, 2014.

Saxe-Fernández, John. "Diseños imperials sobre México y América Latina." *Temas de Nuestra América* 25, no. 47 (2009): 101–14.

Scharrón-del Río, María and Alan A. Aja. "*Latinx*: Inclusive Language as Liberation Praxis." *Journal of Latinx Psychology* 8, no. 1 (2020): 7–20.

Schradie, Jen. *The Revolution that Wasn't: How Digital Activism Favors Conservatives*. Cambridge, MA: Harvard University Press, 2019.

Schreiber, Rebecca M. "The Undocumented Everyday: Migrant Rights and Visual Strategies in the Work of Alex Rivera." *Journal of American Studies* 50, no. 2 (2016): 305–27.

Schwab, William A. *Right to DREAM: Immigration Reform and America's Future*. Fayetteville: University of Arkansas Press, 2013.

Schweitzer, Ivy. "For Gloria Anzaldúa: Collecting America, Performing Friendship." *PMLA* 12, no. 1 (2006): 285–91.

Seed, David. *Science Fiction: A Very Short Introduction.* Oxford: Oxford University Press, 2011.

Segato, Rita Laura. "Territory, Sovereignty, and Crimes of the Second State: The Writing on the Body of Murdered Women." Translated by Sara Koopman. In Fregoso and Bejarano, *Terrorizing Women*, 70–92.

Segre, Erica. "'La desnacionalización de la pantalla': Mexican Cinema in the 1990s." In *Changing Reels: Latin American Cinema against the Odds*, edited by Rob Rix and Roberto Rodríguez-Saona, 33–59. Leeds: Trinity and All Saints University College, 1997.

Segura, Denise A., and Beatriz M. Pesquera. "Beyond Indifference and Antipathy: The Chicana Movement and Chicana Feminist Discourse." In Noriega et al., *The Chicano Studies Reader*, 358–74.

Serafin, Silvana. "Eu-topos/ou-topos: Utopías y futuro." *Oltreoceano-Rivista Sulle Migrazioni* no. 18 (2021): 11–19.

Šesnić, Jelena. "Dreams Deferred: The Concept of the US-Mexican Borderlands between the Global North and the Global South." *Americana: E-Journal of American Studies in Hungary* 7, no. 1 (2011). https://americanaejournal.hu/vol7no1/sesnic.

Shafer, Alexander P. "Queering Bodies: Aliens, Cyborgs, and Spacemen in Mexican and Argentine Science Fiction." PhD diss., University of California, Riverside, 2017.

Shaw, Deborah. *The Three Amigos: The Transnational Filmmaking of Guillermo del Toro, Alejando González Iñárritu, and Alfonso Cuarón.* Manchester: Manchester University Press, 2013.

Shea, Anne. "'Don't Let Them Make You Feel You Did a Crime': Immigration Law, Labor Rights, and Farmworker Testimony." *MELUS* 28, no. 1 (2003): 123–44.

Sierra, Marta. "*Memento Mori*: Photography and Narrative in Cristina Rivera Garza's *Nadie me verá llorar.*" In Ribas-Casasayas and Petersen, *Espectros*, 151–64.

Silver, Patricia. *Sunbelt Diaspora: Race, Class, and Latino Politics in Puerto Rican Orlando.* Austin: University of Texas Press, 2020.

Sim, Hyekyong. "Acting 'Like a Woman': South Korean Female Action Heroines." *Journal of Japanese and Korean Cinema* 12, no. 2 (2020): 110–23.

Sisk, Christina L. "Disembodied and Deportable Labor at the US Mexico-Border: Representations of the Mexican Body in Film." *Transmodernity* 3, no. 2 (2014): 41–58.

———. "Entre el Cha Cha Chá y el Estado: El cine nacional mexicano y sus arquetipos." *A Contracorriente* 8, no. 3 (2011): 163–82.

Slemon, Stephen. "Magic Realism as Postcolonial Discourse." In Zamora and Faris, *Magical Realism*, 407–26.

Smith, Peter H. *Talons of the Eagle: Latin America, the United States, and the World.* Oxford: Oxford University Press, 2008.

Sobchack, Vivian Carol. *Screening Space: The American Science Fiction Film.* New Brunswick, NJ: Rutgers University Press, 1997.

Solis Ybarra, Priscilla. *Writing the Goodlife: Mexican American Literature and the Environment*. Tucson: University of Arizona Press, 2016.

Sondergard, Sidney. "The Ambivalence of Creative Desire: Theogonic Myth and Monstrous Offspring." In Morehead, *Supernatural Cinema*, 93-111.

Sosa Riddell, Adaljiza. "Chicanas and El Movimiento." In Noriega et al., *The Chicano Studies Reader*, 336-44.

Sotelo, Susan Baker. *Chicano Detective Fiction: A Critical Study of Five Novelists*. Jefferson, NC: McFarland, 2005.

Soto Salazar, Isabella. "Ruta para la coproducción en Colombia." Senior thesis, Universidad Autónoma de Occidente, 2017.

Spencer, Grace C. "Her Body is a Battlefield: The Applicability of the Alien Tort Statute to Corporate Human Rights Abuses in Juarez, Mexico." *Gonzaga Law Review* 40, no. 3 (2004): 503-33.

Spitta, Silvia. "Of Brown Buffaloes, Cockroaches, and Others: *Mestizaje* North and South of the Río Bravo." *Revista de Estudios Hispánicos* 35, no. 2 (2001): 333-46.

Spivak, Gayatri Chakravorty. "Can the Subaltern Speak?" In *Marxism and the Interpretation of Culture*, edited by Lawrence Grossberg and Cary Nelson, 271-313. Urbana: University of Illinois Press, 1988.

Starrs, D. Bruno. "Keeping the Faith: Catholicism in *Dracula* and Its Adaptations." *Journal of Dracula Studies*, vol. 6, article 3 (2004): 1-7.

Stock, Anne Marie. "Authentically Mexican? *Mi querido Tom Mix* and *Cronos* Reframe Critical Questions." In *Mexico's Cinema: A Century of Film and Filmakers*, edited by Joanne Hershfield and David R. Maciel, 267-92. Wilmington, DE: Scholarly Resources Books, 2005.

Streeby, Shelley. "Speculative Archives: Histories of the Future of Education." *Pacific Coast Philology* 49, no. 1 (2014): 25-40.

Stuadt, Kathleen, and Howard Campbell. "The Other Side of the Ciudad Juárez Femicide Story." *ReVista: Harvard Review of Latin America* 7, no. 2 (2008): 17-19.

Stuadt, Kathleen, and Irasema Coronado. "Binational Civic Action for Accountability: Antiviolence Organizing in Ciudad Juárez / El Paso." In Gaspar de Alba and Guzmán, *Making a Killing*, 157-82.

Sudhinaraset, Pacharee. "The End of Innocence: Women of Color Literature, Utopia, and the Cultural Politics of U.S. Cold War Racial Liberalism." PhD diss., University of Washington, 2013.

Suppia, Alfredo. "Quando a realidade parece ficção, é hora de fazer mockumentary." *Ciência e Cultura* 65, no. 1 (2013): 60-63.

———. "Remote Exploitations: Alex Rivera's Materialist SF Cinema in the Age of Cognitive Capitalism." In *Red Alert: Marxist Approaches to Science Fiction Cinema*, edited by Ewa Mazierska and Alfredo Suppia, 202-28. Detroit, MI: Wayne State University Press, 2014.

Suppia, Alfredo, and Igor Oliveira. "Cibertíteres: Discurso marxista e a colisão entre o público e privado no cinema de Alex Rivera." *Ciberlegenda* 1, no. 26 (2012): 191-201.

Sussman, Herbert, and Gerhard Joseph. "Prefiguring the Posthuman: Dickens and Prosthesis." *Victorian Literature and Culture* 32, no. 2 (2004): 617–28.
Tabuenca Córdoba, María Socorro. "Ghost Dance in Ciudad Juárez at the End/Beginning of the Millennium." In Gaspar de Alba and Guzmán, *Making a Killing*, 95–119.
———. "Representations of Femicide in Border Cinema." In Corona and Domínguez-Ruvalcaba *Gender Violence*, 81–101.
Tarica, Estelle. "La biopolítica en contra de sí: Víctimas y contravíctimas en el México contemporáneo." In Moraña and Sánchez Prado, *Heridas abiertas*, 203–24.
Taylor, Claire. *Place and Politics in Latin American Digital Culture*. New York: Routledge, 2014.
Taylor, Claire, and Thea Pitman. *Latin American Identity in Online Cultural Production*. New York: Routledge, 2013.
Tekin, İnci Bilgin. *Myths of Oppression Revisited in Cherríe Moraga's and Liz Lochhead's Drama*. Stuggart: Ibidem-Verl, 2012.
Thomas, Elizabeth Arden. "Poisoning the Mother/Land: An Ecofeminist Dramaturgy in José Rivera's *Marisol* and Cherríe Moraga's *Heroes and Saints*." *Theatre History Studies*, no. 35 (2016): 143–60.
Thornton, Niamh. *Tastemakers and Tastemaking: Mexico and Curated Screen Violence*. Albany: State University of New York Press, 2020.
Tierney, Dolores. "Transnational Political Horror in *Cronos* (1993), *El espinazo del diablo* (2001), and *El laberinto del fauno* (2006)." In Davies, Shaw, and Tierney, *The Transnational Fantasies of Guillermo del Toro*, 161–82.
Tinajero, Araceli, and Brian J. Freeman, eds. *Technology and Culture in Twentieth-Century Mexico*. Tuscaloosa: University of Alabama Press, 2013.
Tobin, Stephen C. "Televisual Subjectivities in Pepe Rojo's Speculative Fiction from Mexico: 1996–2003." *Alambique* 4, no. 1 (2016): 1–18.
Tobin, Stephen C., and Libia Brenda. "Genre in Mexico and the Crazy, Joyful Adventure of the Anthology for the Mexicanx Initiative." *Latin American Literature Today* 8, no 12 (2018). http://www.latinamericanliteraturetoday.org/en/2018/november/genre-mexico-and-crazy-joyful-adventure-anthology-mexicanx-initiative-stephen-c-tobin.
Todorov, Tzvetan. *The Fantastic: A Structural Approach to a Literary Genre*. Translated by Richard Howard. Ithaca: Cornell University Press, 1975.
Tonn, Horst. "Imagining the Local and the Global in the Work of Rudolfo A. Anaya." In Cantú, *The Forked Juniper*, 241–52.
Tornero, Angélica. "Discursos híbridos y perspectiva en *2666* de Roberto Bolaño y en *Backyard/El traspatio* de Carlos Carrera." *Cuaderno Internacional de Estudios Humanísticos y Literatura*, no. 20 (2013): 25–37.
———. "La vida dañada: Documentos de cultura sobre Ciudad Juárez." *Elemento*, no. 92 (2013): 31–38.
Torres-Saillant, Silvio. "Inventing the Race: Latinos and the Ethnoracial Pentagon." *Latino Studies* 1, no. 1 (2003): 123–51.

Touami, Sabrina. "Vehicules de Livraison Autonomes: Une Solution pour L'avenir?" Master's thesis, Université Gustave Eiffel, 2020. https://www.lvmt.fr/wp-content/uploads/2020/11/TOUAMI-m%C3%A9moire-version-chaire.pdf.

Tourney, Christopher P. "The Moral Character of Mad Scientists: A Cultural Critique of Science." *Science, Technology, and Human Values* 17, no. 4 (1992): 411–37.

Trigo, Beatriz. "*Cronos* by Guillermo del Toro." *Chasqui: Revista de Literatura Latinoamericana* 30, no. 1 (2001): 176–78.

Trujillo-Pagán, Nicole. "Crossed out by LatinX: Gender Neutrality and Genderblind Sexism." *Latino Studies* 16, no. 3 (2018): 396–406.

Ulibarri, Kristy L. "Speculating Latina Radicalism: Labour and Motherhood in *Lunar Braceros 2125-2148*." *Feminist Review*, no. 116 (2017): 85–100.

Utley, Robert M. *Wanted: The Outlaw Lives of Billy the Kid and Ned Kelly*. New Haven, CT: Yale University Press, 2015.

Valdez, Avelardo, and Charles D. Kaplan. "Deconstructing US Marijuana Prohibition Policies in the Early Twentieth Century: An Intersectional Theoretical Approach." *Aztlán: A Journal of Chicano Studies* 44, no. 1 (2019): 111–40.

Valdez, Hugo. "Los cinefotógrafos creadores de la imagen fílmica en México." *Varia*, no. 20 (2012): 56–69.

Valencia, Sayak. *Gore Capitalism*. Translated by John Pluecker. South Pasadena: Semiotext(e), 2018.

Valencia, Sayak, and Sonia Herrera Sánchez. "From Cinema to the *Live* Regime: Pedagogies of Cruelty and Social Anesthesia in Two Latin American Movies." In *Gender-Based Violence in Latin American and Iberian Cinemas*, edited by Rebeca Maseda García, María José Gámez Fuentes, and Barbara Zecchi, 176–90. New York: Routledge, 2020.

———. "Pornomiseria, violencia machista y mirada colonial en los filmes *Backyard: El traspatio* y *La mujer del animal*." *Anclajes* 34, no. 3 (2020): 7–27.

Valenzuela Arce, José Manuel. "Ciudad Juárez: La frontera más bonita." *Alternativas*, no. 3 (2014): 1–16.

———. 2014. "El *cruising* de la muerte. Biocultura: Biopolíticas, biorresistencias y bioproxemias." In Moraña and Sánchez Prado, *Heridas abiertas*, 165–82.

Valenzuela Arce, José Manuel, and Mabel Moraña. "Vidas carenciadas, y resistencias sociales." In Moraña and Valenzuela Arce, *Precariedades, exclusiones y emergencias*, 15–24.

Valenzuela Arce, José Manuel, and Mabel Moraña. "Entrada: Precariedad y exclusión social: Dispositivos estructurantes del proyecto neoliberal." In Moraña and Valenzuela Arce, *Precariedades, exclusiones y emergencias*, 11–14.

Valverde, Estela. "New Latin American Film: Addressing the Negative Culturescapes and Glocalising Transnational Problems." *Crítica Contemporánea: Revista de Teoría Política*, no. 2 (2012): 135–45.

Valverde Gefaell, Clara. *De la necropolítica neoliberal, a la empatía radical: Violencia discreta, cuerpos excluidos y repolitización*. Madrid: Icaria, 2016.

Vanden Berg, Kristine. *Narcos y sicaros en la ciudad letrada*. Valencia: Albatros, 2019.

Van Hecke, An. "Hybrid Voices in the Borderlands: Translation and Reconstruction of Mexican Images in Rudolfo Anaya." *Confluencia: Revista Hispánica de Cultura y Literatura* 29, no. 2 (2014): 61–69.

Varela Huerta, Amarela, ed. *Necropolítica y migración en la frontera vertical mexicana: Un ejercicio de conocimiento situado*. Mexico City: UNAM, 2020.

Vargas, Arturo. "Movilidades posapocalípticas: Un nuevo acercamiento a la película de la migración irregular." *Nomenclatura: Aproximaciones a los estudios hispánicos*, no. 2, article 1 (2012): 1–21. https://uknowledge.uky.edu/cgi/viewcontent.cgi?article=1015&context=naeh.

Vargas Amésquita, Alicia. "El cuerpo femenino como metáfora del territorio-nación en *Backyard: El traspatio* de Carlos Carrera." In *Mexican Transnational Cinema and Literature*, edited by Maricruz Castro Ricalde, Mauricio Calderón Díaz, and James Ramsey, 271–86. New York: Peter Lang, 2017.

Varona, Alfonso. "Entrevista a Sabina Berman." *Latin American Theatre Review* 47, no. 1 (2013): 133–44.

Vasconcelos, José. *La raza cósmica*. 5th ed. Mexico City: Ediciones Porrúa, 2010.

———. *El monismo estético*. Mexico City: Tip Murguía, 1918.

Vázquez Moyers, Alonso, and Germán Espino Sánchez. "La producción discursiva en la guerra contra el narcotráfico en el sexenio de Calderón: En busca de la legitimidad perdida." *Discurso y Sociedad* 9, no. 4 (2015): 493–518.

Velasco, Juan. "The X in Race and Gender: Rethinking Chicano/a Cultural Production through the Paradigms of Xicanisma and Me(x)icanness." In Chabram-Dernersesian, *The Chicana/o Cultural Studies Reader*, 203–10.

Vélez-Ibáñez, Carlos G. Prólogo to *Tradición, identidad, mito y metáfora: Mexicanos y chicanos en California*, by Mariángela Rodríguez. Mexico City: Centro de Investigaciones y Estudios Superiores en Antropología Social, 5–8.

Villalobos, Elizabeth. "Asesinos fronterizos: *Performance* de transgresión de los derechos humanos en el imaginario social del norte y sur de México." PhD diss., University of Kansas, 2014.

Villalobos-Ruminott, Sergio. "Biopolítica y soberanía: Notas sobre la ambigüedad del corpus literario." In Moraña and Sánchez Prado, *Heridas abiertas*, 47–64.

Villazana, Libia. "Transnational Virtual Mobility as a Reification of Deployment of Power: Exploring Transnational Processes in the Film *Sleep Dealer*." *Transnational Cinemas* 4, no. 2 (2013): 217–30.

Volk, Steven S., and Marian E. Schlotterbeck. "Gender, Order, and Femicide: Reading the Popular Culture of Murder in Ciudad Juárez." In Noriega et al., *The Chicano Studies Reader*, 610–38.

Volpi, Jorge. *El insomnio de Bolívar: Cuatro consideraciones intempestivas sobre América Latina en el siglo XXI*. Mexico City: Random House Mondadori, 2009.

Wald, Sarah D. "Farmworker Activism." In *The Cambridge Companion to Literature and Food*, edited by J. Michelle Coghlan, 197–214. Cambridge: Cambridge University Press, 2020.

Waldkirch, Andreas. "The Effects of Foreign Direct Investment in Mexico since NAFTA." *World Economy* 33, no. 5 (2010): 710–45.

Waldron, John. "Introduction: Culture Monopolies and Criticism: A Way Out?" *Discourse* 26, no. 1–2 (2004): 5–25.

Ward, Cynthia. "*Cortez on Jupiter*, by Ernest Hogan." *Cascadia Subduction Zone* 5, no. 2 (2015): 12–13.

Wark, McKenzie. *Gamer Theory*. Cambridge, MA: Harvard University Press, 2007.

Warnes, Christopher. *Magical Realism and the Postcolonial Novel: Between Faith and Irreverence*. New York: Palgrave MacMillan, 2009.

Watt, Peter, and Roberto Zepeda. *Drug War Mexico: Politics, Neoliberalism and Violence in the New Narcoeconomy*. London: Zed Books, 2012.

Weaver, Angel D., A. Dana Ménard, Christine Cabrera, and Angela Taylor. "Embodying the Moral Code? Thirty Years of Final Girls in Slasher Films." *Psychology of Popular Media Culture* 4, no. 1 (2015): 31–46.

Wehbe Herrera, Aishih. "Performing Masculinity, Performing the Self: Rudolfo Anaya's *Bless Me, Ultima* and *Heart of Aztlan*." *Revista Canaria de Estudios Ingleses*, no. 66 (2013): 111–23.

Weil, Simone. *Gravity and Grace*. Translated by Arthur Wills. New York: Routledge, 2004.

Wellman, Ashley, Michele Bisaccia Meitl, and Patrick Kinkade. "Lady and the Vamp: Roles, Sexualization, and Brutalization of Women in Slasher Films." *Sexuality and Culture* 25, no. 2 (2021): 660–79.

Wells, Sarah Ann. "The Scar and the Node: Border Science Fiction and the Mise-en-scène of Globalized Labor." *Global South* 8, no. 1 (2014): 69–90.

West, Alexandra. "Where the Wild Things Are: Monsters and Children." In Morehead, *Supernatural Cinema*, 130–45.

White, Eric. "Insects and Automata in Hoffmann, Balzac, Carter, and del Toro." *Journal of the Fantastic in the Arts* 19, no. 3 (2008): 363–78.

Williams, Gareth. *The Mexican Exception: Sovereignty, Police, and Democracy*. New York: Palgrave MacMillan, 2011.

Wolf, Sonja, and Gonzalo Celorio Morayta. "La guerra de México contra el narcotráfico y la iniciativa Mérida: Piedras angulares en la búsqueda de legitimidad." *Foro Internacional* 51, no. 4 (2011): 669–714.

Wolfenzon, Carolyn. *Nuevos fantasmas recorren México: Lo espectral en la literatura mexicana del siglo XXI*. Madrid: Iberoamericana, 2020.

Woodruff, Christopher, and Rene Zenteno. "Migration Networks and Microenterprises in Mexico." *Journal of Development Economics* 82, no. 2 (2007): 509–28.

Workman, Amber. "The Uses and Limits of Ethnic Humor and New Media in *¡Ask a Mexican!*" In Chacón, *Online Activism in Latin America*, 151–60.

Worthen, W. B. "Staging América: The Subject of History in Chicano/a Theatre." *Theatre Journal* 49, no. 2 (1997): 101–20.

Wray, Stefan. "On Electronic Civil Disobedience." *Peace Review* 11, no. 1 (1999): 107–11.

Wright, Melissa. "El lucro, la democracia y la mujer pública: Estableciendo las conexiones." In Monárrez Fragoso and Tabuenca Córdoba, *Bordeando la violencia*, 49–82.

———. "The Dialectics of Still Life: Murder, Women, and the Maquiladoras." *Public Culture* 11, no. 3 (1999): 453–73.

Wyble, Sarah. "The Undermining of Queer and Feminist Agendas in Julio Hernández Cordón's *Cómprame un revólver*." Paper presented at the Southeast Conference of Latin American Studies, Charlotte, NC, March 2022.

Yankelevich, Pablo. *Los otros: Raza, normas y corrupción en la gestión de la extranjería en México, 1900–1950*. Mexico City: Colegio de México, 2019.

Yarbro-Bejarano, Yvonne. "Chicana Literature from a Chicana Feminist Perspective." *Americas Review* 15, no. 3–4 (1987): 139–45.

———. *The Wounded Heart: Writing on Cherríe Moraga*. Austin: University of Texas Press, 2001.

Yehya, Naief. *Drone Visions: A Brief Cyberpunk History of Killing Machines*. San Diego, CA: Hyperbole Books, 2020.

———. "Revolt, Confusion, and Cult of the Trivial in Mexican Cyberculture." In Tinajero and Freeman, *Technology and Culture*, 124–40.

Zahniser, Steven and William Coyle. *US-Mexico Corn Trade during the NAFTA Era: New Twists on an Old Story*. US Department of Agriculture, Economic Research Service, FDS-04D-01, May 2004. https://www.ers.usda.gov/webdocs/outlooks/36451/49338_fds04d01.pdf?v=374.2.

Zamora, Lois Parkinson, and Wendy B. Faris, eds. *Magical Realism: Theory, History, Community*. Durham, NC: Duke University Press, 1995.

Zavala, Oswaldo. *Los cárteles no existen: Narcotráfico y cultura en México*. Mexico City: Malpaso, 2018.

Zavala, Pablo M. "La producción antifeminicidista mexicana: Autoría, representación y feminismo en la frontera juarense." *Chasqui* 45, no. 2 (2016): 57–69.

Zermeño Vargas, Carlos Gerardo. "Fantasticidad, encuentros con lo monstruoso e identidades inestables en dos novelas mexicanas: Patricia Laurent Kullick y Guadalupe Nettel." PhD diss., Instituto Tecnologico y Estudios Superiores de Monterrey, 2017. https://repositorio.tec.mx/ortec/bitstream/handle/11285/632777/CZ_Tesis.pdf.

Zulkarnain, Iskandar. "Polyspatial Resistance for the Sake of the 'Real' Subalterns: Electronic Civil Disobedience as a Form of Hacktivism." In *On and Off the Page: Mapping Place in Text and Culture*, edited by M. B. Hackler and Ari J. Adipurwawidjana, 219–42. Cambridge: Cambridge Scholars Press, 2009.

Zylinska, Joanna. "'The Future . . . Is Monstrous': Prosthetics as Ethics." In *The Cyborg Experiments: The Extensions of the Body in the Media Age*, edited by Joanna Zylinska, 214–36. London: Continuum, 2002.

# Index

Page numbers in *italic* indicate figures.

activism, 49, 114, 125, 147; antifeminicide, 172; Chicana, 186; cyborg, 69, 97; digital, 196; environmental, 219n29; online, 69, 192, 194, 197; political, 110; robosacer, 26, 28, 50, 63, 121–23, 150, 161, 193; social, 23, 47, 192; virtual, 193; women's, 249n61
Afrofuturism, 20–21, 68, 200
Agamben, Giorgio, 2–3, 9, 13, 15, 106, 120, 165, 180; criticism of, 211n85; on *homo sacer*, 6, 26–27, 34, 36, 59, 72, 103, 115; on *iustitium*, 61; on state of exception, 171. *See also bios; zoē*
Anaya, Rudolfo, 29, 160–61, 165, 176–78, 184, 189, 261n84, 261n91, 262n98–99, 265n147; on Aztlán, 262n96; ChupaCabra trilogy, 160, 162–66, 176–89, 257nn19–20, 257n22; detective literature of, 181–82; interest in Jung, 181, 264n117; magical realism of, 261n83
Anzaldúa, Gloria, 24–26, 37, 83, 98, 177–78; *Borderlands/La frontera*, 184; "Coatlicue State," 6; desconocimientos, 104; spiritual mestizaje, 36. *See also* mestiza/x consciousness
asexuality, 142–43
Aztlán, 22–23, 86, 119, 161, 165, 262n96; cybernetic, 84–85; New Mexico as spiritual center of, 179

Bachran, Daoine S., 79, 81
*Backyard/El traspatio* (Carrera and Berman), 125–28, 130–45, 156, 245n9, 249n51, 251n93, 251n95; slasher aesthetic and, 28, 131, 136–37, 247n33; technology and, 245n5
bare life, 14, 27, 29, 33–34, 156; in *Backyard/El traspatio* (Carrera and Berman), 132–34, 145; in ChupaCabra trilogy (Anaya), 180, 188–89; *Ciudad desnuda* and, 72–73; in *Cómprame un revolver* (Hernández Cordón), 165, 167, 169; in *Cronos* (del Toro), 55, 59, 61; in *Heroes and Saints* (Moraga), 42, 45; in *Lunar Braceros 2125-2148* (Sánchez and Pita), 114, 121–22; in "Ruido gris" (Rojo), 71, 76; in *Sleep Dealer* (Rivera), 96, 99, 105–7, 110–11; in *Smoking Mirror Blues* (Hogan), 84
Barrera, Cordelia E. 104–5

Bell, Andrea, 66, 73, 77
Berman, Sabrina, 126–27, 129–31, 133, 135–45, 156, 245n9, 249n51, 251n95. *See also Backyard/El traspatio*
biopolitics, 6, 10, 13–15, 106, 151, 169–70; body and, 8; of drug war, 161, 176; of memory, 108; race and, 212n93; right-wing, 200; "Soñarán en el jardín" (Damián Miravete) and, 28; technology and, 192
biopower, 2, 13, 94, 170
*bios*, 2, 8–14, 16, 34–35, 61, 63, 94; activism and, 194; as Aristotelean good life, 209n55; *Ciudad desnuda* and, 72; in *Cómprame un revolver* (Hernández Cordón), 174–75; feminicide and, 130; Global North's separation of *zoē* from, 97; immunological programs and, 147; in *Lunar Braceros 2125–2148* (Sánchez and Pita), 121; in *Sleep Dealer* (Rivera), 101; in *Smoking Mirror Blues* (Hogan), 84–85; in "Soñarán en el jardín" (Damián Miravete), 153–54; technological hegemony of, 70; trials as civil rituals for, 120; weapons and, 164–65, 172
borders, 3, 96, 116; bodies as, 109; cyberspace and, 99, 103; internal, 106–7; NAFTA and, 16; necroliberalism and, 12; politics of, 13; virtual, 100
Braidotti, Rosi, 10, 152
Butler, Octavia E., 24, 216n161

Calderón, Felipe, 15, 161, 256nn13–14
Calvo-Quirós, William A., 178–79, 181, 183
capital, 7, 52, 110, 141, 180, 185; accruement of, 12, 15, 113; drug trade and, 161, 170; global, 6, 18, 96, 100–101, 105, 108; necroliberal, 94, 183; transnational, 26, 62, 102, 107
capitalism, 27, 39, 63, 77–78, 94, 120; in *Cronos* (del Toro), 52–53; dehumanizing ideologies of, 42; excesses of, 25; global, 6, 71, 110–11, 241n125; gore, 12, 211n81; industrialized, 22; international, 38; market-based, 2; necroliberal, 33, 51, 60, 96, 98; necropolitical, 12, 211n81; state, 117; technology and, 69; transnational, 56; US, 18, 111
Carrera, Carlos, 129–33, 135–38, 142–45, 156; Barrio Terrazas and, 249n57. *See also Backyard/El traspatio*
catharsis, 46, 141–42, 144, 169–70, 176
Catholic Church, 47–48, 200, 223n76, 268n33
Catholicism, 35, 181; folk, 26; institutionalized, 49; popular, 166; traditional, 36, 46
Chacón, Mario A., 114–15, *117*. *See also Lunar Braceros 2125–2148*
Chávez, César, 36, 40, 219n29
Chicanismo, 86, 119
Chicano Movement (El Movimiento), 5, 17, 86, 118–19, 233n85, 243n168
*chupacabras*, 179–80
cinema, 196; Central American, 168 (*see also* Hernández Cordón, Julio); commercial, 145, 156, 199; Hollywood, 53–54, 237n44; horror, 38; Latin American, 167; lucha libre, 62; maquiladora, 251n103; Mexican, 51–52, 199; neoliberal, 199; slasher, 142, *143*; South Korean, 268n29; vampire, 53
citizenship, 2–3, 51, 113, 167; cultural, 9; prostheses of, 29, 164, 169, 172, 175–76, 189, 198; rights, 193

*Ciudad desnuda*, 71–73
Ciudad Juárez, 16, 125, 133–34, 174, 244n1; extralegal activities in, 249n56; maquiladora industry of, 123, 246n22; women's activism in, 249n61
Clover, Carol, 136, 144
coloniality, 13, 211n85; of power, 69
corruption, 107, 134, 138; police, 251n95
COVID-19, 1–3, 205n20
*Cronos* (del Toro), 26–27, 33–38, 51–63, 226n136; filming of, 217n1; funding of, 224n100
cybernetics, 112, 114, 183
cyberpunk, 6, 25, 68, 78, 89
cyberspace, 28, 65, 67–68, 70, 79, 86, 110, 113–14; borders and, 99, 103; postcolonial subject positions and, 8
cyborg identity, 7–9, 35, 37, 41, 71, 105, 133, 167; mestizaje and, 216n158
cyborgs, 2, 8, 10, 16, 42, 55, 97, 111, 152; low-tech, 164; medicalized, 226n133; resistant, 89, 196; secularly holy, 27, 36
cyborg subjectivity, 8–11, 14, 41, 63, 116, 177; anti-cyborg subjectivity, 169; biopolitics and, 200; in *Cronos* (del Toro), 55; dehumanizing potential of, 108; illegibility and, 218n11; in *Lunar Braceros 2125–2148* (Sánchez and Pita), 114; revolutionary potential of, 100; technology and, 105; weapons and, 29

Damián Miravete, Gabriela, 126, 129–30, 145, 156; "Soñarán en el jardín," 125, 128, 130, 244n1
Davies, Ann, 52, 55–56
Day, Stuart A., 134, 136
death, 1, 13, 45, 50, 65, 68–69, 126, 153, 159; in *Cronos* (del Toro), 62;
economies of, 178; maquiladora work and, 16; Mexican, 53; in "Ruido gris" (Rojo), 77–78; technology and, 146. *See also* markets of death
de la Reguera, Ana, 127, 142, 251n103
del Campo Ramírez, Elsa, 81–82, 228n6, 232n79
del Toro, Guillermo, 26, 33, 39, 51–54, 56–57, 60, 62, 224n98; cinema of, 38, 58, 228n159. *See also Cronos* (del Toro)
democracy, 196; electoral, 15, 19, 33; radical, 110
desaparecidas, 125, 247n29; *Backyard/ El traspatio* (Carrera and Berman) and, 130–31, 136, 140–41, 143–45, 156; "Soñarán en el jardín" (Damián Miravete) and, 128, 145–46, 151–55. *See also* feminicide (*feminicidio*)
diaspora, 116; Mexican, 4, 22
Domínguez, Ricardo, 11, 97, 193
drug trafficking, 15, 29, 161, 179, 189, 256n14
drug violence, 26, 159, 168, 170, 176
drug war, 29, 159–61, 165–66, 168, 176–79, 189
Durán, María J., 43, 45
dystopian fictions, 17, 20–22, 25, 191, 196; Chicanx, 4, 6–7, 10, 29; Mexican, 4, 6–7, 10–11, 19, 29, 202. *See also* cyberpunk

Electronic Disturbance Theater (EDT), 11, 97
Eljaiek-Rodríguez, Gabriel, 38, 55
embodiment, 8, 48–49, 85–87, 114, 169
Emmelhainz, Irmgard, 12, 19, 25
Esch, Sophie, 29, 164, 171, 176
Esposito, Roberto, 15, 147
ethics of representation: feminicide and, 28, 125, 128; in "Soñarán en

ethics of representation (*continued*)
el jardín" (Damián Miravetes), 145, 156
ethnicity, 7, 14

fantasy (genre), 21, 37, 121; feminist, 146
femicide, 132, 135, 246n23, 246n25; machine, 129, 156
feminicide (*feminicidio*), 125–32, 134–37, 141–42, 146, 149–56, 246nn24–25, 250n70, 252n116; Amnesty International and, 246n21; Chicanx studies and, 245n3; drug cartels and, 174, 259n66; ethics of representation and, 28, 125, 128, 145; Final Girl trope and, 144; immunization and, 245n11; machine, 138; NAFTA and, 123, 132; names of victims and, 172; robo-sacer activism and, 26; slasher aesthetic and, 247n33; state sovereignty and, 253n127; TelMex and, 254n151. See also *Backyard/El traspatio* (Carrera and Berman); Damián Miravete, Gabriela: "Soñarán en el jardín"
feminism: Chicana, 5, 23, 186; ecofeminism, 42; white, 23
Fernández L'Hoeste, Héctor, 73, 75
Final Girl trope, 142–44, 251n101
Foucault, Michel, 2, 13, 116. See also biopolitics
futurity, 25, 98

García, Hernán Manuel, 73, 97–98, 100, 110
gender, 5, 8, 79, 186, 221n38, 263n100; discrimination, 129; drug war and, 168; dynamics, 128; fluidity 162, 173; identity, 172, 174, 260n79; race and, 23; robo sacer and, 14; roles, 48, 132; violence, 85, 126, 131, 150–51, 153, 155

Ginway, M. Elizabeth, 21, 68, 75, 153
Global North, 8, 51, 69, 96–97, 108, 123, 201
Global South, 51, 69, 96, 108, 195, 201, 210n69
González Rodríguez, Sergio, 7, 129, 149, 156
Greater Mexico, 14, 25, 83, 85, 191, 201; cyberspace and, 79; dystopian fictions of, 4, 6, 19, 29; feminicide in and throughout, 126; ne(cr)oliberalism and, 39; racial hybridity and, 22

hacktivism, 97, 113, 116–17, 120, 123; Chicanx, 119; robo-sacer, 244n191
Haraway, Donna, 8, 10, 14, 55, 151–52, 164, 169, 176–77, 208n51; cyborg activism and, 69, 97; Cyborg Manifesto, 24, 41; pleasurably tight couplings, 54, 75, 86. See also cyborgs
hauntology, 148–49
Hayles, N. Katherine, 86–87, 103, 139, 146, 169
Henry, Brittany, 113, 122
Hernández Cordón, Julio, 165–74, 176, 189, 258n38; *Cómprame un revolver*, 29, 160–62, 166–76, 198, 258n42, 260n77
*Heroes and Saints* (Moraga), 26–27, 33–43, 46–50, 63; as nationalist play, 221n46
Herrera Sánchez, Sonia, 133, 137, 140
Hind, Emily, 134, 137, 142
Hogan, Ernest, 27, 66–70, 79, 81–85, 87–89, 206n28, 229n7, 229n11, 232n64; aesthetic of, 82, 232n70; *High Aztech*, 66, 79; *Smoking Mirror Blues*, 27, 64–66, 68–69, 79–89, 198, 233n103
homophobia, 24, 73
*homo sacer*, 2–3, 6, 14–15, 26–27, 34, 63–64, 87, 147, 153; *Backyard/El*

*traspatio* (Carrera and Berman) and, 137; biopolitics, 13; class, 174, 181; expendability of, 63, 71; hybrid subjectivities and, 10; migrant children as, 45; NAFTA and, 72; potential migrants as, 16; of Roman Empire, 103; sacrifice and, 36; sanctity of, 72; women as, 151
horror (genre), 20-21, 37, 52, 131, 143, 201, 214n127; Gothic, 37-38, 63. *See also* Final Girl trope; slasher films (genre)
Huerta, Dolores, 40, 219n29
humanism, 20, 200; liberal, 87. *See also* posthuman, the; posthumanism
hybridity, 63, 103; racial, 22, 24; technological, 24, 41, 57

identity, 5, 98, 177; Chicanx, 86, 198; gender, 172, 260n79; mestizo, 178; Mexican, 51; national, 36; robo-sacer, 6, 54, 194. *See also* cyborg identity
ideology, 14, 19-20, 103
immigrants, 2, 9, 113, 196; 1.5 generation, 193; Indigenous, 133; Mexican, 198; in Mexico, 227n152; undocumented, 268n31; xenophobia toward, 59, 93
immunization, 147-48, 155, 245n11
impunity, 129, 140

Johnson, David E., 149, 172
Jung, Carl G., 83, 181, 232n79, 264n117

Kantaris, Geoffrey, 53, 55
Kingsley, Anna, 133, 136, 250n75

labor, 6-7, 93-96, 99, 180, 195; conditions, 26; in *Cronos* (del Toro), 52, 60; de-unionization of, 229n16; exploitation, 113, 116; gender and, 241n105; maquiladora,

16; NAFTA and, 16, 52, 56, 89, 105-6; necroliberal state and, 27; politics, 122; in "Ruido gris" (Rojo), 73; technology and, 194; women and, 133. *See also Lunar Braceros 2125-2148* (Sánchez and Pita); maquiladoras; *Sleep Dealer* (Rivera)
Lamadrid, Enrique, 178-79
López, Marissa K., 4-5, 7, 111, 114
López-Lozano, Miguel, 17, 22
López Obrador, Andrés Manuel, 3, 17, 205n21
*Lunar Braceros 2125-2148* (Sánchez and Pita), 27, 89, 94-98, 112-23, 198, 241nn124-25, 244nn188-89

machismo, 23, 84, 128, 150, 178
magical realism, 165-67, 173-76, 189, 214n127, 215n137, 218n13; science fiction (SF) and, 20-21, 29, 37-39, 63, 165, 176, 201. *See also* Anaya, Rudolfo: ChupaCabra trilogy; *Heroes and Saints* (Moraga); Hernández Cordón, Julio: *Cómprame un revolver*
Manzanas Calvo, Ana María, 104, 108, 115, 122
maquiladora economy, 129-30, 239n81
maquiladora industry, 123, 129, 134, 140, 145. *See also* feminicide (*feminicidio*)
maquiladoras, 56, 106-7, 125, 127-30, 133-34, 138, 246n16, 246n22. *See also Backyard/El traspatio* (Carrera and Berman); feminicide (*feminicidio*); *Sleep Dealer* (Rivera); workers
Marez, Curtis, 96, 100, 216n161
markets of death, 80, 89, 145, 185, 192, 195; capitalism and, 33; necroliberal, 12, 50, 66, 87; neoliberalism and, 14; televisual, 102
Martínez-Raguso, Michael, 102-3
Marx, Karl, 52, 108, 179, 240n92

Mbembe, Achille, 12–14, 20–21, 69, 96, 200
McLuhan, Marshall, 139–40
mediasphere, 65, 67, 71, 79, 81–82, 84–86, 88–89, 232n64; televisual technologies of, 70
mestizaje, 17, 22, 24, 82–83, 86, 184; cyborg identity and, 216n158; cyborg theory and, 216n159; radical, 9–10, 177–78; spiritual, 36–37, 63
mestiza/x consciousness, 9, 24–25, 119, 177–78, 182, 189
#MeToo, 151, 197
Mexican Miracle, 56, 227n136
Mexican Revolution, 14, 22
misogyny, 150; in Chicano Movement, 233n85
modernity, 20–21, 37, 45, 122, 126, 148, 152, 180; antimodern, 184; Mexican, 15–16, 18, 111
Molina-Gavilán, Yolanda, 66, 73
Moraga, Cherríe, 23, 26, 38–41, 47–50, 219n27; queer sexualities and, 223n76. *See also Heroes and Saints* (Moraga)
Moraña, Mabel, 52, 57, 130, 180
More, Thomas, 17, 121, 213n114
multiculturalism, 5, 82

Namaste, Nina, 133, 137
necroliberalism, 12–14, 53, 57, 78, 189; cybernetic, 71; drug war and, 176. *See also under* capitalism
necropolitics, 12–14, 69, 211n81, 211n88, 255n1
neoliberalism, 5–7, 13–14, 33, 63, 71, 100, 131, 138, 192; feminicide and, 135; NAFTA and, 15, 19, 39
neoliberalization, 52, 71, 133, 139
#NiUnaMás, 126, 151, 197
North America Free Trade Agreement (NAFTA), 14–15, 19, 25–27, 29, 39, 69, 196; *Backyard/El traspatio* (Carrera and Berman) and, 156; *Cronos* (del Toro) and, 51–52, 56, 58; economies of death and, 89; feminicide and, 132; human disposability and, 123; implementation of, 37, 65, 68, 71–72, 97; inflation and, 179; maquiladoras and, 129–30, 246n16; migration and, 4, 16; passage of, 89, 93, 105–6; posthumanist criticisms of, 63; as utopia, 17–18

Obama, Barack, 161, 193
Olguín, B. V., 100, 111, 120–21, 214n135

Partido Revolucionario Institucional (PRI), 15, 71
Patrick, Dan, 1–2
*Peppermint* (Morel), 197–200, 268n29
Pérez-Torres, Rafael, 23, 85
performativity, 8, 48, 57, 142
Pita, Beatrice, 27–28, 89, 94, 96–98, 112, 117–19, 123; Chicano Movement (El Movimiento) and, 243n168. *See also Lunar Braceros 2125-2148* (Sánchez and Pita)
Pitman, Thea, 24, 98, 192
Pitts, Andrea J., 177, 184
polyspatiality, 11, 110, 118
polyspatial solidarity, 11–12, 88, 97, 99, 110, 193
posthuman, the, 87, 103, 114, 148, 183–84; McLuhan and, 139
posthumanism, 7, 42, 54, 87, 148
prosthesis, 129, 169, 177; firearms and, 172, 175–76, 187, 198

race, 5, 7–8, 14, 23, 207n35, 263n100; biopolitics and, 212n93; discrimination, 129; in *Heroes and Saints* (Moraga), 221n38; in *Lunar Braceros 2125-2148*, 119; in *Smoking Mirror Blues* (Hogan), 79, 83

racism, 14, 24, 26, 94, 113, 184;
  environmental, 43, 46
Ramírez, Catherine S., 9, 20
Reagan, Ronald, 39, 219n24
resistance, 4, 27, 34, 51, 117, 129, 174, 201, 245n5; armed, 29, 160–62, 164–65, 244n191; Chicanx, 177; cyborg, 57, 83, 103, 105, 164, 183, 200, 208n51; against necroliberal capitalism, 33; against neoliberalism, 138; polyspatial, 11, 110, 126–27, 139, 151; science fiction and, 20; technology and, 191; violent, 172. *See also* robo-sacer resistance
Rieder, John, 19–20, 196
Rivera, Alex, 28, 96–98, 100, 108, 123; Cybracero Project, 93–94. *See also Sleep Dealer* (Rivera)
Rivera, John-Michael, 185, 188
Rivera, Lysa, 4, 6, 21, 82
Rivera Garza, Cristina, 150, 152, 154, 256n13
robo-sacer resistance, 6–7, 10–11, 14, 29, 64, 69–70, 89, 123, 196–97; armed, 160–61, 164–65, 252n13; in *Backyard/El traspatio* (Carrera and Berman), 28, 131, 137–38, 141–42, 145; in ChupaCabra trilogy (Anaya), 177, 189; citizenship and, 9; countervictimization and, 207n38; in *Cronos* (del Toro), 55, 60–61, 63; in *Heroes and Saints* (Moraga), 40–41; in *Lunar Braceros 2125-2148* (Sánchez and Pita), 113–14, 116, 118, 120; Mexican commercial cinema and, 199–200; polyspatial solidarity and, 12; in "Ruido Gris" (Rojo), 73, 78; in *Sleep Dealer* (Rivera), 98, 106, 111–12; in *Smoking Mirror Blues* (Hogan), 84, 88; in "Soñarán en el jardín" (Damián Miravetes), 147, 151; technology and, 94, 126; *zoē* and, 192

Rodríguez-Hernández, Raúl, 60, 109
Rojo, Pepe, 27, 66, 68–74, 77–79, 89, 228n2; "Ruido gris," 27, 64–71, 73–79, 81, 89, 198, 228n2

Salinas de Gortari, Carlos, 18, 179
Sánchez, Rosaura, 27–28, 89, 94, 96–98, 112, 117–19, 123, 182; on El Movimiento, 243n168. *See also Lunar Braceros 2125-2148* (Sánchez and Pita)
Sánchez Prado, Ignacio M., 7, 54, 56, 62, 131, 137, 199
sanctity, 26, 34, 50, 62; of *homo sacer*, 72; secular, 33, 35–37, 40, 58, 63
Sandoval, Chela, 9–10, 24, 69, 97, 106, 110, 114, 116, 151, 177
Sasser, Kim, 173, 175
Schaefer, Claudia, 60, 109
science fiction (SF), 19–22, 24–25, 201, 214n127, 215n137; borderlands, 94, 100; Chicano, 63, 66, 206n28; from colonial center, 196; farmworker, 95; feminicide and, 145–46; feminism and, 146; Latin American, 215n143; magical realism and, 29, 37–40, 63, 160, 165, 176, 185, 218n13; Mexican, 66, 215n140; Mexican cinema and, 52; subaltern, 200. *See also* Anaya, Rudolfo: ChupaCabra trilogy; Hernández Cordón, Julio: *Cómprama un revolver*; *Heroes and Saints* (Moraga); Hogan, Ernest: *Smoking Mirror Blues*
sexism, 24, 113, 126, 150
sexuality, 5, 8, 79, 110, 131–32, 136, 221n38, 223n74, 233n103;

feminine, 142; interracial, 82; Virgen de Guadalupe and, 48–49; women's, 135
Shaw, Deborah, 54, 56, 62
slasher films (genre), 28, 125, 131–32,

slasher films (genre) (*continued*)
135–38, 142–45, 252n108, 252n112.
See also *Backyard/El traspatio*
(Carrera and Berman)
*Sleep Dealer* (Rivera), 27–28, 89, 94,
96–112, 123, 240n99, 241n108;
alienation in, 238n66; border
fascism and, 243n164; gender
and, 241n105; Hollywood cinema
and, 237n44; KiwiBot and, 194–
95; Marx's vampire and, 240n92;
Mexican Golden Age cinema and,
236n32; pre-emption in, 238n55;
as transnational production,
236n33; water rights in, 238n53
speculative fiction, 20–21, 27, 176, 201,
215n136
state of exception, 3–4, 61, 69, 115,
171, 211n80; Billy the Kid and,
185; biopolitics of memory and,
108; capital and, 15; drug war
and, 159–61, 167, 170; exceptional,
134; immunization and, 148; in
McFarland, 44; NAFTA as, 72;
necroliberal, 1, 10, 12–13, 192; in
*Peppermint* (Morel), 198; profit
maximization as, 40, 96; in
"Soñarán en el jardín" (Damián
Miravete), 147; technology and,
100, 102
subaltern studies, 7, 209n55
subjectivity, 37, 48, 52, 105, 148;
Chicanx, 189; hybrid/hybridized,
25, 39; robo-sacer, 26, 100, 191, 197,
201; vampire, 57. See also cyborg
subjectivity
suicide, 65, 67, 77–78
Taylor, Claire, 24, 98, 192
technology, 4, 6, 8, 26–27, 29, 96, 100,
194–96, 201, 208n48; Afrofuturism

and, 20; in *Backyard/El traspatio*
(Carrera and Berman), 142, 144,
245n5; body and, 191, 197; in
ChupaCabra trilogy (Anaya),
188; in *Cronos* (del Toro), 54, 56;
cyberpunk and, 64; digital, 166;
drone, 102; farming, 41; feminicide
and, 151, 156; femi(ni)cide machine
and, 123; firearms as, 165; hybridity
and, 24; immortality through,
254n149; lack of access to, 63; in
Latin American cyberpunk, 68–
69; in *Lunar Braceros 2125–2148*
(Sánchez and Pita), 95, 112–14,
116, 118, 120–22; necroliberalism
and, 45, 79; necropolitics and,
13; in *Peppermint* (Morel), 198;
radio, 138; resistance and, 10–11,
94, 141, 192, 197, 267n14; in "Ruido
gris" (Rojo), 71, 73–74; in *Sleep
Dealer* (Rivera), 103, 105–6; in
*Smoking Mirror Blues* (Hogan),
81; in "Soñarán en el jardín"
(Damián Miravete), 145–47, 150,
152–55; state of exception and, 100;
subaltern resistance and, 98–99;
subversive articulations of, 66; as
tool for domination/oppression,
25, 37; transnational corporations
and, 111; wireless, 126
Televisa, 71–72, 230n23
Tierney, Dolores, 54, 57, 60–61
Tobin, Stephen C., 73, 214n136
Trump, Donald, 2, 17, 193, 196
TV Azteca, 71–72, 230n23
*2033* (Laresgoiti), 199–200

UFW (United Farm Workers), 50, 119
US Southwest, 22–23, 85, 161, 193
utopia, 17–18, 22–25, 121, 176

Valencia, Sayak, 13–14, 133, 140, 149, 170, 174
Vargas Amésquita, Alicia, 131, 135
Vasconcelianism, 22, 184
Vasconcelos, José, 22, 24, 184
violence, 29, 64, 70, 132, 137–38, 147, 159–60, 164, 196; drug, 26, 159, 168, 170, 176; exotic, 131, 137; feminicidal, 128, 145, 171; gender, 126, 131, 150–51, 153, 155; maquiladora work and, 16; necroliberal, 40; patriarchal, 125; quotidian, 165–67, 170, 172–73, 175; sexual, 135–36, 150, 172, 174; slow, 43; against women, 128, 132, 139, 149, 151, 246n24, 254n144, 259n66 (*see also* feminicide [*feminicidio*])
Virgin of Guadalupe, 35–36, 41–42, 47–50, 223n79

Warnes, Christopher, 166, 173
Williams, Gareth, 15, 147–48
workers, 4, 14, 16, 93–94, 98, 106–7, 194–95; displacement of, 56; expendability of, 122; maquiladora, 127, 133–34; meatpacking, 2, 7, 204n6; migrant, 27, 37, 39, 41, 44, 47, 100, 145, 218n12, 234n5; women, 129–30, 132–33, 141, 245n5

$zo\bar{e}$, 2–3, 8–10, 12–14, 29, 33–34, 36, 72; in *Backyard/El traspatio* (Carrera and Berman), 133; in ChupaCabra trilogy (Anaya), 180, 187–88; in *Cómprame un revolver* (Hernández Cordón), 165, 167, 169–70, 174–75; in *Cronos* (del Toro), 53, 56, 61; hacktivism and, 123; in *Heroes and Saints* (Moraga), 45, 50; in *Lunar Braceros 2125–2148* (Sánchez and Pita), 112, 114, 116; mediasphere and, 65, 89; migrant farmworkers as, 39; NAFTA and, 16, 25–27; robo-sacer resistance and, 192, 196; in "Ruido gris" (Rojo), 71, 73, 76, 79; in *Sleep Dealer* (Rivera), 100, 102, 107–8, 110–11; in *Smoking Mirror Blues* (Hogan), 84–85; in "Soñarán en el jardín" (Damián Miravete), 152–53; technology and, 64, 69–70, 96–97; in *2033* (Laresgoiti), 199; weapons and, 164–65; in "Why Cybraceros?" (Rivera), 94